MLA Style
Manual
and
Guide to
Scholarly Publishing

MLA Style Manual and Guide to Scholarly Publishing

SECOND EDITION

Joseph Gibaldi

THE MODERN LANGUAGE ASSOCIATION OF AMERICA
NEW YORK
1998

Only two books on MLA documentation style are published by the association: the *MLA Handbook for Writers of Research Papers* (for high school and undergraduate students) and the *MLA Style Manual and Guide to Scholarly Publishing* (for graduate students, scholars, and professional writers). These volumes provide the most accurate and complete instructions on MLA style.

If updates of the information in this manual become necessary, they will be posted at the MLA's World Wide Web site (http://www.mla.org/).

© 1985, 1998 by The Modern Language Association of America
All rights reserved

First edition 1985
Second edition 1998

Printed in the United States of America

For information about obtaining permission to reprint material from MLA book publications, send your request by mail (see address below), e-mail (permissions@mla.org), or fax (212 477-9863).

Library of Congress Cataloging-in-Publication Data

Gibaldi, Joseph, 1942–
   MLA style manual and guide to scholarly publishing / Joseph Gibaldi. — 2nd ed.
      p.   cm.
   Includes index.
   ISBN 0-87352-699-6
   1. Authorship—Style manuals.   2. Humanities—Authorship—Handbooks, manuals, etc.   3. Scholarly publishing—Handbooks, manuals, etc.   I. Modern Language Association of America.   II. Title.
   PN147.G444   1998
   808'.027—dc21   97-49983

Text design by Joan Greenfield
Typeset in Palatino and Lucida Typewriter
Printed on acid-free paper

Published by The Modern Language Association of America
10 Astor Place, New York, New York 10003-6981

CONTENTS

FOREWORD by Herbert Lindenberger   xv

ACKNOWLEDGMENTS   xxvii

1   SCHOLARLY PUBLISHING
1.1   Scholars and Scholarly Publishing   2
1.2   Refereed and Nonrefereed Publications   2
1.3   Deciding to Submit the Manuscript   3
1.4   Placing a Manuscript for a Journal Article   5
    1.4.1   Scholarly Journals   5
    1.4.2   Types of Scholarly Articles   5
    1.4.3   Selecting a Journal   6
    1.4.4   Submitting the Manuscript to a Journal   7
    1.4.5   Evaluation of the Manuscript   8
    1.4.6   Acceptance of the Manuscript   10
1.5   Placing a Manuscript for a Book   10
    1.5.1   Scholarly Book Publishers   10
    1.5.2   Types of Scholarly Books   11
    1.5.3   Selecting a Publisher   13
    1.5.4   Submitting the Prospectus for a Book   15
    1.5.5   Submitting the Manuscript to a Publisher   17
    1.5.6   Evaluation of the Manuscript   18
    1.5.7   Acceptance of the Manuscript   20
1.6   Production and Publication   20
    1.6.1   Copyediting   21
    1.6.2   Proofreading   23
    1.6.3   Preparing an Index   24
    1.6.4   Design   26
    1.6.5   Composition, Printing, Binding   27
    1.6.6   Marketing   28
1.7   Conclusion   29

2 **LEGAL ISSUES IN SCHOLARLY PUBLISHING**
by Arthur F. Abelman

2.1   Copyright   34
    2.1.1   Development of Copyright Law in the United States   34
    2.1.2   Scope of Copyright Protection   35
    2.1.3   Works Made for Hire   36
    2.1.4   Co-ownership   37
    2.1.5   Compilations, Including Collective Works   37
    2.1.6   Material Objects   38
    2.1.7   Term of Copyright   38
    2.1.8   Registration of Copyright   39
    2.1.9   Copyright Notice   40
    2.1.10   Renewal of Copyright   41
    2.1.11   Rights of Copyright Owners   42
    2.1.12   Transfers and Terminations   42
    2.1.13   Fair Use of Copyrighted Works   43
    2.1.14   Requesting Permission   45
    2.1.15   Damages for Copyright Infringement   45
    2.1.16   International Copyright   46
    2.1.17   Copyright and Computer Networks   47

2.2   Publishing Contracts   48
    2.2.1   Books   48
    2.2.2   Journal Articles and Contributions to Edited Works   52

2.3   Defamation   53
    2.3.1   Libel   53
    2.3.2   Opinion   55
    2.3.3   Truth as Defense   55
    2.3.4   Actual Malice   56

2.4   Right of Privacy   57
    2.4.1   Emergence of Privacy Law   57
    2.4.2   Unreasonable Publicity of Private Life   58
    2.4.3   Publicity Placing Another in a False Light   58
    2.4.4   Consent as Defense   59

2.5   Further Guidance   59

3 **BASICS OF SCHOLARLY WRITING**

3.1   Audience, Genre, and the Conventions of Scholarship   63

3.2   Language and Style   63

3.3   Spelling   65
    3.3.1   Consistency and Choice of Spelling   65
    3.3.2   Word Division   65
    3.3.3   Plurals   65

3.3.4 Accents 65
3.3.5 Diaereses 66
3.3.6 Ligatures and Other Special Characters 66
3.4 Punctuation 66
3.4.1 Purpose of Punctuation 66
3.4.2 Commas 67
3.4.3 Semicolons 72
3.4.4 Colons 72
3.4.5 Dashes and Parentheses 73
3.4.6 Hyphens 74
3.4.7 Apostrophes 76
3.4.8 Quotation Marks 77
3.4.9 Square Brackets 78
3.4.10 Slashes 79
3.4.11 Periods, Question Marks, and Exclamation Points 79
3.5 Italics (Underlining) 80
3.5.1 Words and Letters Referred to as Words and Letters 81
3.5.2 Foreign Words in an English Text 81
3.5.3 Emphasis 81
3.6 Names of Persons 81
3.6.1 First and Subsequent Uses of Names 81
3.6.2 Titles of Persons 82
3.6.3 Names of Authors and Fictional Characters 82
3.6.4 Dutch and German Names 83
3.6.5 French Names 83
3.6.6 Greek Names 84
3.6.7 Hungarian Names 84
3.6.8 Italian Names 85
3.6.9 Russian Names 86
3.6.10 Spanish Names 86
3.6.11 Latin Names 87
3.6.12 Asian Names 88
3.6.13 Names in Other Languages 89
3.7 Capitalization 89
3.7.1 English 89
3.7.2 French 91
3.7.3 German 92
3.7.4 Italian 93
3.7.5 Portuguese 93
3.7.6 Russian 94
3.7.7 Spanish 95
3.7.8 Latin 96
3.7.9 Other Languages 96

3.8   Titles of Works in the Manuscript   97
    3.8.1   General Guidelines   97
    3.8.2   Underlined Titles   98
    3.8.3   Titles in Quotation Marks   98
    3.8.4   Titles and Quotations within Titles   99
    3.8.5   Exceptions   100
    3.8.6   Shortened Titles   102

3.9   Quotations   102
    3.9.1   Accuracy of Quotations   102
    3.9.2   Prose   103
    3.9.3   Poetry   105
    3.9.4   Drama   106
    3.9.5   Ellipsis   107
    3.9.6   Other Alterations of Sources   111
    3.9.7   Punctuation with Quotations   112
    3.9.8   Translations of Quotations   114

3.10 Numbers   115
    3.10.1   Arabic Numerals   115
    3.10.2   Use of Words or Numerals   115
    3.10.3   Commas in Numbers   116
    3.10.4   Percentages and Amounts of Money   117
    3.10.5   Dates and Times of the Day   117
    3.10.6   Inclusive Numbers   118
    3.10.7   Roman Numerals   119

3.11 Transliteration and Romanization   119

3.12 Further Guidance   123

4   PREPARATION OF SCHOLARLY MANUSCRIPTS
4.1   Divisions of the Text   126
    4.1.1   Articles and Essays   126
    4.1.2   Books   127
    4.1.3   Consistency of Headings   128

4.2   Physical Characteristics of the Printed Manuscript   128
    4.2.1   Printing   128
    4.2.2   Paper   128
    4.2.3   Margins   129
    4.2.4   Spacing   129
    4.2.5   Title and Author's Name   129
    4.2.6   Page Numbers   131
    4.2.7   Tables and Illustrations   131
    4.2.8   Corrections and Revisions   133
    4.2.9   Binding   135

4.3 Manuscripts for Print Publication   135

4.4 Manuscripts for Electronic Publication   136

4.5 Further Guidance on Tagging Electronic Documents   140

5   PREPARATION OF THESES AND DISSERTATIONS

5.1 Student Publications as Professional Publications   141

5.2 Prescribed Guidelines   142

5.3 Selecting a Topic   142

5.4 Preparing a Prospectus   143

5.5 Special Format Requirements   143
    5.5.1 Theses and Dissertations as Published Works   143
    5.5.2 Divisions of the Text   144
    5.5.3 Page Numbers   144
    5.5.4 Margins   145
    5.5.5 Spacing   145
    5.5.6 Binding   145

5.6 Publishing the Dissertation through University Microfilms
International   146
    5.6.1 Terms of Agreement   146
    5.6.2 Abstract   146
    5.6.3 Copyright   146
    5.6.4 Permissions   146

5.7 Electronic Publication   147

6   DOCUMENTATION: PREPARING THE LIST OF WORKS
CITED

6.1 Documentation and Plagiarism   151

6.2 MLA Style   152

6.3 The List of Works Cited and Other Source Lists   153

6.4 Placement of the List of Works Cited   153

6.5 Arrangement of Entries   154

6.6 Citing Books and Other Nonperiodical Publications   155
    6.6.1 The Basic Entry: A Book by a Single Author   155
    6.6.2 An Anthology or a Compilation   159
    6.6.3 Two or More Books by the Same Author   159
    6.6.4 A Book by Two or More Authors   160
    6.6.5 Two or More Books by the Same Authors   162
    6.6.6 A Book by a Corporate Author   162
    6.6.7 A Work in an Anthology   163

6.6.8 An Article in a Reference Book   166
6.6.9 An Introduction, a Preface, a Foreword, or an Afterword   167
6.6.10 Cross-References   167
6.6.11 An Anonymous Book   168
6.6.12 An Edition   168
6.6.13 A Translation   170
6.6.14 A Book Published in a Second or Subsequent Edition   171
6.6.15 A Multivolume Work   172
6.6.16 A Book in a Series   175
6.6.17 A Republished Book   175
6.6.18 A Publisher's Imprint   176
6.6.19 A Book with Multiple Publishers   177
6.6.20 A Pamphlet   177
6.6.21 A Government Publication   177
6.6.22 The Published Proceedings of a Conference   179
6.6.23 A Book in a Language Other Than English   180
6.6.24 A Book Published before 1900   181
6.6.25 A Book without Stated Publication Information or Pagination   181
6.6.26 An Unpublished Dissertation   182
6.6.27 A Published Dissertation   183
6.7 Citing Articles and Other Publications in Periodicals   183
6.7.1 The Basic Entry: An Article in a Scholarly Journal with Continuous Pagination   183
6.7.2 An Article in a Scholarly Journal That Pages Each Issue Separately   186
6.7.3 An Article in a Scholarly Journal That Uses Only Issue Numbers   186
6.7.4 An Article in a Scholarly Journal with More Than One Series   187
6.7.5 An Article in a Newspaper   187
6.7.6 An Article in a Magazine   189
6.7.7 A Review   190
6.7.8 An Abstract in an Abstracts Journal   191
6.7.9 An Anonymous Article   192
6.7.10 An Editorial   192
6.7.11 A Letter to the Editor   193
6.7.12 A Serialized Article   193
6.7.13 A Special Issue   194
6.7.14 An Article in a Microform Collection of Articles   194
6.7.15 An Article Reprinted in a Loose-Leaf Collection of Articles   195

6.8   Citing Miscellaneous Print and Nonprint Sources   195
    6.8.1   A Television or Radio Program   195
    6.8.2   A Sound Recording   197
    6.8.3   A Film or Video Recording   200
    6.8.4   A Performance   201
    6.8.5   A Musical Composition   202
    6.8.6   A Work of Art   203
    6.8.7   An Interview   204
    6.8.8   A Map or Chart   205
    6.8.9   A Cartoon   205
    6.8.10   An Advertisement   205
    6.8.11   A Lecture, a Speech, an Address, or a Reading   206
    6.8.12   A Manuscript or Typescript   206
    6.8.13   A Letter or Memo   207
    6.8.14   A Legal Source   207

6.9   Citing Electronic Publications   209
    6.9.1   Introduction   209
    6.9.2   An Online Scholarly Project, Reference Database, or Professional or Personal Site   211
    6.9.3   An Online Book   214
    6.9.4   An Article in an Online Periodical   216
    6.9.5   A Publication on CD-ROM, Diskette, or Magnetic Tape   219
    6.9.6   A Work in More Than One Publication Medium   223
    6.9.7   A Work in an Indeterminate Medium   224
    6.9.8   Other Electronic Sources   224

7   DOCUMENTATION: CITING SOURCES IN THE TEXT

7.1   Parenthetical Documentation and the List of Works Cited   230

7.2   Information Required in Parenthetical Documentation   231

7.3   Readability   232

7.4   Sample References   235
    7.4.1   Citing an Entire Work   235
    7.4.2   Citing Part of a Work   237
    7.4.3   Citing Volume and Page Numbers of a Multivolume Work   240
    7.4.4   Citing a Work Listed by Title   241
    7.4.5   Citing a Work by a Corporate Author   243
    7.4.6   Citing Two or More Works by the Same Author or Authors   244
    7.4.7   Citing Indirect Sources   245
    7.4.8   Citing Literary Works   246

7.4.9 Citing More Than One Work in a Single Parenthetical Reference 249

7.4.10 Citing a Book with Signatures and No Page Numbers 251

7.5 Using Notes with Parenthetical Documentation 252

7.5.1 Content Notes 252

7.5.2 Bibliographic Notes 253

8 ABBREVIATIONS

8.1 Introduction 255

8.2 Time Designations 256

8.3 Geographic Names 258

8.4 Common Scholarly Abbreviations and Reference Words 261

8.5 Publishers' Names 272

8.6 Titles of Literary and Religious Works 274

8.6.1 Bible 274

8.6.2 Works by Shakespeare 277

8.6.3 Works by Chaucer 278

8.6.4 Other Literary Works 279

8.7 Names of Languages 281

8.8 Proofreading Symbols 283

8.8.1 Symbols Used in the Text 284

8.8.2 Symbols Used in the Margin 285

8.8.3 Sample Marked Proof 287

APPENDIX: OTHER SYSTEMS OF DOCUMENTATION

A Endnotes and Footnotes 289

A.1 Documentation Notes versus the List of Works Cited and Parenthetical References 290

A.2 Note Numbers 290

A.3 Note Form versus Bibliographic Form 290

A.4 Endnotes versus Footnotes 291

A.5 Sample First Note References: Books and Other Nonperiodical Publications 291

A.6 Sample First Note References: Articles and Other Publications in Periodicals 295

A.7 Sample First Note References: Miscellaneous Print and Nonprint Sources 298

A.8 Sample First Note References: Electronic Publications 301

A.9 Subsequent References 305

B   Author-Date System   305
C   Number System   308
D   Specialized Style Manuals   309

SOURCES OF EXAMPLES IN 3.4–5   311

INDEX   315

FOREWORD

Herbert Lindenberger

The *MLA Style Manual and Guide to Scholarly Publishing* is addressed to those of you contemplating serious publication in the field of literature and language. Unlike the *MLA Handbook for Writers of Research Papers*, which is intended primarily for undergraduates, the *Manual* establishes ground rules and provides practical advice for scholars—from advanced undergraduates to authors preparing their first books for publication—in a variety of subfields such as literary history and theory, rhetoric and composition, second-language acquisition, and ethnic and cultural studies. Students and teachers of literature and language, however divergent their research interests and methods, form a distinct disciplinary community sharing certain assumptions about, for instance, the value of contributing new knowledge about a culture's texts and the need to present this knowledge to other members of the community by means of solid evidence and rational argument.

A manual like this one, to the extent that it offers a uniform set of rules and conventions to govern the presentation of scholarship in articles and books, can be viewed as articulating the present highly diversified institutional style of literary and language study. This volume's ancestor was a thin paperbound pamphlet called the *MLA Style Sheet*, which came out in 1951, when I was a graduate student. I remember using it for my dissertation and first publications; indeed, since I do not possess a good memory for textual detail—in what order and with what punctuation, for example, to present the various items in an endnote or a bibliographic entry—I confess having needed to consult the *Style Sheet* and its successors regularly throughout my publishing career. I might further confess that this very day, while preparing the

Herbert Lindenberger, Avalon Foundation Professor of Humanities at Stanford University, was president of the Modern Language Association in 1997.

final manuscript of a book on opera and literature for a university press, I had to look up the rule on when to spell out numbers and when to present them as numerals.

You may wonder whether the uniform rules with which much of the *Style Manual* is concerned are not at odds with one of the central requisites of academic research: the need for originality. Does not the demand to follow an intricate set of codes inhibit, perhaps even stifle, a scholar's thinking? Quite the contrary, for with constraints come opportunities. When you follow a standard manual, you do not need to create a style from scratch, and your readers are not obliged to learn a new system. Standardization of form keeps you from having to worry about nonsubstantive matters, and as a consequence you can concentrate on your genuinely fresh contributions.

Moreover, observing the codes that have been agreed on within our disciplinary community signals your membership in the community. These codes range from the hard-and-fast rules for placing commas to matters that demand a certain discretion—knowing when, for example, to cite a source for a statement you make and when to assume that the source is common knowledge for most of your readers. In a large field such as ours, adherence to these codes allows your writing to be taken seriously, whether by referees who decide the publication of your work or by readers whom you ultimately hope to convince with your evidence and arguments but who are otherwise unacquainted with you. Indeed, it is through the confines imposed by a commonly acknowledged set of practices that readers can judge the competence of your methods and the individuality of what you offer.

As a disciplinary community concerned with the preservation and interpretation of texts, we can trace our roots back well over two millennia to the rhetoricians, critics, and editors of ancient Greece and Rome. The changes that have taken place since that remote time in the interpreter's relation to text and reader, in the purpose and function of interpretation within a culture, and in the technological means by which knowledge is disseminated are so profound that terms such as *critic, scholar*, and *historical* have developed distinct meanings in different settings and times. Similarly, what has counted as an original contribution to knowledge has changed considerably over the years.

In spite of this apparent discontinuity, a conversation among practitioners widely separated in time and place has evolved by means of publication. While the conventions they agree to follow ensure that this conversation will remain disciplined, the original ideas they articulate can give it a liveliness, a sense of the unexpected, that continuingly renews scholarship. As you enter this conversation, you are staking out a claim to membership in a profession with a long, vital, and also often contentious history.

To demonstrate how publication keeps alive the enterprise of scholars in languages and literature—above all, to help you view your professional activities within a large historical spectrum—I propose to look back a little more than two centuries at some commentaries on a much discussed poem, Milton's "Lycidas." Each of these commentaries is not only embedded in the values of its time, each also offers what counted as an original view of "Lycidas" according to the prevailing definitions of the critic's or scholar's role. Consider the following sentences, all of which begin commentaries on this literary text:

> 1779: "One of the poems on which much praise has been bestowed is *Lycidas*; of which the diction is harsh, the rhymes uncertain, and the numbers unpleasing."   (Johnson 224)

> 1859: "What the wits and scholars of England at large were doing for Ben's memory, a select number of wits and scholars, chiefly connected with Cambridge, had resolved to do for the memory of poor Edward King."   (Masson 602)

> 1910: "To most modern readers the pastoral setting of Milton's *Lycidas* is far from being an element of beauty."   (Hanford 403)

> 1933: "It was published in 1638, and therefore I shall not pretend to be offering a fresh tidbit to the moderns; clearly a product of that darkness which preceded our incomparable modernity."
>   (Ransom 179)

> 1958: "I should like to begin with a brief discussion of a familiar poem, Milton's *Lycidas*, in the hope that some of the inferences drawn from the analysis will be relevant to the theme of this conference."   (Frye 44)

> 1962: "My point is that, on the evidence of their own commentaries [on "Lycidas"], critics agree about the excellence of quite different poems."   (Abrams, "Five Ways" 1–2)

> 1996: "When Milton appointed Lycidas 'the Genius of the shore,' he was staking a claim for his nation as well as his poem."
>   (Lipking 205)

The first quotation, because of its author's fame and the resoluteness of its condemnation, may well be the most readily identifiable statement ever made about Milton's poem. Though most of us today are put off by absolute judgments of this sort, a literary critic in Samuel Johnson's time served as a propagator and arbiter of shared values and thus gave cohesion to the new and rapidly growing middle-class reading public. Famous for the dictionary on which he had labored for much of his career, Johnson was granted institutional authority by readers who sought guidance in developing their literary taste and, in the process, maximizing their cultural capital.

If Johnson happens to reject "Lycidas" as belonging to what he calls an untruthful and "disgusting" genre (224), it is not that he was naive about the literary tradition to which the poem belongs but rather that the notion of achieving sympathy with earlier texts and of placing them in their appropriate historical contexts did not emerge until the succeeding century. His task as a critic was not so much to generate new interpretations as to make explicit the values that he and, he assumed, his readers already held.

The second quotation, unlike the others, comes not from an essay on "Lycidas" but from one of the great monuments of Victorian literary biography, David Masson's *Life of John Milton*, in which the treatment of this pastoral elegy takes up only fourteen out of several thousand pages. Note the familiar tone—unthinkable for any of us to use today—with which Masson approaches his readers by referring to "poor Edward King" and calling Ben Jonson by first name alone. Unlike scholars of our century, Masson was writing for a general public, the same educated public that followed the pronouncements of the great Victorian sages, among them his friend, sponsor, and fellow Scot Thomas Carlyle.

Since Masson is writing in the genre long dubbed "life and times," he is unsparing in the number of historical facts he offers, though he makes no attempt to integrate them within his discussion of the poem. Indeed, only a relatively few pages are devoted to what a later generation was to call "the poem itself." What Masson provides would scarcely be labeled criticism in the mid to late twentieth century. Rather, we get a lengthy paraphrase of the poem liberally sprinkled with quotations; in fact, Masson reproduces many of the poem's images not, as in a present-day essay, to illustrate the critic's points but to encourage the reader to reexperience the poem—for example, when he describes the hero's apotheosis: "[Lycidas] is now in a region of groves and streams other and more lovely than those of this earthly Arcady where we are fain to bury him" (614).

Moving forward to James Holly Hanford's essay, of 1910, you will note a radically different conception of what should properly be the study of a poem. The quoted opening sentence makes clear the essay's relatively narrow focus, a narrowness that has marked the scholarship of the twentieth century despite many changes in critical method and even in the notion of what constitutes literature. By reminding us of modern readers' bias against the pastoral mode—a bias that goes back at least to Johnson's condemnation of the mode's artifice—Hanford lays the groundwork for his argument, which will culminate in the conclusion that "the supreme beauty of *Lycidas* lies partly in the very fact of its conventionality" (447).

The scholarly approach that he pursues is what was long called the historical or philological method: it assumed that the primary role of a scholar was not to help readers "appreciate" a literary text but to discover and present new knowledge about it. This knowledge was not of the sort we label interpretive but consisted rather of facts about such subjects as the circumstances surrounding the composition of the text or, as with Hanford's essay, the work's verifiable sources in earlier writings. Innovativeness for Hanford's generation meant limiting yourself to textual demonstration and avoiding at once the value judgments of Johnson and the appreciative rhetoric of Masson.

Although Masson and Hanford were both professors of English literature, the institutional roles they played were profoundly different. Masson had not been formally educated beyond the MA and had gained a considerable reputation as a man of letters before his first academic appointment. Hanford, by contrast, was a product of the American graduate school, an institution whose rationale and methods of instruction had been imported from German universities during the last decades of the nineteenth century and whose model for original research in the humanities derived from the experimental sciences. Whereas Masson's writing reached a large and varied readership, Hanford's was directed to a specialized audience of fellow professors and advanced students who possessed sufficient training to recognize the newness of the facts he had uncovered.

The significant commentary on "Lycidas" offered since Hanford's essay has not, however, been limited to the productions of the research university. Reading the opening phrase of John Crowe Ransom's essay, "It was published in 1638," we recognize that we are not, as the then reigning school of historical scholarship demanded, being presented with a new fact but are being reminded of a long-familiar story. The end of the sentence, "that darkness which preceded our incomparable modernity," jolts us with its brashly expressed value judgments about the relation of the present to the past. Although a college professor as well as a poet, Ransom puts on a defiantly antiprofessional tone: "The Milton scholars know their Italian, and have me at a disadvantage," he writes while demonstrating the origins of Milton's formal irregularities in the Italian *canzone* (185).

In his role as poet-critic, Ransom seeks above all to show the relevance of "Lycidas" to his fellow poets and to readers of modern poetry. Describing the poem as "young, brilliant, insubordinate," Ransom prepares us for his assertion that Milton's poem "has much in common with, for example, *The Waste Land*" (180). Built around Milton's formal irregularities, the essay portrays Milton roughening his language as poets of Ransom's generation were wont to do.

In its informal style, its absence of footnotes, its antiacademic pronouncements, Ransom's essay would seem to be directed to the sort of general readership for whom Masson wrote. But by the 1930s the size of the audience for serious criticism had shrunk from that of its

Victorian forebear just as the audience for serious poetry had become little more than a coterie. Within scarcely more than a decade after the writing of this essay, first published in the *American Review*, a small-circulation journal that mixed politics and literary criticism, the New Criticism, which Ransom named, was itself absorbed within the American university system. The modernist bias of this movement, as well as the skepticism toward historical method and the emphasis on the formal analysis of texts, became thoroughly institutionalized within the classroom, as I can testify, having been assigned Ransom's essay on "Lycidas" in a senior seminar on contemporary criticism at Antioch College.

The statement with which Northrop Frye opens his essay on "Lycidas," first presented as a conference paper, makes clear that he is concerned primarily not with the poem, about which he claims only to offer "a brief discussion," but with the inferences he can draw from a text familiar enough to an audience of diverse specialists. By 1958, the year of Frye's presentation, the academic conference, doubtless because of the increasing rapidity and availability of air travel, was starting to serve as a central means by which a scholar's ideas could be communicated. The members of Frye's audience identified themselves with comparative literature, a discipline that, during the years following the Second World War, sought to break down the barriers separating scholars within various national-literature departments.

In this paper, however, Frye is less concerned with challenging the departmental affiliations of literary scholars than with propounding a large theory of literature that eschews national borders. "Lycidas" provides him the occasion to outline his central theoretical premises. Thus for Frye a complaint such as Johnson's about Milton's failure to portray grief with sincerity is beside the point, for literature occupies its own realm and has its own "structural principles" independent of personal motivations and historical contexts. Nor does he allow for the value judgments central to some earlier modes of criticism such as Johnson's or Ransom's, for these judgments are irrelevant to the larger, "co-ordinated" view of literature that Frye advocates (55).

The confidence with which Frye could proclaim his theory of literature parallels a self-assurance that developed within literary study as a whole in the United States and Canada during the succeeding decade. University enrollments were growing in all fields; faculties were expanding; governments were generous in the support of research and graduate study to a degree that they had not been before —more generous, in fact, than they have proved to be since that time. By the mid–twentieth century a theorist like Frye could build on many decades of work by scholars who, in editions of texts and critical studies of major authors and periods, had provided a detailed framework for the understanding of Western literary traditions.

The boom in literary study in mid-century manifested itself not only in Frye's global theorizing but also in a new self-consciousness of scholars about their activity, above all a concern with how one could properly arrive at the "meaning" of a literary text. Only four years after Frye's essay, his exact contemporary M. H. Abrams wrote an essay entitled "Five Ways of Reading 'Lycidas,'" which asks how it is possible for five scholars and critics (among them Hanford, Ransom, and Frye) to come up with the most diverse and sometimes even contradictory statements of what this poem is all about. Abrams attempts to resolve the problem with his own reading of the poem, which seeks to place the poet in an appropriate historical context as a Christian humanist mediating between classical convention and divine revelation. In this reading Abrams extends the Christian-humanist approach of a slightly earlier essay, by Rosemond Tuve, who, working within the method that Hanford had pioneered for "Lycidas," questioned the more recent approaches that ignored Milton's intellectual and religious background (Tuve 99). By reasserting the need to link the meaning of a work to its historical traditions, Abrams seeks to provide a "safeguard against confusion" ("Five Ways" 22).

Yet, in a 1989 retrospect on his essay, Abrams acknowledges that the five authors he considered may have intended less to "discover [. . .] what *Lycidas* is really about" than "to justify their enterprise" ("Postscript" 216). He thus calls attention to the institutional need within the modern university to lay claim to knowledge that seems both newer and truer than the knowledge offered by earlier practitioners.

The last in the line of essays on "Lycidas" I quoted makes it clear that the attempt to find a fresh significance for Milton's poem has by no means come to an end. To anybody familiar with literary criticism during the 1990s, Lawrence Lipking's reading of the poem as "staking a claim for [Milton's] nation" is part of a larger critical endeavor to uncover the national and imperial motives—what Lipking calls the "collaboration between poetry and nationalism" (205)—central to much writing in early modern Europe. The relation of poetry to nation was of course present for earlier critics: the edition of British poets for which Johnson originally intended his *Lives*, as well as Masson's grounding of Milton in the historical events of the poet's time, constituted an effort to bond British readers with a sense of their common nationhood. By contrast, rather than use poetry to enhance nationalist feelings, Lipking and his contemporaries seek to historicize the national impulses that have motivated literary texts at specific moments.

Like many critical essays of the 1990s, this one is concerned with the material conditions surrounding the composition of the poem, above all with Milton's use of maps to establish the geographic names with which the poem is loaded. Lipking reproduces maps of the British Isles, Europe, and northwest Spain that Milton might have consulted (206–08, 211). The material conditions that Lipking finds relevant to the poem include as well the family tree of Edward King (209), whose involvement in Ireland now becomes a subtext of the elegy. Moreover, whereas Masson and most later commentators kept their discussions of formal and historical detail separate, for Lipking and for most of us working in the new-historicist mode, history is embedded in the literary text itself.

Like Frye, Lipking invokes a comparative literary perspective, but whereas Frye links "Lycidas" to numerous works of various times and places in order to demonstrate the unity of literature, Lipking cites a specific passage, the brief speech of Adamastor, spirit of the Cape of Good Hope in Camões's *The Lusiads*, to place Milton's elegy within the literary ambience of early modern Europe (214–19). Yet Lipking's frame of reference extends beyond this historical period. Just as the allusions to Namancos and Bayona in "Lycidas" suggest a nationalist message by awakening cultural memories of traditional British enmity toward Spain, so Lipking's brief mentions of contemporary analogies in the Balkans and South Africa show how long-standing ethnic resentments feed the growth of national consciousness (213).

Although Lipking's argument is dependent on the richness of his historical detail, it also depends on a theoretical framework, without which this detail could not be interpreted and given significance. But while the theory that Frye invokes claims to be drawn directly from literary texts, Lipking, like many scholars of the 1980s and 1990s, turns to theorists within and outside the area of literary study to help legitimate his argument. Near the end of his essay he names a social scientist, Benedict Anderson, whose *Imagined Communities: Reflections on the Origin and Spread of Nationalism* has provided many recent literary scholars with a model that shows how the bonds holding nations together have been constructed in specific times and places (219).

But Lipking also invokes a literary theorist, Walter Benjamin, who, Lipking notes, is cited by Anderson. Lipking links Benjamin's much discussed image of the Angel of History with Milton's "Genius of the shore" as well as with Camões's Adamastor to suggest "the calamities and grievances that compose their historical myths of nationhood" (219). Juxtaposing Benjamin's image with Milton's and Camões's accomplishes something more than illumination by means of an analogy, for by the 1990s Benjamin's image had become a topos that enabled critics to display their theoretical credentials without having to lay detailed groundwork, just as during the 1930s and 1940s critics such as Ransom could use references to T. S. Eliot's *The Waste Land* as shorthand to place themselves in the mainstream of modernism.

What conclusions can we draw from this story of the fortunes of "Lycidas" among its commentators during the last two centuries? For one thing, the institutional role that critics and scholars play, as well as the way that their creativity and originality are defined, is constantly changing. Unlike the academic critic of our time, Samuel Johnson spoke as a freelancer to a public willing to trust him to voice opinions that they could then, if they chose, assume as their own. Like Ransom, he could not separate his judgments of earlier poetry from his concern for the fate of poetry in his time—indeed, of his own role as poet. The artifice and insincerity that he finds in "Lycidas," which a scholar of the twentieth century might conscientiously seek to justify on historical grounds, are alien to his poetic practice, so he has scarcely any sympathy for Milton's endeavor. The vocation Johnson pursued as poet-critic demanded that he speak out persuasively to a large literate community.

Today academic critics, except for the few who attain star status within the profession, do not ordinarily expect to reach more than a handful of fellow scholars working within areas (defined variously by historical period, genre, or critical orientation) similar to theirs. Most often a critical work is read only when someone notices it in a bibliography while seeking information on a specific problem or text. Even the so-called stars, who constitute a relatively new phenomenon within literary study (see Shumway), do not reach more than a small proportion of the total reading public, although their writings may appear in the most popular multidisciplinary critical journals. However much our methods differ from those in the natural sciences, we share with our colleagues in those fields the assumption that our prospective readers have a certain degree of professional training and familiarity with our specialized vocabulary.

In contrast to the men of letters who flourished in earlier centuries as independent entrepreneurs (or, in even earlier times, as the beneficiaries of patrons whom they courted), scholars within the modern university are subject to bureaucratic constraints. Like the administrative bureaucracies that characterize the modern state, the university bureaucracy is based on commonly accepted rules and procedures by means of which a faculty member's career path is defined rationally and largely predictably. All of us entering the academic profession, whether in the natural sciences or the humanities, are familiar with the stages that make up a career: the completion of course work, examinations, and a dissertation while we are students; the achievement of sufficient distinction as a researcher and teacher during our early post-doctoral years to justify the award of tenure; the demand for continued professional growth to ensure that we remain valuable to our institutions until retirement. Like those who people the corporate and government offices in modern bureaucracies, academic personnel are subject to guidelines intended to guarantee that all competitors are treated evenhandedly. The *MLA Style Manual and Guide to Scholarly Publishing* could, in fact, be viewed as expressing this attempt to keep the profession solidly democratic.

As I indicated at the start, the constraints of a uniform style do not need to inhibit an individual scholar's originality. Indeed, the treatments of "Lycidas" discussed above each succeed in saying something new—sometimes about the poem itself, sometimes about literature in general—without abandoning the norms of critical writing. Yet the pressure to add something new, however differently we may interpret the meaning of originality, poses a special problem in literary study because of the high population of the field. The sheer bulk of literary critical production, as the MLA bibliographies have demonstrated for many years, can easily deter anybody seeking to say something different about a particular phenomenon in literature. Just as the English Romantic poets feared that everything worth doing in poetry had already been accomplished (see Bate), so literary scholars in the later twentieth century have often felt overwhelmed by the weight of commentary that has accumulated on the more important (and many of the less important) works in the Western literatures.

The need to establish one's presence in a crowded and competitive intellectual marketplace can have positive consequences, however. The perception that older forms of knowledge have become saturated has sometimes motivated literary scholars to try out valuable new ideas that seem daring, even outrageous, at first. It is a fact that most of the new perspectives that have emerged in the humanities during the later twentieth century—for example, feminism, deconstruction, the new historicism, ethnically based criticism, gender studies—were first developed in North American departments of modern literatures (whatever the origins of some of these ideas in European thinkers). Only afterward did these perspectives enter the discourses of such long-conservative fields as art history, musicology, classical studies, and even history. Moreover, the circumstances surrounding the production and circulation of knowledge change with new technological developments; just as the increasing frequency of conferences affected intellectual exchange a generation ago, so electronic publishing, a phenomenon of such importance that it has necessitated a new section in the present edition of this manual, may well transform the ways that ideas are articulated.

It has long been a truism that scholars (even those who feel overwhelmed with heavy teaching and administrative duties) need to keep pursuing research interests to prevent their ideas from going stale. In the course of a long career I have found that it is not enough for you simply to reapply the research methods that you mastered in graduate school or even, for that matter, to assume that the literary or cultural texts you studied there will retain the importance for you that they once had. Keeping up with the field demands extending your intellectual antennae to whatever seems new and promising; and what proves most useful to your work may be a way of thinking to be found not in the scholarship of your specialized period or critical approach but in some more distant area of thought, often outside literary study altogether.

The fervor, sometimes even ferocity, with which we uphold our beliefs may well derive from the fact that we view our professional choice as a calling. There are of course other professions—for example, the ministry and the creative and performing arts—whose practitioners see themselves as called on to put their talents to use no matter how meager the remuneration or the chances that they will fully realize their goals. What is common to these professions is a sense of mission, a fervent belief in the value, in the very rightness, of having chosen them. There is a tired joke that controversies among academic professionals assume great import because the financial stakes are pitifully low; in actuality, once we recognize that these controversies are fueled by deep-held beliefs emanating from the pursuit of a mission, the stakes seem high indeed.

What separates the profession of college professor from many other callings is that its practitioners have to perform both as individual operators and as members of a bureaucratic hierarchy. On the one hand, you are the masters of your classrooms and creators of your research agendas (even if you sometimes collaborate with colleagues in these activities); on the other hand, your progress is monitored and sometimes delayed, even stifled, by the ongoing judgments of colleagues, students, and administrators, as well as by referees whose identities you may never learn.

A typical academic career is marked by alternating confidence and anxiety, by a zeal to realize your mission that is all too often compromised by impediments. Serious intellectual work demands a willingness to assume the risk that an idea of yours, sometimes even a whole project you have been pursuing for a considerable period, may not turn out. By the same token, the sense of accomplishment gained from articulating an idea that others perceive as new, an idea that may, in fact, stimulate the work of colleagues you have never known, is immense.

Although these adversities and triumphs are experienced by workers in the social and natural sciences as well as in the humanities, those of us whose mission it is to preserve, interpret, and transmit cultural artifacts such as poems, paintings, and musical works take on ourselves a responsibility and a commitment different in character from those assumed by analysts of the natural world or of society.

However much we may disagree about the value or meaning of particular artifacts, the attention to which we subject these artifacts gives them life over long stretches of time. So historically remote a poem as Milton's pastoral elegy for his acquaintance Edward King remains a living presence for us because of the ongoing dialogue among those who have felt called on to work in the field of literature.

WORKS CITED

Abrams, M. H. "Five Ways of Reading 'Lycidas.'" *Varieties of Literary Experience: Eighteen Essays in World Literature*. Ed. Stanley Burnshaw. New York: New York UP, 1962. 1–29.

———. "Postscript to 'Five Types of "Lycidas."'" *Doing Things with Texts: Essays in Criticism and Critical Theory*. By Abrams. Ed. Michael Fischer. New York: Norton, 1989. 212–16.

Bate, W. Jackson. *The Burden of the Past and the English Poet*. Cambridge: Harvard UP, 1970.

Frye, Northrop. "Literature as Context: Milton's 'Lycidas.'" *Comparative Literature: Proceedings of the Second Congress of the International Comparative Literature Association*. 8–12 Sept. 1958. Ed. Werner P. Friederich. Vol. 1. Chapel Hill: U of North Carolina P, 1959. 44–55. 2 vols.

Hanford, James Holly. "The Pastoral Elegy and Milton's 'Lycidas.'" *PMLA* 25 (1910): 403–47.

Johnson, Samuel. *The Lives of the Most Eminent English Poets; with Critical Observations on Their Works*. Vol. 1. London: C. Bathurst et al., 1781. 4 vols.

Lipking, Lawrence. "The Genius of the Shore: Lycidas, Adamastor, and the Poetics of Nationalism." *PMLA* 111 (1996): 205–21.

Masson, David. *The Life of John Milton: Narrated in Connexion with the Political, Ecclesiastical, and Literary History of His Time*. Vol. 1. Cambridge: Macmillan, 1859. 7 vols. 1859–94.

Ransom, John Crowe. "A Poem Nearly Anonymous." *American Review* 1 (1933): 179–203, 444–67.

Shumway, David R. "The Star System in Literary Studies." *PMLA* 112 (1997): 85–100.

Tuve, Rosemond. "Theme, Pattern, and Imagery in 'Lycidas.'" *Images and Themes in Five Poems by Milton*. Cambridge: Harvard UP, 1957. 73–111.

ACKNOWLEDGMENTS

The creation of this second edition of the *MLA Style Manual and Guide to Scholarly Publishing* has been a collaborative enterprise drawing on and incorporating the thoughts and contributions of numerous persons. Thanks are extended here to the many who generously helped in the development of the project. The efforts and assistance of the persons and institutions cited below are especially acknowledged.

The members of the *MLA Style Manual* Review Committee oversaw preparation of the book: Reinhold Grimm, Joseph C. Harris, John W. Kronik, Ian Lancashire, Janel Mueller, Stephen G. Nichols, and Felicity Nussbaum. The views of the members of the MLA Committee on Computers and Emerging Technologies in Teaching and Research also helped shape the revision. Herbert Lindenberger, the 1997 president of the Modern Language Association, contributed the foreword to the book. Arthur F. Abelman wrote the second chapter, on legal issues.

The following persons read and commented on portions of the manuscript during its development: Katherine M. Arens, Jennifer Crewe, Andrew P. Debicki, Mario A. Di Cesare, Heather Florence, Susan S. Friedman, Stirling Haig, James L. Harner, Patrick Henry, Matthew Kirschenbaum, Gerald R. Kleinfeld, Melinda Koyanis, Holly Laird, Sheila Levine, Leslie Mitchner, Caroline Pari, Geoffrey Rockwell, Robert J. Rodini, Michael N. Salda, Jeffrey L. Sammons, Sanford G. Thatcher, Alan G. Thomas, John M. Unsworth, and Jack Zipes.

Graduate language and literature departments at the following institutions furnished materials that informed chapter 5, on preparing theses and dissertations: Baylor University; Brandeis University; Brown University; University of California, Davis; University of California, Los Angeles; University of California, Santa Barbara; University of Chicago; City University of New York; University of Delaware, Newark; University of Denver; Duke University; Fordham University; Georgetown University; George Washington University; Harvard University; University of Hawaii, Manoa; University of Iowa; Johns

Hopkins University; University of Kansas; Louisiana State University; Loyola University, Chicago; University of Missouri, Columbia; State University of New York, Stony Brook; New York University; Ohio State University, Columbus; University of Pittsburgh, Pittsburgh; Princeton University; Rutgers University, New Brunswick; Saint Louis University; Stanford University; University of Texas, Austin; Texas Tech University; Vanderbilt University; University of Virginia; University of Washington; University of Wisconsin, Madison; and Yale University.

Among MLA staff members, Martha Evans served as the general coordinator of the project; Eric Wirth was the principal copyeditor; Elizabeth Holland enlarged and improved the section on punctuation; and Judith Altreuter advised on chapter 4 and related sections dealing with the preparation of scholarly manuscripts. Other staff members lending assistance and support included Terence Ford, Phyllis Franklin, Judy Goulding, Bettina Huber, Sonia Kane, David Cloyce Smith, and Jennifer Wilson.

1

SCHOLARLY PUBLISHING

1.1   Scholars and Scholarly Publishing

1.2   Refereed and Nonrefereed Publications

1.3   Deciding to Submit the Manuscript

1.4   Placing a Manuscript for a Journal Article
    1.4.1   Scholarly Journals
    1.4.2   Types of Scholarly Articles
    1.4.3   Selecting a Journal
    1.4.4   Submitting the Manuscript to a Journal
    1.4.5   Evaluation of the Manuscript
    1.4.6   Acceptance of the Manuscript

1.5   Placing a Manuscript for a Book
    1.5.1   Scholarly Book Publishers
    1.5.2   Types of Scholarly Books
    1.5.3   Selecting a Publisher
    1.5.4   Submitting the Prospectus for a Book
    1.5.5   Submitting the Manuscript to a Publisher
    1.5.6   Evaluation of the Manuscript
    1.5.7   Acceptance of the Manuscript

1.6   Production and Publication
    1.6.1   Copyediting
    1.6.2   Proofreading
    1.6.3   Preparing an Index
    1.6.4   Design
    1.6.5   Composition, Printing, Binding
    1.6.6   Marketing

1.7   Conclusion

1.1   SCHOLARS AND SCHOLARLY PUBLISHING

To publish is to make public. When scholars make their work public, they educate, enlighten, stimulate learning, and further intellectual pursuit, serving the academic community and society at large. Scholarly publication is also often used within the academy as a measure when professional advancement is decided.

The publication of scholarship takes many forms, depending on field, objective, medium, and audience. Teaching is probably the most common way of making scholarship public. Other ways are contributing to an electronic discussion group and offering a presentation at a local, regional, national, or international meeting. This book primarily concerns itself with the more formal modes of academic publishing in the field of language and literature, especially journal articles and books.

As this chapter indicates, scholarly publication is a collaborative enterprise that comprises diverse and complex relations among numerous persons besides you, as the author, and your reader. Academic authors normally submit their work to editors, who in turn customarily seek the advice and judgment of other scholars—for example, consultant readers (specialists in the field addressed by the author) and members of editorial boards. Various other persons, though perhaps less visible to the author, also play vital roles in making scholarship public; these include publishing professionals in areas like copyediting, design, typesetting, printing, and promotion. Such intermediary figures add value to the author's work by enhancing its intellectual quality and communicative presentation and by helping to bring it to the attention of its potential audience.

Publishers are as intrinsic to the scholarly community as academic institutions and professional organizations are. While institutions provide a forum for teaching and organizations plan meetings that primarily promote the oral exchange of ideas and information between attendees, publishers make possible the dissemination of scholarship in finished forms to varied and broadly dispersed audiences. Book and journal publication, then, exists on a continuum with teaching and convention presentations. Scholars turn to a publisher when they believe they can make a contribution to scholarship that warrants wider circulation than the classroom and the conference hall permit.

1.2   REFEREED AND NONREFEREED PUBLICATIONS

Academic journals and book publishers can be divided into two broad categories: those that seek and rely on the advice of referees or consultant readers and those that do not. The editor of a refereed journal, whether print or electronic, asks specialist readers to review a manuscript before it is accepted or rejected. Each consultant reads the work and sends the editor a report evaluating the manuscript and, in most instances, either recommending or not recommending it for publication. The editor, editorial staff, or editorial board—whichever is appropriate to the journal—refers to the consultants' evaluations and recommendations when deciding whether to publish the article. Most academic presses follow like procedures, soliciting reviews by experts before deciding on publication of a book manuscript. (For more on the refereeing of articles and books, see 1.4.5 and 1.5.6, respectively.)

A nonrefereed journal, by contrast, whether print or electronic, generally publishes a manuscript without specialist review, as do some presses. The use of referees normally adds several months to the time between completion of the manuscript and its publication. Although it is desirable to get your work published as soon as possible, there are many advantages to seeking a publisher committed to a policy of refereeing.

Specialist readings constitute professional service to authors. As experts in the work's general subject, reviewers can identify scholarly errors and omissions and thus save the author the embarrassment of having a flawed manuscript reach publication. In addition, consultants often offer suggestions for revision that improve manuscripts or help make them publishable.

Academic institutions, moreover, invariably attach greater prestige to articles and books that underwent formal review than to those that did not. Hiring, promotion, and tenure committees, whose members are frequently not specialists in the candidate's field, almost always assign a refereed publication significantly more professional standing and scholarly authority than they do a nonrefereed publication. Most scholars believe that the assistance derived from referees' reports and the value and prestige conferred on a published work that successfully passes through rigorous critical examination more than compensate for the publication delay that consultant evaluation necessitates.

1.3   DECIDING TO SUBMIT THE MANUSCRIPT

Professional circumstances tend to press scholars to publish early and abundantly. Before you consider submitting a manuscript for publication, however, no matter the stage of your career, you should always ask a number of colleagues, especially other experts in your field, to read and assess your work, including revised versions of it; to advise you on whether the manuscript is appropriate and ready for publication; and to recommend possible publishers. These readers are likely to provide useful comments on intellectual and scholarly issues and on such matters as the organization and development of ideas, the unity and coherence of the discussion, the cogency of the argument, and the clarity of expression. Some scholars also place drafts—clearly labeled as works in progress—on the Internet and invite comments from interested readers.

You should not consider a work ready for submission to a publisher, moreover, until you have given it a final editorial review that includes, among other things, confirming the accuracy of all paraphrases, quotations, bibliographic references, and textual citations. Your manuscript should also follow the technical specifications discussed in chapter 4 of this manual.

You should be aware that most publishers adhere to a house editorial style, which dictates such features of scholarly presentation as the documentation system and mechanics of writing. Chapters 6 and 7 offer an authoritative and comprehensive explanation of the style followed by the Modern Language Association of America.

The submitted manuscript should also contain clear copies of illustrations you want to publish with the work. It is useful to consider at an early stage whether you will need permission to reproduce any quotation, photograph, chart, or other material that you take from others (see 2.1.13) and whether such permission will be easily obtained. (For samples of letters requesting permission to reproduce printed materials and illustrations, see figs. 2 and 3, at the end of this chapter.)

The author's concerns before submitting a manuscript, then, are many and wide-ranging: they include not only intellectual and scholarly but also stylistic and technical questions. Attention to this full range of authorial considerations before submission will facilitate the passage of the manuscript through the publishing process.

The next two sections discuss the typical ways that journal articles (1.4) and books (1.5) progress toward publication. Because the two paths are not completely dissimilar, there is some inevitable repetition in the two sections that will permit you to consult these sections independently from each other.

1.4   PLACING A MANUSCRIPT FOR A JOURNAL ARTICLE

1.4.1   Scholarly Journals

The scope of scholarly journals ranges from the broadly focused to the more specific. At one end of the spectrum, for example, is a journal like *PMLA*, which, according to its current statement of editorial policy, publishes "essays of interest to those concerned with the study of language and literature" and is "receptive to a variety of topics, whether general or specific, and to all scholarly methods and theoretical perspectives." Most journals, however, are more specialized, focusing on a specific literature, language, culture, period, genre, ethnicity, theory, methodology, theme, author, and so forth.

The editorial staff of a scholarly journal is usually identified on the inside of the front cover or on the copyright page of each printed issue or as part of the journal's home page on the Internet. The roster typically designates at least one editor of the journal, and other persons may be listed as, for example, associate editor, book review editor, managing editor, manuscript editor, production editor, and editorial assistant.

The page also likely names the members of the journal's editorial board, sometimes given a title such as "advisory board" or "board of editorial consultants." This group of scholars, which may range in number from a half dozen to several dozen, assists the editorial staff in setting the direction of the journal as well as in evaluating submissions. Depending on the journal, publication decisions are made by the editor or editors or by the editorial board, sometimes in conjunction with the staff.

Most scholarly journals are associated with a sponsoring organization—a college, university, learned society, library, museum, foundation, research institute, government agency. In addition, some journals have business affiliations with academic presses: the journal staff supplies the copy for each issue, and the press produces and distributes the publication.

1.4.2   Types of Scholarly Articles

The typical issue of a scholarly journal in language and literature is devoted primarily to articles containing new research and original interpretations of texts and data. Some journals also publish book reviews, review essays, reviews of research, and translations. Other contributions include letters to the editor commenting on articles previously published in the journal or on general matters, interviews, notes, conference proceedings, and bibliographies. Most published articles are unsolicited, although some articles and even whole issues may be commissioned by the journal. Book reviews, review essays, reviews of research, and translations are almost always assigned.

When commissioning book reviews, journal editors normally set the format, length, and coverage. A book review tends to be devoted to a single work, which is documented at the beginning (or sometimes at the end) of the review, usually with more information than a reference in a works-cited list gives. Besides the name of the author, title, city of publication, publisher, and date of publication, the reviewer often records the number of pages, price, and, if the book is not published by a major press, ordering information. If you would like to review books for a journal, you should write to the editor or the book review editor, if there is one, indicating your interest, your field of expertise, and your qualifications.

Review essays are extended book reviews, usually covering more than one recent book and giving full publication information for each work discussed. Review essays normally allow the writer greater compass to describe and compare the works under consideration and to place them in perspective. Reviews of research are extended review essays that describe, evaluate, and indicate the importance of significant works in a specific field or on a specific issue published over a broader period of time, often helping to set the terms of discussion for future work in the field. Normally longer than a book review and a review essay, the review of research generally provides only essential bibliographic information for sources (e.g., author, title, city of publication, publisher, and date of publication but not number of pages, price, and so forth). Finally, many journals also present translations of articles and creative works originally published in other languages. If you wish to contribute a review essay, a review of research, or a translation, you should write to an appropriate journal to inquire if there is interest in such a contribution before you embark on it.

1.4.3 Selecting a Journal

One of the keys to successful scholarly publishing is locating the right publishers. Your research will doubtless bring you in contact with numerous journals in your field. Colleagues might direct you to additional suitable journals. To learn of others, consult bibliographies and similar reference works in the discipline, library catalogs, and directories of periodicals.

The *MLA Directory of Periodicals*, which can be found in the reference section of many academic libraries, is a guide to thousands of journals and book series in the fields of language, literature, and folklore. Each entry in this directory is divided into five sections: general information, subscription information, advertising information, editorial description, and submission requirements. The first section gives mailing address, telephone and fax numbers, and date of first publication, among other general information. After data on subscription (e.g., frequency of publication, circulation) and advertising, the entry describes the editorial scope of the periodical and gives such information as whether it reviews books, what languages submissions may be written in, and what its policy on author anonymity is (see 1.4.4). The entry concludes with specifications concerning submission, under categories like the following ones: restrictions on contributors, desired length of articles, editorial style followed, number of manuscript copies required, time between submission and publication decision, time between acceptance and publication, number of reviewers used, number of articles submitted to the periodical in a year, and number of articles published in a year. The *Directory* also contains indexes to subjects, sponsoring organizations, editorial personnel, and languages published as well as a list of periodicals with an author-anonymous submissions policy. Other useful sources include the *Directory of Electronic Journals, Newsletters, and Academic Discussion Lists* and *Ulrich's International Periodicals Directory.*

Once you have identified potential journals for your article, you should consult recent issues of each to determine its nature and quality and to learn about any recent changes in editorial policy, about the editors' special interests, and about details of submission procedures. You might also consult with colleagues whose work has appeared in any of the journals to find out if their experience was professionally satisfactory.

Journals frequently devote entire issues to specific topics. Editors planning special issues may seek submissions by announcing the topics in advance. (Editors' calls for papers can be found, for example, in the Journal Notes section of *PMLA* and in relevant electronic discussion groups and information lists.)

1.4.4   Submitting the Manuscript to a Journal

In submitting a manuscript, follow the instructions in the journal concerning such matters as the number of copies required, encoding (for electronic journals; see 4.4), submission fees (uncommon in the humanities), and any information you are expected to provide along with the manuscript. Be sure that your manuscript falls within the range of lengths requested and follows the appropriate editorial style. For journals published by professional organizations, check that you have the requisite membership status. If the journal has an anonymous-submission policy, your name should appear only on a separate or a duplicate title page (see 4.2.5), and the manuscript should not identify you in any other way; for example, give your name instead of a self-reference such as "See my article [. . .]."

Unless the journal specifies otherwise, submit one hard copy of the manuscript—that is, a version printed or typed on paper—prepared according to the specifications in chapter 4. Electronic journals commonly accept submissions by e-mail, on disk, or on paper. Always keep a paper version of the manuscript and a copy on a backup disk as well.

Address the manuscript to the journal's editor. Include a brief cover letter that states the full title of the article, identifies you and any other author of the work, calls attention to special features (e.g., illustrations, tables), describes permissions that might be required and tells whether they have been or can easily be obtained, and supplies addresses for future correspondence. Send a printed manuscript by first-class mail, indicating in your cover letter if the manuscript is available on disk and enclosing a self-addressed mailer and unattached return postage if you wish the manuscript returned in case it is not accepted.

Journal editors do not have a common policy concerning the submission of manuscripts to more than one periodical at a time. Publications that have each manuscript evaluated by a number of specialist readers often will not consider a submission that is under review elsewhere. If you decide to submit a manuscript to more than one journal simultaneously, you must inform each editor involved.

After submitting the manuscript, you should expect to receive a written acknowledgment of the journal's receipt of it within about two weeks. If there is no response within a month, you should inquire to see whether the manuscript was received.

1.4.5   Evaluation of the Manuscript

The editor of a refereed periodical generally reviews a manuscript soon after submission to verify that it is suitable for the journal. If it is not, the editor rejects the manuscript without further review. If it is suitable, the editor sends the manuscript for evaluation to a number of consultant readers (usually two), sometimes simultaneously and sometimes consecutively. Although the questions asked of readers vary from journal to journal, most editors request comments on the importance of the subject, the originality and soundness of the argument, the accuracy of the facts, the clarity and readability of the style, and the validity of the documentation.

In addition, editors usually ask for a recommendation regarding publication—for example, one of the following choices: recommended without reservations or with only minor changes, not recommended without substantial revision, or not recommended. Consultants are typically encouraged to give specific reasons for their recommendations, to describe reservations in as much detail as possible, and to suggest ways to improve the manuscript.

The readers' reports to a large extent determine whether the editor, editorial staff, or editorial board accepts the manuscript for publication, rejects it, or accepts it pending revision. The last option has the potential for misunderstandings between editors and authors. If the editor asks for revisions, the requested changes and the conditions determining publication should be fully and clearly detailed in writing: you should understand whether the revisions are optional or required, whether there is a deadline for submitting a revised manuscript, whether revision will ensure acceptance or lead to another round of consultant review and publication decision, and, if there is to be a new evaluation, whether the same or different referees will be used. If you are unsure about any of these matters, do not hesitate to ask the editor for clarification.

Consider requests for revision carefully and deliberately. If you choose to undertake the revisions, inform the editor of your intent and give an expected date of resubmission or confirm that you will meet the deadline. When returning the revised manuscript, include in your cover letter a summary of the changes made.

If you do not agree with all the revisions requested, tell the editor in writing which changes you are willing to make and which you are not, giving explicit reasons for your decision, before reworking the article. If the editor does not concur with your plan of revision, you should withdraw the manuscript and submit it elsewhere.

Copies of the consultant readers' reports usually accompany requests for revision. Some journals remove the reviewer's name from each report whether it is favorable or not; others give consultants the option of anonymity. Many journal editors send the author copies of the reports—or excerpts from or summaries of them—regardless of the publication decision. Thus, even if the manuscript is rejected, the author might be able to use the reviews to improve it and make it publishable.

The editor's acknowledgment letter at the start of the process may tell you approximately how long it will take before a decision is made. The typical waiting period is about two or three months, although referees' schedules and the time of the academic year could delay the decision. If you do not hear again from the journal within four months after the initial acknowledgment, feel free to inquire about the status of the manuscript. When an editorial board, rather than an editor or editorial staff, decides on publication, the process can take longer because the board may meet only two or three times a year. If the journal is unable to make a decision after four to six months, depending on the type of journal, and the editor and you cannot agree on a timetable, you may send the manuscript to another journal after notifying the editor of your decision.

1.4.6   Acceptance of the Manuscript

A journal generally accepts an article for publication either as is or subject to revisions that only the editor needs to review. Sometimes editors prescribe changes; sometimes they merely suggest them and allow the author to decide which to perform. Even if your article is accepted without the need for revision, you may receive an opportunity to update the manuscript or make final improvements before copyediting and production begin. Whatever the circumstances, make revisions as expeditiously as possible, carefully observing any deadline the editor sets. Submit the final version of the article in the form or forms required by the journal (e.g., hard copy and disk). When the journal receives the final version, the editor should be able to notify you of the projected date of publication. After accepting a manuscript, the journal usually offers the author a contract, or memorandum of agreement, for publication of the work (see 2.2.2).

Should communication between an author and a journal editor break down at any point, either can appeal to the Council of Editors of Learned Journals, which tries to mediate such misunderstandings and differences of opinion. (See the council's listing in the Directory of Useful Addresses in the annual September issue of *PMLA*.)

On the production and publication of books and journal articles, see 1.6.

1.5   PLACING A MANUSCRIPT FOR A BOOK

1.5.1   Scholarly Book Publishers

Most scholarly books are published by university presses, professional organizations, commercial academic presses, and trade publishers. University presses and book publication programs within professional organizations are usually headed by a director and include staff members in such areas as acquisitions, copyediting, design, production, marketing, sales, and business (e.g., contracts, royalties, rights, permissions). At both types of publishers, editorial boards composed of faculty members or association members normally make final decisions on publication (see 1.5.6, on evaluation).

By contrast, at commercial academic presses and trade publishers, which are rarely affiliated with an educational or a professional institution, decisions are usually made by staff editors rather than academic committees. Both types of publishers are set up to make a profit, but commercial academic presses, such as Blackwell Publishers or Greenwood Press, tend to issue the same kinds of books as university presses and professional organizations, whereas trade publishers, like HarperCollins and Random House, generally seek out books that appeal to a wide general audience. Although commercial publishers are usually headed by presidents and vice presidents rather than directors, their staffs fulfill the same general functions (e.g., editorial, production, business) as those of not-for-profit publishers.

1.5.2 Types of Scholarly Books

Most scholarly books in the field of language and literature fall into one of the following categories: scholarly studies, collections of original essays, collections of previously published essays, translations, scholarly editions, bibliographies and other reference books, and textbooks.

The most common form is the scholarly study, usually by a single author but occasionally by coauthors. The author of a scholarly study typically begins with a clear statement of an original thesis and then explores that thesis by presenting and analyzing a significant body of evidence. In many humanities fields, such books represent the primary means of advancing scholarly knowledge. A number of publishers have established book series, often under series editors or editorial boards, that group studies according to subject.

Scholarly studies embrace works ranging from the monograph—an extended discussion of a narrowly focused topic (e.g., a single author or single text), aimed at a limited audience—to the nonfiction trade book, which reaches general readers as well as scholars. Nearly all presses tend to favor works that have wider scholarly audiences. A book with a small potential readership is more difficult to place than a book that promises to draw readers with different interests from various fields and disciplines. In general, moreover, most publishers will not consider unrevised dissertations, which are unlike books in nature, purpose, objectives, and intended audience, and, with few exceptions, publishers will review a revised dissertation only if it has been reconceived and rewritten to address the interests of a broad range of scholars (see Eleanor Harman and Ian Montagnes, eds., *The Thesis and the Book* [Toronto: U of Toronto P, 1976]). It is likely that in the future works with very limited audiences will only be collected within electronic databases and supplied on demand.

A collection of original essays by different authors offers at its best a breadth of knowledge and diversity of perspectives and methodologies that no book by a single author can. To avoid problems of disunity, incoherence, unevenness, or confusion of purpose, the editor of a collection typically strives to identify a useful and important subject for the book, establish clear and attainable objectives, define the intended audience, divide the book's subject into specific topics, select appropriate contributors for these topics, establish unambiguous guidelines for writing the essays, maintain high scholarly and editorial standards, and communicate these goals and expectations to the contributors. If you are interested in editing such a collection, you might approach possible authors for tentative commitments at an early stage but should not formally invite anyone to contribute until a publisher expresses serious interest in the projected book and invites a manuscript.

Collections of previously published essays bring together studies from diverse sources, often giving wider circulation to important essays published in journals. Many such collections usefully and conveniently present major scholarly trends in an established field over a specific period, focus attention and help give definition and shape to an emergent field, or provide key essays on a certain topic for classroom use. Since identifying the most appropriate works for republication is essential to the success of the collection, its editor needs to consult widely with other scholars before selecting essays. Another consideration for the editor is to obtain permission from—and possibly pay requisite fees to—the holder of the copyright to each essay. If you plan to prepare such a book, you might make preliminary inquiries about permissions before approaching a potential publisher but should pay no fees until publication is certain. In any event, copyright holders usually do not grant permission or set fees until after they receive details of publication, such as the price of the book and the number of copies to be printed.

Translations of scholarly or creative works similarly expand readership. Like those who edit collections of previously published essays, the translator of a work under copyright or the translator's publisher needs to obtain rights from the copyright holder, normally the original publisher or the author, who will likely require a fee. Translations of works in the public domain—no longer protected by copyright law (see 2.1.7)—do not have this problem, but if the work has already been translated, the new translator has the challenge of making a convincing argument that the proposed rendition is necessary. Translators commonly prepare a sample translation to send to potential publishers, sometimes inquiring of the original-language publisher at the same time about the availability of translation rights, but do not translate the entire work or pay fees without a commitment to publish.

The spectrum of scholarly editions ranges from single-text diplomatic editions to eclectic critical editions. The editor of a single-text diplomatic edition reproduces a text (e.g., a manuscript) or version of a text (e.g., an important printed edition of the text) exactly as it originally appeared—that is, as a historical document. The editor of an eclectic critical edition produces an original version of a text by combining the "best readings" drawn from several other versions (e.g., editions, manuscripts). Like translators, scholarly editors usually seek a publication commitment before beginning a project, supplying a sample of the edition, along with a statement of editorial principles, to possible publishers. (For further information, see William Proctor Williams and Craig S. Abbott, *An Introduction to Bibliographical and Textual Studies*, 3rd ed. [New York: MLA, 1999] and D. C. Greetham, ed., *Scholarly Editing: A Guide to Research* [New York: MLA, 1995].)

Authoritative annotated bibliographies and other reference works (e.g., dictionaries, encyclopedias, handbooks) are useful, time-saving research tools for scholars and students. Such works are normally prepared only under contract to a publisher, since they usually involve a considerable investment of time and require close cooperation between author and publisher. Unlike most other scholarly books, reference works adhere to relatively strict editorial policies and follow numerous conventions intended to make them readily accessible to their users. (For further information on annotated bibliographies, see James L. Harner, *On Compiling an Annotated Bibliography*, rev. ed. [New York: MLA, 1991].)

Publishing textbooks allows scholars the opportunity to have their personally developed, perhaps theoretically based teaching approaches adopted by instructors for use in courses in other educational institutions. Textbooks can also be lucrative enterprises for authors as well as publishers. Because of the potential profits involved, commercial textbook publishing is a highly competitive area. To be successful, a textbook has to appeal not only to instructors, who must decide to adopt the book for their classes, often selecting it as a replacement for a previously used text, but also to students, whose experience with the book must be positive if it is to be reordered. Textbook publishers—often the textbook divisions of trade publishers—require extensive reviews of a proposed book at every stage of development. Reviewers number not just the two or three common to other scholarly publications but perhaps dozens, since the review process for textbooks serves both evaluative and marketing functions. If a textbook is accepted, the publisher's staff is likely to work closely with the author in the development of the book.

1.5.3   Selecting a Publisher

Like selecting a journal for an article, identifying an appropriate publisher will facilitate placing a book manuscript successfully. Your scholarly research and conversations with colleagues will help make you knowledgeable about which publishers are apt to be interested in your work. Book advertisements in journals, publishers' catalogs and brochures, and visits to presses' Internet sites and to their exhibition booths at scholarly conferences will provide additional information about publishers' interests. Be especially alert to book series into which your project might fit. Just as journals devote issues to specific topics, many book publishers have series that group books according to kind (e.g., bibliographies, translations) or subject.

A useful reference work for selecting a book publisher is the *MLA Directory of Scholarly Presses in Language and Literature*, which lists more than three hundred publishers from over thirty countries. Each entry in this directory is divided into six sections: general information, scope, submission requirements, editorial information, contract provisions, and publication and distribution information. The first section gives mailing addresses, telephone and fax numbers, year established, and contact person(s), among other general information. The second section describes the publishing interests of the press and covers such questions as the series it sponsors and the languages of the works it publishes. The section on submission requirements includes information on what the preferred form of initial contact is, what editorial style is followed, and whether a subvention is required. The section on editorial requirements gives data on matters like the number of manuscripts or prospectuses received in a year, the number of consultant readers used to evaluate a manuscript, the time between submission and publication decision, and the time between acceptance and publication. The next section, on contracts, deals with copyright ownership, royalty provisions, and responsibility for permissions. The entry concludes with publication and distribution information under such categories as the following ones: forms of publication (e.g., cloth, paper, electronic media), language and literature titles published in a year, typical print run, number of review copies distributed for each title, and number of years a title is usually kept in print. The *Directory* contains indexes to publishing interests, imprints and subsidiary firms, series titles, editorial personnel, and languages of publication.

Similarly useful is the annual directory of the Association of American University Presses (AAUP), which lists the more than one hundred publishers that are members of the association. Each entry in this directory contains general information about the press; a comprehensive listing of staff members by department (e.g., administrative, acquisitions, manuscript editorial, marketing, design and production, business); facts on history and activity (e.g., year established, title output in the previous year, titles in print); and a description of the editorial program, including disciplines covered and book series and journals published. The AAUP directory also includes a helpful subject-area grid that serves as a convenient guide to the interests of individual presses.

Other relevant, though less focused, directories are *Literary Market Place (LMP)*, *International Literary Market Place (ILMP)*, and *Books in Print (BiP)*, all published by R. R. Bowker. *LMP* is a directory of the book publishing industry in the United States and Canada. It contains a listing of virtually all publishers in the United States, offering primarily business-oriented information on each. This listing is indexed by geographic location, type of publication, and subject. The work also has separate sections on Canadian book publishers and foreign publishers with offices in the United States. *ILMP* is a companion directory to *LMP*, with similar data on book publishers in over 170 countries outside the United States and Canada. *Books in Print* lists all books currently published or distributed in the United States and includes general facts on publishers of listed books.

After you have identified potential publishers for your manuscript, you might look at some of their recent books to see the quality of work each produces. You might also learn how efficiently and professionally a press functions by asking colleagues whose work it has published.

1.5.4 Submitting the Prospectus for a Book

Every scholarly publisher includes among its staff an editor or a number of editors responsible for acquiring the manuscripts that the press publishes. Often such editors possess advanced degrees and a good sense of the scholarship in at least one field of learning. The acquisitions editor normally is the author's principal contact with the press; thus it is essential that the two share a productive working relationship. Acquisitions editors at many presses actively solicit manuscripts, especially from well-known and established scholars who have written important and influential books and articles. Acquisitions editors also commonly attend professional meetings and make campus trips to seek manuscripts. Most authors who wish to publish scholarly books take the initiative by approaching editors at conventions, meeting with visiting editors on campus, or writing to presses.

When offering a book manuscript to publishers, submit a brief cover letter and a prospectus for the manuscript to the appropriate acquisitions editors. Since few publishers have the staff to read unsolicited manuscripts, do not send the complete manuscript unless invited to do so. Authors usually send the prospectus to the editor by first-class mail; presses prefer not to receive a prospectus by fax or e-mail or on disk only. To find editors' names, consult the directories cited in section 1.5.3 or inquire directly of the presses. If you cannot discover which editor to approach, write to the director or the editor in chief of the press, who will be able to route the manuscript to the right person. Alternatively, a colleague familiar with the press may be willing to introduce you to the editor who acquires books in your field.

Your prospectus should clearly and concisely describe the manuscript and provide a rationale for its publication. Usually no longer than ten double-spaced pages, the prospectus addresses such questions as the need for the book, its goals and purposes, its scholarly and professional significance, the qualities that distinguish it from other publications on the subject, and its intended audience. The prospectus also incorporates a summary of the book and provides relevant biographical data indicating the author's credentials for the project, including previous publications, as well as information on the status of the manuscript and on relevant physical characteristics—scheduled completion date, expected length, availability on disk, word-processing software used, special features (e.g., illustrations, tables), and so forth. Typically accompanying the prospectus are selected materials from the manuscript, such as the table of contents, the introduction or preface, and a sample chapter. To facilitate future correspondence with the publisher, authors may include a self-addressed, stamped envelope for the acquisitions editor to use in acknowledging receipt of the prospectus and a self-addressed mailer with unattached postage if they wish the submitted materials returned.

After submitting the prospectus, you will likely receive a written acknowledgment of the press's receipt of it within about two weeks. If there is no response within a month, you should inquire whether the prospectus was received.

The acquisitions editor usually reads the prospectus quickly to ascertain whether the proposed book is appropriate for the press. If it is not or if the prospectus seems ill-conceived, the editor normally rejects the proposal immediately with a brief note stating that it does not meet the publisher's current needs or requirements. Otherwise, the editor reads the prospectus more carefully, perhaps circulating it to consultant readers for opinion and advice. After the evaluation, the editor responds to the author either to report that the press is not interested in the proposed book or to invite submission of the manuscript for full review. The consideration of a prospectus usually takes from one to three months. If you do not receive a decision or otherwise hear from the editor about the evaluation after three months, you should feel free to inquire about the status of the prospectus.

Experienced authors usually have a somewhat easier course in placing a book manuscript with a publisher. For one thing, they are more knowledgeable about which presses are apt to be interested in their work and may even have professional relationships with some acquisitions editors. If the scholar's previously published work was successfully received, editors from different presses may actively pursue and compete for the author's current manuscript. Such authors are likely to be offered advance contracts before submission of the manuscript (see 2.2.1) and to have a voice in such matters as how the work is published (e.g., in cloth, paper, or electronic versions) and marketed.

Most academic authors, even experienced ones, seldom use literary agents to place their manuscripts. Since scholarly books rarely sell in large numbers and since agents receive a percentage of royalties as their fee, authors are reluctant to share their modest royalties with agents, and agents are reluctant to invest the time and effort required to place a manuscript for the small fee it will produce. The scholars who tend to use agents are those who write trade books—works that reach a wide general audience. If you wish to find an agent, seek the advice of colleagues who have used agents or consult the most recent editions of such reference works as *Literary Agents of North America* (*LANA*), published by Author Aid / Research Associates International, and *Literary Market Place* (*LMP*) and *International Literary Market Place* (*ILMP*), both published by R. R. Bowker. *LANA* contains profiles of more than one thousand agencies, with information on policies, interests, specialties, and fees. *LMP* lists agents in the United States and Canada; *ILMP*, agents in other countries. Listings in *LMP* indicate whether the agent belongs to the Association of Authors' Representatives (AAR), a professional organization that sets ethical standards for its members.

1.5.5   Submitting the Manuscript to a Publisher

If a publisher invites you to submit a book manuscript for consideration, follow the press's instructions, if any, on the method of submission and the number of copies to send. Unless the publisher specifies otherwise, submit one hard copy of the manuscript prepared according to the specifications in chapter 4. Always keep a paper version of the manuscript and a copy on a backup disk as well.

Send a typescript by first-class mail, addressed to the editor who invited it. Include a brief cover letter that states the full title of the book, identifies you and any other author of the work, indicates if it is available on disk, calls attention to any aspect of the manuscript that significantly differs from what was laid out in the prospectus, and supplies addresses for future correspondence. You should also enclose a self-addressed mailer and unattached return postage if you wish the manuscript returned in case it is not accepted.

Although it is common to send a prospectus simultaneously to more than one press, many publishers will not review a manuscript under consideration elsewhere, because of the time and expense the evaluation exacts. If two or more editors invite you to submit a manuscript and you decide to send it to more than one of them, you must inform each press involved.

After submitting the manuscript, you should expect to receive a written acknowledgment of the press's receipt of it within about two weeks. If there is no acknowledgment within a month, you should inquire to see whether the manuscript was received.

1.5.6   Evaluation of the Manuscript

The acquiring editor generally reviews a manuscript soon after submission to confirm that it fulfills the promise of the prospectus. If it does, the editor sends the manuscript for evaluation to a number of consultant readers (usually two), sometimes simultaneously and sometimes consecutively. Some publishers ask authors for advice and suggestions concerning reviewers. Although the questions asked of readers vary from press to press, most editors seek comments on the importance of the subject, the originality and soundness of the argument, the accuracy of the facts, the logic and effectiveness of the organization, the clarity and readability of the style, and the validity of the documentation. The editor often also asks the readers to compare the work with other books on the subject and to comment on the potential audience for the manuscript.

In addition, editors usually ask for a recommendation regarding publication—for example, one of the following choices: recommended without reservations or with only minor changes, not recommended without substantial revision, or not recommended. Consultants are typically encouraged to give specific reasons for their recommendations, to describe reservations in as much detail as possible, and to offer suggestions on ways to improve the manuscript. Publishers usually pay readers an honorarium or offer them free books for preparing a report on a book-length manuscript.

If the press receives conflicting reports from two consultant readers, it may seek one additional evaluation or more. The readers' reports determine to a large extent whether the press accepts the manuscript for publication, rejects it, or accepts it pending revision. The last option sometimes results in misunderstandings between publishers and authors. If the press asks for revisions, the requested changes and the conditions determining publication should be fully and clearly detailed in writing: you should understand whether the revisions are optional or required, whether there is a deadline for submitting a revised manuscript, whether revision will ensure acceptance or lead to another round of consultant review and publication decision, and, if there is to be a new evaluation, whether the same or different referees will be used. If you are unsure about any of these matters, do not hesitate to communicate with your editor for clarification.

Consider requests for revision carefully and deliberately. If you choose to undertake the revisions, inform the editor of your intent and give an expected date of resubmission or confirm that you will meet the deadline. Notify the press of any subsequent delay, reporting on your progress and giving a new projected submission date. When returning the revised manuscript, include in your cover letter a summary of the changes made.

If you do not agree with all the revisions requested, tell the editor in writing which changes you are willing to make and which you are not, giving explicit reasons for your decision, before reworking the manuscript. If the press does not concur with your plan of revision, you should withdraw the manuscript and submit it elsewhere.

Copies of the consultant readers' reports usually accompany requests for revision. Some publishers remove the reviewer's name from each report whether it is favorable or not; others give consultants the option of anonymity. Many presses send the author copies of the reports—or excerpts from or summaries of them—regardless of the publication decision. Thus, even if the manuscript is rejected, the author might be able to use the reviews to improve it and make it publishable.

When the readers' reports are favorable, the press usually has enough information to decide whether to publish the manuscript. At most academic presses, the acquiring editor presents the manuscript for a publication decision to the editorial committee, normally a board of scholars who are not employed by the press. Faculty members constitute the committee at university presses; professional organizations with book publishing programs appoint association members to the board. The acquisitions editor shares with the committee representative excerpts from the manuscript (or sometimes the entire text), the readers' reports, the author's response to the reports (if deemed necessary), and any other material of importance to the decision. A covering document by the editor usually introduces the manuscript, supplying background information. At commercial academic presses and trade publishing houses, by contrast, staff editors usually make publication decisions.

The editor's acknowledgment letter at the start of the process may tell you approximately how long it will take before a decision is made. The typical waiting period is about two or three months, although referees' schedules and the time of the academic year could delay the decision. When an editorial board meets infrequently, the process can take longer. If you do not hear from the publisher within three months, feel free to inquire about the status of the manuscript. If the publisher is unable to make a decision after four to six months, depending on the type of press, and the editor and you cannot agree on a timetable, you may send the manuscript to another publisher after notifying the editor of your decision.

1.5.7   Acceptance of the Manuscript

A press generally accepts a book manuscript for publication either as is or subject to revisions that only an editor needs to review. Sometimes publishers prescribe changes; sometimes they merely suggest them and allow the author to decide which to perform. Even if your book is accepted without the need for revision, you should expect to receive an opportunity to update the manuscript or make final improvements before copyediting and production begin. Whatever the circumstances, make revisions as expeditiously as possible, carefully observing any deadline the editor sets. If the publisher furnishes a set of editorial guidelines or a handbook for authors, prepare and submit the manuscript as requested. When the press receives the final version of the manuscript, your editor should be able to notify you of the projected date of publication, usually about a year from receipt of the final manuscript, depending on the length and complexity of the work, the time of the year, and the press's publication schedule.

The publisher usually offers the author a contract following acceptance of the book manuscript. Some scholarly book publishers, like most trade book publishers, offer contracts on approving a prospectus and inviting the manuscript for evaluation, but such advance contracts do not guarantee publication, since they normally stipulate that the manuscript must first satisfactorily pass through the evaluation process, including consultant review and approval by the editorial board. Sometimes the publisher offers the author a monetary advance against royalties, along with the contract (see 2.2.1). The press generally expects the author to secure before copyediting any permissions necessary for reproduction of illustrative matter and previously published text, typically asking the author to return a copy of the signed contract with the permission statements attached.

1.6   PRODUCTION AND PUBLICATION

Authors commonly submit the final version of their manuscript, both in hard copy and on disk, to the journal editor or the book acquisitions editor, who reviews the manuscript and transmits it to editorial staff members for copyediting, design, and production. Book publishers normally ask authors to review both a copyedited and a typeset version of the manuscript and to supply an index for the book; journals usually require authors to review the article in at least one of the versions produced before publication.

1.6.1   Copyediting

Copyediting is an important intermediary stage between acceptance and publication. Serving both the publisher and the author, the copyeditor's responsibilities embrace style and mechanics in addition to other aspects of the manuscript.

As Claire Kehrwald Cook notes in her book *Line by Line: How to Edit Your Own Writing* (Boston: Houghton, 1985), a principal task of copyediting is to eliminate "the stylistic faults" that "impede reading and obscure meaning" (viii). Copyeditors concern themselves with questions of grammar, usage, and punctuation as well as with the correctness and consistency of other mechanical matters, such as spelling, capitalization, the treatment of numbers and names, and the documentation of scholarship. This aspect of copyediting frequently centers on making the manuscript conform to the house style the journal or press follows. The copyeditor enables the publisher to ensure consistency in spelling, capitalization, italicization, and the like within a work and from one work to another. The copyeditor also marks up the manuscript for typesetting, specifying such design features as title, subheadings, set-down quotations, notes, and list of works cited.

Besides stylistic and mechanical questions, the copyeditor may call attention to more-substantive matters that may not have been detected by the consultant readers and the acquisitions editor, such as errors of fact or logic, possibly unjustified generalizations, or even potential legal problems in the manuscript. The successful copyeditor, therefore, routinely renders a manuscript more cogent and accessible to its readers and sometimes saves the author and the publisher from various kinds of professional discomfiture.

Copyediting may be done on the paper or the electronic version of the manuscript. When working on hard copy, editors use a set of symbols to indicate changes—deletions, insertions, transpositions, and so forth—in the manuscript. Frequently the symbols are supplemented by explanations or clarifications in the margins or on slips attached to the page. Copyeditors also commonly use margins or slips to address queries to the author, requesting information or explication, for example, or suggesting alternative choices of wording. (See fig. 1.) A copyeditor who works on computer usually produces at the end a new printout incorporating the editorial changes, which are often highlighted to allow the author to compare the original and copyedited versions more easily. Queries to the author are likely to appear not in the margins but elsewhere—for instance, all queries may be collected in a list keyed to numbers embedded in the text.

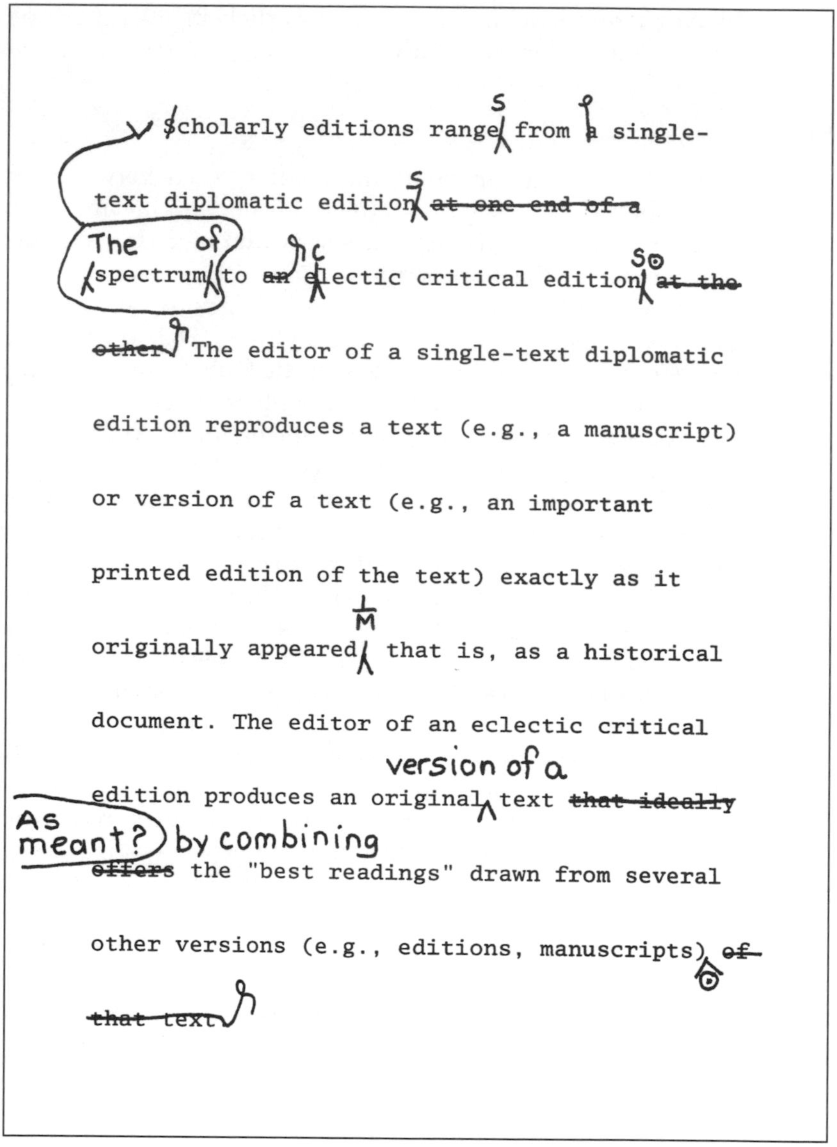

Scholarly editions range from a single-text diplomatic edition at one end of a spectrum to an eclectic critical edition at the other. The editor of a single-text diplomatic edition reproduces a text (e.g., a manuscript) or version of a text (e.g., an important printed edition of the text) exactly as it originally appeared; that is, as a historical document. The editor of an eclectic critical edition produces an original version of a text that ideally offers by combining the "best readings" drawn from several other versions (e.g., editions, manuscripts) of that text.

Fig. 1. A sample from the copyedited manuscript of this manual.

In returning the copyedited manuscript to the author for review, the editor usually sends a cover letter that, among other things, may call attention to special problems or give instructions about responding to changes and queries. The letter also normally specifies a deadline for the return of the manuscript. If you cannot meet the deadline, notify the editor immediately. Otherwise, the publisher will expect to receive the reviewed manuscript within the time requested, so that production can proceed on schedule. If no schedule is set, return the manuscript as quickly as possible.

When you receive a copyedited manuscript from your publisher, read the cover letter first, especially noting the deadline for return. Evaluate each suggested change and either accept the change or explain what is wrong with it and, if the copyeditor has identified a problem, substitute a different revision. If you do not understand a change, ask for clarification. If the copyediting was done on paper, do not erase or otherwise obliterate any change or query. Try to respond unambiguously and as near as possible on the page to the query; if space is insufficient, place replies on a separate sheet, making evident the pages and lines involved.

For works destined for print publication, the review of the copyedited manuscript is normally the author's last chance to make revisions, such as correcting or updating references, for from this time forward, changes become costly (and are often charged to the author or not even made). If your revisions are brief, insert them within the manuscript; when lengthy or likely to lead to confusion if placed directly on the manuscript, revisions should be written on separate pages with clear indications of where they belong in the text.

Before returning the copyedited manuscript to the publisher, make sure you have answered all questions, supplied all requested information, and made all needed changes. Besides meeting the deadline, follow any special instructions the publisher gives for the return of the manuscript. Include a cover letter explaining what you have carried out and noting any specific problems or questions of which the copyeditor should be aware.

If problems remain unresolved, the copyeditor may return to you with further queries. For a text copyedited on computer, the editor normally transfers all final changes to the disk or disks containing the work. (Less frequently, some publishers ask authors to make the changes and to submit the final version on disk for composition.)

1.6.2 Proofreading

After your article or book is typeset—either directly from the final disk version of the manuscript or manually from the paper manuscript —the publisher will send you for correction a set of page proofs (your text converted into printed pages that will eventually constitute the actual publication), usually along with the final version of the manuscript.

Read proofs carefully, word for word against the manuscript. Do not assume that the manuscript was translated into type without omissions or other errors. If you are not an experienced proofreader, it may help to ask someone to read the manuscript aloud while you follow on the proofs. Make corrections on the proofs, using proofreading symbols (see 8.8), and respond to any queries from the editor or typesetter. To reduce production costs, many presses assign authors primary responsibility for proofreading and sometimes suggest they seek the services of a professional proofreader.

Because changes at this stage can prove costly (usually to the author if they are not the typesetter's errors) and also seriously delay the publication schedule, publishers will usually make changes only to remove factual errors and will not permit stylistic refinements. If you want to make alterations, explain their rationale and relative importance in a cover letter when returning the proofs, so that the publisher can make informed decisions about allowing the changes. Be sure to return the corrected proofs within the time agreed on or as quickly as possible if no schedule was set. Often the book publisher sends two sets of page proofs: one to correct and return, the other for preparing an index.

1.6.3   Preparing an Index

Creating the index for a scholarly book is usually the responsibility of the author, the person most familiar with the contents and intentions of the book. In negotiating the contract, the author and editor determine the type of index or indexes required: a name index, a subject index, a combined index of names and subjects, or another kind of index—a scholarly study of poetry, for example, might include an index of titles or an index of first lines. Another consideration is the mode of indexing. Whereas most books are indexed by page number, some works are more useful if indexed another way, such as by section number.

Some authors hire a professional indexer rather than prepare the index themselves. The publisher can probably recommend an indexer if you are unsure about whom to hire. If you intend to have your press help you obtain the services of a freelance indexer, let the publisher know well in advance, so that the indexer's schedule can be coordinated with the publication schedule for the book. Since such an indexer is unlikely to be a specialist in your field, the press will ask you to review the index, deleting or adding entries as needed or making other refinements.

Ordinarily the following parts of the book are indexed: the introduction, text, content notes, and appendixes. The following parts are usually not indexed: the preface and other front matter (e.g., title page, copyright page, dedication, table of contents, acknowledgments) and the list of works cited.

Although you cannot complete the index until page proofs are available, you can begin working on it at any time after acceptance. Before receiving proofs, for example, you can identify the terms for your index and arrange them in alphabetical order. For a subject index, you can select in advance what words and phrases you will use as headings and subheadings. Headings are key terms that guide readers to important ideas and issues discussed in the book; headings are normally divided into subheadings if the headings would otherwise be followed by long strings of undifferentiated page numbers. For a name index, you can extract all personal names from the manuscript and alphabetize them in advance. Once the index has been thus set up, all you then need do is add page numbers when you receive the proofs. Before beginning any such work, be sure to inquire about and follow any instructions the publisher provides for preparing the index.

Computers are useful in the creation of indexes. Special indexing software or the indexing feature of your word-processing program can help produce the index, but you need to use such programs with care. Whereas software performs many valuable functions—for instance, it can automatically index terms the user marks; record headings, subheadings, and page numbers; and alphabetize entries—the indexer nonetheless must perform the most-essential tasks: creating the list of terms to be marked, checking and modifying terms as indexing proceeds, editing entries, adding cross-references, and so forth.

Print out the final index copy double-spaced and in one column. Begin each entry flush with the left margin; indent the second and subsequent lines of the entry one-half inch (or five spaces) from the margin. Use commas to indicate inversions ("artists, reference works on") and qualifying phrases ("authors, as indexers" and "authors, and publishers"). Place a comma after the entry, skip a space, and give the relevant page number or numbers, separated with a comma and a space ("pragmatism, in editing, 489, 519, 536"). Use inclusive numbers if the subject continues for more than one page ("10–11, 110–11"; see 3.10.6, on inclusive numbers). If the page number refers to a note, add the lowercase letter *n* ("286n"). If the page contains more than one note, add the note number or numbers, preceded by the abbreviation *n* or *nn* ("286n3" or "286nn4–5"). Identify cross-references with *See* and *See also*, underlined ("acronyms See abbreviations" and "theater See also plays").

Although most indexes are printed in run-in style, prepare the copy in indented style (in which each subhead appears on a separate line indented under the major head):

```
writing
     guides to, 38-40
     style manuals for, 260-61
```

Number every page of the index in the upper right-hand corner and otherwise follow the recommendations for manuscript preparation in chapter 4.

Indexes generally follow one of two systems of alphabetizing: letter by letter and word by word. The letter-by-letter system ignores spaces between words and alphabetizes by all letters up to the first comma indicating an inversion or a qualifier. The word-by-word system, in contrast, alphabetizes up to the first space and uses the letters that follow only when two entries begin with identical words.

LETTER BY LETTER	WORD BY WORD
Day, Dorothy	Day, Dorothy
daybooks	Day of the Locust,
Day of the Locust,	The (West)
The (West)	daybooks

The letter-by-letter system is more commonly used. In alphabetizing, disregard accents, hyphens, apostrophes, and commas indicating series, and follow the rules for names given in 3.6.

Check your manuscript of the index carefully, for at many presses the author has complete responsibility for the accuracy and correctness of the index. Unless otherwise instructed, submit the manuscript in both print and disk form to the publisher. The manuscript for the index, like that for the rest of the book, will be copyedited and converted into page proofs. Presses usually ask authors to review the copyedited manuscript or the proofs of the index.

There are, of course, many strategies and resources for creating indexes. The procedure detailed in Kenneth L. Pike's "How to Make an Index" (*PMLA* 83 [1968]: 991–93) is primarily recommended for those preparing the index without indexing software but may also be useful for those using such software. *The Chicago Manual of Style* (14th ed. [Chicago: U of Chicago P, 1993] ch. 17) recommends typing each entry on an individual index card (a time-consuming procedure that leaves no way of tracing errors), briefly defines various kinds of indexes, and gives considerable information about the mechanics of preparing an index.

1.6.4 Design

Although publishers, not authors, are responsible for the design, production, and marketing of books and journals, it is useful for scholars to have some notion of what happens to their manuscripts apart from editing.

All books and printed journals must be designed, no matter how simple and straightforward the result. A designer writes specifications that cover every aspect of the typography of the publication. The designer's concerns include:

the trim size (the dimensions of a page of the publication)

the margins (the space at the top, bottom, and sides of the page)

the type page (the area of the page in which type appears, including any footnotes, running heads or running footers, and page numbers)

the text page (the area of the page in which the text appears)

the typeface and the type size for not only the text but also the running heads, chapter numbers, chapter titles, headings within the text, extracts, notes, list of works cited, and so forth

the spacing between letters, words, and lines

the indentation of paragraph beginnings, extracts, notes, the list of works cited, and so forth

The design of a book also includes such features as its cover and jacket (if there is one), the selection of the paper on which it is to be printed, the cloth or paper with which it will be bound, and the method of binding (e.g., case binding, adhesive binding). Publishers sometimes ask authors for design suggestions (e.g., a work of art or a photograph to serve as an illustration for the cover or jacket of the book), but the press has the final say on all aspects of design.

1.6.5   Composition, Printing, Binding

The term *composition* covers a wide range of typesetting processes, old and new. Originally typesetting involved selecting preformed metal characters from a case, arranging them into lines on a composing stick, and then, after laying out the lines in galleys to take a proof impression, locking them into rectangular chases, or frames. The type was then inked and pressed against paper to produce first galley or page proofs and eventually the final printed product. The terminology of publishing still reflects these procedures, which held sway for four centuries. Typesetting was mechanized in the late nineteenth century, with the invention of the Linotype and the Monotype, which automated the selection of the metal characters.

Recent decades have seen rapid changes in composition methods. Current electronic text files—usually originating with the author but sometimes created when the typesetter keyboards a paper manuscript or scans it with an optical character reader (OCR)—are imported into a pagination or page-layout program, where the text can be corrected and formatted and pages generated. Pagination programs vary in their ability to lay out a document. Some are virtually automatic, programmed with rules to create an aesthetically pleasing page. Most programs, however, work through a combination of automation and manual intervention (in page-spread alignment, page breaks, hyphenation, line justification, etc.). A heavily illustrated book, for example, requires more manual work than a book with text only.

The typesetter prints out page proofs for the author to review and correct, makes the changes indicated by the author, and generates new pages. This cycle repeats until there are no further corrections and the pages are deemed ready for printing. This version is then sent—as electronic files, film, or a reproduction proof (a clear, sharp proof)—to the printer for reproduction.

The text pages and endpapers for a clothbound book are sewn or glued together, and the endpapers are pasted to covered boards. Text and sometimes designs are stamped or printed on the covering material before it is glued to the boards. The book may then be wrapped in a printed jacket. The collated pages of a paperbound publication are glued to a printed paper cover.

1.6.6   Marketing

Publishers use marketing to try to bring their publications to the fullest potential audiences. Scholarly publications are usually marketed through promotional mailings to individuals and libraries, advertisements, displays at professional conferences, listings on the press's World Wide Web site, and efforts to have the works reviewed.

The marketing plan for a publication depends on the nature of the work and on its intended audience. For example, for a trade book aimed at a general audience, a press might place an advertisement in the *New York Review of Books* or arrange author interviews and book signings, but for a more specialized book it might rely on direct mailings and reviews in scholarly journals and in periodicals consulted by academic librarians, such as *Choice*.

A book publisher is likely to ask you to play an active advisory role in the marketing of your book. The press will customarily send you a questionnaire or similar form requesting information that will assist the marketing staff. You might be asked, for instance, to supply a brief description of the book and biographical data to be used in the copy for the jacket or cover and for direct-mail materials (flyers, brochures, catalogs).

In addition, you will probably be asked to provide a list of journals whose reviews are respected (and whose advertisements are read) by scholars in your field. Although publishers rely on their own lists of customers as well as lists rented from professional and scholarly associations and from list services, you can assist in direct-mail advertising by telling the press of any organizations and groups whose members might be particularly interested in the book. Similarly, many publishers exhibit their books at meetings of major scholarly associations, but you can help direct the press to specialized meetings that have exhibit opportunities. In addition, you might mention any awards and prizes for which the book is eligible.

Needless to say, it might not be possible for your publisher to pursue every suggestion you offer. Keep in mind that the marketing staff needs to promote many new and backlist titles at the same time, that the costs of advertising are high, and that the plan for each title is limited by budget and largely shaped by the projected income from the book. Nevertheless, you should expect your press to do its best to inform potential readers of the existence and importance of your book.

1.7   CONCLUSION

Scholarly publication ideally constitutes a collaboration between author and publisher, characterized by complementary and mutually supportive and sustaining interests and goals. Authors wish to gain publication of manuscripts that have taken them months and usually years to conceptualize, research, and write. Publishers wish to disseminate new and important ideas and scholarship and thus invest considerable time and money in reviewing, editing, designing, composing, printing, binding, and marketing each work. Authors and publishers alike seek to have the publications they produce reach as wide a readership as possible.

Scholarly publishing typically relies on evaluations and advice from consultant readers or referees. Such specialist readings help the publisher verify the soundness and quality of the submitted work's thought, scholarship, and writing and help the author discover ways in which the manuscript might be improved.

Cooperation between the two parties enhances the efficacy and the efficiency of the publishing process. Toward this end, an author prepares and submits a manuscript for an article or a prospectus for a book in a commonly accepted form or as prescribed by the journal or press; informs the publisher if the work, or any part of it, is being considered elsewhere; agrees to make necessary revisions; reviews the copyedited manuscript and corrects proof; supplies an index, if required; provides advice on design and information for marketing, as requested; and, most important, meets the publisher's deadlines.

For its part, the publisher in this ideal relationship promptly notifies the author of every significant development (and of any delay) during the review stage, from the receipt to the approval of the manuscript; clearly indicates what revisions it wants the author to make and if the revisions are optional or required; keeps the author informed of the publication schedule; and establishes reasonable deadlines for making revisions, reviewing the copyedited manuscript, correcting proof, and preparing an index.

The author and the publisher agree on and enter into a contract for the publication of the manuscript. In book publishing, they commonly share any income derived from the work. And finally, by making important scholarship public in conveniently accessible form, both parties also share in the other rewards—intellectual, professional, and personal—that successful scholarly publication renders.

Dear Permissions Manager:

I would like to reprint the following material from your publication: [author, title, date of publication, page numbers, line numbers, etc.]. This material is to appear in my article/book [title], scheduled for publication in [date] by [name of journal or press]. The journal/press plans a first print run of [number].

Permission to reprint will be acknowledged with the usual credit line, citing author, title, and publisher, unless you specify otherwise.

If you hold the copyright and will grant me nonexclusive world rights for this use, please sign below and return this form to me. A copy is enclosed for your files. If you have your own form for permission requests, I will be glad to fill it out. If I need to apply to someone else for permission, I would appreciate your letting me know.

Thank you very much for attending to this request. I look forward to your prompt reply.

Sincerely yours,

[your name]

_____

The above request is approved on the conditions specified above.

Approved by _____ *Date*_____

Fig. 2. Sample of a letter, sent in duplicate, requesting permission to reproduce printed material.

Dear Permissions Manager:

I would like to reproduce [title, artist, etc.], which appears in [author, title, publisher, date, page numbers, etc.]. The reproduction would be printed in black and white / color in my article/book [title], scheduled for publication in [date] by [name of journal or press]. The journal/press plans a first print run of [number].

The image will be identified in the publication with the usual credit line, citing artist, title, and source, unless you specify otherwise.

If you hold the copyright and will grant me nonexclusive world rights for this use, please sign below and return this form to me. A copy is enclosed for your files. If you have your own form for permission requests, I will be glad to fill it out. If I need to apply to someone else for permission, I would appreciate your letting me know.

If you grant permission, I will need to obtain from you a photograph, slide, or transparency of the image suitable for reproduction. Please inform me of any fee that I must pay for the print.

Thank you very much for attending to this request. I look forward to your prompt reply.

Sincerely yours,

[your name]

_____

The above request is approved on the conditions specified above.

Approved by _____ *Date_____*

Fig. 3. *Sample of a letter, sent in duplicate, requesting permission to reproduce an illustration.*

2

LEGAL ISSUES IN SCHOLARLY PUBLISHING

Arthur F. Abelman

2.1 Copyright
    2.1.1 Development of Copyright Law in the United States
    2.1.2 Scope of Copyright Protection
    2.1.3 Works Made for Hire
    2.1.4 Co-ownership
    2.1.5 Compilations, Including Collective Works
    2.1.6 Material Objects
    2.1.7 Term of Copyright
    2.1.8 Registration of Copyright
    2.1.9 Copyright Notice
    2.1.10 Renewal of Copyright
    2.1.11 Rights of Copyright Owners
    2.1.12 Transfers and Terminations
    2.1.13 Fair Use of Copyrighted Works
    2.1.14 Requesting Permission
    2.1.15 Damages for Copyright Infringement
    2.1.16 International Copyright
    2.1.17 Copyright and Computer Networks
2.2 Publishing Contracts
    2.2.1 Books
    2.2.2 Journal Articles and Contributions to Edited Works
2.3 Defamation
    2.3.1 Libel
    2.3.2 Opinion
    2.3.3 Truth as Defense
    2.3.4 Actual Malice

Arthur F. Abelman, a lawyer at the firm Moses and Singer LLP, in New York City, specializes in the law of copyright and literary property.

2.4   Right of Privacy
    2.4.1   Emergence of Privacy Law
    2.4.2   Unreasonable Publicity of Private Life
    2.4.3   Publicity Placing Another in a False Light
    2.4.4   Consent as Defense
2.5   Further Guidance

Scholars who publish their work inevitably become involved in a network of legal issues, including copyright, contracts, libel, and the right of privacy. These issues have been shaped by a complex history of laws, court decisions, and international agreements that are unfamiliar and often confusing to scholars. Since common sense is not always a reliable guide to proper legal conduct in publishing, it is important for potential authors to protect themselves by an acquaintance with the fundamentals of legal issues in scholarly publishing.

In our information-based society and economy, intellectual property has become the focus of increasing attention. Furthermore, new conditions of publication rendered possible by the electronic exchange of texts are making it necessary to reconsider and redefine longstanding copyright law in the United States and abroad. In addition, the globalization of regional economies is creating pressure for the standardization of intellectual-property laws across national borders. Such developments in copyright law affect scholars both as creators who want to protect their writings from unauthorized uses and changes and as researchers who want to use and build on the writings of others. Although gaining access to and using texts often present obstacles to scholars as researchers, securing copyright for their own works is relatively simple. This is particularly so since, despite the efforts of some scholars to liberalize the use of intellectual property, changes in the law have for the most part increased protection, lengthened copyright duration, and decreased the risk that material could fall into the public domain.

2.1   COPYRIGHT

2.1.1   Development of Copyright Law in the United States

The principal method of protecting the rights of authors and other creators of original material fixed in a tangible medium of expression is copyright. There has been statutory copyright protection since 1710, when the English Parliament enacted the Statute of Anne, the first copyright act. After the American Revolution, most of the former colonies enacted copyright statutes, many influenced by the Statute of Anne. When the nation's founders met in Philadelphia to draft the Constitution, a copyright clause was inserted without opposition or even significant discussion. However, the copyright clause of the Constitution, instead of directly protecting authors' and other creators' interests, gave Congress "power [. . .] to promote the progress of science and useful arts, by securing for limited times to authors and inventors the exclusive right to their respective writings and discoveries [. . .]" (art. I, § 8, cl. 8). By reason of this language in the Constitution, copyright in the United States has developed as a limited monopoly, a group of exclusive rights granted to authors with exceptions or limits for the benefit of the public.

Congress proceeded to enact a series of copyright statutes, the first of which, enacted in 1790, protected maps, charts, and books. By far the most important statute today is the 1976 Copyright Act (Pub. L. 94-553, Title 1, § 101, 19 Oct. 1976, 90 Stat. 2541), the first major revision of copyright law in three-quarters of a century, because it took account of new and emerging technology and because it enabled the United States to afford greater protection of authors' rights through international treaties. Also relevant are the Copyright Act of 1909, which governs the ownership of copyrights before 1 January 1978, the effective date of the 1976 Copyright Act; the Sound Recording Amendment Act of 1971, extending federal protection to sound recordings; the Computer Software Copyright Act of 1980, extending federal protection to software; the Berne Convention Implementation Act of 1988, which provides for the United States to join a larger group of countries that extend a high level of international copyright protection to works of their citizens; and the Copyright Amendments Act of 1992, which clarifies congressional intent about the fair use of unpublished works.

2.1.2   Scope of Copyright Protection

Copyright is based on *authorship* of *original* works that are fixed in any *tangible medium* now known or later developed. The Supreme Court has defined an author as a person "to whom anything owes its origin; originator, maker" (*Burrow-Giles Lithographic Co. v. Sarony*, 111 US 53, 58, 1884). (For the authorship of works made for hire, see 2.1.3.) Originality means that the author's work is of the author's own effort and is not copied from other work, even if the author's effort is only modestly creative. To be fixed in a tangible medium, a work must be able to be perceived, reproduced, or otherwise communicated either directly or with the aid of a machine or other device. The Copyright Act lists the following examples of works of authorship:

35

Literary works, which include literary criticism and scholarly writing

Musical works, including accompanying words

Dramatic works, including accompanying music

Pantomimes and choreographic works

Pictorial, graphic, and sculptural works

Motion pictures and other audiovisual works

Sound recordings

Architectural works   (17 USCA § 102)

The list is not exhaustive: other types of works, such as computer programs, have been added by statute, and their protection has been enforced by the courts. Copyright protection is extended to new material created by an author for a compilation or derivative work—that is, a work (such as a translation, an annotated version, or an abridgment) based on another work. Protection of a compilation or derivative work, however, does not imply an exclusive right in the preexisting material included and does not affect the scope or duration of rights in that material.

Copyright protects only the author's expression and does not extend to facts, ideas, procedures, and methods of operation regardless of the form in which they are embodied or illustrated. For example, theories about history, such as a theory about the destruction of the dirigible *Hindenburg*, or scientific discoveries are unprotectible, but the words in which theories or discoveries are discussed are protected. A 1991 Supreme Court decision (*Feist Publications, Inc., v. Rural Telephone Service, Inc.*) made clear that a simple assembling of facts, such as an alphabetical listing of names and addresses, does not qualify as an original and therefore a copyrightable work, even though considerable labor ("sweat of brow") may be involved.

Questions about whether a particular work is protected by copyright, in whole or in part, can be complex. Authors who plan to use another's work but doubt whether they have the right to do so should refer the question to copyright counsel. In the absence of an opinion from counsel, it is prudent to assume that there is copyright protection. (On fair use of copyrighted works, see 2.1.13.)

2.1.3 Works Made for Hire

The Copyright Act provides that the employer or other person for whom a *work made for hire* is prepared is considered the author of that work. A work made for hire is either a work prepared by an employee within the scope of employment or a commissioned work, such as a contribution to a collective work, a translation, or another kind of supplementary work as defined in section 101 of the United States Copyright Law. Editorial notes and scholarly articles may sometimes fall within this category. A commissioned work is treated as a work made for hire only when there is a written agreement between the writer and the commissioning party that the work is made for hire.

Some universities now claim that writing by faculty members done under university auspices and involving software and patentable inventions is work for hire. Such claims, not of immediate issue in the humanities, will be decided under the definition of a work for hire found in the Copyright Law and under applicable patent law.

2.1.4   Co-ownership

Co-ownership of copyright can result from two situations. The first is the creation of a *joint work*. The Copyright Act of 1976 defines a joint work as one prepared by two or more authors with the intention that their contributions be merged into inseparable or interdependent parts of a unitary whole. If the creative portions of a work attributable to all the authors are intended to be inseparable or interdependent, the work is a joint work, and the authors co-own the copyright. Further, if authors agree before or at the time of creation that their contributions will be regarded as forming a joint work, there is co-ownership of copyright. The most common example of a joint work is a song with words and music by different parties who intend to produce only one work, but co-ownership may exist with any creation. Co-ownership of copyright can also occur when additional persons acquire ownership after the work's creation. For example, the owner of a copyright may transfer a portion of it to another, or children of a deceased author may renew their parent's copyright and thus own it together.

Co-owners of a copyright can transfer their respective interests in the copyright separately, without approval of the other owners, but all the co-owners must join in a grant of the entire copyright. Similarly, any co-owner of a copyright may license the entire copyright on a nonexclusive basis, but all the co-owners must join in a license of exclusive rights. A co-owner who uses or licenses a copyright on a nonexclusive basis without consulting the other co-owners is required to account for the proceeds to the other co-owners and pay them their just shares. As a practical matter, most users of copyrights willing to pay substantial sums for a license will require an exclusive license.

2.1.5   Compilations, Including Collective Works

A *compilation* is defined by the Copyright Act as a work formed by the collection and assembling of preexisting materials in such a way that the result constitutes an original work of authorship. Compilations include *collective works*, defined as journal or periodical issues, anthologies, or encyclopedias in which separate and independent contributions are assembled into a whole. The copyrights in the contributions to collective works remain with the authors unless the copyrights are expressly transferred in writing. The proprietor of a collective work owns the copyright in the collective work, but that right conveys only the privilege of reproducing the contributions together in that collection, in a revision of that collection, or in a later collective work in a series with the former collective work.

2.1.6   Material Objects

Copyright law has long provided that the ownership of a copyright or of any right under a copyright, such as an exclusive license, is separate and distinct from ownership of the material object embodying the copyright. The sale or transfer of the material object does not convey any rights in the copyright unless they are granted in addition. Conversely, the ownership of a copyright or a right under a copyright does not convey any right in the material object embodying the copyright. Accordingly, owners of letters, manuscripts, and original works of art have no rights to the copyright of those works unless the owners specifically acquired copyright rights by an agreement or bill of sale. The owner of a work of art, for example, may not copy the work without having received the right to do so from the copyright owner but may deny access to anyone wishing to copy it, except perhaps the copyright owner.

2.1.7   Term of Copyright

The term of protection under the 1976 Copyright Act is the life of the author plus fifty years after the author's death for works first published on or after 1 January 1978 and for unpublished works. The term of copyright for a joint work is the life of the last surviving author plus fifty years.

Works that are anonymous, pseudonymous, or made for hire (see 2.1.3) have a copyright term of seventy-five years after first publication or one hundred years from creation, whichever terminates first. Works copyrighted before 1 January 1978 have a term of protection of twenty-eight years from the date copyright was secured and a renewal term of forty-seven years (for a potential seventy-five years of copyright protection) when the renewal is secured as provided in the Copyright Act. A copyright falling due for renewal between 31 December 1976, when the new law was passed, and 31 December 1977, when the law went into effect, endures for a term of seventy-five years from the date copyright was originally secured if it was renewed.

In 1994 an amendment to the Copyright Law was enacted to strengthen protection abroad for United States works and uphold the obligations of the United States to member countries of the Berne Convention. This amendment restores copyrights to works of foreign origin that would otherwise be in the public domain and therefore available for copying by anyone without restriction. To be eligible for copyright restoration in the United States, these foreign works must be protected by copyright in the source country and must meet other qualifications. When copyright is restored, it endures for a term of seventy-five years from the date it first began. The scholar should make a careful investigation of the facts before reaching a conclusion about the copyright status of a foreign work. An incomplete list of works whose copyright has been restored is available from the Copyright Office. Copyright restoration vests automatically, and the list contains only the works for which a notice of an intent to enforce rights against a so-called reliance party has been filed in the Copyright Office.

2.1.8   Registration of Copyright

Copyright in an original work eligible for protection begins with the creation of the work. Accordingly, registration of copyright is no longer required and may be done anytime during the life of the copyright. Registration may be effected by the owner of a copyright or of any exclusive right in the copyright and entails a deposit of the work with the Copyright Office (Register of Copyrights, Copyright Office, Library of Congress, Washington, DC 20059-6000), along with an application form and the prescribed fee. The deposit consists of one complete copy of an unpublished work, two complete copies of the best edition of a work published in the United States other than a contribution to a collective work, one complete copy of a work published outside the United States, and one complete copy of the best edition of a contribution to a collective work. Whether or not copyright is registered, however, deposit of the work is required by law within three months of publication. This deposit requirement is intended to build the collection of the Library of Congress, of which the Copyright Office is a division. A single deposit can satisfy both the deposit requirement and the registration procedure. Forms for registration are available from the Copyright Office and vary in accordance with the class of work being registered. Instructions are included with each form.

A reason to register a copyright is that the Copyright Office verifies that the work meets the formal requirements of the Copyright Act.

If the requirements are met, the office registers the claim and issues a certificate of registration. In any judicial proceeding, this certificate, if issued before publication or within five years after, is prima facie evidence that the copyright and the facts stated in the certificate are valid.

Another advantage of registration is that it enables the copyright owner to initiate an action for infringement; without registration no action for infringement may be commenced. Foreign works protected under the Berne Convention are exempt from the registration requirement, however, and an action for infringement of such works may be initiated without registration. Furthermore, in any infringement action for an unpublished work, no award of statutory damages or attorney's fees may be made if the infringement began before the effective date of registration. Similarly, no statutory damages or attorney's fees may be awarded for infringement of a published work if the infringement began after first publication and before the effective date of the registration, unless registration was made within three months after first publication. Of course, whenever the infringement and the registration occurred, the owner of a work infringed is always entitled to actual damages, such as lost income, as well as to the infringer's profits attributable to the infringement, so long as they do not duplicate the award of actual damages (see 2.1.15).

2.1.9   Copyright Notice

Under the 1976 Copyright Act, copies of a work distributed to the public may contain a notice of copyright. The notice should be visible either directly or with the aid of a device. The form of the notice normally consists of three elements:

1. The word *Copyright*, the symbol ©, or the abbreviation *Copr.*

2. The year of first publication of the work

3. The name of the owner of the copyright in the work, an abbreviation by which the name can be recognized, or some other designation of the owner of the copyright   (17 USCA § 401)

Many publishers elect to add the phrase *All rights reserved* to the copyright notice. This phrase protects copyright in countries that are members of the Buenos Aires Convention. The copyright notice is to be affixed to copies in a manner and location that enable it to give reasonable notice of the claim to copyright. In books the traditional place for the notice is the reverse side of the title page, sometimes called the copyright page.

After the effective date of the Berne Convention Implementation Act of 1988—1 March 1989—notice is not required for United States or foreign works claiming copyright pursuant to the Berne Convention.

However, it is advantageous for all works to bear a copyright notice. If such a notice is placed in accordance with the Copyright Act, then a court must give no weight to a defendant's claim that the infringement was innocent and that damages should therefore be mitigated. Further, the use of the symbol ©, though not of the term *Copyright* or *copr.* alone, in a notice gains rights for the copyright owner in countries that belong to the Universal Copyright Convention but not to the Berne Convention. Finally, in works published online, it is advisable for authors to include a copyright notice to alert readers that copyright should be respected.

A notice of copyright on a collective work in the name of the proprietor of the collection protects all the component parts, even if they are of different ownership and were originally published in various years. Of course, separate notices of copyright for component parts may be properly used if the publisher is willing to print them. No special notice of copyright renewal is required for works in which copyright has been renewed. Under the Copyright Act, the year of first publication is the proper year for the notice even in the renewal term.

2.1.10   Renewal of Copyright

Renewal of copyright is now largely pertinent only for older works. It is helpful for authors to be aware of the relevant law, however, whether they are authors of works published before the mid-1960s or whether they are trying to determine whether a work they wish to quote is in the public domain. Before 1992 copyright renewal applications had to be filed in the twenty-eighth year of the copyright for all copyrights in the first term on 1 January 1978. If a copyright was not renewed, the work fell into the public domain. This is still true of copyrights secured before 1964. After an amendment to the Copyright Act in 1992, copyrights secured in 1964 and thereafter renew automatically even if no application is filed. In the case of works that are owned by a proprietor other than by assignment from an author, a post-1963 copyright renews automatically in the name of the proprietor if no application is filed. These works can include posthumous works, periodicals, encyclopedic and composite works owned by the proprietor or its predecessor in interest in the original term, and works created for hire (see 2.1.3).

In the case of copyright in a work owned by an author, the Copyright Act gives the renewal term to the author, if living; to the widow, widower, or children as a class if the author is not living; to the executor of the author if the author is not living and there is no living widow, widower, or children; or to the author's next of kin if there is no will. The renewal follows the order stated in the statute and does not follow state inheritance law. Furthermore, an author may not leave a renewal copyright by will or grant it while living to anyone if the author does not live into the renewal term. The reason for this restriction is that the author does not own the renewal term unless the author is alive when the renewal application is filed in the twenty-eighth year of the copyright or when the renewal term commences. As these arrangements make evident, copyright is not property in the ordinary sense. It is created by Congress, and the renewal term is also created by Congress, which decides who is entitled to the renewal.

2.1.11 Rights of Copyright Owners

The proprietor of copyright in a work is given by statute the exclusive right to do or authorize others to do any of the following actions:

1. Reproduce the work
2. Distribute copies or phonorecords of the work to the public by sale or other transfer of ownership or by rental, lease, or lending
3. Prepare derivative works based on the work
4. Perform the work publicly if it is a literary, musical, dramatic, or choreographic work; a pantomime; or a motion picture or another kind of audiovisual work
5. Display the work publicly if it is a literary, musical, dramatic, or choreographic work; a pantomime; or a pictorial, graphic, or sculptural work, including the individual images of a motion picture or of another kind of audiovisual work   (17 USCA § 106)

Even the exclusive rights stated above are limited by the Copyright Act in a variety of provisions, particularly fair use (see 2.1.13).

The copyright owner of a work listed in item 5 above has the exclusive right to display it publicly on a screen. The question whether the uploading and downloading of copyrighted computer materials by someone who is not the copyright owner constitute a distribution of copies and therefore infringe the owner's rights has not yet been settled by the courts. Legislation has been proposed, however, that would define transmission from computer to computer as a distribution of copies, protected by copyright.

2.1.12 Transfers and Terminations

Copyright ownership resides with the author unless the author transfers it to another party. The term *transfer* includes assignment, exclusive license, and any other conveyance of any of the exclusive rights comprised in a copyright, but it does not include nonexclusive license. Ownership of a copyright may also be bequeathed. By committing a material breach of a work-for-hire agreement, an employer or a commissioning party may lose its rights in the work made for hire.

The 1976 Copyright Act contains provisions for the termination of any transfer of copyright, nonexclusive licenses of copyright, and any right included in copyright assigned by the author on or after 1 January 1978. The purpose of Congress in providing these termination provisions is to protect authors against unremunerative transfers. Termination may be effected during a period of five years after the expiration of thirty-five years from the date of the grant, but if the grant covers the right to publish the work, the five-year period begins thirty-five years after publication of the work or forty years after the date of the grant, whichever is earlier. The Copyright Act also stipulates who may terminate a grant and the type of notice of termination required. Whenever a grant is terminated, all copyright rights that were covered by it revert to the author or other parties owning termination rights. Failure to give proper and timely notice and to file it in the Copyright Office, in Washington, DC, results in an irrevocable lapse of the termination right, and the grant continues for the balance of the copyright term.

2.1.13   Fair Use of Copyrighted Works

The rights of copyright owners are not absolute. The most important limitation on these rights is known as *fair use.* Under this principle, someone who does not own the copyright in a work may be entitled to make limited use of the work without permission of the owner. The principle of fair use was established to advance creative work and public knowledge. The Copyright Act of 1976 for the first time set forth criteria for fair use, which had previously been interpreted primarily through judicial decisions. The law now provides that the fair use of a copyrighted work is not an infringement of copyright. Although the Copyright Act speaks of the use of a work, in practice only use of a small portion of a work is likely to qualify as a fair use. There are no guidelines on the quantity of material protected by copyright that may be taken without permission. The statute provides four factors to be considered in a determination of whether a use of a copyrighted work is fair use:

1. The purpose and character of the use, including whether it is of a commercial nature or for nonprofit educational purposes

2. The nature of the copyrighted work

3. The amount and substantiality of the portion used in relation to the copyrighted work as a whole

4. The effect of the use on the potential market for or value of the
   work   (17 USCA § 107)

Congress intended the statutory provisions above to restate the
fair use doctrine that existed before passage of the act, not to change,
narrow, or enlarge it in any way, as the reports of the House and Senate committees make clear. Accordingly, all decisions of the courts
before and after the enactment of the 1976 Copyright Act are relevant
to determining the application of fair use to any question of copyright
law. This means that factors other than those listed in the statute may
be considered. Furthermore, the Copyright Act makes no statement
about the relative importance of the factors, so in each determination
about fair use all the facts involved must be taken into account.

In discussing the first factor, the purpose and character of the use,
the courts give greater latitude to "transformative use"—which adds
to the original work something new and possibly different in form—
than to mere reproduction of the work. Mere reproduction is more
likely to be infringement. According to the law, fair use includes copying for purposes of criticism, comment, news reporting, teaching,
scholarship, and research. In 1996 Congress added section 121 of
the Copyright Law, which provides that it is not an infringement for
certain nonprofit or government agencies to reproduce or distribute
copies of a nondramatic literary work made for the blind or other persons with disabilities. Like verbatim copying, close paraphrasing of
protected expression can constitute infringement if the borrowing
does not meet the criteria of fair use. The ideas contained in a work,
though, in contrast to the original expression, may be freely used without risk of copyright infringement (see 2.1.2).

Fair use of unpublished works is more restricted than that of published works. Nevertheless, "[t]he fact that a work is unpublished shall
not itself bar a finding of fair use if such finding is made upon consideration of all the above factors." Congress added this sentence in 1992
to section 107 of the Copyright Law after a series of cases in which the
United States Court of Appeals for the Second Circuit denied fair use
to users of unpublished letters by J. D. Salinger and L. Ron Hubbard.
Letters, manuscripts, and other archival materials are examples of
works that may be unpublished.

In 1994 the House Subcommittee on Courts and Intellectual Property adopted in a nonlegislative report certain fair use guidelines
for educators and students, a result of the Conference on Fair Use
(CONFU). Under these guidelines, educational institutions could digi-
tize images not readily available for purchase or license at a fair price.
The guidelines would not permit the reproduction and publishing of
the images, however. Copyrighted books and other media could be
stored for nonlinear retrieval, but there would be limitations both on

the percentages of the works that might be stored and on the duration of storage. These guidelines do not enjoy a consensus of support, though, and they are not the law.

2.1.14 Requesting Permission

Written permission to reproduce copyrighted materials should be obtained if there is a question whether the use is fair. Litigating a fair use question can be enormously expensive since the courts have to examine in detail each of the four factors stated in 2.1.13. A defendant found to have infringed a copyright may be liable for damages (see 2.1.15). An author should allow a substantial amount of time for obtaining permission. It is not a defense against an infringement-of-copyright claim that there was insufficient time to obtain permission or that the publisher failed to respond to an inquiry about permission. A request for permission should specify the full extent of the material intended to be used as well as particulars of the use, including the type of publication in which the material would appear. The name of the publisher, the date of publication, and the price of the projected work are helpful in a permission request if they are known. (Sample permission requests appear on pp. 31–32.)

2.1.15 Damages for Copyright Infringement

A variety of remedies are available to someone whose copyright has been infringed. A court may issue an injunction to prevent or restrain the infringement. While infringement litigation is pending, the court may also order the impounding of copies made in violation of the copyright owner's rights as well as all plates and production materials from which copies could be reproduced. In addition, an infringer is liable for the actual damages that the copyright owner suffered as a result of the infringement and for profits the infringer made from the infringement. However, not all copyright owners whose rights have been infringed can prove that they suffered damages, and not all infringers make profits. The Copyright Act gives the owner the right to elect statutory damages instead of actual damages and profits. For each work, statutory damages consist of not less than $200 or more than $20,000 when the court finds that the infringer had no reason to believe that the acts committed were infringing and not less than $500 or more than $100,000 when the court finds that the infringement was willful. The court determines the exact amount.

In addition to damages, the court may at its discretion award the copyright owner reasonable attorney's fees and other costs of bringing the action. An unsuccessful plaintiff in an infringement action may have to pay the defendant's costs and attorney's fees. No award of statutory damages or attorney's fees may be made for an infringement of an unpublished work that began before copyright registration or for an infringement of a published work that began before the effective date of registration unless registration was made within three months after first publication of the work. (On registration, see 2.1.8.) The award of attorney's fees may be less than the amount actually charged by the attorney, who is not bound by the award to reduce the fee.

The term *plagiarism* is not used in the Copyright Act. Plagiarism brings a moral stigma and penalties in institutions, but it is legally punishable only to the extent that it qualifies as copyright infringement. (On plagiarism, see 6.1.)

2.1.16   International Copyright

For the first one hundred years of American history, the United States was a copyright piracy center, extending no copyright protection to foreigners. Starting in 1891, foreigners were permitted to obtain some copyright rights in the United States by complying with formalities more onerous than the present ones. At the same time the United States began to negotiate with individual countries bilateral treaties affecting copyright. These treaties continued until 1955, when the United States joined a multinational copyright convention it had proposed, the Universal Copyright Convention, called the UCC. It is from this treaty that the copyright world acquired the symbol © as a part of the notice claiming copyright. Previously United States publishers had attempted to secure Berne Convention rights for their works by the so-called back door to Berne, because the United States did not belong to this century-old convention. The Berne Convention, which affords a high level of protection, covers works first or simultaneously published in a Berne member country. As a result, it became common practice for United States publishers to publish their books simultaneously in the United States and Canada, a member of the Berne Convention.

The United States joined the Berne Convention in 1988. Since Berne standards require no formalities, Congress was required to amend the Copyright Act to exempt Berne claimants from procedures such as notice, registration, and deposit. This accession to Berne afforded protection in the United States for works from member countries and protected works of United States origin in those countries, more numerous than the membership of the UCC, without resort to the problematic back door to Berne. Subsequently, the United States signed the Agreement on Trade-Related Aspects of Intellectual Property Rights (TRIPS), which required the restoration of certain foreign copyrights that were in the public domain in the United States but were protected in a country of origin belonging to Berne. This obligation was implemented by the enactment in 1994 of the Uruguay Round Agreements Act. The initial restoration was effective 1 January 1996.

The laws of many European countries, especially France, recognize a series of moral rights of authors, such as the right to claim authorship of one's work, the right to prevent others from using one's work or name in a manner that harms one's reputation as an author, and the right to prevent distortion of one's work. An author may retain these moral rights even after transferring all economic rights in a copyright to another party. The Berne Convention expressly recognizes some moral rights—for example, the rights to claim authorship and to prevent distortion or other modification of the work. United States law extends Berne Convention moral rights to works of visual art, though not to works of other kinds. Still, for any work, claims of severe distortion may be actionable under state laws as defamation or on other grounds.

2.1.17 Copyright and Computer Networks

The Copyright Act of 1976 makes allowances for new technology but does not contain specific provisions dealing with computer networks. The growth of such networks has created some difficult legal problems. Users require guidance on the rights and liabilities of those who upload copyrighted material onto a network or who download it from the network and make a copy of it and on the liability of the network for transmitting the copyrighted work. There have been few court cases to date concerning computer networks and copyright, and none of them has reached the United States Supreme Court. Until the Supreme Court has ruled on these issues, the law is unsettled, and different federal courts of appeal might even reach different decisions on the same issue.

In *MAI Systems Corp. v. Peak Computer, Inc.*, the United States Court of Appeals for the Ninth Circuit found in 1993 that copying within the scope of the Copyright Act occurs when a computer program is transferred from permanent storage to a computer's random-access memory. The court held that when a service company that maintained computer software turned on its customer's computer at the customer's office using licensed software, a copyright infringement was committed. The court noted that the copyright license for the software permitted use by the licensee only for its own information and did not permit use or copying by others. A basic rule of copyright law, established before the advent of computer networks—that any exceeding of a copyright license by the licensee is an infringement—was found to hold in this case.

In a district-court case (*Playboy Enterprises, Inc., v. Frena*), operation of a subscription computer bulletin-board service through which a subscriber distributed copyrighted photographs was held an infringement of copyright by the operator even though the subscriber uploaded the copyrighted material without the operator's knowledge. The court found that the uploading violated two exclusive rights of the copyright owner—the rights of public display and of public distribution. Violation of either right was sufficient to be infringement.

Many copyright experts believe that transmission over computer networks is a right that should belong exclusively to the copyright proprietor. Until Congress or the Supreme Court clarifies the applicability of copyright law to online materials or changes the law, it is prudent to apply the existing principles of the law. The original expression, though not the ideas, contained in works found on the Internet should usually be considered not available for use without permission, except for fair use.

2.2   PUBLISHING CONTRACTS

2.2.1   Books

The most common form of license by which exclusive rights under a copyright are transferred is the contract between author and publisher for publication of a book. Authors of scholarly books and textbooks usually negotiate their own contracts with publishers, whereas authors of trade books are commonly represented by agents. The subjects that must be covered by a publication contract are the grant, the term, the compensation, the acceptability of the manuscript, the correction of proofs, the index, warranties and indemnities, permissions, the publisher's agreement to publish the work, and subsidiary rights and payments for them. Other subjects covered may be revisions and subsequent editions, out-of-print provisions, competing publications, an option on the author's next work, and the publisher's termination of the contract. A brief explanation of these subjects follows.

Grant. The contract for a scholarly book or textbook normally asks the author to transfer the copyright to the publisher, although there is no legal requirement that the author do so. Since publishers cannot accept competition on the same work, most contracts contain a grant of exclusive rights to publish the work in book form. The contract usually calls for the author to "grant and assign" to the publisher "any and all" rights associated with the work for "any and all" purposes in "any and all" languages, forms (e.g., clothbound, paperbound), and media (e.g., print, electronic) throughout the world. As copyright owner or exclusive licensee, the publisher takes on the responsibility of not only filing the proper forms with the Copyright Office and paying the appropriate fee but also guarding against unauthorized use of the work, negotiating subsidiary rights, and looking after administrative work related to licensing (e.g., receiving and responding to requests for permission, setting and collecting fees).

Term. The publisher customarily requests as a term the life of the copyright and any renewals or extensions thereof, including extensions provided for by future legislation.

Compensation. Compensation to the author may take the form of royalties, based on a percentage of sales. Not all publishers offer royalties, and when they do, rates very considerably. Customary rates range from five to fifteen percent. For scholarly books, the rate may be based on the publisher's net receipts from sales, while trade book royalties are often based on the publisher's suggested retail price. The royalty offered on a clothbound edition of a book may be higher than that offered on a paperbound edition. In addition, while some publishers pay the same rate for all copies sold, others use a sliding scale, paying a higher royalty after certain numbers of copies have been sold (e.g., eight percent on the first one thousand clothbound copies sold and ten percent thereafter). For a book with multiple authors, the publisher may divide the royalties among the authors or pay honoraria in lieu of royalties.

The author may receive an advance against royalties, a fixed sum paid before the publication of the book. The publisher deducts the advance from the first royalties due. The author should ensure that an advance is nonreturnable so that if the book does not earn sufficient royalties to cover the advance, the author is not responsible for repaying the publisher. No royalty is paid for works made for hire, but a fixed fee may be paid. Royalty reports should be required once a year for scholarly books and twice a year for trade books. The statement reporting the sales or revenues and computing the royalties for each period precedes or accompanies the check from the publisher to the author. The contract may state that if the royalties for a period fall below a certain amount (e.g., twenty-five dollars), the publisher will hold the sum over until the royalty account reaches the minimum figure. Authors are also commonly given a number of free copies of the book and the opportunity to purchase additional copies at a reduced price.

Acceptability of the Manuscript. The author normally agrees to deliver a manuscript of a specified length, often together with such supplements as "illustrations, maps, and charts" (typically qualified as "camera-ready" or "reproducible without redrawing"), in a specified form (e.g., on computer disks as well as in hard copy) or a specified number of legible copies, on or before a certain date, "time being of the essence." (The latter phrase enables the publisher to cancel the contract and to retrieve any advance against royalties if the author does not deliver the manuscript by the date specified.) Publishers contract for an acceptable literary property, not labor and services. Hence the contract also specifies that the work must be acceptable to the publisher, unless the work is already written before the signing of the contract (and even then the contract form may contain such a clause). Much litigation has arisen over the meaning of the term *acceptable*.

Correction of Proofs. The author will be required to correct proofs within a reasonable time and to share the cost of large changes to the proofs other than corrections of printer's (typesetter's) errors. The author normally further agrees that the publisher may proceed to publish the manuscript if the author does not return the proofs at a specified time. The typical contract does not oblige the publisher to accept any of the author's changes in proof and provides that the publisher may charge the author for the cost of proofreading should the author fail to read and return proofs.

Index. Authors are usually required to provide an index for the book, preparing it themselves or having it prepared at their expense, within a stated number of days after receiving page proofs from the publisher. The contract normally provides that if the author fails to do so, the publisher will have an index prepared and charge the cost to the author's royalty account.

Warranties and Indemnities. The author is typically asked to warrant that the work is original, that the author is the sole author and has full power to make the agreement, that the work has not been published previously, and that it is not the subject of any other publishing agreement. In addition, the author is asked to warrant that the work violates neither the rights of third parties nor the law. There are frequently specific warranties with respect to copyright infringement, libel, and invasion of privacy. There may also be included a warranty that procedures or other matters that the author advises the reader to do or use are not injurious. The contract requires the author to indemnify the publisher against loss from the author's breach of the warranties and to pay reasonable attorney's fees expended by the publisher in defense of the book.

Permissions. The publisher expects the author to obtain written permission to use any copyrighted material included in the book, usually requiring the author to furnish a copy of each permission to the publisher (see 1.3). If there is a question whether the use of copyrighted material is a fair use, the publisher often requires permission.

Publisher's Agreement to Publish the Work. The publisher typically agrees to publish the manuscript in "such manner and style" as the publisher deems "best." The agreement to publish thus makes the publisher the final arbiter of the appropriate design and content of the book and normally gives the publisher the sole right to set the price of the work. Some publishers stipulate an outside date for publication, measured from the signing of the contract.

Subsidiary Rights and Payments. All the rights in other publication forms and media granted by the author to the publisher should be stated in the contract, and the division of proceeds that result from such rights should be specified. Subsidiary rights usually include co-publication by a foreign English-language publisher; translations; republications of parts of the work by other publishers in periodicals, anthologies, and electronic databases; and classroom photocopying of a portion of the work. Often the publisher agrees to split equally with the author proceeds from licensing of subsidiary rights.

Revisions and Subsequent Editions. A revision clause is important to a publisher for certain scholarly and trade books and for all textbooks. The contract may provide that the publisher, when planning, for example, a new edition of the work, may obtain revisions from a third-party expert if the author refuses to make them or disagrees about their necessity and that the cost will be deducted from the author's royalties. The contract should provide that the original author and the revising author be given separate credits.

Out-of-Print Provisions. When an author retains the copyright in a work that has gone out of print, many contracts contain a provision permitting the author to recapture publishing rights from the publisher if, after written notice and the elapse of a reasonable time, usually six to nine months, the publisher fails to reprint the book. Once rights have reverted to the author, they may be licensed to another publisher. However, the first publisher's failure to discern a sufficient demand for the book to justify keeping it in print suggests that a second publishing license may be difficult to achieve.

Competing Publications. Many publishing contracts contain a provision restricting the author from writing, editing, or contributing to a competing publication. The problem with such a provision is that a precise definition of a competing publication is difficult to frame and an overbroad definition is unfair to the author. When an author writes exclusively within a particular field of scholarship, such a clause can hamper all the author's future writing projects. Even in the absence of such a provision, the author makes an implied promise not to deprive the publisher of the benefits of the contract. Writing a second book that captured all or part of the publisher's market for the first book would breach this promise.

Option. Contracts for many trade books and for some scholarly books contain a provision granting the publisher some form of option on the author's next work. An option that defines the author's compensation for the next book deprives the author of the opportunity of gaining a greater royalty if the current work is successful. If possible, therefore, authors should negotiate to delete terms specifying compensation for future work or to limit the option to a right of negotiation rather than to specific terms.

Termination of the Contract. Many contracts give the publisher the right to terminate the contract after a stated number of years following publication of the work, often stipulating that the author then be allowed to purchase any remaining stock of the work. If the author declines to purchase it, the publisher is free to dispose of it at will.

Any negotiations over specific provisions of the contract usually take place before the publisher draws up a final contract. Authors whose books generate significant income and numerous requests for subsidiary rights frequently hire lawyers or agents to negotiate and review contracts.

2.2.2   Journal Articles and Contributions to Edited Works

The agreement covering publication of a journal article or a contribution to an edited work may be a formal contract or a letter of agreement. The publisher often requires an assignment of the copyright to itself. The transfer of copyright allows the publisher to publish and republish the work and to license other uses of it, such as classroom photocopying, translation, and republication in print or electronic forms by others. In return for transfer of copyright, the publisher may grant the author the right to republish the article in any work of which the author is the author or editor, as long as proper credit is given in the new publication. In addition, the publisher may agree to share with the author any fees received from licenses to republish, translate, or photocopy the article. If there is no written transfer of copyright, the publisher acquires from the agreement only the privileges of publishing the article in the journal or collection, of reprinting it, and of including it in compilations.

In the typical formal contract for publishing an article, the author warrants that the manuscript is new, original, and unpublished and that it does not violate the copyright or another right of any person or entity. Commonly the publisher agrees to publish the work and to allow the author an opportunity to review the copyedited manuscript or to correct proofs (or both), and the author agrees to obtain any permissions needed for the reproduction of material from other sources, to pay fees related to those permissions, and to read and return the copyedited manuscript or proofs by a reasonable date set by the publisher. (On fair use and permissions, see 2.1.13–14.)

Authors rarely receive royalties or fees from the original publication of a journal article but may be given free reprints of the contribution, extra copies of the issue, or a year's subscription to the journal, or there may be no compensation. For a contribution to a book, compensation may take the form of a single payment or free books.

2.3	DEFAMATION

2.3.1 Libel

The tort of defamation had been recognized and remedied by English law for hundreds of years before the American Revolution. The concepts underlying the English common law of defamation were taken into American common law early in American history. With the exception of federal decisions in the second half of the twentieth century to protect the freedom of the press guaranteed by the First Amendment to the United States Constitution, there has been little change in the law of defamation since the eighteenth century.

In law defamation is a published false statement of fact about a living person that exposes the person to public hatred, ridicule, contempt, or disgrace, induces an evil opinion of the person in the minds of others, or deprives the person of friendly relations in society. Defamation has traditionally been divided into two branches—slander, or oral defamation, and libel, or written defamation. With the prominence of the broadcast media, the distinction between these two branches of defamation has become confused. Legal treatises have commented on the difficulty of distinguishing between slander and libel. In this chapter, only libel (written defamation) will be discussed. Not all false statements about a person are libelous. False statements that are merely annoying or unpleasant or that subject someone only to jests that hurt feelings are not defamatory and therefore are not legally actionable, even if the statements include words of abuse and epithets.

Libel has been divided by the state courts into two categories—libel per se and libel per quod. Words that are actionable per se are assumed to injure reputation by their very nature. Language that is libelous per se has been delimited by judicial decisions over the years. Libel per se includes, for instance, statements that a person is guilty of a criminal offense involving moral turpitude or disgrace, but not those asserting other violations of law. For example, allegations of speeding would not be libelous per se, but those of hit-and-run driving would be. Another example of libel per se is the claim that someone currently has a loathsome disease, such as leprosy or a sexually transmitted disease. Statements concerning disease in the past, implying that it has been cured, are not actionable per se.

Allegations of sexual misconduct, particularly against women, have traditionally been considered libels per se. Statements about sexual behavior that fall short of asserting sexual misconduct (such as a charge of having posed in the nude) may not be found libelous per se. As social standards and attitudes have changed, the same allegations that were once libelous per se primarily against women have also in recent decisions been found to be libelous per se against men. Questions of sexual libel are still not treated identically for men and women, however. Statements charging that someone is insolvent or bankrupt also fall into the category of libel per se. However, criticism of legal business practices, such as failure to pay a debt, is not libelous per se. Unproved statements alleging incompetence in a business or profession are usually found to be libelous per se, as are statements charging dishonest business practices. By contrast, a statement that a person made a serious mistake in a business or profession is not libelous per se and may not be defamatory at all. The same rules about business libels apply to corporations as well as to individuals.

When a plaintiff successfully proves libel per se, it is usually presumed that the plaintiff was damaged. Consequently, the plaintiff's burden of proof is lightened. The exact parameters of libel rules can vary from state to state because libel is governed by state law.

Under common law, libel per quod was language that was not actionable as libel without an explanation of extrinsic facts. The plaintiff had to prove the extrinsic facts to succeed with the case. The application of this rule varies from state to state. An example of libel per quod would be a statement that a person had been president of a named corporation, when proof could be obtained elsewhere that the former president of that corporation was convicted of theft of its assets.

2.3.2   Opinion

Statements of pure opinion are not actionable no matter how offensive they are. This follows from the definition of defamation as a false statement of fact. However, an opinion that would be libelous if an assertion of fact and that is accompanied by an implication that it is based on undisclosed facts is actionable. Thus, when writing an unflattering opinion, an author should be careful to set forth the facts on which it is based. Rhetoric and hyperbole are closely related to pure opinion and, in the absence of other factors, are not actionable. It is therefore safer to express a harsh judgment or conclusion in the form of hyperbole than as an unsupported statement of fact.

The determination whether an offensive statement is opinion rather than an allegation of fact is a frequent subject of judicial opinions. The determination is based on what an average person reading the statement would understand it to mean. This judgment, difficult at best, is largely a question of the context in which the statement is made. The context in which offensive words appear can alter their status from opinion to fact. For example, words that might be regarded as opinion or rhetoric and not be actionable if uttered in the heat of a dispute could be found to be a statement of fact and therefore actionable if appearing in a book based on research. Verbal qualifications can shift a statement from fact to opinion. A writer without conclusive proof of an offensive statement should not hesitate to say that the statement is the writer's opinion or belief instead of propounding it as factual. Nonetheless, a court may not be bound by qualifying language in extreme cases, such as the accusation of a heinous crime. The type of writing may also make a difference. Offensive language appearing in reviews or humorous writing is likely to be found to be protected opinion. There would be no purpose to such writing if unfavorable comment could not be made. Indeed, one who appears in a public performance, writes a book, or opens a restaurant may even be deemed to have consented to a review, no matter how unfavorable. Not only is such work protected by the common law of most states, but some courts have found it to be constitutionally protected as well.

2.3.3   Truth as Defense

Truth is a complete defense in all actions for libel. However, belief in the truth of an offending statement is different from the ability to prove the truth of such a statement. Government records and believable witnesses with pertinent knowledge are the best proofs of truth. Many publishers are willing to accept a potentially offensive statement as true if it appeared in a publication with a large circulation and if no rebuttal is known to have been made. Nonetheless, such a precedent is not proof of truth; it would at most mitigate damages if an author who repeated the statement lost an action for libel. The judge or jury would have to consider whether it was the prior publication, as well as the author's repetition, that injured the plaintiff's reputation. Publishers may still be justified in refusing to publish such material, since damages are not always mitigated on these grounds and since a libel action carries expenses and risks besides damages, such as the costs of defense. The defense of truth is further complicated because although in some states a plaintiff may be required to prove that an offensive statement is false, in other states the statement may be presumed false without proof. In the latter case, the defendant has the burden of proving the truth of the potentially libelous statement.

2.3.4   Actual Malice

State libel law has not changed much in the last two hundred years. In 1964, however, the United States Supreme Court, deciding the case *New York Times Co. v. Sullivan*, drastically altered the law of libel about persons involved in public matters. The court was asked for the first time the extent to which the United States Constitution limits the power of the states to award libel damages to public officials. In this case, L. B. Sullivan, a public official in Montgomery, Alabama, brought a libel action against the *New York Times* for publication of a political advertisement in support of Martin Luther King, Jr., and placed by a group advocating civil rights in the South. The advertisement, which did not mention Sullivan by name, charged that civil rights were being abridged in the South and specifically referred to actions of public officials in Montgomery. It contained some errors of fact. A jury awarded Sullivan $500,000, and the Alabama Supreme Court affirmed the award. The United States Supreme Court, on appeal, held unanimously that the First Amendment to the Constitution bars any award to a public official for defamatory statements unless the statements were made with what the court called "actual malice," defined by the court as reckless disregard of the truth or as knowledge that the material published was false. As a result of the *Sullivan* case, a public official claiming to have been libeled by statements in a publication protected by the First Amendment has to prove both that the statements are false and that the defendant published them with *actual malice*—that is, in reckless disregard of the truth or with knowledge of their falsity.

In 1967 the Supreme Court decided two cases that expanded the protections of the *Sullivan* case to statements about public figures who were not officials. In *Curtis Publishing Co. v. Butts*, a nationally known football coach and athletic director charged the *Saturday Evening Post* with libeling him because it printed an article accusing him of fixing a football game. The Supreme Court again applied the protection of the

First Amendment and the actual-malice standard. The court found the magazine's investigative practices so bad as to constitute actual malice and permitted recovery for libel, but it also clarified that the rule of the *Sullivan* case applied to public figures who were not public officials. In the second case, *Beckley Newspapers Corp. v. Hanks*, the Supreme Court made it clear that publication with a bad or corrupt motive or out of personal spite did not constitute actual malice under the standard of the *Sullivan* case. Rather, the publication had to have been made with knowledge that the material was false or with reckless disregard of the truth.

Despite the expansion of the actual-malice standard established in the *Sullivan* case, plaintiffs who are public figures have sometimes been able to prove actual malice and to recover damages for libel. Further, the Supreme Court has held that as long as states do not impose liability for defamation without fault, they may define appropriate standards for liability for publication of defamatory material about individuals who are not public figures. Consequently, great care in research and writing is still required. The key to liability for defamation of private individuals, which may vary from state to state, is usually neglect of the procedures of reporting that a prudent journalist or scholar would follow.

To be able to counter accusations of recklessness or negligence, a prudent author should retain careful notes, tapes of interviews, copies of documents in support of contentions made in writing, and copies of reports making the same charges that the author intends to make. Someone who suspects the possibility of defamation in an upcoming publication may ask to see an author's work before publication. The author should discuss such a request with the prospective publisher. It is customary to refuse such a request unless the person making it will provide the author with important facts or material otherwise unavailable.

2.4   RIGHT OF PRIVACY

2.4.1   Emergence of Privacy Law

Unlike copyright and defamation, the law of privacy is a development of the twentieth century. In 1890 Samuel D. Warren and Louis D. Brandeis, later a justice of the United States Supreme Court, wrote an article entitled "The Right to Privacy" (*Harvard Law Review* 4 [1890]), which called for the law to recognize the right of anyone to be let alone. In an early privacy case (*Roberson v. Rochester Folding Box Co.*), involving the use of the plaintiff's likeness in an advertisement for a product, New York's highest court held in 1902 that the right of privacy did not exist in New York in common law or equity. In response to this decision, the New York legislature enacted in 1909 a limited statutory right of privacy that made it a misdemeanor to use the name, portrait, or picture of any living person without permission for advertising or purposes of trade. The New York legislature has resisted adding any further provisions regarding the circumstances actionable as invasion of privacy. Most states proceeded to recognize the right of privacy by statute or case decision in four respects:

1. Unreasonable intrusion on the seclusion of others

2. Appropriation of another's name or likeness without permission for advertising or purposes of trade

3. Unreasonable publicity of another's private life

4. Publicity placing another in a false light

Since invasion of privacy is a relatively new legal concept, it would be unrealistic to assume that the four categories stated above will always be the only types of actionable privacy torts. Moreover, not every state recognizes all four categories of invasion of privacy as legally actionable; New York, for example, recognizes only the second category. Other states have recognized all the types of invasion of privacy but by judicial decision rather than by statute.

2.4.2   Unreasonable Publicity of Private Life

In many states, publication of private facts about someone who is not of public concern is considered an invasion of privacy. Although existing cases in this area involve disclosure in the mass media, it is not impossible that publication to a limited audience, such as the readers of a scholarly book or journal, may be actionable. The facts disclosed must be private, however, to be the basis for an action. When they are in the public record, even if not widely known, there is no invasion of privacy. According to some commentators, the publicized facts must be very offensive to reasonable people. There has been little guidance from the United States Supreme Court concerning this type of invasion of privacy.

2.4.3   Publicity Placing Another in a False Light

Publicity that places the person who is its subject in a false light is an actionable invasion of privacy. This tort seems to be nothing more than a variant form of defamation. To clarify the false-light tort, courts and commentators have added the requirements that the publicity be highly offensive and that the person creating it acted in reckless disregard of the truth or with knowledge of the falsity of the publicity. When there is significant misrepresentation of fact or outright fictionalization, the publicity is clearly actionable. Omission of important facts can also contribute to a false-light claim. Not all states recognize false light as an actionable invasion of privacy, but this area of law is still developing. It is thus unwise to place someone in a false light. Another reason to avoid false-light characterizations is that it is difficult to determine which state law could apply, since a plaintiff may make a claim under the law of the state in which the plaintiff lives at the time of publication.

2.4.4   Consent as Defense

For a defendant in an action of invasion of privacy, proof that the plaintiff consented to the invasion is a complete defense. Some states require that the consent be in writing. Many users of material that may invade privacy, including publishers, require before publication written consent forms from those who are subjects of the material. State laws that recognize consent as a defense against an invasion-of-privacy claim may base this recognition on the existence of a contract. To be enforceable, however, such a contract requires a payment of money or of something else valuable. A consent form given without consideration is revocable at will and could be revoked after substantial funds have been expended on the project. Therefore, publishers and other producers may require both a recitation of consideration in the consent form and a payment to the subject signing the consent.

2.5   FURTHER GUIDANCE

PUBLICATIONS OF THE COPYRIGHT OFFICE

The following publications are available from the Copyright Office, Library of Congress, 101 Independence Ave., SE, Washington, DC 20559. Most of them can be read on the Internet (http://lcweb.loc .gov/copyright/circs/).

Copyright Basics. Circular 1.
Copyright Notice. Circular 3.
Extension of Copyright Terms. Circular 15t.
International Copyright Relations of the United States. Circular 38a.
Renewal of Copyright. Circular 15.
Reproduction of Copyrighted Works by Educators and Librarians. Circular 21.

ON COPYRIGHT AND PUBLISHING AGREEMENTS FOR BOOKS

Abrams, Howard B. *The Law of Copyright*. New York: Clark, 1995.

Balkin, Richard. *How to Understand and Negotiate a Book Contract*. Cincinnati: Writer's Digest, 1985.

Goldstein, Paul. *Copyright*. 2nd ed. Boston: Little, 1996.

Gorman, Robert A., and Jane C. Ginsburg. *Copyright for the Nineties*. 4th ed. Charlottesville: Michie, 1993.

Nimmer, Melville B., and Paul Edward Geller. *International Copyright Law and Practice*. New York: Bender, 1995.

Nimmer, Melville B., and David Nimmer. *Nimmer on Copyright*. New York: Bender, 1996.

Patry, William F. *Copyright Law and Practice*. Washington: Bureau of Natl. Affairs, 1994.

————. *The Fair Use Privilege in Copyright Law*. 2nd ed. Washington: Bureau of Natl. Affairs, 1995.

Poking, Kirk. *Writers' Friendly Legal Guide*. Cincinnati: Writer's Digest, 1989. Washington: Bureau of Natl. Affairs, 1995.

United Nations Educational, Scientific, and Cultural Organization. *Copyright Laws and Treaties of the World*. Washington: Bureau of Natl. Affairs, 1992.

ON DEFAMATION AND PRIVACY

Forer, Lois G. *A Chilling Effect*. New York: Norton, 1987.

McCarthy, J. Thomas. *The Rights of Publicity and Privacy*. New York: Clark, 1996.

Sack, Robert D. *Libel, Slander, and Related Problems*. 2nd ed. New York: Practising Law Inst., 1980.

Sanford, Bruce W. *Libel and Privacy*. 2nd ed. Gaithersburg: Aspen, 1996.

Smolla, Rodney A. *Law of Defamation*. New York: Clark, 1994.

3

BASICS OF SCHOLARLY WRITING

3.1 Audience, Genre, and the Conventions of Scholarship

3.2 Language and Style

3.3 Spelling
    3.3.1 Consistency and Choice of Spelling
    3.3.2 Word Division
    3.3.3 Plurals
    3.3.4 Accents
    3.3.5 Diaereses
    3.3.6 Ligatures and Other Special Characters

3.4 Punctuation
    3.4.1 Purpose of Punctuation
    3.4.2 Commas
    3.4.3 Semicolons
    3.4.4 Colons
    3.4.5 Dashes and Parentheses
    3.4.6 Hyphens
    3.4.7 Apostrophes
    3.4.8 Quotation Marks
    3.4.9 Square Brackets
    3.4.10 Slashes
    3.4.11 Periods, Question Marks, and Exclamation Points

3.5 Italics (Underlining)
    3.5.1 Words and Letters Referred to as Words and Letters
    3.5.2 Foreign Words in an English Text
    3.5.3 Emphasis

3.6 Names of Persons
    3.6.1 First and Subsequent Uses of Names
    3.6.2 Titles of Persons
    3.6.3 Names of Authors and Fictional Characters
    3.6.4 Dutch and German Names
    3.6.5 French Names

      3.6.6   Greek Names
      3.6.7   Hungarian Names
      3.6.8   Italian Names
      3.6.9   Russian Names
      3.6.10 Spanish Names
      3.6.11 Latin Names
      3.6.12 Asian Names
      3.6.13 Names in Other Languages

3.7   Capitalization
      3.7.1   English
      3.7.2   French
      3.7.3   German
      3.7.4   Italian
      3.7.5   Portuguese
      3.7.6   Russian
      3.7.7   Spanish
      3.7.8   Latin
      3.7.9   Other Languages

3.8   Titles of Works in the Manuscript
      3.8.1   General Guidelines
      3.8.2   Underlined Titles
      3.8.3   Titles in Quotation Marks
      3.8.4   Titles and Quotations within Titles
      3.8.5   Exceptions
      3.8.6   Shortened Titles

3.9   Quotations
      3.9.1   Accuracy of Quotations
      3.9.2   Prose
      3.9.3   Poetry
      3.9.4   Drama
      3.9.5   Ellipsis
      3.9.6   Other Alterations of Sources
      3.9.7   Punctuation with Quotations
      3.9.8   Translations of Quotations

3.10 Numbers
      3.10.1 Arabic Numerals
      3.10.2 Use of Words or Numerals
      3.10.3 Commas in Numbers
      3.10.4 Percentages and Amounts of Money
      3.10.5 Dates and Times of the Day
      3.10.6 Inclusive Numbers
      3.10.7 Roman Numerals

3.11 Transliteration and Romanization

3.12 Further Guidance

3.1   AUDIENCE, GENRE, AND THE CONVENTIONS OF SCHOLARSHIP

Scholarly writing takes various shapes and forms, depending on genre (e.g., research article, book review) and audience. An accurate assessment of your intended audience will help you answer many of the formal and stylistic questions that arise in preparing a manuscript. For a general audience, such as that for a book review in a newspaper, you would usually keep documentation to a minimum and give only in English translation any quotations from works originally written in other languages; for somewhat more knowledgeable readers, such as those for an article in a periodical like the *American Scholar*, you might mention sources, either in the text or in a bibliography, and offer occasional words and phrases in another language, along with English translations; but a scholarly audience expects full and precise documentation and quotations in the original language (with translation subordinated, if provided at all).

This book assumes a scholarly audience and presents recommended guidelines for scholarly publication. At times you may need to or choose to consider variations of these guidelines, but since conventions by definition are general agreements about basic principles and since conventional practices are readily understood by others, most scholars do not depart from such guidelines without weighing advantages against disadvantages.

In some situations, departures from convention result in greater clarity or enable you to meet the needs of a particular audience. Normally, you should alter established practices only by expanding them —for instance, by giving publishers' names in full or by not using abbreviations. Where conventions do not exist or are not firmly established, you should adopt clear, workable, and consistent procedures. In general, closely follow the conventions outlined in this manual when you write articles for periodicals (or essays for collections) addressed to other scholars. Publishers usually allow more latitude for books; some types of manuscripts, such as scholarly editions and reference works, often require special practices.

3.2   LANGUAGE AND STYLE

Whereas conventions govern such matters as documentation and format of scholarly manuscripts, there are no special directives for prose style. Scholars usually aim for the qualities that distinguish all effective expository prose. (The works listed in 3.12 provide guidance.) Like most other authors of nonfiction prose, scholars generally work toward writing that is direct and clear, organized and coherent, lively and persuasive. In presenting arguments, they strive for fairness and balance while maintaining clarity and focus. In addition, the scholarly authors who have been most influential over a long period have usually conveyed their ideas without jargon, which presumes a closed audience, seeking instead terminology comprehensible to a wide range of educated readers, no matter how complex the subject.

Careful writers do not use language that implies unsubstantiated or irrelevant generalizations about such personal qualities as age, economic class, ethnicity, political or religious belief, race, sex, or sexual orientation. Many journals and book publishers have strong editorial policies concerning the avoidance of such language. Since 1981, for example, *PMLA*'s statement of editorial policy has urged "its contributors to be sensitive to the social implications of language and to seek wording free of discriminatory overtones."

Discussions and statements about nondiscriminatory language have generally focused on wording that could be labeled sexist. For example, many writers no longer use *he*, *him*, or *his* to express a meaning that includes women as well as men. The use of *she*, *her*, and *hers* to refer to a person of no particular sex is not a widely accepted alternative. Both usages can be distracting and momentarily confusing. They can often be avoided through revision that recasts the sentence into the plural or that eliminates the pronoun altogether. Another technique is to make the discussion refer to a person who is identified, so that there is a reason to use a specific singular pronoun. *He or she* as subject, *her or his* as possessive, and *her or him* as object are cumbersome alternatives to be used sparingly. Many authors now also avoid terms that unnecessarily integrate a person's sex with a job or role. For instance, *anchorman, policewoman, stewardess*, and *poetess* are commonly replaced with *anchor, police officer, flight attendant*, and *poet*, which can apply to both men and women. For advice on current practices, see the guides to nonsexist language listed in 3.12.

Effective scholarly writing, then, depends on clarity and readability as well as on content. The organization and development of ideas, unity and coherence of presentation, and fitness of sentence structure, grammar, and diction are all essential considerations, as is the correctness of the mechanics of writing—capitalization, punctuation, spelling, and so on. Although the scope of this book precludes a detailed discussion of grammar, usage, and related aspects of writing, the sections that follow address mechanical questions scholarly authors encounter in their writing: spelling, punctuation, italics (underlining), names of persons, capitalization, titles of works, quotations, numbers, and transliteration and romanization.

3.3   SPELLING

3.3.1   Consistency and Choice of Spelling

Spelling, including hyphenation, should be consistent throughout the manuscript—except in quotations, which must retain the spelling of the original, whether correct or incorrect. To ensure accuracy and consistency, always use a single widely recognized authority for spelling, such as *Merriam-Webster's Collegiate Dictionary* or, if the word is not listed there, *Webster's Third New International Dictionary*. Other standard dictionaries are *The American Heritage Dictionary* and *Random House Dictionary of the American Language*.

Where entries show variant spellings, use the form given first or, if the variants have separate listings, the form that appears with the full definition. Inform your editor, before copyediting begins, of any necessary deviations from this practice—for example, a variant commonly used in your discipline.

3.3.2   Word Division

Dividing words at the ends of lines makes the manuscript less readable and can cause typesetting errors. If a word will not fit on a line, leave the line short and begin the word on the next line. The "word-wrap" feature of word-processing programs performs this operation automatically, provided that any automatic-hyphenation option is turned off. If you choose to divide a word, consult your dictionary about where the break should occur.

3.3.3   Plurals

The plurals of English words are generally formed by adding the suffix *-s* or *-es* (*laws, taxes*), with several exceptions (e.g., *children, halves, mice, sons-in-law, bison*). The tendency in American English is to form the plurals of words naturalized from other languages in the standard manner. The plurals *librettos* and *formulas* are therefore now more common in American English than *libretti* and *formulae*. But some adopted words, like *alumni* and *phenomena*, retain the original plurals. Consult a dictionary for guidance. If the dictionary gives more than one plural form for a word (*appendixes, appendices*) use the first listed. (See 3.4.7 for plurals of letters and for possessive forms of plurals.)

3.3.4   Accents

In quoting, reproduce all accents and other diacritical marks exactly as they appear in the original. Handwrite marks that your word processor or typewriter lacks. Accented letters do not always retain the accent mark when capitalized (the accent in the French word *école* may be omitted in *Ecole*, for example), but an accent is never unacceptable over a capital letter that would require one if it were lowercase (*École*). When transcribing words that appear in all capitals and changing them to lowercase (as in transcribing a title from a title page), insert the necessary accents.

3.3.5   Diaereses

In German words the diaeresis, not *e*, should be used for the umlaut (*ä*, *ö*, *ü* rather than *ae*, *oe*, *ue*), even for initial capitals (*Über*). But common usage must be observed for names: *Götz*, but *Goethe*. In alphabetizing such words, Germanists treat an umlauted vowel as if the letter were followed by an *e*; thus *Götz* would be alphabetized as *Goetz* and would precede *Gott* in an alphabetical listing. Nonspecialists, however, and many libraries in English-speaking countries alphabetize such words without regard to the diaeresis.

3.3.6   Ligatures and Other Special Characters

A ligature is a combination of letters that is united in print: æ and Æ in Danish, Norwegian, and Old English; œ and Œ in French; and ß in German. When addressing a specialist audience, you should reproduce these characters in your manuscript, through your word processor or by hand notation, if they appear in the source you are duplicating. When addressing a general readership, you may omit the connection between letters (*ae*, *Ae*, *oe*, *Oe*, *ss*). Other special characters —for example, Old English and Middle English letters that are not used in modern English—should be reproduced from the source regardless of your audience.

3.4   PUNCTUATION

3.4.1   Purpose of Punctuation

The primary purpose of punctuation is to ensure the clarity and readability of writing. Punctuation clarifies sentence structure, separating some words and grouping others. It adds meaning to written words and guides the understanding of readers as they move through sen-

---

Most of the usage examples in 3.4–5 are quotations or adaptations of quotations. The sources are listed on pages 311–13.

tences. The rules set forth here cover many of the situations common in scholarly writing. For the punctuation of quotations in the text, see 3.9.7. For the punctuation of parenthetical references and bibliographies, see chapters 6 and 7. See also the individual listings in the index for specific punctuation marks.

3.4.2   Commas

a. Use a comma before a coordinating conjunction (*and, but, for, nor, or, yet,* or *so*) joining independent clauses in a sentence.

> Synonyms have a basic similarity of meaning, but at the margins they can differ greatly.

> Inexpensive examples of literary annuals still turn up in secondhand stores, for the craze leaped the Atlantic, and the books became as popular in the United States as in England.

b. Use commas to separate words, phrases, and clauses in a series.

WORDS

> Priests, conjurers, magicians, and shamans have long known the importance of using words correctly in prayers, petitions, hexes, and incantations.

PHRASES

> To some writers the computer is a subtle saboteur, subverting their intentions, reconstituting their words, and redirecting their attention to the layout of the page.

CLAUSES

> Originally the plantations were rather small, there were fewer slaves than colonists, and social discrimination was less harsh than in the eighteenth century.

But use semicolons when items in a series have internal commas.

> Perhaps the most ambitious English-language poem of the decolonized Third World, Walcott's Omeros fills

```
hundreds of pages with rolling hexameters in terza
rima; alludes abundantly to Homer, James Joyce, and
Aimé Césaire; and ranges historically from
precolonial Africa to contemporary Ireland and Saint
Lucia.
```

c. Use a comma between coordinate adjectives—that is, adjectives that separately modify the same noun.

```
For men, heroism was usually described as bravery and
the active, successful overcoming of adversity. (The
```
adjectives *active* and *successful* each modify *overcoming*.)

But note:

```
The dialogue soon reveals the reason for her mysterious
daily sojourns there. (The adjective *mysterious* modifies *daily*
sojourns.)
```

d. Use commas to set off a parenthetical comment, or an aside, if it is brief and closely related to the rest of the sentence. (For punctuation of longer, more intrusive, or more complex parenthetical elements, see 3.4.5.)

```
A title or a headline, for instance, functions as a
signal and determines our approach to the ensuing
text.
```

```
It is not, I submit, about the body at all.
```

e. Use commas to set off a nonrestrictive modifier—that is, a modifier that is not essential to the meaning of the sentence. A nonrestrictive modifier, unlike a restrictive one, could be dropped without changing the main sense of the sentence. Modifiers in the following three categories are either nonrestrictive or restrictive. (For the use of parentheses and dashes around complex nonrestrictive modifiers, see 3.4.5b.)

Words in apposition

NONRESTRICTIVE

```
Baron François-Pascal-Simon Gérard, court painter to
Louis XVIII, made Duras's heroine the subject of a
painting.
```

RESTRICTIVE

The painter Baron François-Pascal-Simon Gérard made Duras's heroine the subject of a painting.

Clauses that begin with *who, whom, whose, which,* and *that*

NONRESTRICTIVE

All these subjects seemed irrelevant to Seneca, who thought that the only valid use of literature was as a model for conduct.

A brief comparison with the most famous chivalric drama, which was written fifteen years earlier, clarifies the uniqueness of Thon's play.

RESTRICTIVE

All these subjects seemed irrelevant to philosophers who thought that the only valid use of literature was as a model for conduct.

A brief comparison with a chivalric drama that was written fifteen years earlier clarifies the uniqueness of Thon's play.

Note that some writers prefer to use *which* to introduce nonrestrictive clauses and *that* to introduce restrictive clauses.

Adverbial phrases and clauses

NONRESTRICTIVE

After the separation, she moved to Lunéville, where she was under the protection of the ducal court.

RESTRICTIVE

After the separation, she moved to a town where she was under the protection of the ducal court.

f. Use a comma after a long introductory phrase or clause.

PHRASE

In this charged atmosphere of cultural victory and cultural defeat, Americanists undertook the search for a central myth of America.

CLAUSE

When Zilia begins learning how to write French, she is writing to Aza.

g. Use commas to set off alternative or contrasting phrases.

Fin de siècle Spain was simply not receptive to feminism, especially not to the fundamental feminism that formed the basis of Pardo Bazán's thought on sex roles.

Sometimes this is where the deeper motives for the work are most clearly, if inadvertently, revealed.

But note:

Alexander Pope uses classical myths and allusions for incidental yet incisive contributions to his overarching satiric design. (The conjunction *yet* links *incidental* and *incisive*, making commas unnecessary.)

h. Do not use a comma between subject and verb.

What makes Sartre's theory of commitment relevant to our discussion [no comma] is its insistence that choice in today's world can be only political.

i. Do not use a comma between verb and object.

In 1947 Allen Walker Read devoted to dialect geography [no comma] only the fifth day of his twenty-eight-day course.

j. Do not use a comma between the parts of a compound subject, compound object, or compound verb.

COMPOUND SUBJECT

Bakhtin's notion of novelistic languages as "ideologically saturated" [no comma] and his conception of them as "rejoinders" in a dialogue with the extraliterary (271, 274) are heuristic tools that can be applied not only to the analysis of prose

fiction but also to the interpretation of poetic
texts.

COMPOUND OBJECT

Miller has taken pride in citing the civic function
of the theater [no comma] and the way in which the
spectacle influences the private tensions of the
individual.

COMPOUND VERB

In the afterlife, the poem suggests, African artists
such as Wheatley will have "gem-blaz'd" crowns of their
own [no comma] and will take their rightful places in
"the heav'nly choirs."

k. Do not use a comma between two parallel subordinate
elements.

From his darkness, Lear has gained insight into himself
as fallible man and negligent king [no comma] and into
the evil of Goneril and Regan.

The current political and cultural climate has given
rise to a public that demands training in basic
literacy [no comma] but that is unwilling to pay for
it.

l. Use a comma in a date whose order is month, day, and year. If
such a date comes in the middle of a sentence, include a comma after
the year.

Martin Luther King, Jr., was born on January 15, 1929,
and died on April 4, 1968.

But commas are not used with dates whose order is day, month, and
year.

Martin Luther King, Jr., was born on 15 January 1929
and died on 4 April 1968.

m. Do not use a comma between a month and a year or between a
season and a year.

> The events of July 1789 are as familiar to the French
> as those of July 1776 are to Americans.

See 3.9.7 for commas with quotations.

3.4.3 Semicolons

a. Use a semicolon between independent clauses not linked by a conjunction.

> Shelley remarks that "the blank incapability of
> invention [. . .] is the greatest misery of authorship"
> (x); that misery overcome, she is pleased to write the
> "Author's Introduction" to a tale in which authorship
> proves a misery to her protagonist.

b. Use semicolons between items in a series when the items contain commas.

> Thérèse, the washerwoman; Sethe, the cook; Eva, the
> shelter giver and caretaker; and Baby Suggs, the
> churchless preacher, negotiate this paradox
> successfully within the narrative context.

3.4.4 Colons

The colon is used between two parts of a sentence when the first part creates a sense of anticipation about what follows in the second. Leave only one space after a colon, not two.

a. Use a colon to introduce a list, an elaboration of what was just said, or the formal expression of a rule or principle.

LIST

> All five of the relatively distinct types of early
> Japanese religious belief and practice are present in
> the book: Shinto, Buddhism, Taoism, Confucianism, and
> folk religion.

ELABORATION

> As Emerson's friend at Walden Pond suggested, it takes
> two to speak the truth: one to speak and another to
> hear.

RULE OR PRINCIPLE

> Most such standards no doubt point to the <u>delectare</u> and <u>prodesse</u> of Horace's advice to the poet: Delight and benefit your reader! (A rule or principle after a colon should begin with a capital letter.)

But a verb (e.g., *includes*) or preposition that performs the same introductory function as a colon makes the colon unnecessary.

> Atwood's other visual art includes a drawing for the cover of <u>Good Bones</u>, collages in <u>The Journals of Susanna Moodie</u>, and comic strips.

b. Use a colon to introduce a quotation that is independent from the structure of the main sentence.

> The new art relation of modernism is a concept that was most memorably given expression by Walter Pater: "All art constantly aspires towards the condition of music" (140).

A quotation that is integral to the sentence structure is generally preceded by no punctuation or, if a verb of saying (*says, exclaims, notes, writes*) introduces the quotation, by a comma. A colon is used after a verb of saying, however, if the verb introduces certain kinds of formal literary quotations, such as long quotations set off from the main text (see 3.9.2–4, 3.9.8). On colons separating titles and subtitles, see 3.8.1.

3.4.5   Dashes and Parentheses

Dashes make a sharper break in the continuity of the sentence than commas do, and parentheses make a still sharper one. To indicate a dash in typing, use two hyphens, with no space before, between, or after. (Some word processors have a dash, and you may use it instead of hyphens.) Your writing will be smoother and more readable if you use dashes and parentheses sparingly. Limit the number of dashes in a sentence to two paired dashes or one unpaired dash.

a. Use dashes or parentheses to enclose a sentence element that interrupts the train of thought.

> The human race has survived, and the planet seems to have replenished itself--there are fish, oceans, forests--but what kind of society exists in 2195?

b. Use dashes or parentheses to set off a parenthetical element that contains a comma and that might be misread if set off with commas.

> Most newcomers to both states soon accommodate to the "correct" pronunciation--that is, to the pronunciation used by most westerners.

> The Italian sonnet (which is exemplified in Petrarch's Canzoniere, along with other kinds of poems) developed into the English sonnet.

c. Use a dash to introduce words that summarize a preceding series.

> Whether we locate meaning in the text, in the act of reading, or in some collaboration between reader and text--whatever our predilection, let us not generate from it a straitjacket.

A dash may also be used instead of a colon to introduce a list or an elaboration of what was just said (see 3.4.4a).

3.4.6   Hyphens

Compound words of all types—nouns, verbs, adjectives, and so on— are written as separate words (*hard drive, hard labor*), with hyphens (*hard-and-fast, hard-boiled*), and as single words (*hardcover, hardheaded*). The dictionary shows how to write many compounds. A compound not in the dictionary should usually be written as separate words unless a hyphen is needed to prevent readers from misunderstanding the relation between the words. Following are some rules to help you decide whether you need a hyphen in compounds and other terms that may not appear in the dictionary.

a. Use a hyphen in a compound adjective beginning with an adverb such as *better, best, ill, lower, little,* or *well* when the adjective precedes a noun.

> better-prepared ambassador
> best-known work
> ill-informed reporter
> lower-priced tickets
> well-dressed announcer

But do not use a hyphen when the compound adjective comes after the noun it modifies.

    The ambassador was better prepared than the other
    delegates.

b. Do not use a hyphen in a compound adjective beginning with an adverb ending in -*ly* or with *too, very,* or *much.*

    thoughtfully presented thesis
    very contrived plot
    too hasty judgment
    much maligned performer

c. Use a hyphen in a compound adjective ending with the present participle (e.g., *loving*) or the past participle (e.g., *inspired*) of a verb when the adjective precedes a noun.

    sports-loving throng
    fear-inspired loyalty

d. Use a hyphen in a compound adjective formed by a number and a noun when the adjective precedes a noun.

    second-semester courses
    early-thirteenth-century architecture

e. Use hyphens in other compound adjectives before nouns to prevent misreading.

    continuing-education program (The hyphen indicates that the
        term refers to a program of continuing education and not to an
        education program that is continuing.)
    Portuguese-language student (The hyphen makes it clear that the
        term refers to a student who is studying Portuguese and not to a
        language student who is Portuguese.)

f. Do not use hyphens in familiar unhyphenated compound terms, such as *social security, high school,* and *liberal arts,* when they appear before nouns as modifiers.

    social security tax
    high school reunion
    liberal arts curriculum

75

g. Use hyphens to join coequal nouns.

```
writer-critic
scholar-athlete
```

But do not use a hyphen in a pair of nouns in which the first noun modifies the second.

```
father figure
opera lover
```

h. In general, do not use hyphens after prefixes (e.g., *anti-, co-, multi-, non-, over-, post-, pre-, re-, semi-, sub-, un-, under-*).

```
antiwar          overpay         semiretired
coworker         postwar         subsatellite
multinational    prescheduled    unambiguous
nonjudgmental    reinvigorate    underrepresented
```

But sometimes a hyphen is called for after a prefix.

```
post-Victorian
```
(Use a hyphen before a capital letter.)

```
re-cover
```
(The hyphen distinguishes this verb, meaning "cover again," from *recover*, meaning "get back.")

```
anti-icing
```
(Without the hyphen, the doubled vowel would make the term hard to recognize.)

3.4.7 Apostrophes

A principal function of apostrophes is to indicate possession. They are also used to form contractions (*can't, wouldn't*), which are rarely acceptable in scholarly writing, and the plurals of the letters of the alphabet (*p's and q's, three A's*).

a. To form the possessive of a singular noun, add an apostrophe and an *s*.

```
a poem's meter
```

b. To form the possessive of a plural noun ending in *s*, add only an apostrophe.

```
photographers' exhibit
```

c. To form the possessive of an irregular plural noun not ending in
s, add an apostrophe and an *s*.

```
women's studies
```

d. To form the possessive of nouns in a series, add a single apostrophe and an *s* if the ownership is shared.

```
Palmer and Colton's book on European history
```

But if the ownership is separate, place an apostrophe and an *s* after
each noun.

```
Palmer's and Colton's books on European history
```

e. To form the possessive of any singular proper noun, add an
apostrophe and an *s*.

```
Dickens's reputation
Descartes's philosophy
Marx's precepts
```

f. To form the possessive of a plural proper noun, add only an
apostrophe.

```
the Dickenses' economic woes
```

g. Do not use an apostrophe to form the plural of an abbreviation
or a number.

```
MAs        fours
PhDs       GRE score in the 1400s
1990s
```

On using apostrophes to abbreviate dates, see 3.10.5.

3.4.8   Quotation Marks

a. Place quotation marks around a word or phrase given in someone else's sense or in a special sense or purposefully misused.

```
Teachers often make use of visual "texts" from current
exhibits at the college's art gallery.
```

> Baillie relies on metaphors that contrast "bad" ancien
> régime-style formal gardens to "good" British natural
> landscapes.

> One commentator would go so far as to say that
> nothing is less traditional than "primitive"
> societies.

If introduced unnecessarily, this device can make writing heavy-handed. Quotation marks are redundant after *so-called*.

> One commentator would go so far as to say that
> nothing is less traditional than so-called primitive
> societies.

b. Use quotation marks for a translation of a foreign word or phrase.

> From its inception in the tragosodos, the "goat songs"
> whose dithyrambic intensity galvanized early Greek
> audiences of tragedy, the tragic has served this self-
> reflexive purpose.

> During the Meiji period, the emperor was recuperated as
> a divine monarch embodying the national polity
> (kokutai, literally "national body").

You may use single quotation marks for a translation that follows the original directly, without intervening words or punctuation.

> In a 1917 letter to the publisher Kurt Wolff, for
> example, Kafka refers to "[der] tief in mir sitzende
> Beamte" 'the deep-seated bureaucrat inside me' (Briefe,
> 1902-1924 158; Letters 134).

On quotation marks with titles, see 3.8.3–4. On quotation marks with quotations and with translations of quotations, see 3.9.7 and 3.9.8, respectively.

3.4.9 Square Brackets

Use square brackets around a parenthesis within a parenthesis, so that the levels of subordination can be easily distinguished. Insert square brackets by hand if they are not available on your word processor or typewriter.

```
The editor decided to use the Leningrad Codex
(preserved in the Saltykov-Shchedrin State Public
Library in Leningrad [now Saint Petersburg]).
```

For square brackets around an ellipsis or an interpolation in a quotation, see 3.9.5 and 3.9.6, respectively. For square brackets around missing, unverified, or interpolated data in documentation, see 6.6.1, 6.6.23, and 6.6.25.

3.4.10 Slashes

The slash, or diagonal, is rarely necessary in formal prose. Other than in quotations of poetry (see 3.9.3), the slash has a place mainly between two terms paired as opposites or alternatives and used together as a noun.

```
The essay traces a number of crossings over
hypothetical borders or divisions: East/West,
female/male, homosexual/heterosexual,
colonized/colonizer, among others.
```

```
The class studies Meyer Schapiro's discussion of such
pictorial properties of painting as right/left or
frame/center.
```

But use a hyphen when such a compound precedes and modifies a noun.

```
nature-nurture conflict
either-or situation
East-West relations
```

3.4.11 Periods, Question Marks, and Exclamation Points

A sentence can end with a period, a question mark, or an exclamation point. Periods end declarative sentences. (For the use of periods with ellipsis points, see 3.9.5.) Question marks follow interrogative sentences. Except in direct quotation, avoid exclamation points in scholarly writing.

Place a question mark inside a closing quotation mark if the quoted passage is a question. Place a question mark outside if the quotation ends a sentence that is a question. If a question mark occurs where a comma or period would normally be required, omit the comma or period. Note the use of the question mark and other punctuation marks in the following sentences:

```
Whitman asks, "Have you felt so proud to get at the
meaning of poems?"
```

```
Where does Whitman speak of "the meaning of poems"?
```

```
"Have you felt so proud to get at the meaning of
poems?" Whitman asks.
```

3.5   ITALICS (UNDERLINING)

Most word-processing programs and computer printers permit the reproduction of italic type. In manuscripts that will be edited for publication, however, the type style of every letter and punctuation mark must be easily recognizable to copyeditors, designers, typesetters, and production editors. Italic type is sometimes not distinctive enough for this purpose. In printed scholarly manuscripts submitted for editing, therefore, words that would be italicized in a publication (*Candide*) are usually underlined:

```
Candide
```

If you wish to use italics rather than underlining, check your editor's preferences.

When preparing a manuscript for electronic publication, consult your editor on how to represent italicization. In electronic environments that do not permit text formatting, it is common to place one underline before and after each word or group of words that would be italicized in print:

```
_Candide_
_The Uses of Literature_
```

The rest of this section discusses using italics for words and letters referred to as words and letters (3.5.1), foreign words in an English text (3.5.2), and emphasis (3.5.3). (See 3.8.2 for the italicizing of titles.)

3.5.1   Words and Letters Referred to as Words and Letters

Underline words and letters that are referred to as words and letters.

> The exercise is designed to help students understand
> critical terms like <u>irony</u>, <u>symbol</u>, and <u>metaphor</u>.

> Shaw spelled <u>Shakespeare</u> without the final <u>e</u>.

3.5.2   Foreign Words in an English Text

In general, underline foreign words used in an English text.

> The Renaissance courtier was expected to display
> <u>sprezzatura</u>, or nonchalance, in the face of adversity.

The numerous exceptions to this rule include quotations entirely in another language ("Julius Caesar said, 'Veni, vidi, vici'"); non-English titles of short works (poems, short stories, essays, articles), which are placed in quotation marks and not underlined ("El sueño," the title of a poem by Quevedo); proper names (Marguerite de Navarre); and foreign words anglicized through frequent use. Since American English rapidly naturalizes words, use a dictionary to decide whether a foreign expression requires italics. Following are some adopted foreign words, abbreviations, and phrases commonly not underlined:

ad hoc	et al.	lieder
cliché	etc.	raison d'être
concerto	genre	sic
e.g.	hubris	versus

3.5.3   Emphasis

Italics for emphasis is a device that rapidly becomes ineffective. It is rarely appropriate in scholarly writing.

3.6   NAMES OF PERSONS

3.6.1   First and Subsequent Uses of Names

In general, the first time you use a person's name in the text of your manuscript, state it fully and accurately, exactly as it appears in your source.

```
Arthur George Rust, Jr.
Victoria M. Sackville-West
```

Do not change Arthur George Rust, Jr., to Arthur George Rust, for example, or drop the hyphen in Victoria M. Sackville-West. In subsequent references to the person, you may give the last name only (Rust, Sackville-West)—unless, of course, you refer to two or more persons with the same last name—or you may give the most common form of the name (e.g., Garcilaso for Garcilaso de la Vega). In casual references to the very famous—say, Mozart, Shakespeare, or Michelangelo—it is not necessary to give the full name initially. In some languages (e.g., Chinese, Hungarian, Japanese, Korean, and Vietnamese), surnames precede given names (see 3.6.7 and 3.6.12).

3.6.2   Titles of Persons

In general, do not use formal titles (Mr., Mrs., Miss, Ms., Dr., Professor, Reverend) in first or subsequent references to men or women, living or dead (Churchill, not Mr. Churchill; Mead, not Professor Mead; Hess, not Dame Hess; Montagu, not Lady Montagu). A few women in history are traditionally known by their titles as married women (e.g., Mrs. Humphry Ward, Mme de Staël), although the tendency is to omit such titles (Lafayette, not Mme de Lafayette). Treat other women's names the same as men's.

The appropriate way to refer to persons with titles of nobility can vary. For example, the full name and title of Henry Howard, earl of Surrey, should be given at first mention, and thereafter Surrey alone may be used. In contrast, for Benjamin Disraeli, first earl of Beaconsfield, it is sufficient to give Benjamin Disraeli initially and Disraeli subsequently. Follow the example of your sources in citing titles of nobility.

3.6.3   Names of Authors and Fictional Characters

It is common and acceptable to use simplified names of famous authors (Vergil for Publius Vergilius Maro, Dante for Dante Alighieri). Also acceptable are pseudonyms of authors.

```
Molière (Jean-Baptiste Poquelin)
Voltaire (François-Marie Arouet)
George Sand (Amandine-Aurore-Lucie Dupin)
George Eliot (Mary Ann Evans)
Mark Twain (Samuel Clemens)
```

> Stendhal (Marie-Henri Beyle)
>
> Novalis (Friedrich von Hardenberg)

Refer to fictional characters in the same way that the work of fiction does. You need not always use their full names, and you may retain titles (Dr. Jekyll, Mme Defarge).

3.6.4   Dutch and German Names

With some exceptions, especially in English-language contexts, Dutch *van*, *van der*, and *van den* and German *von* are generally not used with the last name alone.

> Beethoven (Ludwig van Beethoven)
>
> Droste-Hülshoff (Annette von Droste-Hülshoff)
>
> Kleist (Heinrich von Kleist)
>
> Vondel (Joost van den Vondel)

but

> Van Dyck (Anthony Van Dyck)
>
> Von Braun (Wernher Von Braun)

See 3.3.5 for German names with an umlaut.

3.6.5   French Names

With some exceptions, especially in English-language contexts, French *de* following a first name or a title such as *Mme* or *duc* is not used with the last name alone.

> La Boétie (Etienne de La Boétie)
>
> La Bruyère (Jean de La Bruyère)
>
> Maupassant (Guy de Maupassant)
>
> Nemours (Louis-Charles d'Orléans, duc de Nemours)
>
> Ronsard (Pierre de Ronsard)
>
> Scudéry (Madeleine de Scudéry)

but

> De Quincey (Thomas De Quincey)

When the last name has only one syllable, however, *de* is usually retained.

```
de Gaulle  (Charles de Gaulle)
de Man  (Paul de Man)
```

The preposition also remains, in the form *d'*, when it elides with a last name beginning with a vowel.

```
d'Arcy  (Pierre d'Arcy)
d'Arsonval  (Arsène d'Arsonval)
```

The forms *du* and *des*—combinations of *de* with *le* and *les*—are always used with last names and are capitalized.

```
Des Périers  (Bonaventure Des Périers)
Du Bos, Charles  (Charles Du Bos)
```

A hyphen is frequently used between French given names, as well as between their initials (Marie-Joseph Chénier, M.-J. Chénier). Note that *M.* and *P.* before names may be abbreviations for the titles *Monsieur* and *Père* (M. René Char, P. J. Reynard).

3.6.6   Greek Names

In Greek books, the author's name appears on the title page in the genitive case ("Hypo ["by"] Perikleous Alexandrou Argyropoulou"). The first name and usually the surname of a man are nominative (some surnames, however, are always genitive). The second, or patronymic, remains genitive because it means "son of" (Periklēs Alexandrou Argyropoulos, Konstantinos Petrou Kavafis). The first name of a woman is nominative, the patronymic and surname both genitive (Roxanes Demetriou Argyropoulu). On transliterating Greek, see 3.11.

3.6.7   Hungarian Names

In Hungarian, the surname precedes the given name.

```
Bartók Béla
Bessenyei György
Illyés Gyula
Molnár Ferenc
Nagy László
Szabó Magda
```

In English texts, Hungarian names usually appear with given name first and the surname last.

    Béla Bartók

    György Bessenyei

    Gyula Illyés

    Ferenc Molnár

    László Nagy

    Magda Szabó

3.6.8   Italian Names

The names of many Italians who lived before or during the Renaissance are alphabetized by first name.

    Bonvesin da la Riva

    Cino da Pistoia

    Dante Alighieri

    Iacopone da Todi

    Michelangelo Buonarroti

But other names of the period follow the standard practice.

    Boccaccio, Giovanni

    Cellini, Benvenuto

    Stampa, Gaspara

The names of members of historic families are also usually alphabetized by last name.

    Este, Beatrice d'

    Medici, Lorenzo de'

In modern times, Italian *da, de, del, della, di,* and *d'* are usually capitalized and used with the last name alone.

    Da Ponte (Lorenzo Da Ponte)

    D'Azeglio (Massimo D'Azeglio)

    Del Buono (Oreste Del Buono)

    Della Casa (Giovanni Della Casa)

    De Sica (Vittorio De Sica)

    Di Costanzo (Angelo Di Costanzo)

3.6.9 Russian Names

See J. Thomas Shaw, *The Transliteration of Modern Russian for English-Language Publications* (1967; New York: MLA, 1979), for a more extended discussion of which system of transliteration to use for Russian names in various circumstances and when to use common Western forms of names. The following is adopted from Shaw.

Russian names have three parts: prename, patronymic, and surname (Anton Pavlovich Chekhov). Prenames of Russians should be transliterated according to the appropriate system rather than given in their English equivalents (Ivan, not John). The only exception is the prename of a Russian ruler used alone (without the patronymic); in this case, use the English equivalent (Michael I, but Mikhail Pavlovich).

The form of patronymics in Russian varies by sex, as the form of surnames often does. For example, Aleksandr Sergeevich Pushkin was the husband of Natalia Nikolaevna Pushkina. The treatment of such names in an English text depends on the audience, on the predominance of masculine or feminine names in the text, and particularly on whether the text uses names without prenames. In general, the feminine forms should be used for the feminine names and the masculine forms for the masculine names. On occasion, however, especially in a casual reference to Russians in a work not on Russian studies, some modifications may be acceptable. Scholars not familiar with Russian names must exercise care in balancing accuracy with clarity.

3.6.10 Spanish Names

Spanish *de* is not used before the last name alone.

> `Las Casas` (Bartolomé de Las Casas)
>
> `Madariaga` (Salvador de Madariaga)
>
> `Rueda` (Lope de Rueda)
>
> `Timoneda` (Juan de Timoneda)

Spanish *del*, formed from the fusion of the preposition *de* and the definite article *el*, is capitalized and used with the last name alone.

> `Del Río` (Angel Del Río)

A Spanish surname may include both the paternal name and the maternal name, with or without the conjunction *y*. The surname of a married woman usually includes her paternal surname and her husband's paternal surname, connected by *de*. Alphabetize Spanish names by the full surnames (consult your sources or a biographical dictionary for guidance in distinguishing surnames and given names).

```
Carreño de Miranda, Juan
Cervantes Saavedra, Miguel de
Díaz del Castillo, Bernal
García Márquez, Gabriel
Larra y Sánchez de Castro, Mariano José
López de Ayala, Pero
Matute, Ana María
Ortega y Gasset, José
Quevedo y Villegas, Francisco Gómez de
Sinues de Marco, María del Pilar
Zayas y Sotomayor, María de
```

Even persons commonly known by the maternal portions of their surnames, such as Galdós and Lorca, should be indexed under their full surnames.

```
García Lorca, Federico
Pérez Galdós, Benito
```

3.6.11 Latin Names

Roman male citizens generally had three names: a praenomen (given name), a nomen (clan name), and a cognomen (family or familiar name). Men in this category are usually referred to by nomen, cognomen, or both; your source or a standard reference book such as *The Oxford Classical Dictionary* will provide guidance.

```
Brutus  (Marcus Iunius Brutus)
Calpurnius Siculus  (Titus Calpurnius Siculus)
Cicero  (Marcus Tullius Cicero)
Lucretius  (Titus Lucretius Carus)
Plautus  (Titus Maccius Plautus)
```

Roman women usually had two names—a nomen (the clan name in the feminine form) and a cognomen (often derived from the father's cognomen): Livia Drusilla (daughter of Marcus Livius Drusus). Sometimes a woman's cognomen indicates her chronological order among the daughters of the family: Antonia Minor (younger daughter of Marcus Antonius). Most Roman women are referred to by nomen:

Calpurnia, Clodia, Octavia, Sulpicia. Some, however, are better known by cognomen: Agrippina (Vipsania Agrippina).

When citing Roman names, use the forms most common in English.

Horace (Quintus Horatius Flaccus)

Julius Caesar (Gaius Iulius Caesar)

Juvenal (Decimus Iunius Iuvenalis)

Livy (Titus Livius)

Ovid (Publius Ovidius Naso)

Quintilian (Marcus Fabius Quintilianus)

Terence (Publius Terentius Afer)

Vergil (Publius Vergilius Maro)

Finally, some medieval and Renaissance figures are best known by their adopted or assigned Latin names.

Albertus Magnus (Albert von Bollstädt)

Comenius (Jan Amos Komenský)

Copernicus (Niklas Koppernigk)

Paracelsus (Theophrastus Bombast von Hohenheim)

3.6.12 Asian Names

In Chinese, Japanese, Korean, and Vietnamese, surnames precede given names.

CHINESE

Deng Nan

Deng Xiaoping

JAPANESE

Ueda Akinari

Ueda Makoto

KOREAN

Kim Jong-gil

Kim Nam-ju

VIETNAMESE

Nguyen Du

Nguyen Trai

Western authors should follow known preferences, however, even if the preferred forms do not accord with normal practice or standard romanization (Y. R. Chao, Syngman Rhee). (On transliterating Asian languages, see 3.11.)

In the older Wade-Giles system of romanizing Chinese, the given name appears in two syllables, separated by a hyphen (Huang Tso-lin, Mao Tse-tung); in the pinyin system, the given name appears without a hyphen (Huang Zuolin, Mao Zedong). Scholars presenting Chinese names need to balance the sometimes conflicting goals of consistency and clarity. In general, if you use the pinyin system, add the Wade-Giles spelling, in parentheses, for the names of persons who died before 1950 or who are better known by the older spelling. This practice allows a reader unfamiliar with the systems of romanization to become acquainted with the differences between them and to locate in other scholarly works information you cite. Many figures from the past are known by names of only two syllables, sometimes hyphenated: Lao-tzu, Han-shan, Li Po, Wang Wei.

3.6.13 Names in Other Languages

For the names of persons in a language with which you are not familiar, consult relevant reference works or knowledgeable scholars for guidance on the order of names and on the use of prefixes (as in Arabic names). When a work you cite includes a transliteration of the author's name on the title page, spell the author's name in your bibliography according to the system of transliteration recommended in 3.11, and follow the name by the transliteration (in parentheses) printed on the title page, if it is different.

3.7 CAPITALIZATION

3.7.1 English

Capitalized in English are (1) the first word of a sentence, (2) the subject pronoun *I*, (3) the names and initials of persons (except for some particles), (4) the names of months and days of the week, (5) titles that immediately precede personal names (President Wilson) but not persons' titles used alone (*the president, a professor of English*), (6) other proper nouns, and (7) most adjectives derived from proper nouns.

In titles and subtitles of works, capitalize the first words, the last words, and all principal words, including those that follow hyphens in compound terms. Therefore, capitalize the following parts of speech:

- Nouns (e.g., *flowers* and *Europe* as in *The Flowers of Europe*)
- Pronouns (e.g., *our* as in *Save Our Children, that* as in *The Mouse That Roared*)
- Verbs (e.g., *watches* as in *America Watches Television, is* as in *What Is Literature?*)
- Adjectives (e.g., *more* as in *No More Parades, that* as in *Who Said That Phrase?*)
- Adverbs (e.g., *slightly* as in *Only Slightly Corrupt, down* as in *Go Down, Moses*)
- Subordinating conjunctions (e.g., *after, although, as if, as soon as, because, before, if, that, unless, until, when, where, while* as in *One If by Land* and *Anywhere That Chance Leads*)

Do not capitalize the following parts of speech when they fall in the middle of a title:

- Articles (*a, an, the* as in *Felix Holt, the Radical*)
- Prepositions (e.g., *against, as, between, in, of, to* as in *The Merchant of Venice* and "A Dialogue between the Soul and Body")
- Coordinating conjunctions (*and, but, for, nor, or, so, yet* as in *Romeo and Juliet*)
- The *to* in infinitives (as in *The Courage to Be*)

Use a colon and a space to separate a title from a subtitle, unless the title ends in a question mark, an exclamation point, or a dash. Include other punctuation only if it is part of the title.

The following examples illustrate how to capitalize and punctuate a variety of titles. For a discussion of which titles to underline and which to place in quotation marks, see 3.8.2–3.

> <u>Death of a Salesman</u>
> <u>The Teaching of Spanish in English-Speaking Countries</u>
> <u>Storytelling and Mythmaking: Images from Film and</u>
>   <u>Literature</u>
> <u>Life As I Find It</u>
> <u>The Artist as Critic</u>
> <u>What Are You Doing in My Universe?</u>
> <u>Whose Music? A Sociology of Musical Language</u>
> <u>Where Did You Go? Out. What Did You Do? Nothing.</u>
> "Ode to a Nightingale"
> "Italian Literature before Dante"

```
"What Americans Stand For"
"Why Fortinbras?"
```

When the first line of a poem serves as the title of the poem, reproduce the line exactly as it appears in the text.

```
Dickinson's poem "I heard a Fly buzz--when I died--"
contrasts the mundane and the momentous.
```

In the name of a periodical, an initial definite article is usually not
treated as part of the title (the *Washington Post*). Capitalize the word
series or *edition* only when it is part of a title (Norton Critical Edition,
Twayne World Authors Series; but Penguin edition, *Oxford Companion*
series). Do not capitalize the descriptive name for a part of a work—
for example, *preface*, *introduction*, or *appendix*—unless it is a well-
known title, such as Wordsworth's Preface to *Lyrical Ballads*.

Do not capitalize a noun, spelled out or abbreviated, followed by a
numeral or letter indicating place in a sequence (*act 5, version A, ch. 3,
no. 20, pl. 4, vol. 2*). Never capitalize entire words (i.e., every letter) in
titles, even if the words are capitalized on the title page, except for
terms composed of initials (*MLN*).

3.7.2   French

In prose and verse, French capitalization is the same as English except
that the following terms are not capitalized in French unless they
begin sentences or, sometimes, lines of verse: (1) the subject pronoun *je*
'I,' (2) the names of months and days of the week, (3) the names of languages, (4) adjectives derived from proper nouns, (5) titles preceding
personal names, and (6) the words meaning "street," "square," "lake,"
"mountain," and so on, in most place-names.

```
Un Français m'a parlé anglais près de la place de la
Concorde.

Hier j'ai vu le docteur Maurois qui conduisait une
voiture Ford.

Le capitaine Boutillier m'a dit qu'il partait pour
Rouen le premier jeudi d'avril avec quelques amis
normands.
```

In a title or subtitle, capitalize the first word and all proper nouns.

> L'ami du peuple
>
> Du côté de chez Swann
>
> Le grand Meaulnes
>
> La guerre de Troie n'aura pas lieu
>
> La jeune parque
>
> Nouvelle revue d'onomastique

Some editors and presses follow other rules. When the title of a book begins with an article, they also capitalize the first noun and any preceding adjectives: *L'Ami du peuple*, *La Jeune Parque*. In titles of series and periodicals, they capitalize all major words: *Nouvelle Revue d'Onomastique*.

3.7.3 German

In prose and verse, German capitalization differs considerably from English. Always capitalized in German are all nouns—including adjectives, infinitives, pronouns, prepositions, and other parts of speech when used as nouns—as well as the pronoun *Sie* 'you' and its possessive, *Ihr* 'your,' and their inflected forms. Not capitalized except at the beginning of sentences and, usually, of lines of verse are (1) the subject pronoun *ich* 'I,' (2) the names of languages and of days of the week used as adjectives, adverbs, or complements of prepositions, and (3) adjectives and adverbs formed from proper nouns, unless the proper nouns are names of persons and the adjectives and adverbs refer to the persons' works or deeds.

> Ich glaube an das Gute in der Welt.
>
> Er schreibt, nur um dem Auf und Ab der Buch-Nachfrage zu entsprechen.
>
> Fahren Sie mit Ihrer Frau zurück?
>
> Ein französischer Schriftsteller, den ich gut kenne, arbeitet sonntags immer an seinem neuen Buch über die platonische Liebe.
>
> Der Staat ist eine der bekanntesten Platonischen Schriften.

In letters and ceremonial writings, the pronouns *du* and *ihr* 'you' and their derivatives are capitalized.

In a title or subtitle, capitalize the first word and all words normally capitalized.

> Thomas Mann und die Grenzen des Ich
>
> Ein treuer Diener seines Herrn
>
> Zeitschrift für vergleichende Sprachforschung

3.7.4 Italian

In prose and verse, Italian capitalization is the same as English except that in Italian centuries and other large divisions of time are capitalized (*il Seicento*) and the following terms are not capitalized unless they begin sentences or, usually, lines of verse: (1) the subject pronoun *io* 'I,' (2) the names of months and days of the week, (3) the names of languages and nationalities, (4) nouns, adjectives, and adverbs derived from proper nouns, (5) titles preceding personal names, and (6) the words meaning "street," "square," and so on, in most place-names.

> Un italiano parlava francese con uno svizzero in piazza di Spagna.
>
> Il dottor Bruno ritornerà dall'Italia giovedì otto agosto e io partirò il nove.

In a title or subtitle, capitalize only the first word and all words normally capitalized.

> L'arte tipografica in Urbino
>
> Bibliografia della critica pirandelliana
>
> Collezione di classici italiani
>
> Dizionario letterario Bompiani
>
> Studi petrarcheschi

3.7.5 Portuguese

In prose and verse, Portuguese capitalization is the same as English except that the following terms are not capitalized in Portuguese unless they begin sentences or, sometimes, lines of verse: (1) the subject pronoun *eu* 'I,' (2) the names of days of the week, (3) the names of months in Brazil (they are capitalized in Portugal), (4) adjectives derived from proper nouns, (5) titles preceding personal names in Portugal (they are capitalized in Brazil), and (6) the words meaning "street," "square," and so on, in most place-names in Portugal (they are capitalized in Brazil). As in English, points of the compass are not capitalized when indicating direction (*ao norte da América*), but they are capitalized when indicating regions (*os americanos do Norte*). Braziian Portuguese capitalizes nouns used to refer to abstract concepts, to institutions, or to branches of knowledge (*a Igreja, a Nação, a Matemática*).

PENINSULAR USAGE

Vi o doutor Silva na praça da República.

BRAZILIAN USAGE

O francês falava da História do Brasil na Praça Tiradentes, utilizando o inglês.

Ontem eu vi o Doutor Garcia, aquêle que tem um carro Ford.

Então me disse Dona Teresa que pretendia sair para o Recife a primeira segunda-feira de abril com alguns amigos mineiros.

In a title or subtitle, capitalize only the first word and all words normally capitalized.

O bico da pena

O espírito das leis

Gabriela, cravo e canela

Problemas das linguagem e do estilo

Boletim de filologia

Revista lusitana

Correio da manhã

Some editors and presses, however, capitalize all major words: *Gabriela, Cravo e Canela* and *Boletim de Filologia*.

3.7.6 Russian

In prose and verse, Russian capitalization is the same as English except that the following terms are not capitalized in Russian unless they begin sentences or, sometimes, lines of verse: (1) the subject pronoun *ja* 'I,' (2) the names of months and days of the week, (3) the names of languages, (4) adjectives derived from proper nouns, (5) titles preceding personal names, and (6) the words meaning "street," "square," and so on, in most place-names. Transliterated Russian should follow the same usage (on transliteration, see 3.11).

```
V subbotu, trinadcatogo aprelja, prazdnuja svoj den'
roždenija, doktor Petuxov vnov' vspomnil o svoej
vstreče s francuzom iz Liona na ulice Marata.

V to vremja peterburgskaja znat' predpočitala govorit'
pofrancuzski.

Naprasno ia pytalsja ugovorit' ego ne delat' ètogo.
```

In a title or subtitle and in the name of an organization or institution, capitalize the first word and all words normally capitalized.

```
"K istorii obrazovanija vostočnoslavjanskix jazykov:
Po dannym Galickogo evangelija 1266-1301 gg."

Obščestvennye nauki za rubežom: Literaturovedenie

Voprosy literatury
```

3.7.7 Spanish

In prose and verse, Spanish capitalization is the same as English except that the following terms are not capitalized in Spanish unless they begin sentences or, sometimes, lines of verse: (1) the subject pronoun *yo* 'I,' (2) the names of months and days of the week, (3) the names of languages and nationalities, (4) nouns and adjectives derived from proper nouns, (5) titles preceding personal names, and (6) the words meaning "street," "square," and so on, in most place-names.

```
El francés hablaba inglés en la plaza Colón.

Ayer yo vi al doctor García en un coche Ford.

Me dijo don Jorge que iba a salir para Sevilla el
primer martes de abril con unos amigos neoyorkinos.
```

In a title or subtitle, capitalize only the first word and words normally capitalized.

```
Breve historia del ensayo hispanoamericano
Extremos de América
La gloria de don Ramiro
Historia verdadera de la conquista de la Nueva España
```

95

Revista de filología española

Trasmundo de Goya

Some editors and presses follow other rules. In titles of series and periodicals, they capitalize all major words: *Revista de Filología Española.*

3.7.8   Latin

Although practice varies, Latin most commonly follows the English rules for capitalization, except that *ego* 'I' is not capitalized.

Semper ego auditor tantum? Numquamne reponam / Vexatus totiens rauci Theseide Cordi?

Quidquid id est, timeo Danaos et dona ferentes.

Nil desperandum.

Quo usque tandem abutere, Catilina, patientia nostra?

In a title or subtitle, however, capitalize only the first word and all words normally capitalized.

De senectute

Liber de senectute

Medievalia et humanistica

3.7.9   Other Languages

In transliterating or romanizing languages that do not have capital letters (e.g., Arabic, Chinese, Japanese), capitalize the first words of sentences and, sometimes, of lines of poetry and all names of persons and places. (On transliteration and romanization, see 3.11.) In Arabic, the article *al* (and its forms) is lowercase except when it begins a sentence. Capitalize transliterated or romanized names of institutions, religions, movements, and the like if comparable names are capitalized in English. A lowercase transliterated or romanized term appearing in English text is underlined; a capitalized transliterated or romanized name (other than a title of a work) in English text is not underlined, unless it is part of an expression that is otherwise lowercase. In a title or subtitle, capitalize only the first word and all words normally capitalized.

   For additional information on capitalization in a variety of languages, consult *The Chicago Manual of Style* (14th ed. [Chicago: U of Chicago P, 1993]), the United States Government Printing Office *Style Manual* (rev. ed. [Washington: GPO, 1984]), *ALA-LC Romanization*

Tables: Transliteration Schemes for Non-Roman Scripts (comp. and ed. Randall K. Barry [Washington: Lib. of Congress, 1991]), *Words into Type* (by Marjorie E. Skillin, Robert M. Gay, et al., 3rd ed. [Englewood Cliffs: Prentice, 1974]; new ed. in preparation), and Georg F. von Ostermann's *Manual of Foreign Languages for the Use of Librarians, Bibliographers, Research Workers, Editors, Translators, and Printers* (4th ed. [New York: Central, 1952]).

3.8   TITLES OF WORKS IN THE MANUSCRIPT

3.8.1   General Guidelines

Whenever you cite the title of a published work in your manuscript, take the title from the title page, not from the cover or from the top of a page. Do not reproduce any unusual typographic characteristics, such as special capitalization or lowercasing of letters. Place a colon between a title and a subtitle, unless the title ends in a question mark, an exclamation point, or a dash. A title page may present a title designed like one of the following examples:

MODERNISM & NEGRITUDE

BERNARD BERENSON
The Making of a Connoisseur

Turner's early sketchbooks

These titles should appear in a manuscript as follows:

Modernism and Negritude

Bernard Berenson: The Making of a Connoisseur

Turner's Early Sketchbooks

To indicate titles in your manuscript, whether in English or in another language, either underline them or enclose them in quotation marks. In general, underline the titles of works published independently (see 3.8.2) and use quotation marks for titles of works published within larger works and for unpublished works (see 3.8.3).

3.8.2   Underlined Titles

Underline the names of books, plays, long poems published as books, pamphlets, periodicals (newspapers, magazines, and journals), films, radio and television programs, compact discs, audiocassettes, record albums, ballets, operas and other long musical compositions (except those identified simply by form, number, and key; see 3.8.5), paintings, works of sculpture, ships, aircraft, and spacecraft. In the following examples, note that the underlining is not broken between words. While there is no need to underline the spaces between words, a continuous line is often the default in word-processing programs, and it guards against the error of failing to underline the punctuation within a title.

<u>The Awakening</u> (book)

<u>The Piano Lesson</u> (play)

<u>The Waste Land</u> (long poem published as a book)

<u>New Jersey Driver Manual</u> (pamphlet)

<u>Wall Street Journal</u> (newspaper)

<u>Time</u> (magazine)

<u>Die bitteren Tränen der Petra von Kant</u> (film)

<u>Star Trek</u> (television program)

<u>Sgt. Pepper's Lonely Hearts Club Band</u> (compact disc, audiocassette, record album)

Ailey's <u>Revelations</u> (ballet)

<u>Rigoletto</u> (opera)

Berlioz's <u>Symphonie fantastique</u> (long musical composition identified by name)

Chagall's <u>I and My Village</u> (painting)

French's <u>The Minute Man</u> (sculpture)

HMS <u>Vanguard</u> (ship)

<u>Spirit of St. Louis</u> (aircraft)

3.8.3   Titles in Quotation Marks

Enclose in quotation marks the titles of such published works as articles, essays, short stories, short poems, chapters of books, individual episodes of television and radio programs, and short musical compositions (e.g., songs). Also use quotation marks for unpublished works, such as lectures, papers delivered at conferences, manuscripts of any length, and dissertations.

"Literary History and Sociology" (journal article)

"Etruscan" (encyclopedia article)

"The Fiction of Langston Hughes" (essay in a book)

"The Lottery" (short story)

"Kubla Khan" (poem)

"Contemporary Theory, the Academy, and Pedagogy" (chapter in a book)

"The Trouble with Tribbles" (episode of the television program *Star Trek*)

"Mood Indigo" (song)

"Adapting to the Age of Information" (lecture)

3.8.4   Titles and Quotations within Titles

Underline a title normally indicated by underlining when it appears within a title enclosed in quotation marks.

"<u>Romeo and Juliet</u> and Renaissance Politics" (an article about a play)

"Language and Childbirth in <u>The Awakening</u>" (an article about a novel)

Enclose in single quotation marks a title normally indicated by quotation marks when it appears within another title requiring quotation marks.

"Lines after Reading 'Sailing to Byzantium'" (a poem about a poem)

"The Uncanny Theology of 'A Good Man Is Hard to Find'" (an article about a short story)

Also place single quotation marks around a quotation that appears within a title requiring quotation marks.

"Emerson's Strategies against 'Foolish Consistency'" (an article with a quotation in its title)

Use quotation marks around a title normally indicated by quotation marks when it appears within an underlined title.

> <u>"The Lottery" and Other Stories</u> (a book of short stories)
>
> <u>New Perspectives on "The Eve of St. Agnes"</u> (a book about a poem)

If a period is required after an underlined title that ends with a quotation mark, place the period before the quotation mark.

> The study appears in <u>New Perspectives on "The Eve of St. Agnes."</u>

Do not underline or enclose in quotation marks a normally underlined title when it appears within another underlined title.

> <u>Approaches to Teaching Murasaki Shikibu's</u> The Tale of Genji (a book about a novel)
>
> <u>From</u> The Lodger <u>to</u> The Lady Vanishes: Hitchcock's Classic British Thrillers (a book about films)

Some scholars, editors, and presses follow a rule different from the preceding one. They underline and place quotation marks around all titles within underlined titles: *Approaches to Teaching Murasaki Shikibu's "The Tale of Genji," From "The Lodger" to "The Lady Vanishes": Hitchcock's Classic British Thrillers.*

There are shortcomings to both methods of handling titles within underlined titles. In the first method, when the part of the title not underlined falls at the beginning or end of the title, there is little typographic differentiation between that part and any text adjacent to it. In the second method, works published within larger works and works published independently are not distinguished. In addition, this approach causes a single class of works to be treated two ways: titles of works published independently are placed in quotation marks when part of underlined titles but not in other contexts.

3.8.5   Exceptions

The convention of using underlining and quotation marks to indicate titles does not generally apply to the names of sacred writings (including all books and versions of the Bible); of laws, acts, and similar political documents; of instrumental musical compositions identified by form, number, and key; of series, societies, buildings, and monuments; and of conferences, seminars, workshops, and courses. These terms all appear without underlining or quotation marks.

SACRED WRITINGS

Bible   Gospels

King James Version   Talmud

Old Testament   Koran

Genesis   Upanishads

But underline titles of individual published editions of sacred writings (*The Interlinear Bible, The Talmud of the Land of Israel: A Preliminary Translation and Explanation, The Upanishads: A Selection for the Modern Reader*) and treat the editions in the works-cited list like any other published book.

LAWS, ACTS, AND SIMILAR POLITICAL DOCUMENTS

Magna Carta

Declaration of Independence

Bill of Rights

Treaty of Trianon

INSTRUMENTAL MUSICAL COMPOSITIONS IDENTIFIED BY FORM, NUMBER, AND KEY

Beethoven's Symphony no. 7 in A, op. 92

Vivaldi's Concerto for Two Trumpets and Strings in C, RV539

SERIES

Bollingen Series

University of North Carolina Studies in Comparative Literature

Masterpiece Theatre

SOCIETIES

American Historical Association

Renaissance Society of America

BUILDINGS AND MONUMENTS

Moscone Center

Sears Tower

Arch of Constantine

CONFERENCES, SEMINARS, WORKSHOPS, AND COURSES

The Social Poem: A Conference on Contemporary Poetry in
  the Public Sphere
Canadian Writers' Workshop
MLA Annual Convention
Introduction to Linguistics
Portuguese 102

Words designating the divisions of a work are also not underlined or put within quotation marks, nor are they capitalized when used in the text ("The author says in her preface [. . .]," "In canto 32 Ariosto writes [. . .]").

preface	bibliography	act 4
introduction	appendix	scene 7
list of works cited	index	stanza 20
chapter 2	canto 32	

3.8.6 Shortened Titles

If you cite a title often in the text of your manuscript, you may, after stating the title in full at least once, use a shortened form, preferably a familiar or obvious one (e.g., "Nightingale" for "Ode to a Nightingale"), or an abbreviation (for standard abbreviated titles of literary and religious works, see 8.6).

3.9   QUOTATIONS

3.9.1 Accuracy of Quotations

The accuracy of quotations is extremely important. They must reproduce the original sources exactly. Unless indicated in brackets or parentheses (see 3.9.6), changes must not be made in the spelling, capitalization, or interior punctuation of the source. You must construct a clear, grammatically correct sentence that allows you to introduce or incorporate a quotation with complete accuracy. Alternatively, you may paraphrase the original and quote only fragments, which may be easier to integrate into the text. If you change a quotation in any way, make the alteration clear to the reader, following the rules and recommendations below.

3.9.2   Prose

If a prose quotation runs no more than four lines and requires no special emphasis, put it in quotation marks and incorporate it into the text.

> "It was the best of times, it was the worst of times,"
> wrote Charles Dickens about the eighteenth century.

You need not always reproduce complete sentences. Sometimes you may want to quote just a word or phrase as part of your sentence.

> For Charles Dickens the eighteenth century was both
> "the best of times" and "the worst of times."

You may put a quotation at the beginning, middle, or end of your sentence or, for the sake of variety or better style, divide it by your own words.

> Joseph Conrad writes of the company manager in Heart of
> Darkness, "He was obeyed, yet he inspired neither love
> nor fear, nor even respect."

or

> "He was obeyed," writes Joseph Conrad of the company
> manager in Heart of Darkness, "yet he inspired neither
> love nor fear, nor even respect."

If a quotation ending a sentence requires a parenthetical reference, place the sentence period after the reference. (For more information on punctuating quotations, see 3.9.7.)

> For Charles Dickens the eighteenth century was both
> "the best of times" and "the worst of times" (35).

> "He was obeyed," writes Joseph Conrad of the company
> manager in Heart of Darkness, "yet he inspired neither
> love nor fear, nor even respect" (87).

If a quotation runs to more than four lines in the manuscript, set it off from your text by beginning a new line, indenting one inch (or ten spaces) from the left margin, and typing it double-spaced, without adding quotation marks. A colon generally introduces a quotation displayed in this way, though sometimes the context may require a different mark of punctuation or none at all. If you quote only a single paragraph or part of one, do not indent the first line more than the rest. A parenthetical reference to a prose quotation set off from the text follows the last line of the quotation.

> At the conclusion of <u>Lord of the Flies</u>, Ralph and the other boys realize the horror of their actions:
>
>> The tears began to flow and sobs shook him. He gave himself up to them now for the first time on the island; great, shuddering spasms of grief that seemed to wrench his whole body. His voice rose under the black smoke before the burning wreckage of the island; and infected by that emotion, the other little boys began to shake and sob too. (186)

If you need to quote two or more paragraphs, indent the first line of each paragraph an additional quarter inch (or three spaces). If the first sentence quoted does not begin a paragraph in the source, however, do not indent it the additional amount. Indent only the first lines of the successive paragraphs.

> In <u>Moll Flanders</u> Defoe maintains the pseudoautobiographical narration typical of the picaresque tradition:
>
>> My true name is so well known in the records, or registers, at Newgate and in the Old Bailey, and there are some things of such consequence still depending there relating to my particular conduct, that it is not to be expected I should set my name or the account of my family to this work [. . .].
>>> It is enough to tell you, that [. . .] some of my worst comrades, who are out of the way of doing me harm [. . .] know me by the name of Moll Flanders [. . .]. (1)

On omitting words within quotations, see 3.9.5. For translations of quotations, see 3.9.8.

3.9.3   Poetry

If you quote part or all of a single line of verse that does not require special emphasis, put it in quotation marks within your text. You may also incorporate two or three lines in this way, using a slash with a space on each side (/) to separate them.

> Bradstreet frames the poem with a sense of mortality:
> "All things within this fading world hath end" (1).

> Reflecting on the "incident" in Baltimore, Cullen
> concludes, "Of all the things that happened
> there / That's all that I remember" (11-12).

Verse quotations of more than three lines should begin on a new line. Unless the quotation involves unusual spacing, indent each line one inch (or ten spaces) from the left margin and double-space between lines, adding no quotation marks that do not appear in the original. A parenthetical reference for a verse quotation set off from the text follows the last line of the quotation (as in quotations of prose); a parenthetical reference that will not fit on the line should appear on a new line, flush with the right margin of the page.

> Elizabeth Bishop's "In the Waiting Room" is rich in
> evocative detail:
>> It was winter. It got dark
>> early. The waiting room
>> was full of grown-up people,
>> arctics and overcoats,
>> lamps and magazines. (6-10)

A line that is too long to fit within the right margin should be continued on the next line and the continuation indented an additional quarter inch (or three spaces). You may reduce the indentation of the quotation to less than one inch (or ten spaces) from the left margin if doing so will eliminate the need for such continuations. If the spatial arrangement of the original lines, including indentation and spacing within and between them, is unusual, reproduce it as accurately as possible.

> E. E. Cummings concludes the poem with this vivid
> description of a carefree scene, reinforced by the
> carefree form of the lines themselves:

```
it's

spring

and

     the

          goat-footed
balloonMan          whistles

far

and

wee (16-24)
```

When a verse quotation begins in the middle of a line, the partial line should be positioned where it is in the original and not shifted to the left margin.

```
In a poem on Thomas Hardy ("T. H."), Molly Holden
recalls her encounter with a "young dog fox" one
morning:
                                        I remember
       he glanced at me in just that way,
            independent
       and unabashed, the handsome sidelong look
       that went round and about but never
            directly
       met my eyes, for that would betray his
            soul.
       He was not being sly, only careful. (43-48)
```

For translations of quotations, see 3.9.8.

3.9.4   Drama

If you quote dialogue between two or more characters in a play, set the quotation off from your text. Begin each part of the dialogue with the appropriate character's name indented one inch (or ten spaces) from the left margin and written in all capital letters: HAMLET. Follow the name with a period, and start the quotation. Indent all subsequent lines in that character's speech an additional quarter inch (or three spaces). When the dialogue shifts to another character, start a new line indented one inch (or ten spaces) from the left margin. Maintain this pattern throughout the entire quotation. For the other aspects of formatting, follow the recommendations above for quoting prose and poetry (3.9.2–3).

Marguerite Duras's screenplay for <u>Hiroshima mon amour</u>
suggests at the outset the profound difference between
observation and experience:

> HE. You saw nothing in Hiroshima. Nothing.
>
> SHE. I saw <u>everything</u>. <u>Everything</u>. [. . .]
>   The hospital, for instance, I saw it.
>   I'm sure I did. There is a hospital in
>   Hiroshima. How could I help seeing it?
>
> HE. You did not see the hospital in
>   Hiroshima. You saw nothing in
>   Hiroshima. (2505-06)

A short time later Lear loses the final symbol of his
former power, the soldiers who make up his train:

> GONERIL.   Hear me, my lord.
>   What need you five-and-twenty, ten or
>   five,
>   To follow in a house where twice so many
>   Have a command to tend you?
>
> REGAN.   What need one?
>
> LEAR. O, reason not the need! (2.4.254-58)

3.9.5   Ellipsis

Whenever you wish to omit a word, a phrase, a sentence, or more from
a quoted passage, you should be guided by two principles: fairness to
the author quoted and the grammatical integrity of your writing. A
quotation should never be presented in a way that could cause a
reader to misunderstand the sentence structure of the original source.
If you quote only a word or a phrase, it will be obvious that you left
out some of the original sentence.

> In his inaugural address, John F. Kennedy spoke of a
> "new frontier."

But if omitting material from the original sentence or sentences leaves
a quotation that appears to be a sentence or a series of sentences,
you must use ellipsis points, or three spaced periods, to indicate that
your quotation does not completely reproduce the original. To distinguish between your ellipses and the spaced periods that sometimes
appear in works, place square brackets around the ellipsis points that
you add. Leave a space before the second and third periods but

no space before the first or after the third. Whenever you omit words from a quotation, the resulting passage—your prose and the quotation integrated into it—should be grammatically complete and correct.

For an ellipsis within a sentence, leave a space before the first bracket and a space after the last bracket.

ORIGINAL

Medical thinking, trapped in the theory of astral influences, stressed air as the communicator of disease, ignoring sanitation or visible carriers. (Barbara W. Tuchman, *A Distant Mirror: The Calamitous Fourteenth Century* [1978; New York: Ballantine, 1979] 101–02)

QUOTATION WITH AN ELLIPSIS IN THE MIDDLE

In surveying various responses to plagues in the Middle Ages, Barbara W. Tuchman writes, "Medical thinking [. . .] stressed air as the communicator of disease, ignoring sanitation or visible carriers."

QUOTATION WITH AN ELLIPSIS IN THE MIDDLE AND
A PARENTHETICAL REFERENCE

In surveying various responses to plagues in the Middle Ages, Barbara W. Tuchman writes, "Medical thinking [. . .] stressed air as the communicator of disease, ignoring sanitation or visible carriers" (101-02).

When the ellipsis coincides with the end of your sentence, leave a space before the first bracket, and immediately follow the last bracket with the sentence period and the closing quotation mark.

QUOTATION WITH AN ELLIPSIS AT THE END

In surveying various responses to plagues in the Middle Ages, Barbara W. Tuchman writes, "Medical thinking, trapped in the theory of astral influences, stressed air as the communicator of disease [. . .]."

If a parenthetical reference follows the ellipsis at the end of your sentence, however, leave a space before the first bracket, and immediately follow the last bracket with the closing quotation mark, a space, the parenthetical reference, and the sentence period.

QUOTATION WITH AN ELLIPSIS AT THE END FOLLOWED BY
A PARENTHETICAL REFERENCE

In surveying various responses to plagues in the Middle
Ages, Barbara W. Tuchman writes, "Medical thinking,
trapped in the theory of astral influences, stressed
air as the communicator of disease [. . .]" (101-02).

In a quotation of more than one sentence, an ellipsis in the middle
can indicate the omission of any amount of text. With such an omission, the first bracket of the ellipsis is always preceded by a space, but
what comes before this space and after the last bracket varies, depending on the material that the ellipsis replaces.

ORIGINAL

Presidential control reached its zenith under Andrew Jackson, the
extent of whose attention to the press even before he became a candidate is suggested by the fact that he subscribed to twenty newspapers. Jackson was never content to have only one organ grinding out
his tune. For a time, the *United States Telegraph* and the *Washington
Globe* were almost equally favored as party organs, and there were
fifty-seven journalists on the government payroll. (William L. Rivers,
The Mass Media: Reporting, Writing, Editing, 2nd ed. [New York:
Harper, 1975] 7)

QUOTATION OMITTING A SENTENCE

In discussing the historical relation between politics
and the press, William L. Rivers notes, "Presidential
control reached its zenith under Andrew Jackson, the
extent of whose attention to the press even before he
became a candidate is suggested by the fact that he
subscribed to twenty newspapers. [. . .] For a time, the
United States Telegraph and the Washington Globe were
almost equally favored as party organs, and there were
fifty-seven journalists on the government payroll" (7).

QUOTATION WITH AN OMISSION FROM THE MIDDLE OF ONE
SENTENCE TO THE END OF ANOTHER

In discussing the historical relation between politics
and the press, William L. Rivers notes, "Presidential
control reached its zenith under Andrew Jackson

```
[. . .]. For a time, the United States Telegraph and
the Washington Globe were almost equally favored as
party organs, and there were fifty-seven journalists on
the government payroll" (7).
```

QUOTATION WITH AN OMISSION FROM THE MIDDLE OF ONE
SENTENCE TO THE MIDDLE OF ANOTHER

```
In discussing the historical relation between politics
and the press, William L. Rivers notes that when
presidential control "reached its zenith under Andrew
Jackson, [. . .] there were fifty-seven journalists on
the government payroll" (7).
```

The omission of words and phrases from quotations of poetry is also indicated by three periods within brackets (as in quotations of prose).

ORIGINAL

In Worcester, Massachusetts,
I went with Aunt Consuelo
to keep her dentist's appointment
and sat and waited for her
in the dentist's waiting room.
It was winter. It got dark
early. The waiting room
was full of grown-up people,
arctics and overcoats,
lamps and magazines.
(Elizabeth Bishop, "In the Waiting Room," lines 1–10)

QUOTATION WITH AN ELLIPSIS AT THE END

```
Elizabeth Bishop's "In the Waiting Room" is rich in
evocative detail:

        In Worcester, Massachusetts,
        I went with Aunt Consuelo
        to keep her dentist's appointment
        and sat and waited for her
        in the dentist's waiting room.
        It was winter. It got dark
        early. The waiting room
        was full of grown-up people [. . .]. (1-8)
```

The omission of a line or more in the middle of a poetry quotation that is set off from the text is indicated by a line of spaced periods, within square brackets, approximately the length of a complete line of the quoted poem.

QUOTATION OMITTING A LINE OR MORE IN THE MIDDLE

```
Elizabeth Bishop's "In the Waiting Room" is rich in
evocative detail:
          In Worcester, Massachusetts,
          I went with Aunt Consuelo
          to keep her dentist's appointment
          [. . . . . . . . . . . . . .]
          It was winter. It got dark
          early. (1-3, 6-7)
```

3.9.6   Other Alterations of Sources

Occasionally, you may decide that a quotation will be unclear or confusing to your reader unless you provide supplementary information. For example, you may need to insert material missing from the original, to add *sic* ("thus," "so") to assure readers that the quotation is accurate even though the spelling or logic might make them think otherwise, or to underline words for emphasis. While such contributions to a quotation are permissible, you should keep them to a minimum and make sure to distinguish them from the original, usually by explaining them in parentheses after the quotation or by putting them in square brackets within the quotation.

A comment or an explanation that immediately follows the closing quotation mark appears in parentheses.

```
Shaw admitted, "Nothing can extinguish my interest in
Shakespear" (sic).
```

```
Lincoln specifically advocated a government "for the
people" (emphasis added).
```

A comment or an explanation that goes inside the quotation must appear within square brackets, not parentheses. (If your keyboard does not include square brackets, insert them by hand.)

```
He claimed he could provide "hundreds of examples [of
court decisions] to illustrate the historical tension
between church and state."
```

```
Milton's Satan speaks of his "study [pursuit] of
revenge."
```

Similarly, if a pronoun in a quotation seems unclear, you may add an identification in square brackets.

```
      Why she would hang on him [Hamlet's father]
As if increase of appetite had grown
By what it fed on [. . .].
```

3.9.7   Punctuation with Quotations

Whether set off from the text or run into it, quoted material is usually preceded by a colon if the quotation is formally introduced and by a comma or no punctuation if the quotation is an integral part of the sentence structure.

```
Shelley held a bold view: "Poets are the unacknowledged
legislators of the World" (794).

Shelley thought poets "the unacknowledged legislators
of the World" (794).

"Poets," according to Shelley, "are the unacknowledged
legislators of the World" (794).
```

Do not use opening and closing quotation marks to enclose quotations set off from the text. Use double quotation marks around quotations incorporated into the text, single quotation marks around quotations within those quotations.

```
In "Memories of West Street and Lepke," Robert Lowell,
a conscientious objector (or "C.O."), recounts meeting
a Jehovah's Witness in prison: "'Are you a C.O.?' I
asked a fellow jailbird. / 'No,' he answered, 'I'm a
J.W.'" (38-39).
```

Except for changing internal double quotation marks to single ones when you incorporate quotations into your text, you should reproduce internal punctuation exactly as in the original. The closing punctuation, though, depends on where the quoted material appears in your sentence. Suppose, for example, that you want to quote the following sentence: "You've got to be carefully taught." If you begin your sentence with this line, you have to replace the closing period with a punctuation mark appropriate to the new context.

> "You've got to be carefully taught," wrote Oscar
> Hammerstein II about how racial prejudice is
> perpetuated.

If the quotation ends with a question mark or an exclamation point, however, the original punctuation is retained, and no comma is required.

> "How can I describe my emotions at this catastrophe, or
> how delineate the wretch whom with such infinite pains
> and care I had endeavoured to form?" wonders the doctor
> in Mary Shelley's <u>Frankenstein</u> (42).

> "What a wonderful little almanac you are, Celia!"
> Dorothea Brooke responds to her sister (7).

By convention, commas and periods that directly follow quotations go inside the closing quotation marks, but a parenthetical reference should intervene between the quotation and the required punctuation. Thus, if a quotation ends with a period, the period appears after the reference.

> N. Scott Momaday's <u>House Made of Dawn</u> begins with an
> image that also concludes the novel: "Abel was
> running" (7).

If a quotation ends with both single and double quotation marks, the comma or period precedes both.

> "Read 'Kubla Khan,'" he told me.

All other punctuation marks—such as semicolons, colons, question marks, and exclamation points—go outside a closing quotation mark, except when they are part of the quoted material.

> ORIGINAL
> I believe taxation without representation is tyranny!

> QUOTATIONS
> He attacked "taxation without representation" (32).
> Did he attack "taxation without representation"?
> What dramatic events followed his attack on "taxation
>   without representation"!

but

> He declared, "I believe taxation without representation
> is tyranny!"

If a quotation ending with a question mark or an exclamation point concludes your sentence and requires a parenthetical reference, retain the original punctuation within the quotation mark and follow with the reference and the sentence period outside the quotation mark.

> In Mary Shelley's <u>Frankenstein</u>, the doctor wonders,
> "How can I describe my emotions at this catastrophe, or
> how delineate the wretch whom with such infinite pains
> and care I had endeavoured to form?" (42).

> Dorothea Brooke responds to her sister, "What a
> wonderful little almanac you are, Celia!" (7).

3.9.8 Translations of Quotations

If you believe that a significant portion of your audience will not be familiar with the language of a quotation you present, you should add a translation. If the translation is not yours, give its source in addition to the source of the quotation. In general, the translation should immediately follow the quotation whether they are run into or set off from the text, although their order may be reversed if most readers will not likely be able to read the orginal. If the quotation is run into the text, use double quotation marks around a translation placed in parentheses following the quotation but single quotation marks around a translation that immediately follows without intervening punctuation.

> Chaucer's setting is April, the time of "shoures soote"
> ("sweet showers"; GP 1).
> Chaucer's setting is April, the time of "shoures soote"
> 'sweet showers' (GP 1).

Do not use quotation marks around quotations and translations set off from the text.

> Dante's <u>Inferno</u> begins literally in the middle of
> things:
>
> > Nel mezzo del cammin di nostra vita
> > mi ritrovai per una selva oscura,

```
ché la diritta via era smarrita.
Ahi quanto a dir qual era è cosa dura
esta selva selvaggia e aspra e forte
che nel pensier rinova la paura! (1.1-6)
Midway in our life's journey, I went astray
from the straight road and woke to find
    myself
alone in a dark wood. How shall I say
what wood that was! I never saw so drear,
so rank, so arduous a wilderness!
Its very memory gives a shape to fear.
    (Ciardi 28)
```

See also 3.4.8 for guidelines on translating a foreign word or phrase within a sentence.

3.10 NUMBERS

3.10.1 Arabic Numerals

Although there are still a few well-established uses for roman numerals (see 3.10.7), virtually all numbers not spelled out are commonly represented today by arabic numerals. If your keyboard does not have the number *1*, use a small letter el (*l*), not capital *I*, for the arabic numeral. If your keyboard has the number *1*, do not substitute the small el.

3.10.2 Use of Words or Numerals

In discussions that require few numbers, you may spell out numbers written in a word or two and represent other numbers by numerals (*one, thirty-six, ninety-nine, one hundred, fifteen hundred, two thousand, three million*, but *2½, 101, 137, 1,275*). To form the plural of a spelled-out number, treat the word like an ordinary noun (*sixes, sevens*).

Do not begin a sentence with a numeral, including a date.

```
Nineteen eighty-one began with several good omens.
```

Except at the beginning of a sentence, always use numerals in the following instances:

WITH ABBREVIATIONS OR SYMBOLS

```
6 lbs.          4:20 p.m.          3%
8 KB            $9                 2"
```

IN ADDRESSES

```
4401 13th Avenue
```

IN DATES

```
1 April 1998
April 1, 1998
```

IN DECIMAL FRACTIONS

```
8.3
```

IN PAGE REFERENCES

```
page 7
```

For large numbers, you may use a combination of numerals and words.

```
4.5 million
```

Express related numbers in the same style.

```
only 5 of the 250 delegates
exactly 3 automobiles and 129 trucks
from 1 billion to 1.2 billion
```

3.10.3 Commas in Numbers

Commas are usually placed between the third and fourth digits from the right, the sixth and seventh, and so on.

```
1,000
20,000
7,654,321
```

Following are some of the exceptions to this practice:

PAGE AND LINE NUMBERS

```
On page 1014 [. . .]
```

ADDRESSES

At 4132 Broadway [. . .]

FOUR-DIGIT YEAR NUMBERS

In 1999 [. . .]

But commas are added in year numbers of five or more figures.

In 20,000 BC [. . .]

3.10.4 Percentages and Amounts of Money

Treat percentages and amounts of money like other numbers: use numerals with the appropriate symbols.

1%	$5.35	68¢
45%	$35	
100%	$2,000	

In discussions involving infrequent use of numbers, you may spell out a percentage or an amount of money if you can do so in three words or fewer (*five dollars, forty-five percent, two thousand dollars, sixty-eight cents*). Do not combine spelled forms of numbers with symbols.

3.10.5 Dates and Times of the Day

Be consistent in writing dates: use either the day-month-year style (*22 July 1997*) or the month-day-year style (*July 22, 1997*) but not both. If you begin with the month, be sure to add a comma after the day and also after the year, unless another punctuation mark goes there, such as a period or a question mark.

April 15, 1997, was the fiftieth anniversary of the
racial integration of baseball.

Do not use a comma between month and year (*August 1996*). European usage gives all dates in day-month-year order. In abbreviated dates, the intended order is sometimes ambiguous (e.g., in *7-3-56*). To give a date in two systems, put one set in parentheses.

3 November 1693 (K'ang hsi 32/10/6)

Spell out centuries in lowercase letters.

the twentieth century

Hyphenate centuries when they are used as adjectives before nouns.

```
eighteenth-century thought
nineteenth- and twentieth-century literature
```

Decades are usually written out without capitalization (*the nineties*), but it is acceptable to express them in figures (*the 1990s, the '60s*). Whichever form you use, be consistent.

The abbreviation *BC* follows the year, but *AD* precedes it.

```
19 BC
AD 565
```

Instead of *BC* and *AD*, some writers prefer to use *BCE*, "before the common era," and *CE*, "common era," both of which follow the year.

Numerals are used to indicate most times of the day (*2:00 p.m., the 6:20 flight*). Exceptions include time expressed in quarter and half hours and in hours followed by *o'clock*.

```
a quarter to twelve
half past ten
five o'clock
```

3.10.6 Inclusive Numbers

In a range of numbers, such as page references, give the second number in full for numbers through ninety-nine.

```
2-3          21-48
10-12        89-99
```

For larger numbers, give only the last two digits of the second number, unless more are necessary.

```
96-101       923-1003
103-04       1003-05
395-401      1608-774
```

In a range of years, write both in full unless they are within the same century AD.

```
1898-1901
1898-99
```

3.10.7 Roman Numerals

Use capital roman numerals for the primary divisions of an outline and after the names of individuals in a series.

```
Elizabeth II
John D. Rockefeller IV
John Paul II
```

Use lowercase roman numerals for citing pages of a book that are so numbered (e.g., the pages in a preface). Treat inclusive roman numerals like inclusive arabic numerals (see 3.10.6): *xxv–vi, xlvi–li*. Some scholars, editors, and presses prefer to use roman numerals to designate acts and scenes of plays (see 7.4.8, on citing literary works).

3.11   TRANSLITERATION AND ROMANIZATION

In most general studies, quotations and documentation in languages using alphabets other than the Latin alphabet should be transliterated and the spoken forms of nonalphabetic languages should be romanized. In studies with extensive quotations from Greek, however, the Greek alphabet is usually used.

Listed below are the primary sources for the systems of transliteration or romanization commonly used in general scholarly studies. The most comprehensive single source is *ALA-LC Romanization Tables: Transliteration Schemes for Non-Roman Scripts*, compiled and edited by Randall K. Barry (Washington: Lib. of Congress, 1991), designated in the listing below by *ALA-LC*. Approved by both the Library of Congress and the American Library Association, this work supersedes all previous ALA-LC romanization tables.

Amharic

ALA-LC 2–3.

Arabic

ALA-LC 4–13.
American National Standard System for the Romanization of Arabic. New York: Amer. Natl. Standards Inst., 1972.

Armenian

ALA-LC 14–15.
American National Standard System for the Romanization of Armenian. New York: Amer. Natl. Standards Inst., 1979.

Assamese

ALA-LC 16–17.

Belorussian

ALA-LC 18–19.

American National Standard System for the Romanization of Slavic Cyrillic Characters. New York: Amer. Natl. Standards Inst., 1976.

Shaw, J. Thomas. *The Transliteration of Modern Russian for English-Language Publications.* 1967. New York: MLA, 1979.

Bengali

ALA-LC 20–21.

Bulgarian

ALA-LC 22–23.

American National Standard System for the Romanization of Slavic Cyrillic Characters. New York: Amer. Natl. Standards Inst., 1976.

Shaw, J. Thomas. *The Transliteration of Modern Russian for English-Language Publications.* 1967. New York: MLA, 1979.

Burmese

ALA-LC 24–26.

Chinese

ALA-LC 27–39. Uses the older Wade-Giles system with modifications.

Reform of the Chinese Written Language. Peking: Foreign Langs., 1958. Uses the modern pinyin system.

Church Slavonic

ALA-LC 40–42.

American National Standard System for the Romanization of Slavic Cyrillic Characters. New York: Amer. Natl. Standards Inst., 1976.

Shaw, J. Thomas. *The Transliteration of Modern Russian for English-Language Publications.* 1967. New York: MLA, 1979.

Divehi

ALA-LC 43–45.

Georgian

ALA-LC 46–47.

Greek

ALA-LC 48–49.

Gujarati

ALA-LC 50–51.

Hebrew

ALA-LC 52–53.

American National Standard System for the Romanization of Hebrew. New York: Amer. Natl. Standards Inst., 1975.

Hindi

ALA-LC 54–56.

Japanese

ALA-LC 57–69. Uses the system employed in *Kenkyusha's New Japanese-English Dictionary*.
American National Standard System for the Romanization of Japanese. New York: Amer. Natl. Standards Inst., 1972.
Kenkyusha's New Japanese-English Dictionary. 4th ed. 1974. Tokyo: Kenkyusha, 1991.

Kannada

ALA-LC 70–71.

Kashmiri

ALA-LC 72–75.

Khmer

ALA-LC 76–78.
American National Standard System for the Romanization of Lao, Khmer, and Pali. New York: Amer. Natl. Standards Inst., 1979.

Korean

ALA-LC 79–93. Uses McCune-Reischauer system.

Kurdish

ALA-LC 94–95.

Lao

ALA-LC 96–99.
American National Standard System for the Romanization of Lao, Khmer, and Pali. New York: Amer. Natl. Standards Inst., 1979.

Lepcha

ALA-LC 100–01.

Limbu

ALA-LC 102–03.

Macedonian

ALA-LC 166–67.

Malayalam

ALA-LC 104–05.

Marathi

ALA-LC 106–07.

Mongolian
ALA-LC 108–09.

Moplah
ALA-LC 110–13.

Non-Slavic Languages in Cyrillic Script
ALA-LC 114–31.

Oriya
ALA-LC 132–33.

Ottoman Turkish
ALA-LC 134–39.

Pali
ALA-LC 140–44.
American National Standard System for the Romanization of Lao, Khmer, and Pali.
　　New York: Amer. Natl. Standards Inst., 1979.

Persian
ALA-LC 145–51.

Prakrit
ALA-LC 162–63.

Punjabi
ALA-LC 152–53.

Pushto
ALA-LC 154–59.

Russian
ALA-LC 160–61.
Shaw, J. Thomas. *The Transliteration of Modern Russian for English-Language*
　　Publications. 1967. New York: MLA, 1979.

Sanskrit
ALA-LC 162–63.

Santali
ALA-LC 164–65.

Serbian
ALA-LC 166–67.

Sindhi
ALA-LC 168–69.

Sinhalese

ALA-LC 170–71.

Tamil

ALA-LC 172–73.

Telugu

ALA-LC 174–75.

Thai

ALA-LC 176–91.
American National Standard System for the Romanization of Lao, Khmer, and Pali.
New York: Amer. Natl. Standards Inst., 1979.

Tibetan

ALA-LC 192–93.

Tigrinya

ALA-LC 194–95.

Uighur

ALA-LC 196–99.

Ukrainian

ALA-LC 200–01.
American National Standard System for the Romanization of Slavic Cyrillic Characters. New York: Amer. Natl. Standards Inst., 1976.

Urdu

ALA-LC 202–09.

Yiddish

ALA-LC 52–53.

3.12   FURTHER GUIDANCE

DICTIONARIES OF USAGE

Bernstein, Theodore M. *The Careful Writer: A Modern Guide to English Usage.*
New York: Atheneum, 1965.
Bryant, Margaret M. *Current American Usage: How Americans Say It and Write It.*
New York: Funk, 1962.
Copperud, Roy H. *American Usage and Style: The Consensus.* New York: Van Nostrand, 1980.
Evans, Bergen, and Cornelia Evans. *A Dictionary of Contemporary American Usage.* New York: Random, 1957.

Follett, Wilson. *Modern American Usage: A Guide*. Ed. Jacques Barzun. New York: Hill, 1966.

Fowler, H[enry] W. *A Dictionary of Modern English Usage*. Oxford: Clarendon, 1926.

———. *A Dictionary of Modern English Usage*. Ed. Ernest Gowers. 2nd ed. New York: Oxford UP, 1965.

———. *The New Fowler's Modern English Usage*. Ed. R. W. Burchfield. 3rd ed. Oxford: Oxford UP, 1996.

Mager, Nathan H., and Sylvia K. Mager. *Prentice Hall Encyclopedic Dictionary of English Usage*. 2nd ed. Englewood Cliffs: Prentice, 1992.

Morris, William, and Mary Morris. *Harper Dictionary of Contemporary Usage*. 2nd ed. New York: Harper, 1985.

Nicholson, Margaret. *A Dictionary of American-English Usage Based on Fowler's Modern English Usage*. New York: Oxford UP, 1957.

Weiner, Edmund S., and Joyce M. Hawkins. *The Oxford Guide to the English Language*. New York: Oxford UP, 1984.

GUIDES TO NONSEXIST LANGUAGE

American Psychological Association. "Guidelines to Reduce Bias in Language." *Publication Manual of the American Psychological Association*. 4th ed. Washington: Amer. Psychological Assn., 1994. 46–60.

Frank, Francine Wattman, and Paula A. Treichler, with others. *Language, Gender, and Professional Writing: Theoretical Approaches and Guidelines for Nonsexist Usage*. New York: MLA, 1989.

International Association of Business Communication. *Without Bias: A Guidebook for Nondiscriminatory Communication*. Ed. J. E. Pickens, P. W. Rao, and L. C. Roberts. 2nd ed. New York: Wiley, 1982.

Maggio, Rosalie. *The Dictionary of Bias-Free Usage: A Guide to Nondiscriminatory Language*. Phoenix: Oryx, 1991.

———. *The Nonsexist Word Finder: A Dictionary of Gender-Free Usage*. 1987. Boston: Beacon, 1989.

Miller, Casey, and Kate Swift. *The Handbook of Nonsexist Writing*. 2nd ed. New York: Harper, 1988.

Schwartz, Marilyn, and the Task Force of the Association of American University Presses. *Guidelines for Bias-Free Writing*. Bloomington: Indiana UP, 1995.

Sorrells, Bobbye D. *The Nonsexist Communicator: Solving the Problem of Gender and Awkwardness in Modern English*. Englewood Cliffs: Prentice, 1983.

Warren, Virginia L. "Guidelines for the Nonsexist Use of Language." *American Philosophical Association Proceedings* 59 (1986): 471–84.

BOOKS ON STYLE

Barzun, Jacques. *Simple and Direct: A Rhetoric for Writers*. Rev. ed. New York: Harper, 1984.

Beardsley, Monroe C. *Thinking Straight: Principles of Reasoning for Readers and Writers*. 4th ed. Englewood Cliffs: Prentice, 1975.

Cook, Claire Kehrwald. *Line by Line: How to Edit Your Own Writing*. Boston: Houghton, 1985.

Eastman, Richard M. *Style: Writing and Reading as the Discovery of Outlook*. 3rd ed. New York: Oxford UP, 1984.

Elbow, Peter. *Writing without Teachers*. New York: Oxford UP, 1973.

———. *Writing with Power: Techniques for Mastering the Writing Process*. New York: Oxford UP, 1981.

Gibson, Walker. *Tough, Sweet, and Stuffy: An Essay on Modern American Prose Styles*. Bloomington: Indiana UP, 1966.

Gowers, Ernest. *The Complete Plain Words*. Ed. Sidney Greenbaum and Janet Whitcut. Rev. ed. Boston: Godine, 1990.

Lanham, Richard A. *Style: An Anti-textbook*. New Haven: Yale UP, 1974.

Smith, Charles K. *Styles and Structures: Alternative Approaches to College Writing*. New York: Norton, 1974.

Strunk, William, Jr., and E. B. White. *The Elements of Style*. 3rd ed. New York: Macmillan, 1979.

Williams, Joseph M. *Style: Ten Lessons in Clarity and Grace*. 4th ed. New York: Harper, 1994.

———. *Style: Toward Clarity and Grace*. Chicago: U of Chicago P, 1990.

4

PREPARATION OF
SCHOLARLY MANUSCRIPTS

4.1 Divisions of the Text
    4.1.1 Articles and Essays
    4.1.2 Books
    4.1.3 Consistency of Headings

4.2 Physical Characteristics of the Printed Manuscript
    4.2.1 Printing
    4.2.2 Paper
    4.2.3 Margins
    4.2.4 Spacing
    4.2.5 Title and Author's Name
    4.2.6 Page Numbers
    4.2.7 Tables and Illustrations
    4.2.8 Corrections and Revisions
    4.2.9 Binding

4.3 Manuscripts for Print Publication

4.4 Manuscripts for Electronic Publication

4.5 Further Guidance on Tagging Electronic Documents

In preparing your final manuscript for publication, follow any formatting requirements your editor or publisher supplies. The recommendations in this chapter are common. (See chapter 5 for preparing theses and dissertations.)

4.1   DIVISIONS OF THE TEXT

4.1.1 Articles and Essays

Scholarly articles and essays in the humanities often have no formal divisions. Sometimes an author inserts extra space (a blank line) at one point or more to divide the text into groups of related paragraphs. When such a break falls at the bottom or top of a page in your final printed manuscript, write "[extra space]" by hand in the blank line.

If an article or essay is made up of unified sections of thought, they may be labeled with numbers, headings, or both. When creating such designations, always use arabic numerals, and do not add extra spacing above or below the line containing the number or heading. A number alone is usually centered, but type a heading or combined number and heading flush left. Separate a heading from a preceding number by a period and a space.

> 2. From 1900 to 1940

See also 4.1.3, on the consistency of headings.

4.1.2   Books

The major divisions of a book usually appear in the order listed below. Each division should begin on a new page. Although only the words not given in brackets serve as formal titles, you can aid your editor by typing the others, in square brackets as shown, flush left and one inch from the tops of the first pages of the appropriate divisions.

[title page]

[copyright page]

[dedication] (optional)

[epigraph] (optional)

Contents (the table of contents)

Illustrations (a list of the illustrations, if applicable)

Tables (a list of the tables, if applicable)

Foreword (optional)

Preface (optional)

Acknowledgments (optional)

Introduction (optional)

[text]

Appendix (optional)

Notes (optional)

Glossary (optional)

Contributors (notes on the contributors, if applicable)

127

Works Cited (the list of the works cited)

Index (optional)

Chapters are the most common divisions within the text of a book. Sometimes chapters are subdivided into unified sections of thought (see 4.1.1). Some books are also divided into "parts," each of which contains a number of related chapters. Chapters should be numbered consecutively throughout the text, whether or not they are grouped into parts, and are normally given titles. Parts should also be numbered consecutively and may be given titles.

4.1.3   Consistency of Headings

Titles of parts, of chapters, and of sections within a chapter or essay are generally referred to as headings or heads. Insofar as possible, make parallel heads grammatically similar (e.g., avoid shifting from sentences to single words for parallel heads within a chapter). If you adopt number and letter designations for heads, be consistent, and do not use a "1" unless there is a "2" or use an "a" unless there is a "b."

If your manuscript has a complex organization with many levels of heads, you might assist your editor by not only carefully working out the organizational system and clearly distinguishing the levels of heads in the manuscript but also supplying a list of all heads in outline form to establish their coordination and subordination.

4.2   PHYSICAL CHARACTERISTICS OF THE PRINTED MANUSCRIPT

4.2.1   Printing

Use a high-quality printer. Always choose a standard, easily readable typeface. Do not justify the lines of the manuscript at the right margin; turn off your word processor's automatic hyphenation feature. Print on only one side of the paper. Be sure to keep a hard copy of the manuscript, as well as electronic copies on at least two disks.

4.2.2   Paper

Use only white, 8½-by-11-inch paper of good quality. If you cannot obtain 8½-by-11-inch paper, use the closest size available. In any case, do not print the text of the manuscript in an area larger than 6½ by 9 inches. (For margins, see 4.2.3.)

4.2.3   Margins

Except for running heads (containing, e.g., your last name and the page number), leave margins of one inch at the top and bottom and on both sides of the text. (For running heads, see 4.2.6.) Indent the first word of a paragraph one-half inch (or five spaces) from the left margin. Indent set-off quotations one inch (or ten spaces) from the left margin.

4.2.4   Spacing

Set your word processor to double-space the entire manuscript, including title, table of contents, quotations, notes, and list of works cited. Do not single-space any part of a manuscript intended for editing or typesetting.

4.2.5   Title and Author's Name

If you are preparing a manuscript for a particular journal or publisher, follow any given instructions or, in the absence of instructions, the relevant recommendations below. If you plan to submit a manuscript seriatim to journals and publishers until it is accepted, prepare it in accordance with the instructions for anonymous submission.

A manuscript for a journal with a policy of anonymous submission should include a separate, unnumbered page giving the title and your full name, postal and e-mail addresses, and telephone and fax numbers. Repeat the title, without author's name, on the first page of the manuscript proper, centered and one inch from the top of the page (see fig. 4). Ensure that your word processor double-spaces between the lines of the title and between the title and the first line of the text. There is no need to add other space between the lines.

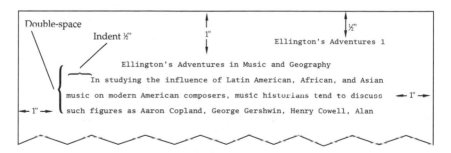

Fig. 4. The top of the first numbered page of a manuscript submitted anonymously.

A separate title page is not needed for an article manuscript submitted to a journal that does not require anonymity or for a chapter or an essay in a collection by more than one author. Instead, beginning one inch from the top of the first page and flush with the left margin, type on separate lines your name, postal and e-mail addresses, and telephone and fax numbers. Then, on separate lines, center the title and your name, as you wish them to appear in the publication. The beginning of the text follows your name on a new line (see fig. 5). Your word processor should double-space all these lines. Do not add any extra space between them.

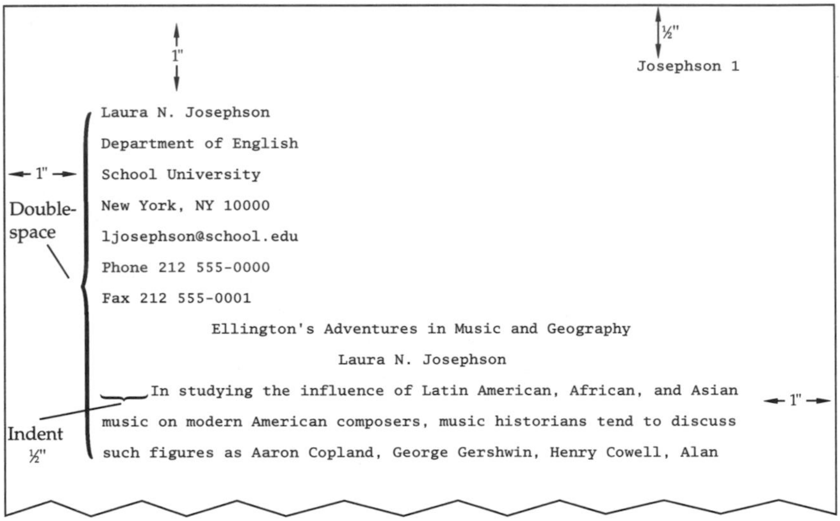

Fig. 5. *The top of the first page of a manuscript not submitted anonymously.*

A manuscript for a book should have a separate title page with the same information given to a journal requiring anonymous submission —title, name, postal and e-mail addresses, telephone and fax numbers. Individual chapters should not have separate title pages, but each should begin on a new page. Starting one inch from the top of the page, type flush left the word *Chapter* followed by the chapter number and, on the next line, the title of the chapter. The text starts on the following line. Your word processor should double-space these lines; do not add extra space.

Do not underline the title of your manuscript, put it in quotation marks, type it in all capital letters, or print it in any special font. Follow the rules for capitalization in 3.7, and underline only the words that you would underline in the text (see 3.5 and 3.8.2).

Violence in Burgess's <u>A Clockwork Orange</u>

The Words <u>Fair</u> and <u>Foul</u> in <u>Macbeth</u>

Romanticism in England and the <u>Scapigliatura</u> in Italy

Do not use a period after the title or after any heading, including numerals used alone as section heads (see 4.1.1). A title ordinarily does not carry a symbol or number referring to a note; if the work was previously published, the editor may add a note to the title that cites the source.

4.2.6   Page Numbers

Number all pages consecutively throughout the manuscript. In the upper right-hand corner, one-half inch from the top and flush with the right margin, create a running head that consists of your last name followed by a space and the page number (see fig. 6) or, for a publication with an anonymous-submission policy, a shortened title of the work followed by a space and the page number. Do not use the abbreviation *p.* before a page number or add a period, a hyphen, or any other mark or symbol. Position the first line of the text one inch from the top of the page.

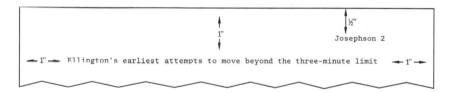

Fig. 6.   The running head of a manuscript not submitted anonymously.

Although in writing the chapters of a book or separate essays for a collection, you may paginate each chapter or essay separately, the final version of the manuscript submitted for production should be numbered consecutively from beginning to end. In a work with several authors, the name preceding each page number should be that of the author who is to receive the copyedited manuscript or proof of that page.

4.2.7   Tables and Illustrations

Place tables and illustrations as close as possible to the parts of the text to which they relate. A table is usually labeled *Table*, given an arabic numeral, and captioned. Type both label and caption flush left on sep-

131

arate lines above the table, and capitalize them as you would a title (do not use all capital letters). Give the source of the table and any notes immediately below the table. To avoid confusion between notes to the text and notes to the table, designate notes to the table with superscript lowercase letters rather than with numerals. Make dividing lines as needed, and ensure that your word processor double-spaces all lines (see fig. 7).

Any other type of illustrative visual material—for example, a pho-

Table 1

Earned Degrees in Modern Foreign Languages Conferred by
Institutions of Higher Education in the United States[a]

Year	Bachelor's Degrees	Master's Degrees	Doctor's Degrees
1984-85	9,675	1,611	387
1985-86	9,808	1,655	426
1986-87	9,858	1,692	403
1987-88	9,790	1,795	380
1988-89	10,498	1,821	389
1989-90	11,092	1,931	475
1990-91	11,724	1,973	477
1991-92	12,367	2,119	537
1992-93	12,819	2,353	535
1993-94	12,785	2,343	578

Source: United States, Dept. of Educ., Office of Educ.
  Research and Improvement, Natl. Center for Educ.
  Statistics, Digest of Education Statistics, 1996
  (Washington: GPO, 1996) table 282.

  [a] These figures include degrees conferred in a
single modern foreign language or a combination of
modern foreign languages and exclude degrees in
linguistics, Latin, classical Greek, and some not
commonly taught modern languages.

Fig. 7. A table in a manuscript.

tograph, map, line drawing, graph, or chart—should be labeled *Figure* (usually abbreviated *Fig.*), assigned an arabic numeral, and given a title or caption: "Fig. 1. Mary Cassatt, *Mother and Child*, Wichita Museum, Wichita." A label and title or caption ordinarily appear directly below the illustration and have the same one-inch margins as the text of the manuscript (see fig. 8).

Fig. 1. Manticore, woodcut from Edward Topsell, <u>The History of Four-Footed Beasts and Serpents</u> [. . .] (London, 1658) 344; rpt. in Konrad Gesner, <u>Curious Woodcuts of Fanciful and Real Beasts</u> (New York: Dover, 1971) 8.

Fig. 8. A figure in a manuscript.

Musical illustrations are labeled *Example* (usually abbreviated *Ex.*), assigned an arabic numeral, and given a title or caption: "Ex. 1. Pyotr Ilich Tchaikovsky, Symphony no. 6 in B, op. 74 (*Pathétique*), finale." A label and title or caption ordinarily appear directly below the example and have the same one-inch margins as the text of the manuscript (see fig. 9).

4.2.8 Corrections and Revisions

Proofread and correct your manuscript carefully before submitting it to a publisher. Software spelling and usage checkers can be helpful, but they should be used with caution. On the one hand, a spelling

Ex. 1. Ludwig van Beethoven, Symphony no. 3 in E flat, op. 55 (Eroica), first movement, opening.

Fig. 9. A musical example in a manuscript.

checker will call attention to words that are correctly spelled if they are not in its dictionary. On the other, it will not point out misspellings that match words in the dictionary (e.g., *their* used for *there*). Recommendations by usage checkers have to be evaluated critically. If you find a mistake in the final copy or decide to make a last-minute revision, reopen the file, make the change, and reprint the corrected page or pages. Be sure to save the changed file.

If you are working with a copyeditor or if a journal editor or publisher has accepted your manuscript but requests revisions before copyediting, it may be convenient to make changes by hand on the printed manuscript until there is complete agreement on the revisions. In such works, make all changes clear, legible, and unambiguous. Insert corrections and revisions directly above the lines involved, using carets (ᴧ) to indicate where they go; do not write a change below the line it affects. If the revised version will not fit on the page, continue it on a separate page identified with the same page number followed by the letter *A* (e.g., "32A," to follow page 32). Indicate at the bottom of the original page that a specially numbered page follows (e.g., write, "Page 32A follows"). You may also write an insertion entirely on a separate page (labeled, e.g., "Insert to page 32") and clearly mark the manuscript to show where the addition goes. When all revisions are accepted, follow the directions of your editor, who may ask you to enter the changes in the file and produce a new printout of the complete corrected version or a copy of the new version on a floppy disk or both.

4.2.9   Binding

Secure manuscripts of articles and essays by paper clips—never by staples. Use a rubber band around a book-length manuscript, and do not secure individual chapters in any way.

4.3   MANUSCRIPTS FOR PRINT PUBLICATION

Most scholarly journals and books are produced directly from computer disks supplied by their authors. Although editors, consultant readers, and editorial boards usually evaluate a manuscript in printed form, once the manuscript is accepted for publication, the editor commonly asks for the final version of the manuscript in electronic form.

After receiving the manuscript on disk, the compositor or production editor usually converts the disk's files to the publisher's system, corrects any technical problems in the files, and inserts appropriate formatting codes. Some journals and presses copyedit the manuscript electronically, and some copyedit a hard copy and transfer changes to the disk.

The compositor subsequently incorporates the designer's specifications for typefaces, type sizes, margins, and so forth, into the coded files and uses typesetting equipment to transform the files into sets of proofs that the author reads and corrects. From the corrected proofs, the compositor prepares a final version from which the printer produces the published book or journal.

Ask your publisher for guidelines on preparing the manuscript on disk. If you do not have a publisher, follow the general principles below, which are derived from guidelines developed by the Association of American University Presses.

Prepare your entire manuscript on the same type of computer and with the same word-processing program throughout, and inform your editor of both the hardware and the software used. Do not add any formatting that is not essential to the manuscript. For example, do not engage your word processor's hyphenation feature or justify right margins, and use only one font. Underline material that would be italicized in a publication (see 3.5). Delete any running head you create for the printed manuscript.

Type only the spaces and hyphens that are to appear in print—for example, the spaces between words and the hyphens in certain compound words. Use one space after a period or colon; two hyphens constitute a dash. To indent paragraphs, use the tab key, not the space bar or your word processor's automatic indent feature; specify a left-margin indention for quotations set off from the text.

Each key must have only one meaning: the letter *l* cannot serve as the numeral one; the letter *O* cannot be used as a zero; any special characters must have a single purpose. For titles and headings within the manuscript, use the standard combination of capital and lowercase letters—not all capital letters.

You should ordinarily use a single file for an article or essay, but create a new file for each chapter or other major division of a book and for each computer-generated table and illustration. Create a single file for all endnotes. Use the tab key to indent the first line of each note. In a single file of notes for a book, carefully indicate the chapters to which the notes belong, and begin each chapter with note 1 unless the book has few notes. Do not use footnotes.

Name related files sequentially (*ch1, ch2; appA, appB*), and transmit them on as few disks as possible. The disk labels should indicate the author's name, the title of the manuscript, the name and release number of your word-processing software, your computer's operating system (e.g., Windows, Mac, Unix), and the date you completed work on the disk. The editor of a collection with more than one author must submit all contributions in the format of one software program, adding authors' last names to the file names. Supply your editor with a list of the file names when you submit the disk version of the manuscript. If your manuscript has accents or special characters not available on your computer, give your editor a list of them, pointing out how you indicated them on the hard copy and on disk.

Finally, the hard copy and the disk version you send to your editor must be identical. Inform your publisher of any subsequent revisions you wish to make, and the publisher will make the necessary changes on the disk.

4.4   MANUSCRIPTS FOR ELECTRONIC PUBLICATION

If you are writing for a specific electronic publisher or publication (e.g., an electronic journal), obtain the required guidelines for formatting, submission, and so forth, and follow them closely. It is important to state within the document, not only on your disk label, the name of the author or editor, the title of the work, the document's version number, the date of the version, and information concerning copyright and permission.

To facilitate documentation in scholarly research, your text should incorporate a system of reference markers, so that other scholars can cite a specific portion of your work and direct their readers to it. Numbering paragraphs is becoming common in electronic publications.

Authors usually place the appropriate number, in brackets—"[12]"—at the beginning of each paragraph. Another practice is to incorporate into the text the page numbers of a print version of the manuscript; typically, where pages end in the print version, the numbers of the concluding and beginning pages are inserted in the text, enclosed in brackets and separated by a slash: "[7/8]."

If you are going to publish electronically, you will doubtless become familiar with document tagging. To create an electronic text that can be universally read, authors need to avoid software-specific formatting. For this purpose, electronic texts are commonly written in characters from a standard subset of the American Standard Code for Information Interchange (ASCII). Files limited to these basic characters are often called *ASCII-text files* or just *text files*. The author or an editor adds to an ASCII text groups of characters that serve as codes or tags marking such aspects of the document as format, content, and foreign or special characters. Marking a textual element commonly entails giving it a beginning tag and a concluding tag expressed in a consistent, unambiguous, easily recognizable pattern, such as "<author>" to mark the beginning of an author's name and "</author>" to mark the end.

```
<author>Mary Shelley</author>
```

Format tags determine the appearance of a text in print or electronic form or describe the preexisting structure of a document. These tags define such elements as subheads, main text, set-off quotations, and lists. Format tags for print publication vary with the software for which they are intended, whether publishing programs for Microsoft Windows or Macintosh systems (e.g., *QuarkXPress*) or proprietary typesetting system software (e.g., Penta). Following is a pair of tags that might be used with *QuarkXPress* to mark an extract, or a quotation set off from the text:

```
@Extract:It isn't over until it's over.
@Bodytext: [. . .]
```

Format tags for a document on the World Wide Web are usually in Hypertext Markup Language (HTML) and can include linking tags that connect files at the same location or across the network. Following are sample HTML tags:

A SET-OFF QUOTATION

```
<BLOCKQUOTE>It isn't over until it's
over.</BLOCKQUOTE>
```

BOLD-STYLE TEXT

`<B>Related Theoretical Issues</B>`

LINK TO ANOTHER FILE AT THE SAME WEB SITE

`<A HREF="nextpage.htm">Go to the next page.</A>`

LINK TO THE HOME PAGE AT ANOTHER WEB SITE

`<A HREF="http://www.utoronto.ca/">University of Toronto Web page</A>`

Content, or logic, tags are concerned primarily with the substance of the text, not with its design. Thus different content tags can mark elements that have the same formatting; for example, the name of a person and the name of a place could receive different content tags although they are both formatted the same in the text. Moreover, the same content tag can define elements with different formatting; a quotation, for instance, may receive the same content tag whether it is integrated into the text or set off from it.

Content tags enhance the ways in which a document can be searched or analyzed by computer. For example, if quoted material throughout the text is tagged differently from the rest of the text, you can search for keywords—or count words or identify collocations of words—only in the quoted material or only in the rest of the text. Similarly, if a play is tagged by speaker, you can search, say, for the number of times a certain speaker uses a certain phrase.

Standard Generalized Markup Language (SGML) is an established system for encoding electronic texts with a set of tags that denote information of potential use to a reader. Developed in 1986, SGML is a standard of the International Organization for Standardization (ISO). HTML is an application of SGML designed for formatting documents and creating hypertextual links on the World Wide Web, but the functions of HTML are often too limited for scholarly textual analysis. The Text Encoding Initiative (TEI) has developed an application of SGML especially for humanities texts and scholarship. The TEI is an international research project sponsored by the Association for Computing in the Humanities, the Association for Computational Linguistics, and the Association for Literary and Linguistic Computing. TEI tags describe the overall structure of a document as well as its internal elements. They are most suitable for texts with strict hierarchical formats.

Following are examples of TEI tags:

STRUCTURAL TAGS

```
<TEI.2>
    <teiHeader>[TEI Header information]</teiHeader>
    <text>
        <front>[front matter . . .]</front>
        <body>[body of text . . .]</body>
        <back>[back matter . . .]</back>
    </text>
</TEI.2>
```

ELEMENT TAGS

Name

```
<name type=place>London</name>
```

Language

```
<foreign lang=deu>Gesamtkunstwerk</foreign>
```

Quotation

```
<q>It isn't over until it's over.</q>
```

Links or Cross-References

```
<ref target=chap2>See chapter 2.</ref>
```

Accented Characters

```
&agrave; la mode
```

TEI-SGML tagging is increasingly accepted in humanities electronic texts. Yet it is a rigorous and complex procedure, even with the aid of tagging software. Once a document has been correctly tagged, however, users can sort, search, and analyze the text in a variety of ways.

Other tagging systems are COCOA and the scheme developed for the text-analysis program *WordCruncher*, but you do not have to use a preexisting markup system to tag a text; you can make up your own system. If your text is intended for public use, however, the markup should be readily accessible to users and should be accompanied by a complete list of the tags and their meanings.

4.5   FURTHER GUIDANCE ON TAGGING ELECTRONIC DOCUMENTS

SGML

ArborText, Inc. *Getting Started with SGML: A Guide to the Standard Generalized Markup Language and Its Role in Information Management.* 1995. 3 Nov. 1997 <http://commerce4.best.com/~sgml/getstart.htm>.

Goldfarb, Charles F. *The SGML Handbook.* Oxford: Clarendon, 1990.

SGML Open. *The SGML Open Library.* 3 Nov. 1997 <http://commerce4.best .com/~sgml/library.htm>.

———. *SGML Open Web Site.* 3 Nov. 1997 <http://www.sgmlopen.org/>.

TEXT ENCODING INITIATIVE

Burnard, Lou. *Text Encoding for Information Interchange: An Introduction to the Text Encoding Initiative.* TEI J31. July 1995. 3 Nov. 1997 <http://www .uic.edu/orgs/tei/info/teij31/>.

Ide, Nancy, and Jean Véronis, eds. *The Text Encoding Initiative: Background and Context.* Dordrecht: Kluwer, 1995.

Plotkin, Wendy, and C. M. Sperberg-McQueen. *Text Encoding Initiative Home Page.* 27 Oct. 1997. 3 Nov. 1997 <http://www.uic.edu/orgs/tei/>.

Sperberg-McQueen, C. M., and Lou Burnard, eds. *Guidelines for Electronic Text Encoding and Interchange.* TEI P3. Chicago: Assn. for Computing in the Humanities; Assn. for Computational Linguistics; Assn. for Literary and Linguistic Computing, 1994. CD-ROM. Providence: Electronic Book Technologies, 1994.

HTML

Learning HTML. Oct. 1997. 3 Nov. 1997 <http://www.hypernews.org/ HyperNews/get/www/ html/learning.html>.

Musciano, Chuck, and Bill Kennedy. *HTML: The Definitive Guide.* 2nd ed. Sebastopol: O'Reilly, 1997.

National Center for Supercomputing Applications. *A Beginner's Guide to HTML.* Apr. 1996. 3 Nov. 1997 <http://www.ncsa.uiuc.edu/General/ Internet/WWW/ HTMLPrimer.html>.

OTHER TYPES OF ENCODING

Lancashire, Ian, et al. *Using* TACT *with Electronic Texts: A Guide to* Text-Analysis Computing Tools. New York: MLA, 1996.

5

PREPARATION OF THESES
AND DISSERTATIONS

5.1   Student Publications as Professional Publications

5.2   Prescribed Guidelines

5.3   Selecting a Topic

5.4   Preparing a Prospectus

5.5   Special Format Requirements
      5.5.1   Theses and Dissertations as Published Works
      5.5.2   Divisions of the Text
      5.5.3   Page Numbers
      5.5.4   Margins
      5.5.5   Spacing
      5.5.6   Binding

5.6   Publishing the Dissertation through University Microfilms
      International
      5.6.1   Terms of Agreement
      5.6.2   Abstract
      5.6.3   Copyright
      5.6.4   Permissions

5.7   Electronic Publication

5.1	STUDENT PUBLICATIONS AS PROFESSIONAL PUBLICATIONS

Student publications—such as class presentations, research and interpretive papers, the master's thesis, the doctoral dissertation—typically form a continuum with a scholar's postdoctoral publications, just as teaching, conference lectures, and published articles and books compose another related sequence within an academic's professional career (see 1.1). Most student work shares with later scholarly work

141

the same general concerns: conceptualization, investigation, organization, and presentation. The experience of writing a thesis or dissertation especially embraces many activities, practices, and conventions common to subsequent professional publishing. This chapter discusses similarities as well as differences between preparing manuscripts for books and articles (see ch. 4) and preparing theses and dissertations.

5.2   **PRESCRIBED GUIDELINES**

While sometimes requesting adherence to special requirements, a scholarly journal or book publisher usually permits authors to prepare their manuscripts according to style authorities that are standard in their fields. Authors of theses and dissertations, however, must often follow specific guidelines prescribed by their departments, schools, or universities. Before you begin work on a thesis or dissertation, therefore, it is essential to inquire about and obtain any such set of guidelines, which may take the form of a simple photocopied handout or an elaborately designed handbook.

In addition to supplying information like degree requirements, deadlines, administrative procedures, fees, and number of thesis or dissertation copies to submit, such guidelines usually also prescribe formal aspects of the work— for example, documentation style, format, and mechanics. The following sections describe common, but by no means universal, practices in the preparing of theses and dissertations. Consult the earlier chapters for information applicable to all scholarly writing. But should you find conflicting recommendations, follow those issued at your school.

5.3   **SELECTING A TOPIC**

Innovative in subject matter or method, your thesis or dissertation should make a substantial contribution to scholarship and learning. The courses you have taken will doubtless suggest potential topics. Further reading in areas of interest and preliminary discussions with instructors will probably prove invaluable as you make your selection. While the topic should be broad enough to produce significant conclusions, it should also be narrow enough that you can complete the thesis or dissertation within a reasonable period of time. Just as you will, of course, seek an adviser with whom you are compatible, try to choose a topic you think will engage you for the considerable time it will take to complete the work.

Before presenting the topic for formal approval, verify its originality by identifying previous studies in the area. Consult all relevant print and electronic sources for this information, including library catalogs, bibliographies in the field, *Dissertation Abstracts* (1952–69), *Dissertation Abstracts International*, and the *Comprehensive Dissertation Index*. This search will help you not only to modify and redefine the topic but also to compile the basic bibliography for the project. Your thesis or dissertation adviser and other professors can assist you in defining objectives, setting the limits of research, testing the soundness of arguments and conclusions, and improving the bibliography.

5.4   PREPARING A PROSPECTUS

The preparation of a prospectus is an important stage between the selection and approval of a topic and the writing of the thesis or dissertation (cf. 1.5.4, on book prospectuses). Consult the school guidelines for directions concerning length, content, and format of the prospectus. Expected length varies widely, but most guidelines ask that the prospectus address the following aspects of the project: its main focus and the basic questions addressed; its significance, contribution, and place within the larger scholarly context; and its methodological foundation. The prospectus also typically contains an annotated projected table of contents and may offer a preliminary bibliography of primary and secondary sources. The prospectus must receive the approval of all members of the thesis or dissertation committee—and sometimes other department members and university officials as well.

5.5   SPECIAL FORMAT REQUIREMENTS

5.5.1   Theses and Dissertations as Published Works

Modern scholarship considers theses and dissertations forms of publications. Nearly all doctoral dissertations are in fact recorded microphotographically by University Microfilms International (see 5.6) and are readily accessible to other scholars. Graduate school guidelines therefore generally require that the pages of these works be more similar to the pages of a printed book than to those of a manuscript.

Consequently, authors of theses and dissertations are responsible for many formatting procedures that a professional publishing staff usually performs during the copyediting, design, typesetting, and production of a printed book. Guidelines often prescribe, for example, the quality of paper, kind of printer, and type style and size and require that the work be free of typing errors and handwritten corrections. The sections that follow discuss a number of other special format requirements for theses and dissertations.

5.5.2   Divisions of the Text

The major divisions of the thesis or dissertation are similar to those of a book (see 4.1.2), with a few important differences. Both types of works contain a title page, but the title page of a thesis or dissertation includes not only the title and the author's name but also such information as the names of the faculty adviser and committee members, a statement indicating that the work has been submitted in partial fulfillment of degree requirements, and the date (e.g., the month and year the work is submitted or the degree is conferred).

Some guidelines require the inclusion of components that have no parallel in book manuscripts, such as an approval page, an abstract page, and a page offering a short biography of the candidate. The approval (or signature) page contains the names and signatures of all members of the thesis or dissertation committee accepting the work; this page usually follows and is sometimes combined with the title page. The abstract, occasionally preceded by an abstract title page, reproduces the summary submitted for publication in *Dissertation Abstracts International* (see 5.6.2). The desired placement of the abstract and the biography varies according to individual guidelines; these pages typically appear among either the front matter (e.g., before the table of contents) or the back matter (e.g., after the bibliography or works-cited list).

Graduate school guidelines sometimes prescribe the insertion of blank sheets between certain divisions, in emulation of a printed book. Theses and dissertations, however, usually do not include indexes.

5.5.3   Page Numbers

Your guidelines will probably require you to number pages according to the system common in published books. Lowercase roman numerals appear on most of the pages containing the front matter or preliminary parts of the work: dedication (optional), epigraph (optional), table of contents, lists of illustrations and tables (if applicable), preface, and acknowledgments (often combined with the preface). Arabic numerals are used to paginate the rest of the work, including the text and the bibliography as well as any endnotes, appendix, glossary, and index.

Page numbers do not usually appear on the title page and copyright page and sometimes do not appear on the first pages of chapters, the endnotes section, the bibliography, and other major divisions, although all are considered in the page count of the work. Numbers normally appear on all other pages, with the occasional exception of the approval page, abstract page, and biography page, which are sometimes neither numbered nor counted in the pagination.

The required position of the page numbers varies. Guidelines commonly prescribe that they appear centered at the bottom or the top or in the upper right-hand corner of the page.

5.5.4   Margins

Nearly all guidelines ask for a margin of at least one and a half inches from the left side of each page to allow for binding (see 5.5.6). The other margins—at the top, bottom, and right side of the page—are normally one inch or slightly more (e.g., one and a quarter inches) to ensure successful photographing of the work (see 5.6). Page numbers must also fall within these marginal limits. The numbers are separated from the text by approximately one-half inch or three lines.

5.5.5   Spacing

Your guidelines will ask you to double-space the text of the thesis or dissertation but may request the use of single-spacing within one or more of the following types of material: a quotation set off from the text, an entry in the bibliography or list of works cited, an endnote or a footnote, a caption for a table or an illustration, and an item in the table of contents or in a list of tables or illustrations. Always skip a line, however, after each set-off quotation, bibliographic entry, note, caption, and listed item.

5.5.6   Binding

Whereas authors normally use no more than paper clips and rubber bands to secure manuscripts submitted to journals and book publishers, graduate school guidelines require more-formal binding of theses and dissertations. Yet requirements differ considerably, from a simple black spring binder purchased at a bookstore to a professional library binding. Universities that, for a fee, have the work bound for the candidate usually ask that each copy be submitted only in a box or other protective container.

5.6   PUBLISHING THE DISSERTATION THROUGH UNIVERSITY MICROFILMS INTERNATIONAL

5.6.1   Terms of Agreement

Most graduate schools require doctoral candidates to publish their dissertations through University Microfilms International (UMI). The author signs a publishing agreement with UMI, which in turn lists the work in the computerized index *Dissertation Database* and in the printed reference works *Comprehensive Dissertation Index* and *American Doctoral Dissertations*, publishes an abstract of it (see 5.6.2), and photographs and stores it for publication on demand. UMI currently makes dissertations available for purchase in microform and paper versions. The agreement with UMI does not preclude your subsequently publishing the dissertation with a press.

5.6.2   Abstract

UMI requires the candidate to submit with the agreement an abstract, or summary, of the dissertation. The abstract, which must be no longer than 350 words, is published in *Dissertation Abstracts International* (*DAI*), in print, CD-ROM, and online formats. The abstract generally describes the problem studied, the materials and methods used, and the conclusions reached.

5.6.3   Copyright

Most graduate school guidelines normally make it optional whether the copyright in theses and dissertations is registered with the Copyright Office at the Library of Congress (see 2.1.8) but strongly recommend registration for the dissertation. For a fee, UMI will have the dissertation copyright registered for you, or you may submit the application on your own. MA candidates are generally responsible for registering their copyrights themselves. Whether or not your copyright is registered, place a copyright notice on the copyright page (see 2.1.9).

5.6.4   Permissions

Since theses and dissertations are considered published works, their authors must be scrupulous about seeking necessary permission to reproduce material taken from others. The agreement with UMI requires authors to certify that permission has been obtained in writing from copyright holders when unpublished material is borrowed or when fair use has been exceeded (see 2.1.13–14). Permission letters must be attached to the UMI agreement form.

For each permission you obtain, you must insert a statement at an appropriate place in the thesis or dissertation. The typical statement consists of a full bibliographic reference (i.e., author, title, city of publication, publisher, year of publication), followed by a standard credit line (e.g., "Reprinted by permission of [. . .]") or wording stipulated by the copyright holder in the permission letter. Permission statements may appear individually in the text where the reprinted materials occur, or, especially if numerous, they may be given collectively in the acknowledgments section or on the copyright page.

5.7   ELECTRONIC PUBLICATION

As of this writing, relatively few theses and dissertations in the humanities have been or are being prepared specifically for electronic publication. Yet it seems clear that publication of theses and dissertations in digital form could provide many benefits for scholarship.

Electronic publication would make theses and dissertations more accessible—if, for example, they were available through the Internet—and would permit searches that are difficult to perform with the printed text. Further, electronic publication has hypertextual capabilities that many researchers would welcome; for instance, a reference to a primary or secondary source might provide a link to the full text of the source, depending on its copyright situation and its availability and accessibility in digital form. In addition, images and sounds could be integrated with the electronic thesis or dissertation, useful additions to, say, a study on film or phonetics. Again, the dissertation writer would need to be aware of copyright laws relevant to images, sound, and video. Finally, since most authors prepare their work on computers, the digital foundation for universal publication in electronic form virtually exists already.

Given these possibilities, it is not surprising that humanities scholars have begun showing increasing interest in electronic theses and dissertations. There is, for example, a site on the World Wide Web that serves as a kind of clearinghouse for electronic theses and dissertations in the humanities (http://etext.lib.virginia.edu/ETD/ETD.html), and some universities now accept or require electronic submission of theses and dissertations and are seeking to establish mechanisms for making these works available through computer to other scholars. The United States Department of Education has funded a proposal for the establishment of a national digital archive of theses and dissertations, and University Microfilms International has begun an initiative to make theses and dissertations available online.

Although many complex issues concerning copyright protection, software, format, markup language, distribution, subsequent publication possibilities, and so forth, still need to be addressed and resolved locally (e.g., within departments, on campuses) and nationally, not to mention internationally, it is likely that a future edition of this book will discuss preparing theses and dissertations in not only print but also electronic form.

6

DOCUMENTATION: PREPARING THE LIST OF WORKS CITED

6.1 Documentation and Plagiarism

6.2 MLA Style

6.3 The List of Works Cited and Other Source Lists

6.4 Placement of the List of Works Cited

6.5 Arrangement of Entries

6.6 Citing Books and Other Nonperiodical Publications

    6.6.1 The Basic Entry: A Book by a Single Author

    6.6.2 An Anthology or a Compilation

    6.6.3 Two or More Books by the Same Author

    6.6.4 A Book by Two or More Authors

    6.6.5 Two or More Books by the Same Authors

    6.6.6 A Book by a Corporate Author

    6.6.7 A Work in an Anthology

    6.6.8 An Article in a Reference Book

    6.6.9 An Introduction, a Preface, a Foreword, or an Afterword

    6.6.10 Cross-References

    6.6.11 An Anonymous Book

    6.6.12 An Edition

    6.6.13 A Translation

    6.6.14 A Book Published in a Second or Subsequent Edition

    6.6.15 A Multivolume Work

    6.6.16 A Book in a Series

    6.6.17 A Republished Book

    6.6.18 A Publisher's Imprint

    6.6.19 A Book with Multiple Publishers

    6.6.20 A Pamphlet

    6.6.21 A Government Publication

    6.6.22 The Published Proceedings of a Conference

    6.6.23 A Book in a Language Other Than English

    6.6.24 A Book Published before 1900

6.6.25 A Book without Stated Publication Information or Pagination
6.6.26 An Unpublished Dissertation
6.6.27 A Published Dissertation

6.7 Citing Articles and Other Publications in Periodicals
6.7.1 The Basic Entry: An Article in a Scholarly Journal with Continuous Pagination
6.7.2 An Article in a Scholarly Journal That Pages Each Issue Separately
6.7.3 An Article in a Scholarly Journal That Uses Only Issue Numbers
6.7.4 An Article in a Scholarly Journal with More Than One Series
6.7.5 An Article in a Newspaper
6.7.6 An Article in a Magazine
6.7.7 A Review
6.7.8 An Abstract in an Abstracts Journal
6.7.9 An Anonymous Article
6.7.10 An Editorial
6.7.11 A Letter to the Editor
6.7.12 A Serialized Article
6.7.13 A Special Issue
6.7.14 An Article in a Microform Collection of Articles
6.7.15 An Article Reprinted in a Loose-Leaf Collection of Articles

6.8 Citing Miscellaneous Print and Nonprint Sources
6.8.1 A Television or Radio Program
6.8.2 A Sound Recording
6.8.3 A Film or Video Recording
6.8.4 A Performance
6.8.5 A Musical Composition
6.8.6 A Work of Art
6.8.7 An Interview
6.8.8 A Map or Chart
6.8.9 A Cartoon
6.8.10 An Advertisement
6.8.11 A Lecture, a Speech, an Address, or a Reading
6.8.12 A Manuscript or Typescript
6.8.13 A Letter or Memo
6.8.14 A Legal Source

6.9 Citing Electronic Publications
6.9.1 Introduction
6.9.2 An Online Scholarly Project, Reference Database, or Professional or Personal Site

6.9.3   An Online Book
6.9.4   An Article in an Online Periodical
6.9.5   A Publication on CD-ROM, Diskette, or Magnetic Tape
6.9.6   A Work in More Than One Publication Medium
6.9.7   A Work in an Indeterminate Medium
6.9.8   Other Electronic Sources

6.1   DOCUMENTATION AND PLAGIARISM

Scholarly authors generously acknowledge their debts to predecessors by carefully giving credit to each source. Whenever you draw on another's work, you must specify what you borrowed—whether facts, opinions, or quotations—and where you borrowed it from. Using another person's ideas or expressions in your writing without acknowledging the source constitutes plagiarism.

Derived from the Latin word *plagiarius* ("kidnapper"), *plagiarism* refers to a form of intellectual theft that has been defined as "the false assumption of authorship: the wrongful act of taking the product of another person's mind, and presenting it as one's own" (Alexander Lindey, *Plagiarism and Originality* [New York: Harper, 1952] 2). In short, to plagiarize is to give the impression that you wrote or thought something that you in fact borrowed from someone, and to do so is a violation of professional ethics.

Forms of plagiarism include the failure to give appropriate acknowledgment when repeating another's wording or particularly apt phrase, paraphrasing another's argument, and presenting another's line of thinking. You may certainly use other persons' words and thoughts, but the borrowed material must not appear to be your creation.

In your writing, then, you must document everything that you borrow: not only direct quotations and paraphrases but also information and ideas. Of course, common sense as well as ethics determines what you document. For example, you rarely need to give sources for familiar proverbs ("You can't judge a book by its cover"), well-known quotations ("We shall overcome"), or common knowledge ("Shakespeare was born during the Elizabethan age"). But you must indicate the source of any appropriated material that readers might otherwise mistake for yours.

Plagiarism is a moral and ethical offense rather than a legal one. Most instances of plagiarism fall outside the scope of copyright infringement, a legal offense. Plagiarism remains an offense even if the plagiarized work is not covered by copyright law or if the amount of material used and the nature of the use fall within the scope of fair use;

copyright infringement remains a legal offense even if the violator acknowledges the source (see 2.1.13–15). The penalties for plagiarism can be severe, ranging from loss of respect to loss of degrees, tenure, or even employment. At all stages of research and writing, guard against the possibility of inadvertent plagiarism by keeping careful notes that distinguish between your musings and thoughts and the material you gather from others.

Another issue related to plagiarism concerns not outside sources but the author's own earlier writing. Whereas reprinting one's published work, such as having a journal article appear in a subsequent book of essays, is professionally acceptable—as long as appropriate permission is secured and complete bibliographic information about the original publication accompanies the reprint—professionals generally disapprove if previously published work is reissued, whether verbatim or slightly revised, under another title or in some other manner that gives the impression it is a new work. Although not the same as plagiarizing someone else's writing, this practice nonetheless qualifies as a kind of self-plagiarism and constitutes another type of unethical activity. If your current work draws on a previously published work of yours, you must give full bibliographic information about the earlier publication.

6.2   # MLA STYLE

Although all fields of research agree on the need to document scholarly borrowings, they do not all agree on the form documentation should take, and different fields generally follow different documentation styles. MLA style is widely used in the humanities, especially in the field of language and literature. Generally simpler and more economical than other styles, MLA style shares with most others its central feature: brief parenthetical citations in the text keyed to an alphabetical list of works cited that appears at the end of the work.

Unlike documentation in other systems, a citation in MLA style contains only enough information to enable readers to find the source in the works-cited list, so that interruptions in the reading are kept to a minimum. A typical citation consists of an author's last name and a page reference: "(Marcuse 197)." If the author's name is mentioned in the text, only the page number appears in the citation: "(197)." If more than one work by the author is in the list of works cited, a shortened version of the title is given, but this too may be omitted from the citation if the title appears in the text. (See ch. 7 for a fuller discussion of parenthetical citations in MLA style.)

Chapters 6 and 7 offer an authoritative and comprehensive presentation of MLA style. For descriptions of other systems of documentation, including one using endnotes and footnotes, see the appendix.

6.3   THE LIST OF WORKS CITED AND OTHER SOURCE LISTS

Although the list of works cited appears at the end of your text, you need to draft the section in advance, so that you will know what information to give in parenthetical references as you write—for example, whether you need to add a shortened title if you cite two or more works by the same author or to give an initial or first name if two of the cited authors have the same last name: "(K. Roemer 123–24)," "(M. Roemer 67)." This chapter explains how to prepare a list of works cited, and the next chapter demonstrates how to document sources where you use them in your text.

As the heading *Works Cited* indicates, this list contains all the works that you will cite in your text. The list simplifies documentation by permitting you to make only brief references to these works in the text. Other names for such a listing are *Bibliography* (literally, "description of books") and *Literature Cited*. Usually, however, the broader title *Works Cited* is most appropriate, since scholarly work often draws on not only books and articles but also nonprint sources.

Titles used for other kinds of source lists include *Annotated Bibliography*, *Works Consulted*, and *Selected Bibliography*. An annotated bibliography, also called *Annotated List of Works Cited*, contains descriptive or evaluative comments on the sources. (For more information on such listings, see James L. Harner, *On Compiling an Annotated Bibliography*, rev. ed. [New York: MLA, 1991].)

The title *Works Consulted* indicates that the list is not confined to works cited. The heading *Selected Bibliography* or *Selected List of Works Consulted* is appropriate for lists that suggest readings.

6.4   PLACEMENT OF THE LIST OF WORKS CITED

The list of works cited appears at the end of the scholarly work; in a book or dissertation the list precedes only the index. Occasionally, as in textbooks or collections of pieces by different authors, each chapter or essay ends with its own list.

Begin the list of works cited on a new page and number each page in a running head (see 4.2.6), continuing the page numbers of the text. Center the title, *Works Cited*, an inch from the top of the page. Double-space between the title and the first entry. Begin each entry flush with the left margin; if an entry runs more than one line, indent the subsequent line or lines one-half inch (or five spaces) from the left margin. Double-space the entire list, both between and within entries (see fig. 10). Continue the list on as many pages as necessary.

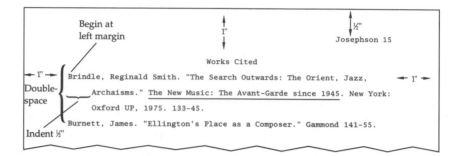

Fig. 10. The top of the first page of a works-cited list.

6.5   ARRANGEMENT OF ENTRIES

Entries in a works-cited list are arranged in alphabetical order to make it easy for the reader to find the entry corresponding to a citation in the text. In general, alphabetize entries in the list by the author's last name, using the letter-by-letter system. In this system, the alphabetical order of names is determined by the letters before the commas that separate last names and first names. Spaces and other punctuation marks are ignored. The letters following the commas are considered only when two or more last names are identical. The following examples are alphabetized letter by letter. (For more information on alphabetizing names, see 3.6.4–13.)

```
Descartes, René
De Sica, Vittorio

MacDonald, George
McCullers, Carson

Morris, Robert
Morris, William
Morrison, Toni

Saint-Exupéry, Antoine de
St. Denis, Ruth
```

If two or more entries citing coauthors begin with the same name, alphabetize by the last names of the second authors listed.

```
Scholes, Robert, and Robert Kellogg
Scholes, Robert, Carl H. Klaus, and Michael Silverman
Scholes, Robert, and Eric S. Rabkin
```

If the author's name is unknown, alphabetize by the title, ignoring any initial *A*, *An*, or *The* or the equivalent in another language. For example, the title *An Encyclopedia of the Latin American Novel* would be alphabetized under the letter *e* rather than *a*, the title *Le théâtre en France au Moyen Age* under *t* rather than *l*.

Other kinds of bibliographies may be arranged differently. An annotated list, a list of works consulted, or a list of selected readings for a historical study, for example, may be organized chronologically by publication date. Some bibliographies are divided into sections and the items alphabetized in each section. A list may be broken down into primary and secondary sources or into different research media (books, articles, films). Alternatively, it may be arranged by subject matter (literature and law, law in literature, law as literature), by period (classical utopia, Renaissance utopia), or by area (Egyptian mythology, Greek mythology, Norse mythology).

6.6   CITING BOOKS AND OTHER NONPERIODICAL PUBLICATIONS

6.6.1   The Basic Entry: A Book by a Single Author

One of the most common items in works-cited lists is the entry for a book by a single author. Such an entry characteristically has three main divisions, each followed by a period and a space except the last, which ends with a period:

```
Author's name. Title of the book. Publication
    information.
```

Here is an example:

```
Cressy, David. Birth, Marriage, and Death: Ritual,
    Religion, and the Life Cycle in Tudor and Stuart
    England. New York: Oxford UP, 1997.
```

Author's Name. Reverse the author's name for alphabetizing, adding a comma after the last name (Porter, Katherine Anne). Put a period after the complete name.

```
Cressy, David.
```

Apart from reversing the order, give the author's name as it appears on the title page. Never abbreviate a name given in full. If, for example, the title page lists the author as "Carleton Brown," do not enter the name as "Brown, C." But use initials if the title page does.

```
Eliot, T. S.
McLuhan, H. Marshall.
```

You may spell out a name abbreviated on the title page if you think the additional information would be helpful to readers. Put square brackets around the material you add.

```
Lewis, C[live] S[taples].
Nesbit, E[dith].
Tolkien, J[ohn] R[onald] R[euel].
```

Similarly, you may give the real name of an author listed under a pseudonym, enclosing the added name in square brackets.

```
Eliot, George [Mary Ann Evans].
Novalis [Friedrich von Hardenberg].
```

If the name of the author is known but not stated on the title page, give the name in brackets. Add a question mark if the authorship is not universally accepted.

```
[Medici, Lorenzo de'?].
```

In general, omit titles, affiliations, and degrees that precede or follow names.

ON TITLE PAGE	IN WORKS-CITED LIST
Anthony T. Boyle, PhD	Boyle, Anthony T.
Sister Jean Daniel	Daniel, Jean.
Gerard Manley Hopkins, SJ	Hopkins, Gerard Manley.
Lady Mary Wortley Montagu	Montagu, Mary Wortley.
Sir Philip Sidney	Sidney, Philip.
Saint Teresa de Jesús	Teresa de Jesús.

A suffix that is an essential part of the name—like *Jr.* or a roman numeral—appears after the given name, preceded by a comma.

```
Rockefeller, John D., IV.
Rust, Arthur George, Jr.
```

Title of the Book. In general, follow the recommendations for titles given in 3.8. State the full title of the book, including any subtitle. If the book has a subtitle, put a colon directly after the main title, unless the main title ends in a question mark, an exclamation point, or a dash. Place a period after the entire title (including any subtitle), unless it ends in another punctuation mark. Underline the entire title, including any colon, subtitle, and punctuation in the title, but do not underline the period that follows the title.

```
Cressy, David. Birth, Marriage, and Death: Ritual,
     Religion, and the Life Cycle in Tudor and Stuart
     England.
```

Extremely long titles or titles usually condensed may be shortened. In shortening a title, include the beginning words of the title up to the first noun and the words by which the work is customarily known. Indicate any omissions by three spaced periods in brackets (see 3.9.5, on ellipsis). For example, *Some Thoughts concerning the Present Revival of Religion in New-England, and the Way in Which It Ought to Be Acknowledged and Promoted, Humbly Offered to the Publick, in a Treatise on That Subject, in Five Parts* may be cited as

```
Some Thoughts concerning the Present Revival of
     Religion in New-England [. . .].
```

Publication Information. In general, give the city of publication, publisher's name, and year of publication. Take these facts directly from the book, not from a source such as a bibliography or a library catalog. The publisher's name that appears on the title page is generally the name to cite. The name may be accompanied there by the city and date. Any publication information not available on the title page can usually be found on the copyright page (i.e., the reverse of the title page) or, particularly in books published outside the United States, in the colophon at the back of the book. Use a colon between the place of publication and the publisher, a comma between the publisher and the date, and a period after the date.

```
Cressy, David. Birth, Marriage, and Death: Ritual,
     Religion, and the Life Cycle in Tudor and Stuart
     England. New York: Oxford UP, 1997.
```

If several cities are listed in the book, give only the first. For cities outside the United States, add an abbreviation of the country (or of the province for cities in Canada) if the name of the city may be ambiguous or unfamiliar to your reader (see 8.3 for abbreviations of geographic names).

```
Manchester, Eng.
Sherbrooke, PQ
```

Shorten the publisher's name, following the guidelines in 8.5. If the year of publication is not recorded on the title page, use the latest copyright date.

Additional examples of the basic book entry follow. (For citing books in languages other than English, see 6.6.23.)

```
Burgess, Anthony [John Burgess Wilson]. A Dead Man in
     Deptford. New York: Carroll, 1995.
Dubrow, Heather. Echoes of Desire: English Petrarchism
     and Its Counterdiscourses. Ithaca: Cornell UP,
     1995.
Metcalf, John. What Is a Canadian Literature? Guelph:
     Red Kite, 1988.
Mitchell, William J. City of Bits: Space, Place, and
     the Informationbahn. Cambridge: MIT P, 1995.
Nobles, Gregory H. American Frontiers: Cultural
     Encounters and Continental Conquest. New York:
     Hill, 1997.
Tatar, Maria. Off with Their Heads! Fairy Tales and the
     Culture of Childhood. Princeton: Princeton UP,
     1992.
```

Sometimes additional information is required. This list shows most of the possible components of a book entry and the order in which they are normally arranged:

1. Author's name

2. Title of a part of the book (see esp. 6.6.7–9)

3. Title of the book

4. Name of the editor, translator, or compiler (see esp. 6.6.7 and 6.6.12–13)

5. Edition used (see 6.6.14)

6. Number(s) of the volume(s) used (see 6.6.15)

7. Name of the series (see 6.6.16)

8. Place of publication, name of the publisher, and date of publication

9. Page numbers (see esp. 6.6.7)

10. Supplementary bibliographic information and annotation (see esp. 6.6.13 and 6.6.15)

The rest of 6.6 explains how to cite these items.

6.6.2   An Anthology or a Compilation

To cite an anthology or a compilation (e.g., a bibliography) that was edited or compiled by someone whose name appears on the title page, begin your entry with the name of the editor or compiler, followed by a comma and the abbreviation *ed.* or *comp.* If the person named performed more than one function—serving, say, as editor and translator —give both roles in the order in which they appear on the title page.

> Kepner, Susan Fulop, ed. and trans. The Lioness in
>   Bloom: Modern Thai Fiction about Women. Berkeley:
>   U of California P, 1996.
> Lopate, Phillip, ed. The Art of the Personal Essay: An
>   Anthology from the Classical Era to the Present.
>   New York: Anchor-Doubleday, 1994.
> Sevillano, Mando, comp. The Hopi Way: Tales from a
>   Vanishing Culture. Flagstaff: Northland, 1986.
> Spafford, Peter, comp. and ed. Interference: The Story
>   of Czechoslovakia in the Words of Its Writers.
>   Cheltenham: New Clarion, 1992.

See also the sections on works in an anthology (6.6.7); introductions, prefaces, and similar parts of books (6.6.9); editions (6.6.12); and translations (6.6.13).

6.6.3   Two or More Books by the Same Author

To cite two or more books by the same author, give the name in the first entry only. Thereafter, in place of the name, type three hyphens, followed by a period and the title. The three hyphens stand for exactly the same name as in the preceding entry. If the person named edited, translated, or compiled the book, place a comma (not a period) after the three hyphens, and write the appropriate abbreviation (*ed., trans.,* or *comp.*) before giving the title. If the same person served as, say, the editor of two or more works listed consecutively, the abbreviation *ed.* must be repeated with each entry. This sort of label does not affect the order in which entries appear; works listed under the same name are alphabetized by title.

> Borroff, Marie. Language and the Poet: Verbal Artistry
>   in Frost, Stevens, and Moore. Chicago: U of
>   Chicago P, 1979.
> ---, trans. Pearl. New York: Norton, 1977.
> ---, ed. Wallace Stevens: A Collection of Critical
>   Essays. Englewood Cliffs: Prentice, 1963.
> Frye, Northrop. Anatomy of Criticism: Four Essays.
>   Princeton: Princeton UP, 1957.
> ---, ed. Design for Learning: Reports Submitted to the
>   Joint Committee of the Toronto Board of Education
>   and the University of Toronto. Toronto: U of
>   Toronto P, 1962.
> ---. The Double Vision: Language and Meaning in
>   Religion. Toronto: U of Toronto P, 1991.
> ---, ed. Sound and Poetry. New York: Columbia UP, 1957.

6.6.4   A Book by Two or More Authors

To cite a book by two or three authors, give their names in the same order as on the title page—not necessarily in alphabetical order. Reverse only the name of the first author, add a comma, and give the other name or names in normal form (Wellek, René, and Austin Warren). Place a period after the last name. Even if the authors have the same last name, state each name in full (Durant, Will, and Ariel Durant). If the persons listed on the title page are editors, translators, or compilers, place a comma (not a period) after the final name and add the appropriate abbreviation (*eds., trans.,* or *comps.* for "editors," "translators," or "compilers").

> Jakobson, Roman, and Linda R. Waugh. The Sound Shape of
>   Language. Bloomington: Indiana UP, 1979.
> Rabkin, Eric S., Martin H. Greenberg, and Joseph D.
>   Olander, eds. No Place Else: Explorations in
>   Utopian and Dystopian Fiction. Carbondale:
>   Southern Illinois UP, 1983.

> Welsch, Roger L., and Linda K. Welsch. <u>Cather's</u>
> <u>Kitchens: Foodways in Literature and Life</u>.
> Lincoln: U of Nebraska P, 1987.

If there are more than three authors, you may name only the first and add *et al.* ("and others"), or you may give all names in full in the order in which they appear on the title page.

> Gilman, Sander, et al. <u>Hysteria beyond Freud</u>. Berkeley:
> U of California P, 1993.
>
> Quirk, Randolph, et al. <u>A Comprehensive Grammar of the</u>
> <u>English Language</u>. London: Longman, 1985.

or

> Gilman, Sander, Helen King, Roy Porter, George
> Rousseau, and Elaine Showalter. <u>Hysteria beyond</u>
> <u>Freud</u>. Berkeley: U of California P, 1993.
>
> Quirk, Randolph, Sidney Greenbaum, Geoffrey Leech, and
> Jan Svartvik. <u>A Comprehensive Grammar of the</u>
> <u>English Language</u>. London: Longman, 1985.

If a single author cited in an entry is also the first of multiple authors in the following entry, repeat the name in full; do not substitute three hyphens. Repeat the name in full whenever you cite the same person as part of a different authorship. The three hyphens are never used in combination with persons' names.

> Scholes, Robert. <u>Protocols of Reading</u>. New Haven: Yale
> UP, 1989.
>
> ---. <u>Textual Power: Literary Theory and the Teaching of</u>
> <u>English</u>. New Haven: Yale UP, 1985.
>
> Scholes, Robert, and Robert Kellogg. <u>The Nature of</u>
> <u>Narrative</u>. New York: Oxford UP, 1966.
>
> Scholes, Robert, and Eric S. Rabkin. <u>Science Fiction:</u>
> <u>History, Science, Vision</u>. New York: Oxford UP,
> 1977.
>
> Tannen, Deborah, ed. <u>Gender and Conversational</u>
> <u>Interaction</u>. New York: Oxford UP, 1993.
>
> ---. <u>You Just Don't Understand: Women and Men in</u>
> <u>Conversation</u>. New York: Morrow, 1990.

161

> Tannen, Deborah, and Roy O. Freedle, eds. Linguistics
>   in Context: Connecting Observation and
>   Understanding. Norwood: Ablex, 1988.
> Tannen, Deborah, and Muriel Saville-Troike, eds.
>   Perspectives on Silence. Norwood: Ablex, 1985.

6.6.5   Two or More Books by the Same Authors

To cite two or more books by the same authors, give the names in the first entry only. Thereafter, in place of the names, type three hyphens, followed by a period and the title. The three hyphens stand for exactly the same names as in the preceding entry.

> Durant, Will, and Ariel Durant. The Age of Voltaire.
>   New York: Simon, 1965.
> ---. A Dual Autobiography. New York: Simon, 1977.
> Gilbert, Sandra M. Blood Pressure. New York: Norton,
>   1989.
> ---. Emily's Bread: Poems. New York: Norton, 1984.
> Gilbert, Sandra M., and Susan Gubar, eds. The Female
>   Imagination and the Modernist Aesthetic. New York:
>   Gordon, 1986.
> ---. The Madwoman in the Attic: The Woman Writer and
>   the Nineteenth-Century Literary Imagination. New
>   Haven: Yale UP, 1979.

6.6.6   A Book by a Corporate Author

A corporate author may be a commission, an association, a committee, or any other group whose individual members are not identified on the title page. Cite the book by the corporate author, even if the corporate author is the publisher. (On citing government publications, see 6.6.21.)

> American Council of Learned Societies. Teaching the
>   Humanities: Essays from the ACLS Elementary and
>   Secondary Schools Teacher Curriculum Development
>   Project. New York: ACLS, 1994.
> Carnegie Foundation for the Advancement of Teaching.
>   Campus Life: In Search of Community. Princeton:
>   Carnegie Foundation for the Advancement of
>   Teaching, 1990.

6.6.7   A Work in an Anthology

If you are citing an essay, a short story, a poem, or another work that appears within an anthology or some other book collection, you need to add the following information to the basic book entry (6.6.1).

Author, title, and (if relevant) translator of the part of the book being cited. Begin the entry with the author and title of the piece, normally enclosing the title in quotation marks.

        Allende, Isabel. "Toad's Mouth."

But if the work was originally published independently (as, e.g., autobiographies, plays, and novels generally are), underline its title instead (see the sample entries below for Douglass, Hansberry, and Sastre). Follow the title of the part of the book with a period. If the anthology contains the work of more than one translator, give the translator's name next, preceded by the abbreviation *Trans.* ("Translated by").

        Allende, Isabel. "Toad's Mouth." Trans. Margaret Sayers
            Peden.

Then state the title of the anthology (underlined).

        Allende, Isabel. "Toad's Mouth." Trans. Margaret Sayers
            Peden. A Hammock beneath the Mangoes: Stories from
            Latin America.

Name of the editor, translator, or compiler of the book being cited. If all the works in the collection have the same translator or if the book has an editor or compiler, write *Trans., Ed.,* or *Comp.* ("Translated by," "Edited by," or "Compiled by"), as appropriate, after the book title and give that person's name.

        Allende, Isabel. "Toad's Mouth." Trans. Margaret Sayers
            Peden. A Hammock beneath the Mangoes: Stories from
            Latin America. Ed. Thomas Colchie.

If someone served in more than one role—say, as editor and translator—state the roles in the order in which they appear on the title page (e.g., "Ed. and trans."; see the entry below for Hanzlík). Similarly, if more than one person served in different roles, give the names in the order in which they appear on the title page: "Trans. Jessie Coulson. Ed. George Gibian."

Page numbers of the cited piece. Give the inclusive page numbers of the piece you are citing. Be sure to provide the page numbers for the entire piece, not just for the material you used. Inclusive page numbers, usually without any identifying abbreviation, follow the publication date and a period. (If the book has no page numbers, see 6.6.25.)

```
Allende, Isabel. "Toad's Mouth." Trans. Margaret Sayers
     Peden. A Hammock beneath the Mangoes: Stories from
     Latin America. Ed. Thomas Colchie. New York:
     Plume, 1992. 83-88.
```

Here are additional sample entries for works in anthologies:

```
Calvino, Italo. "Cybernetics and Ghosts." The Uses of
     Literature: Essays. Trans. Patrick Creagh. San
     Diego: Harcourt, 1982. 3-27.
Hansberry, Lorraine. A Raisin in the Sun. Black
     Theater: A Twentieth-Century Collection of the
     Work of Its Best Playwrights. Ed. Lindsay
     Patterson. New York: Dodd, 1971. 221-76.
Hanzlík, Josef. "Vengeance." Trans. Ewald Osers.
     Interference: The Story of Czechoslovakia in the
     Words of Its Writers. Comp. and ed. Peter
     Spafford. Cheltenham: New Clarion, 1992. 54.
Sastre, Alfonso. Sad Are the Eyes of William Tell.
     Trans. Leonard Pronko. The New Wave of Spanish
     Drama. Ed. George Wellwarth. New York: New York
     UP, 1970. 165-321.
"A Witchcraft Story." The Hopi Way: Tales from a
     Vanishing Culture. Comp. Mando Sevillano.
     Flagstaff: Northland, 1986. 33-42.
```

Often the works in anthologies have been published before. If you wish to inform your reader of the date when a previously published piece other than a scholarly article first appeared, you may follow the title of the piece with the year of original publication and a period.

```
Douglass, Frederick. Narrative of the Life of Frederick
     Douglass, an American Slave, Written by Himself.
     1845. Classic American Autobiographies. Ed.
     William L. Andrews. New York: Mentor, 1992.
     229-327.
```

> Franklin, Benjamin. "Emigration to America." 1782. The
>   Faber Book of America. Ed. Christopher Ricks and
>   William L. Vance. Boston: Faber, 1992. 24-26.

To cite a previously published scholarly article in a collection, give the complete data for the earlier publication and then add *Rpt. in* ("Reprinted in"), the title of the collection, and the new publication facts. (On citing articles in periodicals, see 6.7.)

> Frye, Northrop. "Literary and Linguistic Scholarship in
>   a Postliterate Age." PMLA 99 (1984): 990-95. Rpt.
>   in Myth and Metaphor: Selected Essays, 1974-88.
>   Ed. Robert D. Denham. Charlottesville: UP of
>   Virginia, 1990. 18-27.
> Roberts, Sheila. "A Confined World: A Rereading of
>   Pauline Smith." World Literature Written in
>   English 24 (1984): 232-38. Rpt. in Twentieth-
>   Century Literary Criticism. Ed. Dennis Poupard.
>   Vol. 25. Detroit: Gale, 1988. 399-402.

If the article was originally published under a different title, first state the new title and publication facts, followed by *Rpt. of* ("Reprint of"), the original title, and the original publication facts.

> Lewis, C. S. "Viewpoints: C. S. Lewis." Twentieth-
>   Century Interpretations of Sir Gawain and the
>   Green Knight. Ed. Denton Fox. Englewood Cliffs:
>   Prentice, 1968. 100-01. Rpt. of "The
>   Anthropological Approach." English and Medieval
>   Studies Presented to J. R. R. Tolkien on the
>   Occasion of His Seventieth Birthday. Ed. Norman
>   Davis and C. L. Wrenn. London: Allen, 1962.
>   219-23.

If you refer to more than one piece from the same collection, you may wish to cross-reference each citation to a single entry for the book (see 6.6.10). On citing articles in reference books, see 6.6.8. On citing introductions, prefaces, and the like, see 6.6.9. On citing a piece in a multivolume anthology, see 6.6.15.

6.6.8   An Article in a Reference Book

Treat an encyclopedia article or a dictionary entry as you would a piece in a collection (6.6.7), but do not cite the editor of the reference work. If the article is signed, give the author first (often articles in reference books are signed with initials identified elsewhere in the work); if it is unsigned, give the title first. If the encyclopedia or dictionary arranges articles alphabetically, you may omit volume and page numbers.

When citing familiar reference books, especially those that frequently appear in new editions, do not give full publication information. For such works, list only the edition (if stated) and the year of publication.

> "Azimuthal Equidistant Projection." Merriam-Webster's
>   Collegiate Dictionary. 10th ed. 1993.
> "Ginsburg, Ruth Bader." Who's Who in America. 51st ed.
>   1997.
> "Mandarin." The Encyclopedia Americana. 1994 ed.
> Mohanty, Jitendra N. "Indian Philosophy." The New
>   Encyclopaedia Britannica: Macropaedia. 15th ed.
>   1987.
> "Noon." Oxford English Dictionary. 2nd ed. 1989.

If you are citing a specific definition, among several, add the abbreviation *Def.* ("Definition") and the appropriate designation (e.g., number, letter).

> "Noon." Def. 4b. Oxford English Dictionary. 2nd ed.
>   1989.

When citing less familiar reference books, however, especially those that have appeared in only one edition, give full publication information.

> Bram, Jean Rhys. "Moon." The Encyclopedia of Religion.
>   Ed. Mircea Eliade. 16 vols. New York: Macmillan,
>   1987.
> Le Patourel, John. "Normans and Normandy." Dictionary
>   of the Middle Ages. Ed. Joseph R. Strayer. 13
>   vols. New York: Scribner's, 1987.

6.6.9 An Introduction, a Preface, a Foreword, or an Afterword

To cite an introduction, a preface, a foreword, or an afterword, begin with the name of its author and then give the name of the part being cited, capitalized but neither underlined nor enclosed in quotation marks (*Introduction, Preface, Foreword, Afterword*). If the writer of the piece is different from the author of the complete work, cite the author of the work after its title, giving the full name, in normal order, preceded by the word *By*. If the writer of the piece is also the author of the complete work, use only the last name after *By*. If the complete work is a translation, add the name of the translator next. Continue with full publication information and, finally, the inclusive page numbers.

> Borges, Jorge Luis. Foreword. Selected Poems, 1923–
>   1967. By Borges. Ed. Norman Thomas Di Giovanni.
>   New York: Delta-Dell, 1973. xv-xvi.
>
> Drabble, Margaret. Introduction. Middlemarch. By George
>   Eliot. New York: Bantam, 1985. vii-xvii.
>
> Elliott, Emory. Afterword. The Jungle. By Upton
>   Sinclair. New York: Signet, 1990. 342-50.
>
> Knox, Bernard. Introduction. The Odyssey. By Homer.
>   Trans. Robert Fagles. New York: Viking, 1996.
>   3-64.
>
> Marsalis, Wynton. Foreword. Beyond Category: The Life
>   and Genius of Duke Ellington. By John Edward
>   Hasse. New York: Simon, 1993. 13-14.

6.6.10 Cross-References

To avoid unnecessary repetition in citing two or more works from the same collection, you may create a complete entry for the collection and cross-reference individual pieces to the entry. In a cross-reference, state the author and the title of the piece, the last name of the editor of the collection, and the inclusive page numbers. If the piece is a translation, add the name of the translator after the title, unless one person translated the entire volume.

> Hamill, Pete. Introduction. Sexton and Powers xi-xiv.
> Mayakovsky, Vladimir. "Brooklyn Bridge." Trans. Max
>   Hayward and George Reavey. Sexton and Powers
>   136-41.
> McCullers, Carson. "Brooklyn Is My Neighborhood."
>   Sexton and Powers 143-47.

```
Sexton, Andrea Wyatt, and Alice Leccese Powers, eds.
    The Brooklyn Reader: Thirty Writers Celebrate
    America's Favorite Borough. New York: Harmony,
    1994.
Walcott, Derek. "A Letter from Brooklyn." Sexton and
    Powers 264-65.
Whitman, Walt. "Crossing Brooklyn Ferry." Sexton and
    Powers 267-74.
```

If you list two or more works under the editor's name, however, add the title (or a shortened version of it) to the cross-reference.

```
Angelou, Maya. "Pickin Em Up and Layin Em Down." Baker,
    Norton 276-78.
Baker, Russell, ed. The Norton Book of Light Verse. New
    York: Norton, 1986.
---, ed. Russell Baker's Book of American Humor. New
    York: Norton, 1993.
Hurston, Zora Neale. "Squinch Owl Story." Baker,
    Russell Baker's Book 458-59.
Lebowitz, Fran. "Manners." Baker, Russell Baker's Book
    556-59.
Lennon, John. "The Fat Budgie." Baker, Norton 357-58.
```

6.6.11 An Anonymous Book

If a book has no author's or editor's name on the title page, begin the entry with the title. Do not use either *Anonymous* or *Anon.* Alphabetize the entry by the title, ignoring any initial *A*, *An*, or *The*. (Note in the sample entries that *A Guide to Our Federal Lands* is alphabetized under *g*.)

```
Encyclopedia of Virginia. New York: Somerset, 1993.
A Guide to Our Federal Lands. Washington: Natl.
    Geographic Soc., 1984.
New York Public Library Student's Desk Reference. New
    York: Prentice, 1993.
```

6.6.12 An Edition

Every published book is, in at least one sense, an edition; for example, a book may be a first edition, a second edition, and so forth (see 6.6.14). The term *edition* is also used to denote a work prepared for publication by someone other than the author—by an editor. For example, for a 1998 printing of Shakespeare's *Hamlet,* an editor would have selected a version of the play from the various versions available, decided on any changes in spelling or punctuation, and perhaps added explanatory notes or written an introduction. This version of *Hamlet* would be called an "edition," and the editor's name would most likely appear on the title page along with Shakespeare's.

To cite an edition, begin with the author (or the title, for an anonymous work) if you refer primarily to the text itself; give the editor's name, preceded by the abbreviation *Ed.* ("Edited by"), after the title. If for clarity you wish to indicate the original date of publication, place the year directly after the title (see the entry for Crane).

> Crane, Stephen. The Red Badge of Courage: An Episode of
>   the American Civil War. 1895. Ed. Fredson Bowers.
>   Charlottesville: UP of Virginia, 1975.
>
> Edgeworth, Maria. Castle Rackrent and Ennui. Ed.
>   Marilyn Butler. London: Penguin, 1992.
>
> Octovian. Ed. Frances McSparran. Early English Text
>   Soc. 289. London: Oxford UP, 1986.
>
> Shakespeare, William. Hamlet. Ed. Barbara A. Mowat and
>   Paul Werstine. New York: Washington Square-Pocket,
>   1992.
>
> Smith, Charlotte. The Poems of Charlotte Smith. Ed.
>   Stuart Curran. New York: Oxford UP, 1993.
>
> Twain, Mark. Roughing It. Ed. Harriet E. Smith and
>   Edgar M. Branch. Berkeley: U of California P,
>   1993.
>
> Wollstonecraft, Mary. A Vindication of the Rights of
>   Woman. Ed. Carol H. Poston. New York: Norton,
>   1975.

To cite a facsimile edition, follow the author's name and title with the original publication information (see 6.6.24 for a book published before 1900), the abbreviation *Facsim. ed.* ("Facsimile edition"), and the new publication information.

> Milton, John. Poems. London, 1645. Facsim. ed. Oxford:
>   Clarendon, 1924.

If you are citing a specific work in a facsimile edition, treat it as you would a piece in a collection (see 6.6.7), giving inclusive page numbers at the end of the entry. If you wish to indicate the date of the specific work, place the year directly after the title of the piece.

> Milton, John. "Lycidas." 1638. <u>Poems</u>. London, 1645.
> Facsim. ed. Oxford: Clarendon, 1924. 57-65.

If your citations are generally to the work of the editor (e.g., the introduction, the notes, or editorial decisions regarding the text), begin the entry with the editor's name, followed by a comma and the abbreviation *ed.* ("editor"), and give the author's name, preceded by the word *By*, after the title.

> Bowers, Fredson, ed. <u>The Red Badge of Courage: An</u>
> <u>Episode of the American Civil War</u>. By Stephen
> Crane. 1895. Charlottesville: UP of Virginia,
> 1975.

Consult 6.6.15 if you are citing more than one volume of a multivolume work or if the book is a part of a multivolume edition—say, *The Works of Mark Twain*—and you wish to give supplementary information about the entire project.

6.6.13 A Translation

To cite a translation, state the author's name first if you refer primarily to the work itself; give the translator's name, preceded by *Trans.* ("Translated by"), after the title. If the book has an editor as well as a translator, give the names, with appropriate abbreviations, in the order in which they appear on the title page (see the sample entry for Dostoevsky).

> Dostoevsky, Feodor. <u>Crime and Punishment</u>. Trans. Jessie
> Coulson. Ed. George Gibian. New York: Norton,
> 1964.
> Esquivel, Laura. <u>Like Water for Chocolate: A Novel in</u>
> <u>Monthly Installments, with Recipes, Romances, and</u>
> <u>Home Remedies</u>. Trans. Carol Christensen and Thomas
> Christensen. New York: Doubleday, 1992.
> Homer. <u>The Odyssey</u>. Trans. Robert Fagles. New York:
> Viking, 1996.
> Murasaki Shikibu. <u>The Tale of Genji</u>. Trans. Edward G.
> Seidensticker. New York: Knopf, 1976.

If your citations are mostly to the translator's comments or choice of wording, begin the bibliographic entry with the translator's name, followed by a comma and the abbreviation *trans.* ("translator"), and give the author's name, preceded by the word *By*, after the title. (On citing anthologies of translated works by different authors, see 6.6.7.)

Coulson, Jessie, trans. Crime and Punishment. By Feodor
    Dostoevsky. Ed. George Gibian. New York: Norton,
    1964.

Although not required, some or all of the original publication facts may be added as supplementary information at the end of the entry.

Genette, Gérard. The Work of Art: Immanence and
    Transcendence. Trans. G. M. Goshgarian. Ithaca:
    Cornell UP, 1997. Trans. of L'oeuvre d'art:
    Immanence et transcendence. Paris: Seuil, 1994.
Levi, Primo. Survival in Auschwitz: The Nazi Assault on
    Humanity. Trans. Stuart Woolf. New York: Collier-
    Macmillan, 1987. Trans. of Se questo è un uomo.
    Torino: Einaudi, 1958.

On citing a book in a language other than English, see 6.6.23.

6.6.14   A Book Published in a Second or Subsequent Edition

A book with no edition number or name on its title page is probably a first edition. Unless informed otherwise, readers assume that bibliographic entries refer to first editions. When you use a later edition of a work, identify the edition in your entry by number (*2nd ed., 3rd ed., 4th ed.*), by name (*Rev. ed.*, for "Revised edition"; *Abr. ed.*, for "Abridged edition"), or by year (*1998 ed.*)—whichever the title page indicates. The specification of edition comes after the name of the editor, translator, or compiler, if there is one, or otherwise after the title of the book. (On citing encyclopedias, dictionaries, and similar works revised regularly, see 6.6.8.)

Cavafy, C. P. Collected Poems. Trans. Edmund Keeley and
    Philip Sherrard. Ed. George Savidis. Rev. ed.
    Princeton: Princeton UP, 1992.
Chaucer, Geoffrey. The Works of Geoffrey Chaucer. Ed.
    F. W. Robinson. 2nd ed. Boston: Houghton, 1957.

> Gross, Harvey, and Robert McDowell. <u>Sound and Form in</u>
> <u>Modern Poetry</u>. 2nd ed. Ann Arbor: U of Michigan P,
> 1996.
>
> Murasaki Shikibu. <u>The Tale of Genji</u>. Trans. Edward G.
> Seidensticker. Abr. ed. New York: Vintage-Random,
> 1985.
>
> Newcomb, Horace, ed. <u>Television: The Critical View</u>. 5th
> ed. New York: Oxford UP, 1994.

6.6.15 A Multivolume Work

If you are using two or more volumes of a multivolume work, cite the total number of volumes in the work ("5 vols."). This information comes after the title—or after any editor's name or identification of edition—and before the publication information. Specific references to volume and page numbers ("3: 212–13") belong in the text. (See ch. 7 for parenthetical documentation.)

> Blanco, Richard L., ed. <u>The American Revolution, 1775-</u>
> <u>1783: An Encyclopedia</u>. 2 vols. Hamden: Garland,
> 1993.
>
> Doyle, Arthur Conan. <u>The Oxford Sherlock Holmes</u>. Ed.
> Owen Dudley Edwards. 9 vols. New York: Oxford UP,
> 1993.
>
> Lauter, Paul, et al., eds. <u>The Heath Anthology of</u>
> <u>American Literature</u>. 2nd ed. 2 vols. Lexington:
> Heath, 1994.
>
> Sadie, Stanley, ed. <u>The New Grove Dictionary of Music</u>
> <u>and Musicians</u>. 20 vols. London: Macmillan, 1980.
>
> Schlesinger, Arthur M., gen. ed. <u>History of U.S.</u>
> <u>Political Parties</u>. 4 vols. New York: Chelsea,
> 1973.
>
> Weinberg, Bernard. <u>A History of Literary Criticism in</u>
> <u>the Italian Renaissance</u>. 2 vols. Chicago: U of
> Chicago P, 1961.

If the volumes of the work were published over a period of years, give the inclusive dates at the end of the citation ("1955–92"). If the work is still in progress, write *to date* after the number of volumes ("3 vols. to date") and leave a space after the hyphen that follows the beginning date ("1982– ").

```
Boswell, James. The Life of Johnson. Ed. George
    Birkbeck Hill and L. F. Powell. 6 vols. Oxford:
    Clarendon, 1934-50.
Cassidy, Frederic, ed. Dictionary of American Regional
    English. 3 vols. to date. Cambridge: Belknap-
    Harvard UP, 1985- .
Churchill, Winston S. A History of the English-Speaking
    Peoples. 4 vols. New York: Dodd, 1956-58.
Crane, Stephen. The University of Virginia Edition of
    the Works of Stephen Crane. Ed. Fredson Bowers. 10
    vols. Charlottesville: UP of Virginia, 1969-76.
Wellek, René. A History of Modern Criticism, 1750-1950.
    8 vols. New Haven: Yale UP, 1955-92.
```

If you are using only one volume of a multivolume work, state the number of the volume in the bibliographic entry ("Vol. 2") and give publication information for that volume alone; then you need give only page numbers when you refer to that work in the text.

```
Doyle, Arthur Conan. The Oxford Sherlock Holmes. Ed.
    Owen Dudley Edwards. Vol. 8. New York: Oxford UP,
    1993.
Parker, Hershel. Melville: A Biography. Vol. 1.
    Baltimore: Johns Hopkins UP, 1996.
Stowe, Harriet Beecher. "Sojourner Truth, the Libyan
    Sibyl." 1863. The Heath Anthology of American
    Literature. Ed. Paul Lauter et al. 2nd ed. Vol. 1.
    Lexington: Heath, 1994. 2425-33.
Wellek, René. A History of Modern Criticism, 1750-1950.
    Vol. 5. New Haven: Yale UP, 1986.
```

Although not required, the complete number of volumes may be added as supplementary information at the end of the listing, along with other relevant publication facts, such as inclusive dates of publication if the volumes were published over a period of years (see the sample entry for Wellek).

```
Doyle, Arthur Conan. The Oxford Sherlock Holmes. Ed.
    Owen Dudley Edwards. Vol. 8. New York: Oxford UP,
    1993. 9 vols.
```

Stowe, Harriet Beecher. "Sojourner Truth, the Libyan
Sibyl." 1863. The Heath Anthology of American
Literature. Ed. Paul Lauter et al. 2nd ed. Vol. 1.
Lexington: Heath, 1994. 2425-33. 2 vols.

Wellek, René. A History of Modern Criticism, 1750-1950.
Vol. 5. New Haven: Yale UP, 1986. 8 vols. 1955-92.

If you are using only one volume of a multivolume work and the
volume has an individual title, you may cite the book without reference to the other volumes in the work.

Churchill, Winston S. The Age of Revolution. New York:
Dodd, 1957.

Durant, Will, and Ariel Durant. The Age of Voltaire.
New York: Simon, 1965.

Although not required, supplementary information about the complete multivolume work may follow the basic citation: the volume
number, preceded by *Vol.* and followed by the word *of*; the title of the
complete work; the total number of volumes; and, if the work
appeared over a period of years, the inclusive publication dates.

Churchill, Winston S. The Age of Revolution. New York:
Dodd, 1957. Vol. 3 of A History of the English-
Speaking Peoples. 4 vols. 1956-58.

Durant, Will, and Ariel Durant. The Age of Voltaire.
New York: Simon, 1965. Vol. 9 of The Story of
Civilization. 11 vols. 1935-75.

If the volume you are citing is part of a multivolume scholarly edition
(see 6.6.12), you may similarly give supplementary information about
the entire edition. Follow the publication information for the volume
with the appropriate volume number, preceded by *Vol.* and followed
by the word *of*; the title of the complete work; the name of the general
editor of the multivolume edition, followed by a comma and *gen. ed.*;
the total number of volumes; and the inclusive publication dates for
the edition (see the entry for Howells). If the entire edition was edited
by one person, state the editor's name after the title of the edition
rather than after the title of the volume (see the entry for Crane).

Crane, Stephen. The Red Badge of Courage: An Episode of
the American Civil War. 1895. Charlottesville: UP
of Virginia, 1975. Vol. 2 of The University of

Virginia Edition of the Works of Stephen Crane.
Ed. Fredson Bowers. 10 vols. 1969-76.

Howells, W. D. Their Wedding Journey. Ed. John K.
Reeves. Bloomington: Indiana UP, 1968. Vol. 5 of A
Selected Edition of W. D. Howells. Edwin H. Cady,
gen. ed. 32 vols. 1968-83.

6.6.16   A Book in a Series

If the title page or the preceding page (the half-title page) indicates
that the book you are citing is part of a series, include the series name,
neither underlined nor enclosed in quotation marks, and the series
number, followed by a period, before the publication information. Use
common abbreviations for words in the series name (see 8.4), including *Ser.* if *Series* is part of the name.

Charrière, Isabelle de. Letters of Mistress Henley
Published by Her Friend. Trans. Philip Stewart and
Jean Vaché. Texts and Trans. 1. New York: MLA,
1993.

Neruda, Pablo. Canto General. Trans. Jack Schmitt.
Latin Amer. Lit. and Culture 7. Berkeley: U of
California P, 1991.

Pihl, Marshall R. The Korean Singer of Tales. Harvard-
Yenching Inst. Monograph Ser. 37. Cambridge:
Harvard UP, 1994.

Wilson, Sharon R., Thomas B. Friedman, and Shannon
Hengen, eds. Approaches to Teaching Atwood's The
Handmaid's Tale and Other Works. Approaches to
Teaching World Lit. 56. New York: MLA, 1996.

6.6.17   A Republished Book

To cite a republished book—for example, a paperback version of a
book originally published in a clothbound version—give the original
publication date, followed by a period, before the publication information for the book you are citing.

Atwood, Margaret. Surfacing. 1972. New York: Fawcett,
1987.

Doctorow, E. L. Welcome to Hard Times. 1960. New York:
Vintage-Random, 1988.

> Holier, Denis, ed. A New History of French Literature.
> 1989. Cambridge: Harvard UP, 1994.

Although not required, supplementary information pertaining to the original publication may precede the original publication date.

> Ishiguro, Kazuo. The Remains of the Day. London: Faber,
> 1989. New York: Knopf, 1990.

New material added to the republication, such as an introduction, should be cited after the original publication facts.

> Dreiser, Theodore. Sister Carrie. 1900. Introd. E. L.
> Doctorow. New York: Bantam, 1982.

To cite a republished book that was originally issued under a different title, first state the new title and publication facts, followed by *Rpt. of* ("Reprint of"), the original title, and the original date.

> The WPA Guide to 1930s New Jersey. New Brunswick:
> Rutgers UP, 1986. Rpt. of New Jersey: A Guide to
> Its Past and Present. 1939.

6.6.18 A Publisher's Imprint

Publishers often group some of their books under imprints, or special names. If an imprint appears on a title page along with the publisher's name, state the imprint and follow it by a hyphen and the name of the publisher ("Anchor-Doubleday," "Collier-Macmillan," "Vintage-Random").

> Cassidy, Frederic, ed. Dictionary of American Regional
> English. 3 vols. to date. Cambridge: Belknap-
> Harvard UP, 1985- .
> Findlater, Mary, and Jane Findlater. Crossriggs. 1908.
> Introd. Paul Binding. New York: Virago-Penguin,
> 1986.
> Lopate, Phillip, ed. The Art of the Personal Essay: An
> Anthology from the Classical Era to the Present.
> New York: Anchor-Doubleday, 1994.
> Ondaatje, Michael. The English Patient. New York:
> Vintage-Random, 1992.

6.6.19 A Book with Multiple Publishers

If the title page lists two or more publishers—not just two or more offices of the same publisher—include all of them, in the order given, as part of the publication information, putting a semicolon after the name of each but the last.

> Duff, J. Wight. A Literary History of Rome: From the
> Origins to the Close of the Golden Age. Ed. A. M.
> Duff. 3rd ed. 1953. London: Benn; New York:
> Barnes, 1967.
> Wells, H. G. The Time Machine. 1895. London: Dent;
> Rutland: Tuttle, 1992.

6.6.20 A Pamphlet

Treat a pamphlet as you would a book.

> London. New York: Trip Builder, 1996.
> Renoir Lithographs. New York: Dover, 1994.

6.6.21 A Government Publication

Government publications emanate from many sources and so present special problems in bibliographic citation. In general, if you do not know the writer of the document, cite as author the government agency that issued it—that is, state the name of the government first, followed by the name of the agency, using an abbreviation if the context makes it clear. (But see below for citing a document whose author is known.)

> California. Dept. of Industrial Relations.
> United States. Cong. House.

If you are citing two or more works issued by the same government, substitute three hyphens for the name in each entry after the first. If you also cite more than one work by the same government agency, use an additional three hyphens in place of the agency in the second entry and each subsequent one.

> United States. Cong. House.
> ---. ---. Senate.
> ---. Dept. of Health and Human Services.

The title of the publication, underlined, should follow immediately.

In citing the *Congressional Record* (abbreviated *Cong. Rec.*), give only the date and page numbers.

```
Cong. Rec. 7 Feb. 1973: 3831-51.
```

In citing other congressional documents, include such information as the number and session of Congress, the house (*S* stands for Senate, *H* and *HR* for House of Representatives), and the type and number of the publication. Types of congressional publications include bills (S 33, HR 77), resolutions (S. Res. 20, H. Res. 50), reports (S. Rept. 9, H. Rept. 142), and documents (S. Doc. 333, H. Doc. 222, Misc. Doc. 67).

The usual publication information comes next (i.e., place, publisher, and date). Most federal publications, regardless of the branch of government issuing them, are published by the Government Printing Office (GPO), in Washington, DC; its British counterpart is Her (or His) Majesty's Stationery Office (HMSO), in London. Documents issued by the United Nations and most local governments, however, do not all emanate from a central office; give the publication information that appears on the title page.

```
Great Britain. Ministry of Agriculture, Fisheries, and
     Food. Radionuclide Levels in Food, Animals, and
     Agricultural Products: Post-Chernobyl Monitoring
     in England and Wales. London: HMSO, 1987.
New York State. Commission on the Adirondacks in the
     Twenty-First Century. The Adirondack Park in the
     Twenty-First Century. Albany: State of New York,
     1990.
---. Committee on State Prisons. Investigation of the
     New York State Prisons. 1883. New York: Arno,
     1974.
United Nations. Consequences of Rapid Population Growth
     in Developing Countries. New York: Taylor, 1991.
---. Centre on Transnational Corporations. Foreign
     Direct Investment, the Service Sector, and
     International Banking. New York: United Nations,
     1987.
---. Economic Commission for Africa. Industrial Growth
     in Africa. New York: United Nations, 1963.
```

United States. Cong. Joint Committee on the
Investigation of the Pearl Harbor Attack.
Hearings. 79th Cong., 1st and 2nd sess. 32 vols.
Washington: GPO, 1946.

---. ---. Senate. Subcommittee on Constitutional
Amendments of the Committee on the Judiciary.
Hearings on the "Equal Rights" Amendment. 91st
Cong., 2nd sess. S. Res. 61. Washington: GPO,
1970.

---. Dept. of Labor. Child Care: A Workforce Issue.
Washington: GPO, 1988.

---. Dept. of State. The Global 2000 Report to the
President: Entering the Twenty-First Century. 3
vols. Washington: GPO, 1981.

If known, the name of the document's author may either begin the entry or, if the agency comes first, follow the title and the word *By* or an abbreviation (such as *Ed.* or *Comp.*).

Poore, Benjamin Perley, comp. A Descriptive Catalogue
of the Government Publications of the United
States, September 5, 1774-March 4, 1881. US 48th
Cong., 2nd sess. Misc. Doc. 67. Washington: GPO,
1885.

or

United States. Cong. A Descriptive Catalogue of the
Government Publications of the United States,
September 5, 1774-March 4, 1881. Comp. Benjamin
Perley Poore. 48th Cong., 2nd sess. Misc. Doc. 67.
Washington: GPO, 1885.

6.6.22 The Published Proceedings of a Conference

Treat the published proceedings of a conference like a book, but add pertinent information about the conference (unless the book title includes such information).

Freed, Barbara F., ed. Foreign Language Acquisition
Research and the Classroom. Proc. of Consortium

for Language Teaching and Learning Conference,
Oct. 1989, U of Pennsylvania. Lexington: Heath,
1991.

Hall, Kira, Michael Meacham, and Richard Shapiro, eds.
Proceedings of the Fifteenth Annual Meeting of the
Berkeley Linguistics Society, February 18-20,
1989: General Session and Parasession on
Theoretical Issues in Language Reconstruction.
Berkeley: Berkeley Linguistics Soc., 1989.

Cite a presentation in the proceedings like a work in a collection of
pieces by different authors (see 6.6.7).

Mann, Jill. "Chaucer and the 'Woman Question.'" This
Noble Craft: Proceedings of the Tenth Research
Symposium of the Dutch and Belgian University
Teachers of Old and Middle English and Historical
Linguistics, Utrecht, 19-20 January 1989. Ed. Erik
Kooper. Amsterdam: Rodopi, 1991. 173-88.

6.6.23 A Book in a Language Other Than English

Cite a book published in a language other than English like any other
book. Give the author's name, title, and publication information as
they appear in the book. You may need to look in the colophon, at the
back of the book, for some or all of the publication information found
on the title or copyright page of English-language books. If it seems
necessary to clarify the title, provide a translation, in brackets: "*Gen-
gangere* [*Ghosts*]." Similarly, you may use brackets to give the English
name of a foreign city—"Wien [Vienna]"—or you may substitute the
English name, depending on your readers' knowledge of the language. Shorten the publisher's name appropriately (see 8.5). For capitalization in languages other than English, see 3.7.2–9.

Bessière, Jean, ed. Mythologies de l'écriture: Champs
critiques. Paris: PUF, 1990.

Dahlhaus, Carl. Musikästhetik. Köln: Gerig, 1967.

Eco, Umberto. Il nome della rosa. Milano: Bompiani,
1980.

Esquivel, Laura. Como agua para chocolate: Novelas de
entregas mensuales, con recetas, amores y remedios
caseros. Madrid: Mondadori, 1990.

Poche, Emanuel. Prazské Palace. Praha [Prague]: Odeon,
    1977.

6.6.24 A Book Published before 1900

When citing a book published before 1900, you may omit the name of
the publisher and use a comma, instead of a colon, after the place of
publication.

Brome, Richard. The Dramatic Works of Richard Brome. 3
    vols. London, 1873.

Dewey, John. The School and Society. Chicago, 1899.

Segni, Bernardo. Rettorica et poetica d'Aristotile.
    Firenze, 1586.

6.6.25 A Book without Stated Publication Information or Pagination

When a book does not indicate the publisher, the place or date of publication, or pagination, supply as much of the missing information
as you can, using brackets to show that it did not come from the
source.

New York: U of Gotham P, [1998].

If the date can only be approximated, put it after a *c.*, for *circa* 'around':
"[c. 1998]." If you are uncertain about the accuracy of the information
you supply, add a question mark: "[1998?]." Use the following abbreviations for information you cannot supply.

n.p.	No place of publication given
n.p.	No publisher given
n.d.	No date of publication given
n. pag.	No pagination given

Inserted before the colon, the abbreviation *n.p.* indicates *no place;* after
the colon, it indicates *no publisher. N. pag.* explains the absence of page
references in citations of the work.

NO PLACE

N.p.: U of Gotham P, 1998.

NO PUBLISHER

New York: n.p., 1998.

181

NO DATE

New York: U of Gotham P, n.d.

NO PAGINATION

New York: U of Gotham P, 1998. N. pag.

The examples above are hypothetical; the following ones are entries for actual books.

> Bauer, Johann. Kafka und Prag. [Stuttgart]: Belser,
>   [1971?].
> Malachi, Zvi, ed. Proceedings of the International
>   Conference on Literary and Linguistic Computing.
>   [Tel Aviv]: [Fac. of Humanities, Tel Aviv U], n.d.
> Michelangelo. The Sistine Chapel. New York: Wings,
>   1992. N. pag.
> Photographic View Album of Cambridge. [Eng.]: n.p.,
>   n.d. N. pag.
> Sendak, Maurice. Where the Wild Things Are. New York:
>   Harper, 1963. N. pag.

6.6.26 An Unpublished Dissertation

Enclose the title of an unpublished dissertation in quotation marks; do not underline it. Then write the descriptive label *Diss.*, and add the name of the degree-granting university, followed by a comma and the year.

> Boyle, Anthony T. "The Epistemological Evolution of
>   Renaissance Utopian Literature, 1516-1657." Diss.
>   New York U, 1983.
> Stephenson, Denise R. "Blurred Distinctions: Emerging
>   Forms of Academic Writing." Diss. U of New Mexico,
>   1996.

For citing a dissertation abstract published in *Dissertation Abstracts* or *Dissertation Abstracts International*, see 6.7.8. For documenting other unpublished writing, see 6.8.12.

6.6.27   A Published Dissertation

Cite a published dissertation like a book, but add pertinent dissertation information before the publication facts. If the dissertation was privately printed, state *privately printed* in place of the publisher's name. If the work was published by University Microfilms International (UMI), you may add the order number as supplementary information.

> Dietze, Rudolf F. <u>Ralph Ellison: The Genesis of an</u>
> <u>Artist</u>. Diss. U Erlangen-Nürnberg, 1982. Erlanger
> Beiträge zur Sprach- und Kunstwissenschaft 70.
> Nürnberg: Carl, 1982.
>
> Valentine, Mary-Blair Truesdell. <u>An Investigation of</u>
> <u>Gender-Based Leadership Styles of Male and Female</u>
> <u>Officers in the United States Army</u>. Diss. George
> Mason U, 1993. Ann Arbor: UMI, 1993. 9316566.
>
> Wendriner, Karl Georg. <u>Der Einfluss von Goethes</u> Wilhelm
> Meister <u>auf das Drama der Romantiker</u>. Diss. U
> Bonn, 1907. Leipzig: privately printed, 1907.

6.7   CITING ARTICLES AND OTHER PUBLICATIONS IN PERIODICALS

6.7.1   The Basic Entry: An Article in a Scholarly Journal with Continuous Pagination

Periodicals—newspapers, magazines, journals—appear regularly at fixed intervals. Unlike newspapers and magazines, which typically appear daily, weekly, or monthly, printed scholarly and professional journals usually are issued no more than about four times a year. Also unlike newspapers and magazines, most print journals are paginated continuously throughout each annual volume—that is, if the first issue for a year ends on page 130, the second issue begins on page 131 and so forth.

The works-cited-list entry for an article in a scholarly journal with continuous pagination, like that for a book, has three main divisions:

> Author's name. "Title of the article." Publication
> information.

Here is an example:

```
Henderson, Andrea. "Passion and Fashion in Joanna
      Baillie's 'Introductory Discourse.'" PMLA 112
      (1997): 198-213.
```

Author's Name. In general, follow the recommendations for citing names of authors of books (6.6.1). Take the author's name from the beginning or the end of the article. Reverse the name for alphabetizing, and put a period after it.

```
Henderson, Andrea.
```

Title of the Article. In general, follow the recommendations for titles given in 3.8. State the full title of the article, enclosed in quotation marks (not underlined). Unless the title has its own concluding punctuation (e.g., a question mark), put a period before the closing quotation mark.

```
Henderson, Andrea. "Passion and Fashion in Joanna
      Baillie's 'Introductory Discourse.'"
```

Publication Information. In general, after the title of the article, give the journal title (underlined), the volume number, the year of publication (in parentheses), a colon, the inclusive page numbers, and a period.

```
Henderson, Andrea. "Passion and Fashion in Joanna
      Baillie's 'Introductory Discourse.'" PMLA 112
      (1997): 198-213.
```

Take these facts directly from the journal, not from a source such as a bibliography. Publication information usually appears on the cover or title page of a journal. Omit any introductory article in the title of an English-language journal (*William and Mary Quarterly*, not *The William and Mary Quarterly*), but retain articles before titles of non-English-language journals (*La rivista dalmatica*). For newspaper titles, see 6.7.5. Do not precede the volume number with the word *volume* or the abbreviation *vol.*

In addition to the volume number, the journal's cover or title page may include an issue number ("Number 3") or a month or season before the year ("January 1998," "Fall 1997"). In general, the issues of a journal published in a single year compose one volume. Volumes are usually numbered in continuous sequence—each new volume is numbered one higher than its predecessor—while the numbering of issues starts over with 1 in each new volume. You may ignore the issue number and the month or season if the journal's pages are numbered continuously throughout each annual volume.

Some scholarly journals do not use continuous pagination throughout the annual volume, however, and some use issue numbers alone without volume numbers; on citing articles in such journals, see 6.7.2–3. Entries for newspapers and magazines do not require volume numbers (see 6.7.5–6).

The inclusive page numbers cited should encompass the complete article, not just the portion you used. (Specific page references appear parenthetically at appropriate places in your text; see ch. 7.) Follow the rules for writing inclusive numbers in 3.10.6. Write the page reference for the first page exactly as shown in the source ("198–232," "A32–34," "lxii–lxv"). If an article is not printed on consecutive pages—if, for example, after beginning on page 6 it skips to page 10—write only the first page number and a plus sign, leaving no intervening space: "6+." (See examples in 6.7.5–6.)

Here are some additional examples of the basic entry for an article in a scholarly journal with continuous pagination:

> Bauer, Karin. "Tabus der Wahrnehmung: Reflexion und Geschichte in Herta Müllers Prosa." German Studies Review 19 (1996): 257-78.
>
> Bradford, James H., and Paulette Côté-Laurence. "An Application of Artificial Intelligence to the Choreography of Dance." Computers and the Humanities 29 (1995): 233-40.
>
> Koen, Jacoba. "Ficción e historia en Historia de Mayta de Mario Vargas Llosa." Revista de estudios hispánicos 21 (1994): 189-95.
>
> Weinert, Regina. "The Role of Formulaic Language in Second Language Acquisition: A Review." Applied Linguistics 16 (1995): 180-205.
>
> Yeh, Michelle. "The 'Cult of Poetry' in Contemporary China." Journal of Asian Studies 55 (1996): 51-80.

Sometimes additional information is required in an entry. This list shows most of the possible components of an entry for an article in a periodical and the order in which they are normally arranged:

1. Author's name
2. Title of the article
3. Name of the periodical
4. Series number or name (if relevant; see 6.7.4)
5. Volume number (for a scholarly journal)
6. Issue number (if needed; see 6.7.2–3)
7. Date of publication
8. Page numbers
9. Supplementary information (see esp. 6.7.12)

The rest of 6.7 explains how to cite these items.

6.7.2   An Article in a Scholarly Journal That Pages Each Issue Separately

Some scholarly journals do not number pages continuously throughout an annual volume but begin each issue on page 1. For such journals, you must include the issue number to identify the source. Add a
period and the issue number directly after the volume number, without any intervening space: "14.2" signifies volume 14, issue 2; "10.3–4,"
volume 10, issues 3 and 4 combined.

> Barthelme, Frederick. "Architecture." Kansas Quarterly
>   13.3-4 (1981): 77-80.
>
> Forti-Lewis, Angelica. "Virginia Woolf, Dacia Maraini e
>   Una stanza per noi: L'autocoscienza politica e il
>   testo." Rivista di studi italiani 12.2 (1994):
>   29-47.
>
> Vickeroy, Laurie. "The Politics of Abuse: The
>   Traumatized Child in Toni Morrison and Marguerite
>   Duras." Mosaic 29.2 (1996): 91-109.

6.7.3   An Article in a Scholarly Journal That Uses Only Issue Numbers

Some scholarly journals do not use volume numbers at all, numbering
issues only. Treat the issue numbers of such journals as you would volume numbers.

> Chauí, Marilena. "Política cultural, cultura política."
>   Brasil 13 (1995): 9-24.

> Stein, Karen. "Margaret Atwood's Modest Proposal: The
> Handmaid's Tale." Canadian Literature 148 (1996):
> 57-73.

6.7.4   An Article in a Scholarly Journal with More Than One Series

Some scholarly journals have been published in more than one series.
In citing a journal with numbered series, write the number (an arabic
digit with the appropriate ordinal suffix: *2nd, 3rd, 4th,* etc.) and the
abbreviation *ser.* between the journal title and the volume number (see
the sample entry for Striner). For a journal divided into a new series
and an original series, indicate the series with *ns* or *os* before the volume number (see the entry for Spivack).

> Spivack, Kathleen. "Between Two Cultures." Kenyon
> Review ns 17.3-4 (1995): 118-26.
> Striner, Richard. "Political Newtonism: The Cosmic
> Model of Politics in Europe and America." William
> and Mary Quarterly 3rd ser. 52 (1995): 583-608.

6.7.5   An Article in a Newspaper

To cite an English-language newspaper, give the name as it appears on
the masthead but omit any introductory article (*New York Times,* not
The New York Times). Retain articles before the names of non-English-
language newspapers (*Le monde*). If the city of publication is not
included in the name of a locally published newspaper, add the city
in square brackets, not underlined, after the name: "*Star-Ledger*
[Newark]." For nationally published newspapers (e.g., *Wall Street Journal, Chronicle of Higher Education*), you need not add the city of publication. Next give the complete date—day, month, and year. Abbreviate
the names of all months except May, June, and July (see 8.2). Do not
give the volume and issue numbers even if they are listed. If an edition
is named on the masthead, add a comma after the date and specify the
edition (e.g., *natl. ed., late ed.*). It is important to state the edition
because different editions of the same issue of a newspaper contain
different material. Follow the edition—or the date if there is no edition
—with a colon and the page number or numbers. Here are examples
illustrating how an article appeared in different sections of two editions of the *New York Times* on the same day:

> Rosenberg, Geanne. "Electronic Discovery Proves an
> Effective Legal Weapon." New York Times 31 Mar.
> 1997, late ed.: D5.

> Rosenberg, Geanne. "Electronic Discovery Proves an
> Effective Legal Weapon." New York Times 31 Mar.
> 1997, natl. ed.: C5.

If each section is paginated separately, include the appropriate section number or letter. Determining how to indicate a section can sometimes be complicated. The *New York Times*, for example, is currently divided in two distinct ways, depending on the day of the week, and each system calls for a different method of indicating section and page. Monday through Saturday there are normally several sections, labeled *A, B, C, D,* and so forth, and paginated separately, and the section letter is part of each page number: "A1," "B1," "C5," "D3." Whenever the pagination of a newspaper includes a section designation, copy the page number or numbers exactly.

DAILY *NEW YORK TIMES*

> Smith, Dinitia. "After Four Centuries, Still Gaining
> Devotees." New York Times 22 Apr. 1997, late ed.:
> C12.

The Sunday edition contains numerous individually paged sections (covering the arts and entertainment, business, sports, travel, and so on) designated not by letters but by numbers ("Section 4," "Section 7"), which do not appear as parts of the page numbers. Whenever the section designation of a newspaper is not part of the pagination, put a comma after the date (or after the edition, if any) and add the abbreviation *sec.*, the appropriate letter or number, a colon, and the page number or numbers.

SUNDAY *NEW YORK TIMES*

> Goldberg, Vicki. "Photographing a Mexico Where Silence
> Reigned." New York Times 23 Mar. 1997, late ed.,
> sec. 2: 39+.

Newspaper articles are often not printed on consecutive pages—for example, an article might begin on page 1, then skip to page 16. For such articles, write only the first page number and a plus sign, leaving no intervening space: "6+," "C3+." The parenthetical reference in the text tells readers the exact page from which material was used.

Here are some additional examples from different newspapers:

> Heller, Scott. "From 'Pagan Rites' to Gifts in the
> Parlor: How America Reinvented Christmas."

Chronicle of Higher Education 20 Dec. 1996:
A13-14.

Melikian, Souren. "Fading Charms of 1700s Decor."
International Herald Tribune 24-25 May
1997: 8.

Perrier, Jean-Louis. "La vie artistique de Budapest
perturbée par la loi du marché." Le monde 26 Feb.
1997: 28.

Taylor, Paul. "Keyboard Grief: Coping with Computer-
Caused Injuries." Globe and Mail [Toronto] 27 Dec.
1993: A1+.

Trachtenberg, Jeffrey A. "What's in a Movie Soundtrack?
Catchy Tunes and Big Business." Wall Street
Journal 1 Apr. 1994, eastern ed.: B1.

6.7.6   An Article in a Magazine

To cite a magazine published every week or every two weeks, give the
complete date (beginning with the day and abbreviating the month,
except for May, June, and July), followed by a colon and the inclusive
page numbers of the article. If the article is not printed on consecutive
pages, write only the first page number and a plus sign, leaving no
intervening space. Do not give the volume and issue numbers even if
they are listed.

Kaminer, Wendy. "The Last Taboo." New Republic 14 Oct.
1996: 24+.

Peterson, Thane, and Julia Flynn. "A Beautiful Market
for Art." Business Week 30 Dec. 1996-6 Jan. 1997:
148-49.

To cite a magazine published every month or every two months,
give the month or months and year. If the article is not printed on consecutive pages, write only the first page number and a plus sign, leaving no intervening space. Do not give the volume and issue numbers
even if they are listed.

Csikszentmihalyi, Mihaly. "The Creative Personality."
Psychology Today July-Aug. 1996: 36-40.

Giovannini, Joseph. "Fred and Ginger Dance in Prague."
Architecture Feb. 1997: 52-62.

Perlstein, Rick. "Abridged Too Far?" Lingua Franca
    Apr.-May 1997: 23-24.

6.7.7   A Review

To cite a review, give the reviewer's name and the title of the review (if
there is one); then write *Rev. of* (neither underlined nor enclosed in
quotation marks), the title of the work reviewed, a comma, the word
by, and the name of the author. If the work of someone other than an
author—say, an editor, a translator, or a director—is under review, use
the appropriate abbreviation, such as *ed.*, *trans.*, or *dir.*, instead of *by*.
For a review of a performance, add pertinent information about the
production (see the sample entry for Tommasini). If more than one
work is under review, list titles and authors in the order given at the
beginning of the review (see the entry for Bordewich). Conclude the
entry with the name of the periodical and the rest of the publication
information.

If the review is titled but unsigned, begin the entry with the title of
the review and alphabetize by that title (see the entry for "The Cooling
of an Admiration"). If the review is neither titled nor signed, begin the
entry with *Rev. of* and alphabetize it under the title of the work
reviewed (see the entry for *Anthology of Danish Literature*).

Rev. of Anthology of Danish Literature, ed. F. J.
    Billeskov Jansen and P. M. Mitchell. Times
    Literary Supplement 7 July 1972: 785.
Bordewich, Fergus M. Rev. of Once They Moved like the
    Wind: Cochise, Geronimo, and the Apache Wars, by
    David Roberts, and Brave Are My People: Indian
    Heroes Not Forgotten, by Frank Waters. Smithsonian
    Mar. 1994: 125-31.
"The Cooling of an Admiration." Rev. of Pound/Joyce:
    The Letters of Ezra Pound to James Joyce, with
    Pound's Essays on Joyce, ed. Forrest Read. Times
    Literary Supplement 6 Mar. 1969: 239-40.
Kauffmann, Stanley. "A New Spielberg." Rev. of
    Schindler's List, dir. Steven Spielberg. New
    Republic 13 Dec. 1993: 30.
Rosenthal, Bernice Glatzer. Rev. of Wagner and Russia,
    by Rosamund Bartlett. Slavic Review 55 (1996):
    505-06.

Smarr, Janet Levarie. Rev. of <u>Authorizing Petrarch</u>, by
William J. Kennedy. <u>Journal of English and</u>
<u>Germanic Philology</u> 95 (1996): 544-46.

Tommasini, Anthony. "In G. and S., Better to Have More
Words, Less Voice." Rev. of <u>The Mikado</u>, by William
S. Gilbert and Arthur Sullivan. New York City
Opera. New York State Theater, New York. <u>New York</u>
<u>Times</u> 10 Mar. 1997, late ed.: C22.

Updike, John. "Fine Points." Rev. of <u>The New Fowler's</u>
<u>Modern English Usage</u>, ed. R. W. Burchfield. <u>New</u>
<u>Yorker</u> 23-30 Dec. 1996: 142-49.

6.7.8   An Abstract in an Abstracts Journal

An abstracts journal publishes summaries of journal articles and of
other literature. If you are citing an abstract, begin the entry with the
publication information for the original work. Then add the relevant
information for the journal from which you derived the abstract—title
(underlined), volume number, year (in parentheses), and either item
number or page number, depending on how the journal presents its
abstracts. Of the journals cited below, *Current Index to Journals in Education, Psychological Abstracts*, and *Sociological Abstracts* use item numbers; *Dissertation Abstracts* and *Dissertation Abstracts International* use
page numbers. Precede an item number with the word *item*. If the title
of the journal does not make clear that you are citing an abstract, add
the word *Abstract*, neither underlined nor in quotation marks, immediately after the original publication information (see the sample entry
for McCabe).

Dissertation Abstracts International (DAI) has a long and complex
history that might affect the way you cite an abstract in it. Before volume 30 (1969), *Dissertation Abstracts International* was titled *Dissertation
Abstracts (DA)*. From volume 27 to volume 36, *DA* and *DAI* were paginated in two series: *A*, for humanities and social sciences, and *B*,
for sciences and engineering. With volume 37, *DAI* added a third
separately paginated section: *C*, for abstracts of European dissertations; in 1989, this section expanded its coverage to include institutions
throughout the world. (For recommendations on citing dissertations
themselves, see 6.6.26–27.)

Bishop, Bernadine. "<u>Othello</u>: Faith and Doubt in the
Good Object." <u>British Journal of Psychotherapy</u> 12
(1996): 323-31. <u>Psychological Abstracts</u> 84 (1997):
item 7118.

191

Gans, Eric L. "The Discovery of Illusion: Flaubert's Early Works, 1835-1837." Diss. Johns Hopkins U, 1967. DA 27 (1967): 3046A.

McCabe, Donald L. "Faculty Responses to Academic Dishonesty: The Influence of Student Honor Codes." Research in Higher Education 34 (1993): 647-58. Abstract. Current Index to Journals in Education 26 (1994): item EJ471017.

Pozas Horcasitas, Ricardo. "La libertad en el ensayo político de Octavio Paz." Revista mexicana de sociología 58.2 (1996): 3-20. Sociological Abstracts 45 (1997): item 9701489.

Stephenson, Denise R. "Blurred Distinctions: Emerging Forms of Academic Writing." Diss. U of New Mexico, 1996. DAI 57 (1996): 1700A.

6.7.9 An Anonymous Article

If no author's name is given for the article you are citing, begin the entry with the title. Ignore any initial *A, An,* or *The* when you alphabetize the entry.

"The Decade of the Spy." Newsweek 7 Mar. 1994: 26-27.
"Dubious Venture." Time 3 Jan. 1994: 64-65.

6.7.10 An Editorial

If you are citing a signed editorial, begin with the author's name, give the title, and then add the descriptive label *Editorial*, neither underlined nor enclosed in quotation marks. Conclude with the appropriate publication information. If the editorial is unsigned, begin with the title and continue in the same way.

"Death of a Writer." Editorial. New York Times 20 Apr. 1994, late ed.: A18.
Zuckerman, Mortimer B. "Are Order and Liberty at Odds?" Editorial. US News and World Report 5 Aug. 1996: 64.

6.7.11 A Letter to the Editor

To identify a letter to the editor, add the descriptive label *Letter* after the name of the author, but do not underline the word or place it in quotation marks.

```
Ozick, Cynthia. Letter. Partisan Review 57 (1990):
    493-94.
Safer, Morley. Letter. New York Times 31 Oct. 1993,
    late ed., sec. 2: 4.
```

Identify a published response to a letter as "Reply to letter of [. . .]," adding the name of the writer of the initial letter. Do not underline this phrase or place it in quotation marks.

```
Lipking, Lawrence. Reply to letter of Edgar C.
    Knowlton, Jr. PMLA 112 (1997): 124.
```

6.7.12 A Serialized Article

To cite a serialized article or a series of related articles published in more than one issue of a periodical, include all bibliographic information in one entry if each installment has the same author and title.

```
Gillespie, Gerald. "Novella, Nouvelle, Novelle, Short
    Novel? A Review of Terms." Neophilologus 51
    (1967): 117-27, 225-30.
Meserole, Harrison T., and James M. Rambeau. "Articles
    on American Literature Appearing in Current
    Periodicals." American Literature 52 (1981):
    688-705; 53 (1981): 164-80, 348-59.
```

If the installments bear different titles, list each one separately. You may include a brief supplementary description at the end of the entry to indicate that the article is part of a series.

```
Dillon, Sam. "Special Education Absorbs School
    Resources." New York Times 7 Apr. 1994, late ed.:
    A1+. Pt. 2 of a series, A Class Apart: Special
    Education in New York City, begun 6 Apr. 1994.
Richardson, Lynda. "Minority Students Languish in
    Special Education System." New York Times
    6 Apr. 1994, late ed.: A1+. Pt. 1 of a series,
```

> A Class Apart: Special Education in New York
> City.
> Winerip, Michael. "A Disabilities Program That 'Got out
> of Hand.'" New York Times 8 Apr. 1994, late ed.:
> A1+. Pt. 3 of a series, A Class Apart: Special
> Education in New York City, begun 6 Apr. 1994.

6.7.13 A Special Issue

To cite an entire special issue of a journal, begin the entry with the name of the person who edited the issue (if given on the title page), followed by a comma and the abbreviation *ed.* Next give the title of the special issue (underlined), followed by "Spec. issue of" and the name of the journal (underlined). Conclude the entry with the journal's volume number as well as the issue number (separated by a period: "9.1"), the year of publication (in parentheses), a colon, a space, and the complete pagination of the issue. If the issue has been republished in book form, add the relevant information about the book (city of publication, publisher, and date of publication).

> Appiah, Kwame Anthony, and Henry Louis Gates, Jr., eds.
> Identities. Spec. issue of Critical Inquiry 18.4
> (1992): 625-884. Chicago: U of Chicago P, 1995.
> Perret, Delphine, and Marie-Denise Shelton, eds. Maryse
> Condé. Spec. issue of Callaloo 18.3 (1995):
> 535-711.
> Topographies. Spec. issue of MLN 109.3 (1994): 345-581.

If you are citing one article from a special issue and wish to indicate complete publication information about the issue, use the following form:

> Makward, Christiane. "Reading Maryse Condé's Theater."
> Maryse Condé. Ed. Delphine Perret and Marie-Denise
> Shelton. Spec. issue of Callaloo 18.3 (1995):
> 681-89.

6.7.14 An Article in a Microform Collection of Articles

If you are citing an article that was provided by a reference source such as *Newsbank,* which selects periodical articles and makes them available on microfiche, begin the entry with the original publication information. Then add the relevant information concerning the microform from which you derived the article—title of source (underlined), volume number, year (in parentheses), and appropriate identifying numbers ("fiche 42, grids 5–6").

> Chapman, Dan. "Panel Could Help Protect Children."
>
>   Winston-Salem Journal 14 Jan. 1990: 14. Newsbank:
>
>   Welfare and Social Problems 12 (1990): fiche 1,
>
>   grids A8-11.

6.7.15 An Article Reprinted in a Loose-Leaf Collection of Articles

If you are citing a reprinted article that was provided by an information service such as the Social Issues Resources Series (SIRS), which selects articles from periodicals and publishes them in loose-leaf volumes, each dedicated to a specific topic, begin the entry with the original publication information. Then add the relevant information for the loose-leaf volume in which the article is reprinted, treating the volume like a book (see 6.6)—title (underlined), name of editor (if any), volume number (if any), city of publication, publisher, year of publication, and article number (preceded by the abbreviation *Art.*).

> Edmondson, Brad. "AIDS and Aging." American
>
>   Demographics Mar. 1990: 28+. The AIDS Crisis. Ed.
>
>   Eleanor Goldstein. Vol. 2. Boca Raton: SIRS, 1991.
>
>   Art. 24.

6.8 CITING MISCELLANEOUS PRINT AND NONPRINT SOURCES

6.8.1 A Television or Radio Program

The information in an entry for a television or radio program usually appears in the following order:

1. Title of the episode or segment, if appropriate (in quotation marks)
2. Title of the program (underlined)
3. Title of the series, if any (neither underlined nor in quotation marks)
4. Name of the network
5. Call letters and city of the local station (if any)
6. Broadcast date

For instance, among the examples below, "Frederick Douglass" is an episode of the program *Civil War Journal*; *The Buccaneers* is a program in the series Masterpiece Theatre. Use a comma between the call letters and the city ("KETC, St. Louis"). A period follows each of the other items. For the inclusion of other information that may be pertinent (e.g., performers, director, narrator, number of episodes), see the sample entries.

> The Buccaneers. By Edith Wharton. Adapt. Maggie Wadey.
>   Perf. Mira Sorvino, Alison Elliott, and Carla
>   Gugino. 3 episodes. Masterpiece Theatre. Introd.
>   Russell Baker. PBS. WGBH, Boston. 27 Apr.-11 May
>   1997.
>
> Don Giovanni. By Wolfgang Amadeus Mozart. Perf. James
>   Morris, Bryn Terfel, and Carol Vaness. Cond. Yakov
>   Kreizberg. Lyric Opera of Chicago. Nuveen-Lyric
>   Opera of Chicago Radio Network. WFMT, Chicago. 8
>   June 1996.
>
> "Frankenstein: The Making of the Monster." Great Books.
>   Narr. Donald Sutherland. Writ. Eugenie Vink. Dir.
>   Jonathan Ward. Learning Channel. 8 Sept. 1993.
>
> "Frederick Douglass." Civil War Journal. Narr. Danny
>   Glover. Dir. Craig Haffner. Arts and Entertainment
>   Network. 6 Apr. 1993.
>
> Passion. By Stephen Sondheim. Dir. James Lapine. Perf.
>   Donna Murphy, Jere Shea, and Marin Mazzie. Amer.
>   Playhouse. PBS. WNET, New York. 7 Mar. 1996.
>
> "Shakespearean Putdowns." Narr. Robert Siegel and Linda
>   Wertheimer. All Things Considered. Natl. Public
>   Radio. WNYC, New York. 6 Apr. 1994.
>
> "Yes . . . but Is It Art?" Narr. Morley Safer. Sixty
>   Minutes. CBS. WCBS, New York. 19 Sept. 1993.

If your reference is primarily to the work of a particular individual, cite that person's name before the title.

> Wadey, Maggie, adapt. The Buccaneers. By Edith Wharton.
>   Perf. Mira Sorvino, Alison Elliott, and Carla
>   Gugino. 3 episodes. Masterpiece Theatre. Introd.

> Russell Baker. PBS. WGBH, Boston. 27 Apr.-11 May
> 1997.
> Welles, Orson, dir. The War of the Worlds. By H. G.
> Wells. Adapt. Howard Koch. Mercury Theatre on the
> Air. CBS Radio. WCBS, New York. 30 Oct. 1938.

If you are citing a transcript of a program, add the description *Transcript* at the end of the entry.

> "Shakespearean Putdowns." Narr. Robert Siegel and Linda
> Wertheimer. All Things Considered. Natl. Public
> Radio. WNYC, New York. 6 Apr. 1994. Transcript.

See 6.8.7 for interviews on television and radio programs; see also 6.8.2–3 for sound, film, and video recordings, 6.8.4 for performances, and 6.9.8a for television and radio programs online or on CD-ROM.

6.8.2   A Sound Recording

In an entry for a commercially available recording, which person is cited first (e.g., the composer, conductor, or performer) depends on the desired emphasis. List the title of the recording (or the titles of the works included), the artist or artists, the manufacturer ("Capitol"), and the year of issue (if the year is unknown, write *n.d.*). Place a comma between the manufacturer and the date; periods follow the other items. If you are not using a compact disc, indicate the medium, neither underlined nor enclosed in quotation marks, before the manufacturer's name: *Audiocassette* (see the sample entry for Marsalis), *Audiotape* (reel-to-reel tape; see the entry for Wilgus), or *LP* (long-playing record; see the entry for Ellington).

In general, underline titles of recordings (*Romances for Saxophone*), but do not underline or enclose in quotation marks the titles of musical compositions identified only by form, number, and key (see the entry for Abbado). You may wish to indicate, in addition to the year of issue, the date of recording (see the entry for Ellington).

> Abbado, Claudio, cond. Symphony no. 6 in F, op. 68, and
> Symphony no. 8 in F, op. 93. By Ludwig van
> Beethoven. Vienna Philharmonic. Deutsche
> Grammophon, 1987.
> Ellington, Duke, cond. Duke Ellington Orch. First
> Carnegie Hall Concert. Rec. 23 Jan. 1943. LP.
> Prestige, 1977.

> Gabriel, Peter. <u>Passion: Music for</u> The Last Temptation
> of Christ<u>, a Film by Martin Scorsese</u>. Geffen,
> 1989.
>
> Holiday, Billie. <u>The Essence of Billie Holiday</u>.
> Columbia, 1991.
>
> Joplin, Scott. <u>Treemonisha</u>. Perf. Carmen Balthrop,
> Betty Allen, and Curtis Rayam. Houston Grand Opera
> Orch. and Chorus. Cond. Gunther Schuller. Deutsche
> Grammophon, 1976.
>
> Marsalis, Branford. <u>Romances for Saxophone</u>. English
> Chamber Orch. Cond. Andrew Litton. Audiocassette.
> CBS, 1986.
>
> Simon, Paul. <u>The Rhythm of the Saints</u>. Warner Bros.,
> 1990.
>
> Sondheim, Stephen. <u>Passion</u>. Orch. Jonathan Tunick.
> Perf. Donna Murphy, Jere Shea, and Marin Mazzie.
> Cond. Paul Gemignani. Angel, 1994.

If you are citing a specific song, place its title in quotation marks.

> Bartoli, Cecilia. "Les filles de Cadix." By Pauline
> Viardot. <u>Chant d'amour</u>. London, 1996.
>
> Bono, Brian Eno, the Edge, and Luciano Pavarotti. "Miss
> Sarajevo." <u>Pavarotti and Friends for the Children
> of Bosnia</u>. London, 1996.
>
> Gabriel, Peter. "A Different Drum." Perf. Gabriel,
> Shankar, and Youssou N'Dour. <u>Passion: Music for
> The Last Temptation of Christ</u>, a Film by Martin
> Scorsese. Geffen, 1989.
>
> Holiday, Billie. "God Bless the Child." Rec. 9 May
> 1941. <u>The Essence of Billie Holiday</u>. Columbia,
> 1991.
>
> Simon, Paul, and Milton Nascimento. "Spirit Voices."
> <u>The Rhythm of the Saints</u>. Warner Bros., 1990.

Treat a spoken-word recording as you would a musical recording.
Begin with the speaker, the writer, or the production director, depending on the desired emphasis. You may add the original publication
date of the work immediately after the title.

Burnett, Frances Hodgson. The Secret Garden. 1911. Read
    by Helena Bonham Carter. Audiocassette. Penguin-
    High Bridge, 1993.

Kingsley, Ben, narr. Buddhism. Audiocassette.
    Carmichael, 1994.

Shakespeare, William. Othello. Perf. Laurence Olivier,
    Maggie Smith, Frank Finley, and Derek Jacobi. Dir.
    John Dexter. LP. RCA Victor, 1964.

Welles, Orson, dir. The War of the Worlds. By H. G.
    Wells. Adapt. Howard Koch. Mercury Theatre on the
    Air. Rec. 30 Oct. 1938. LP. Evolution, 1969.

Whitman, Walt. "America." In Their Own Voices: A
    Century of Recorded Poetry. Rhino, 1996.

Do not underline or enclose in quotation marks the title of a private or archival recording or tape. Include the date recorded (if known) and the location and identifying number of the recording.

Wilgus, D. K. Southern Folk Tales. Rec. 23-25 Mar.
    1965. Audiotape. U of California, Los Angeles,
    Archives of Folklore. B.76.82.

In citing the libretto, the booklet, the liner notes, or other material accompanying a recording, give the author's name, the title of the material (if any), and a description of the material ("Libretto"). Then provide the usual bibliographic information for a recording.

Colette. Libretto. L'enfant et les sortilèges. Music by
    Maurice Ravel. Orch. National Bordeaux-Aquitaine.
    Cond. Alain Lombard. Valois, 1993.

Lawrence, Vera Brodsky. "Scott Joplin and Treemonisha."
    Booklet. Treemonisha. By Scott Joplin. Deutsche
    Grammophon, 1976.

Lewiston, David. Liner notes. The Balinese Gamelan:
    Music from the Morning of the World. LP. Nonesuch,
    n.d.

See 6.9.8b for sound recordings online.

6.8.3   A Film or Video Recording

A film entry usually begins with the title, underlined, and includes the director, the distributor, and the year of release. You may include other data that seem pertinent—such as the names of the writer, performers, and producer—between the title and the distributor.

> It's a Wonderful Life. Dir. Frank Capra. Perf. James
> Stewart, Donna Reed, Lionel Barrymore, and Thomas
> Mitchell. RKO, 1946.
>
> Like Water for Chocolate [Como agua para chocolate].
> Screenplay by Laura Esquivel. Dir. Alfonso Arau.
> Perf. Lumi Cavazos, Marco Lombardi, and Regina
> Torne. Miramax, 1993.

If you are citing the contribution of a particular individual, begin with that person's name.

> Chaplin, Charles, dir. Modern Times. Perf. Chaplin and
> Paulette Goddard. United Artists, 1936.
>
> Jhabvala, Ruth Prawer, adapt. A Room with a View. By E.
> M. Forster. Dir. James Ivory. Prod. Ismail
> Merchant. Perf. Maggie Smith, Denholm Eliot,
> Helena Bonham Carter, and Daniel Day-Lewis.
> Cinecom Intl., 1985.
>
> Mifune, Toshiro, perf. Rashomon. Dir. Akira Kurosawa.
> Daiei, 1950.
>
> Rota, Nino, composer. Juliet of the Spirits [Giulietta
> degli spiriti]. Dir. Federico Fellini. Perf.
> Giulietta Masina. Rizzoli, 1965.

Cite a videocassette, videodisc, slide program, or filmstrip like a film, but include the original release date (if relevant) and the medium, neither underlined nor enclosed in quotation marks, before the name of the distributor.

> Don Carlo. By Giuseppe Verdi. Dir. Franco Zeffirelli.
> Perf. Luciano Pavarotti and Samuel Ramey. La Scala
> Orch. and Chorus. Cond. Riccardo Muti.
> Videocassette. EMI, 1994.

Hitchcock, Alfred, dir. Suspicion. Perf. Cary Grant and
    Joan Fontaine. 1941. Videodisc. Turner, 1995.

It's a Wonderful Life. Dir. Frank Capra. Perf. James
    Stewart, Donna Reed, Lionel Barrymore, and Thomas
    Mitchell. 1946. Videocassette. Republic, 1996.

Looking at Our Earth: A Visual Dictionary. Sound
    filmstrip. Natl. Geographic Educ. Services, 1992.

Mifune, Toshiro, perf. Rashomon. Dir. Akira Kurosawa.
    1950. Videocassette. Embassy, 1986.

Renoir, Jean, dir. Grand Illusion [La grande illusion].
    Perf. Jean Gabin and Erich von Stroheim. 1938.
    Videodisc. Voyager, 1987.

See 6.9.8c for films or film clips online or on CD-ROM.

6.8.4   A Performance

An entry for a performance (play, opera, ballet, concert) usually begins
with the title, contains facts similar to those given for a film (see 6.8.3),
and concludes with the site of the performance (usually the theater
and city, separated by a comma and followed by a period) and the date
of the performance.

Hamlet. By William Shakespeare. Dir. John Gielgud.
    Perf. Richard Burton. Shubert Theatre, Boston. 4
    Mar. 1964.

Medea. By Euripides. Trans. Alistair Elliot. Dir.
    Jonathan Kent. Perf. Diana Rigg. Longacre Theatre,
    New York. 7 Apr. 1994.

The River. Chor. Alvin Ailey. Dance Theater of Harlem.
    New York State Theater, New York. 15 Mar. 1994.

The Siege of Paris. Marionettes of the Cooperativa
    Teatroarte Cuticchio. Sylvia and Danny Kaye
    Playhouse, New York. 22 Mar. 1997.

Les vêpres siciliennes. By Giuseppe Verdi. Libretto by
    Eugène Scribe and Charles Duveyrier. Dir. Federico
    Tiezzi. Cond. John Nelson. Perf. Daniela Dessì,
    David Kuebler, and Ferruccio Furlanetto. Teatro
    dell' Opera, Rome. 17 Jan. 1997.

If you are citing the contribution of a particular individual or group, begin with the appropriate name.

> Ars Musica Antiqua. <u>In Praise of Women: Music by Women
> Composers from the Twelfth through the Eighteenth
> Centuries</u>. Concert. Scotch Plains Public Lib., NJ.
> 5 Apr. 1994.
>
> Freni, Mirella, soprano. <u>Fedora</u>. By Umberto Giordano.
> Cond. Roberto Abbado. Metropolitan Opera.
> Metropolitan Opera House, New York. 26 Apr. 1997.
>
> Joplin, Scott. <u>Treemonisha</u>. Dir. Frank Corsaro. Cond.
> Gunther Schuller. Perf. Carmen Balthrop, Betty
> Allen, and Curtis Rayam. Houston Grand Opera.
> Miller Theatre, Houston. 18 May 1975.
>
> Rigg, Diana, perf. <u>Medea</u>. By Euripides. Trans. Alistair
> Elliot. Dir. Jonathan Kent. Longacre Theatre, New
> York. 7 Apr. 1994.

For television and radio broadcasts of performances, see 6.8.1; for sound recordings of performances, see 6.8.2; for video recordings of performances, see 6.8.3.

6.8.5   A Musical Composition

To cite a musical composition, begin with the composer's name. Underline the title of an opera, a ballet, or a piece of instrumental music identified by name (*Symphonie fantastique*), but do not underline or enclose in quotation marks the form, number, and key when used to identify an instrumental composition.

> Beethoven, Ludwig van. Symphony no. 8 in F, op. 93.
> Berlioz, Hector. <u>Symphonie fantastique</u>, op. 14.
> Wagner, Richard. <u>Götterdämmerung</u>.

Treat a published score, however, like a book. Give the title, underlined, as it appears on the title page, and capitalize the abbreviations *no.* and *op.*

> Beethoven, Ludwig van. <u>Symphony No. 8 in F, Op. 93</u>.
> Mainz: Schott, 1989.

If you wish to indicate when a musical composition was written, add the date immediately after the title.

202

```
Beethoven, Ludwig van. Symphony No. 8 in F, Op. 93.
     1812. Mainz: Schott, 1989.
```

See 6.8.2 for sound recordings of musical compositions, 6.8.1 for television and radio programs of music, and 6.8.4 for performances of music.

6.8.6   A Work of Art

To cite a work of art, state the artist's name first. In general, underline the title of a painting or sculpture. Name the institution that houses the work (e.g., a museum) or, for a work in a private collection, the individual who owns it, and follow the name by a comma and the city.

```
Bearden, Romare. The Train. Carole and Alex Rosenberg
     Collection, New York.
Bernini, Gianlorenzo. Ecstasy of St. Teresa. Santa
     Maria della Vittoria, Rome.
Rembrandt van Rijn. Aristotle Contemplating the Bust of
     Homer. Metropolitan Museum of Art, New York.
```

If you use a photograph of the work, indicate not only the institution or private owner and the city but also the complete publication information for the source in which the photograph appears, including the page, slide, figure, or plate number, whichever is relevant.

```
Cassatt, Mary. Mother and Child. Wichita Art Museum,
     Wichita. American Painting: 1560-1913. By John
     Pearce. New York: McGraw, 1964. Slide 22.
El Greco. Burial of Count Orgaz. San Tomé, Toledo.
     Renaissance Perspectives in Literature and the
     Visual Arts. By Murray Roston. Princeton:
     Princeton UP, 1987. 274.
```

If you wish to indicate when a work of art was created, add the date immediately after the title.

```
Bearden, Romare. The Train. 1974. Carole and Alex
     Rosenberg Collection, New York.
Cassatt, Mary. Mother and Child. 1890. Wichita Art
     Museum, Wichita. American Painting: 1560-1913. By
     John Pearce. New York: McGraw, 1964. Slide 22.
```

See 6.9.8d for photographs of works of art online or on CD-ROM.

6.8.7   An Interview

For purposes of documentation, there are three kinds of interviews:

- Published or recorded interviews
- Interviews broadcast on television or radio
- Interviews conducted by the researcher

Begin with the name of the person interviewed. If the interview is part of a publication, recording, or program, enclose the title of the interview, if any, in quotation marks; if the interview was published independently, underline the title. If the interview is untitled, use the descriptive label *Interview*, neither underlined nor enclosed in quotation marks. The interviewer's name may be added if known and pertinent to your work (see the sample entries for Blackmun and Updike). Conclude with the appropriate bibliographic information.

Blackmun, Harry. Interview with Ted Koppel and Nina
      Totenberg. Nightline. ABC. WABC, New York. 5 Apr.
      1994.

Fellini, Federico. "The Long Interview." Juliet of
      the Spirits. Ed. Tullio Kezich. Trans. Howard
      Greenfield. New York: Ballantine, 1966. 17-64.

Gordimer, Nadine. Interview. New York Times 10 Oct.
      1991, late ed.: C25.

Lansbury, Angela. Interview. Off-Camera: Conversations
      with the Makers of Prime-Time Television. By
      Richard Levinson and William Link. New York:
      Plume-NAL, 1986. 72-86.

Updike, John. Interview with Scott Simon. Weekend
      Edition. Natl. Public Radio. WBUR, Boston.
      2 Apr. 1994.

Wolfe, Tom. Interview. The Wrong Stuff: American
      Architecture. Dir. Tom Bettag. Videocassette.
      Carousel, 1983.

To cite an interview that you conducted, give the name of the person interviewed, the kind of interview (*Personal interview, Telephone interview*), and the date.

```
Pei, I. M. Personal interview. 22 July 1993.
Poussaint, Alvin F. Telephone interview. 10 Dec. 1990.
```

See 6.9.8e for interviews online.

6.8.8 A Map or Chart

In general, treat a map or chart like an anonymous book (6.6.11), but add the appropriate descriptive label (*Map*, *Chart*).

```
Japanese Fundamentals. Chart. Hauppauge: Barron, 1992.
Washington. Map. Chicago: Rand, 1995.
```

See 6.9.8f for maps online. For guidance on how to cite such sources as dioramas, flash cards, games, globes, kits, and models, see Eugene B. Fleischer, *A Style Manual for Citing Microform and Nonprint Media* (Chicago: ALA, 1978).

6.8.9 A Cartoon

To cite a cartoon, state the cartoonist's name; the title of the cartoon (if any), in quotation marks; and the descriptive label *Cartoon*, neither underlined nor enclosed in quotation marks. Conclude with the usual publication information.

```
Chast, Roz. Cartoon. New Yorker 7 Apr. 1997: 72.
Trudeau, Garry. "Doonesbury." Cartoon. Star-Ledger
     [Newark] 2 Apr. 1997: 19.
```

See 6.9.8g for cartoons online.

6.8.10 An Advertisement

To cite an advertisement, state the name of the product, company, or institution that is the subject of the advertisement, followed by the descriptive label *Advertisement*, neither underlined nor enclosed in quotation marks. Conclude with the usual publication information.

```
Air Canada. Advertisement. CNN. 1 Apr. 1997.
The Fitness Fragrance by Ralph Lauren. Advertisement.
     GQ Apr. 1997: 111-12.
```

See 6.9.8h for advertisements online.

6.8.11   A Lecture, a Speech, an Address, or a Reading

In a citation of an oral presentation, give the speaker's name; the title of the presentation (if known), in quotation marks; the meeting and the sponsoring organization (if applicable); the location; and the date. If there is no title, use an appropriate descriptive label (*Address, Lecture, Keynote speech, Reading*), neither underlined nor enclosed in quotation marks.

> Atwood, Margaret. "Silencing the Scream." Boundaries of the Imagination Forum. MLA Convention. Royal York Hotel, Toronto. 29 Dec. 1993.
>
> Hyman, Earle. Reading of <u>Othello</u>, by William Shakespeare. Symphony Space, New York. 28 Mar. 1994.
>
> Terkel, Studs. Address. Conf. on Coll. Composition and Communication Convention. Palmer House, Chicago. 22 Mar. 1990.

6.8.12   A Manuscript or Typescript

To cite a manuscript or a typescript, state the author, the title or a description of the material (e.g., *Notebook*), the form of the material (*ms.* for a manuscript, *ts.* for a typescript), and any identifying number assigned to it. Give the name and location of any library or other research institution housing the material.

> Chaucer, Geoffrey. <u>The Canterbury Tales</u>. Harley ms. 7334. British Lib., London.
>
> <u>Octovian</u>. Ms. 91. Dean and Chapter Lib., Lincoln, Eng.
>
> Salviati, Lionardo. <u>Poetica d'Aristotile parafrasata e comentata</u>. Ms. 2.2.11. Biblioteca Nazionale Centrale, Firenze.
>
> Smith, Sonia. "Shakespeare's Dark Lady Revisited." Unpublished essay, 1998.
>
> Twain, Mark. Notebook 32, ts. Mark Twain Papers. U of California, Berkeley.

See 6.9.8i for manuscripts and working papers online.

6.8.13   A Letter or Memo

As bibliographic entries, letters fall into three general categories:

- Published letters
- Unpublished letters in archives
- Letters received by the researcher

Treat a published letter like a work in a collection (see 6.6.7), adding the date of the letter and the number (if the editor assigned one).

> Woolf, Virginia. "To T. S. Eliot." 28 July 1920. Letter
>   1138 of The Letters of Virginia Woolf. Ed. Nigel
>   Nicolson and Joanne Trautmann. Vol. 2. New York:
>   Harcourt, 1976. 437-38.

If you use more than one letter from a published collection, however, provide a single entry for the entire work and cite the letters individually in the text, following the form recommended for cross-references in works-cited lists (see 6.6.10).

In citing an unpublished letter, follow the guidelines for manuscripts and typescripts (see 6.8.12).

> Benton, Thomas Hart. Letter to Charles Fremont.
>   22 June 1847. John Charles Fremont Papers.
>   Southwest Museum Lib., Los Angeles.

Cite a letter that you received as follows:

> Morrison, Toni. Letter to the author. 19 Mar. 1997.

Treat memos similarly: give the name of the writer of the memo, a description of the memo that includes the recipient, and the date of the document. Any title of the memo should be enclosed in quotation marks and placed immediately after the writer's name.

> Cahill, Daniel J. Memo to English dept. fac., Brooklyn
>   Technical High School, Brooklyn, NY. 29 May 1996.

See 6.9.8j for e-mail communications.

6.8.14   A Legal Source

The citation of legal documents and law cases may be complicated. If your work requires many such references, consult the most recent edition of *The Blue Book: A Uniform System of Citation* (Cambridge: Harvard Law Rev. Assn.), an indispensable guide in this field.

In general, do not underline or enclose in quotation marks the titles of laws, acts, and similar documents in either the text or the list of works cited (Declaration of Independence, Constitution of the United States, Taft-Hartley Act). Such titles are usually abbreviated, and the works are cited by sections. The years are added if relevant. Although lawyers and legal scholars adopt many abbreviations in their citations, use only familiar abbreviations when writing for a more general audience (see ch. 8).

```
21 US Code. Sec. 1401a. 1988.
US Const. Art. 1, sec. 1.
```

Note that references to the United States Code, which is often abbreviated *USC*, begin with the title number; in the above USC entry, for example, title 21 refers to laws concerned with food and drugs. Alphabetize USC entries under *United States Code* even if you use the abbreviation. When including more than one reference to the code, list the individual entries in numerical order.

If you are citing an act, state the name of the act, its Public Law number, the date it was enacted, and its Statutes at Large cataloging number. Use the abbreviations *Pub. L.* for Public Law and *Stat.* for Statutes at Large.

```
Pesticide Monitoring Improvements Act of 1988. Pub. L.
    100-418. 23 Aug. 1988. Stat. 102.1412.
```

Names of law cases are similarly abbreviated ("Brown v. Board of Ed.," for the case of Oliver Brown versus the Board of Education of Topeka, Kansas), but the first important word of each party's name is always spelled out. Names of cases, unlike those of laws, are underlined in the text but not in bibliographic entries. In citing a case, include, in addition to the names of the first plaintiff and the first defendant, the volume, name (not underlined), and page (in that order) of the law report cited; the name of the court that decided the case; and the year of the decision. Once again, considerable abbreviation is the norm. The following citation, for example, refers to page 755 of volume 148 of the *United States Patent Quarterly*, dealing with the case of Stevens against the National Broadcasting Company, which was decided by the California Superior Court in 1966.

```
Stevens v. National Broadcasting Co. 148 USPQ 755. CA
    Super. Ct. 1966.
```

6.9   CITING ELECTRONIC PUBLICATIONS

6.9.1   Introduction

Scholars need to evaluate the quality of any source before using and citing it. Assessing electronic resources is a particular challenge. Whereas the print publications scholars depend on are generally issued by reputable journal and book publishers that accept account-ability for the quality and reliability of the works they distribute, rela-tively few electronic publications currently have comparable authority. Most materials on the Internet, for instance, are not refereed; many are self-published.

Just as scholars strive to avoid using print sources based on incor-rect or outdated information, on poor logic, and on narrow opinions, so they must be concerned about the accuracy, reputation, and cur-rency of the electronic sources they use. Scholars should therefore rely on sources that were written or created by authors or editors whose credentials can be verified as authoritative; that were approved by referees or sponsored by known bodies such as educational institu-tions or professional organizations; and that clearly indicate the dates, where relevant, of composition, revision, and electronic publica-tion. (Jan Alexander and Marsha Tate, reference librarians at the Wolf-gram Memorial Library of Widener University, have created a World Wide Web site collecting useful information and materials on the eval-uation of electronic resources; see <http://www.science.widener.edu/ ~withers/webeval.htm>.)

Citations of electronic sources and those of print sources should accomplish the same ends and have analogous formats. Both types of citations identify a source and give sufficient information to allow a reader to locate it. Yet each type requires a different kind and amount of information to fulfill these objectives. Print culture has developed standard reference tools (library catalogs, bibliographies, and so on) for locating published works. Electronic media, in contrast, so far lack agreed-on means of organizing works. Moreover, electronic texts are not as fixed and stable as their print counterparts. References to elec-tronic works therefore must provide more information than print cita-tions generally offer.

Publication Dates. Most bibliographic references to printed works contain only one date of publication; rare exceptions are an article reprinted in a collection of essays (see 6.6.7) and a republished book (see 6.6.17). A citation of an electronic work, however, may require two and sometimes more publication dates to be identified fully. Since electronic texts can be readily altered, any accessed version of an online source is potentially different from any past or future version and therefore must be considered unique. Typically, then, a citation for an online text contains the date assigned to the document in the source as well as the date on which the researcher accessed the document. If the work originally had a print existence, it may be necessary to give the date of the original print publication, if provided, along with the date of electronic publication and the date of access, for the document may have been different at each stage. On citing dates for publications on CD-ROM, diskette, and magnetic tape, see 6.9.5.

Uniform Resource Locator (URL). The most efficient way to find an online publication at present is through its network address, or uniform resource locator (URL). This edition of the *MLA Style Manual and Guide to Scholarly Publishing* recommends including URLs in citations of online works. Since addresses can change, however, and their length and complexity can result in transcription errors, it is crucial to be as accurate as possible in supplying not only URLs but also other identifying information (e.g., author's name, title), so that the reader who cannot locate the material through the stated address might be able to find it with a network searching tool. Moreover, since Internet sites and resources sometimes disappear altogether, you should consider downloading or printing the material you use, so that you can verify it if it is inaccessible later. Enclose URLs in angle brackets. If a URL must be divided between two lines, break it only after a slash; do not introduce a hyphen at the break or allow your word-processing program to do so. Give the complete address, including the access-mode identifier (*http, ftp, gopher, telnet, news*) and, after the first single slash, any relevant path and file names:

```
<http://www.princeton.edu/~lancelot/>
```

The recommendations in this section largely tend to treat sources for which a considerable amount of relevant publication information is available. In truth, though, many sources do not supply all desired information, for few standards currently govern the presentation of electronic publications—for instance, many texts do not include reference markers, such as paragraph numbers, so it is difficult if not impossible to direct a reader to the exact location of the material you are citing. Thus, while aiming for comprehensiveness, writers must often settle for citing whatever information is available to them.

These recommendations are aimed not at specialists in academic computing but primarily at scholars in the field of literature and language who use ideas and facts from electronic sources to complement those derived from traditional print sources. Moreover, since this section cannot possibly cover all materials available in electronic form, its emphasis, like that of the rest of this manual, is on refereed, authoritative sources as well as on historical texts. Needless to say, this edition's recommendations on citing electronic works are necessarily not definitive and will doubtless change as technology, scholarly uses of electronic materials, and electronic publication practices evolve.

This section discusses citing the following kinds of electronic publications: online scholarly projects, reference databases, and professional and personal sites (6.9.2); online books (6.9.3); articles in online periodicals (6.9.4); publications on CD-ROM, diskette, and magnetic tape (6.9.5); works published in more than one medium (6.9.6); publications in an indeterminate medium (6.9.7); and other electronic sources (e.g., audiovisual materials, manuscripts and working papers, e-mail communications, online postings; 6.9.8).

6.9.2   An Online Scholarly Project, Reference Database, or Professional or Personal Site

The typical entry for a complete online scholarly project or reference database consists of the following items:

1. Title of the project or database (underlined)
2. Name of the editor of the project or database (if given)
3. Electronic publication information, including version number (if relevant and if not part of the title), date of electronic publication or of the latest update, and name of any sponsoring institution or organization
4. Date of access and electronic address

If you cannot find some of this information, cite what is available.

> Britannica Online. Vers. 97.1.1. Mar. 1997.
>   Encyclopaedia Britannica. 29 Mar. 1997 <http://
>   www.eb.com/>.
> The Charrette Project. Ed. Karl D. Uitti. 1994. Dept.
>   of Romance Langs., Princeton U. 7 Feb. 1997
>   <http://www.princeton.edu/~lancelot/>.
> The Cinderella Project. Ed. Michael N. Salda. Vers.
>   1.0. Feb. 1995. De Grummond Children's Lit.
>   Research Collection, U of Southern Mississippi. 18
>   Mar. 1997 <http://www-dept.usm.edu/~engdept/
>   cinderella/cinderella.html>.
> Duecento: Repertorio elettronico della poesia italiana
>   dalle origini a Dante. Ed. Francesco Bonomi. 1996.

Si.Lab, Firenze. 19 Apr. 1997 <http://
www.silab.it/frox/200/pwhomita.htm>.

<u>Early Modern English Dictionaries Database</u>. Ed. Ian
Lancashire. Apr. 1996. U of Toronto. 1 May 1997
<http://www.chass.utoronto.ca:8080/english/emed/
patterweb.html>.

<u>The Electronic Text Center</u>. Ed. David Seaman. May 1995.
Alderman Lib., U of Virginia. 14 Feb. 1997
<http://etext.lib.virginia.edu/>.

<u>Nineteenth-Century German Stories</u>. Ed. Robert Godwin-
Jones. 1994. Foreign Lang. Dept., Virginia
Commonwealth U. 10 Jan. 1997 <http://
www.fln.vcu.edu/menu.html>.

<u>Project Bartleby</u>. Ed. Steven van Leeuwen. Dec. 1995.
Columbia U. 5 Jan. 1997 <http://www.columbia.edu/
acis/bartleby/>.

<u>Romantic Chronology</u>. Ed. Laura Mandell and Alan Liu.
Oct. 1996. U of California, Santa Barbara. 22 Nov.
1996 <http://humanitas.ucsb.edu/projects/pack/
rom-chrono/chrono.htm>.

<u>Sí, España</u>. Ed. José Félix Barrio. Vers. 2.0. Oct.
1996. Embassy of Spain, Ottawa. 3 Dec. 1996
<http://www.docuweb.ca/SiSpain/>.

<u>Victorian Women Writers Project</u>. Ed. Perry Willett.
Apr. 1997. Indiana U. 26 Apr. 1997 <http://
www.indiana.edu/~letrs/vwwp/>.

To cite a poem, short story, or similar short work within a
scholarly project, begin the citation with the author's name and, in
quotation marks, the title of the work. Continue with the relevant
information for the project, the date of access, and the URL; be sure to
give the URL of the short work rather than that of the project if they
are different. (On citing the texts of printed books in online scholarly
projects, see 6.9.3.)

Giacomo da Lentini. "Amor è uno desio che ven da core."
<u>Duecento: Repertorio elettronico della poesia
italiana dalle origini a Dante</u>. Ed. Francesco
Bonomi. 1996. Si.Lab, Firenze. 19 Apr. 1997
<http://www.silab.it/frox/200/tree128.htm>.

    Hoffmann, Heinrich. "Struwwelpeter." Trans. Mark Twain.
        Nineteenth-Century German Stories. Ed. Robert
        Godwin-Jones. 1994. Foreign Lang. Dept., Virginia
        Commonwealth U. 10 Jan. 1997 <http://
        www.fln.vcu.edu/struwwel/twpete.html>.

If you are citing a translator, say, instead of the author, place the appropriate abbreviation (*trans.*) after the name, and give the author's name after the title, preceded by the word *By*.

    Twain, Mark, trans. "Struwwelpeter." By Heinrich
        Hoffmann. Nineteenth-Century German Stories. Ed.
        Robert Godwin-Jones. 1994. Foreign Lang. Dept.,
        Virginia Commonwealth U. 10 Jan. 1997 <http://
        www.fln.vcu.edu/struwwel/twpete.html>.

To cite an anonymous article or other short anonymous material from a reference database, begin the citation with the title of the article or material, in quotation marks. Continue with the relevant information for the project, the date of access, and the URL; be sure to give the URL of the article if it differs from that of the database.

    "Catalán." Sí, España. Ed. José Félix Barrio. Vers.
        2.0. Oct. 1996. Embassy of Spain, Ottawa. 3 Dec.
        1996 <http://www.docuweb.ca/SiSpain/spanish/
        language/language/catalan.html>.
    "Fresco." Britannica Online. Vers. 97.1.1. Mar. 1997.
        Encyclopaedia Britannica. 29 Mar. 1997 <http://
        www.eb.com:180>.
    "Selected Seventeenth-Century Events." Romantic
        Chronology. Ed. Laura Mandell and Alan Liu. Oct.
        1996. U of California, Santa Barbara. 22 Nov. 1996
        <http://humanitas.ucsb.edu/projects/pack/
        rom-chrono/chrono1a.htm>.

To document an online professional or personal site, begin the entry with the name of the person who created it (if given and relevant), reversed for alphabetizing and followed by a period. Continue with the title of the site (underlined) or, if there is no title, with a description such as *Home page* (neither underlined nor in quotation marks); the name of any institution or organization associated with the site; the date of access; and the electronic address.

> Dawe, James. <u>Jane Austen Page</u>. 15 Sept. 1997 <http://
> nyquist.ee.ualberta.ca/~dawe/austen.html>.
> Lancashire, Ian. Home page. 1 May 1997 <http://
> www.chass.utoronto.ca:8080/~ian/index.html>.
> <u>Portuguese Language Page</u>. U of Chicago. 1 May 1997
> <http://humanities.uchicago.edu/romance/port/>.

6.9.3   An Online Book

The texts of some printed books are available online, independently or as part of scholarly projects. The typical entry for a complete online book available independently consists of the following items:

1. Author's name (if given). If only an editor, a compiler, or a translator is identified, cite that person's name, followed by the appropriate abbreviation (*ed., comp., trans.*).

2. Title of the work (underlined)

3. Name of the editor, compiler, or translator (if relevant); see, for example, the entries for Hawthorne and Pascal.

4. Publication information. If the version of the text online has not been published before, give the date of electronic publication and the name of any sponsoring institution or organization. State the publication facts about the original print version if they are given in the source (e.g., city of publication, name of publisher, year of publication). You may add in brackets relevant information not stated in the source; see the entry for Pascal.

5. Date of access and electronic address

If you cannot find some of this information, cite what is available.

> Austen, Jane. <u>Pride and Prejudice</u>. Ed. Henry
> Churchyard. 1996. 10 Sept. 1997 <http://
> www.pemberley.com/janeinfo/pridprej.html>.
> Barsky, Robert F. <u>Noam Chomsky: A Life of Dissent</u>.
> Cambridge: MIT P, 1997. 8 May 1997 <http://
> mitpress.mit.edu/chomsky/>.
> Douglass, Frederick. <u>Narrative of the Life of Frederick
> Douglass</u>. Boston, 1845. 30 Jan. 1997 <gopher://
> gopher.vt.edu:10010/02/73/1>.

Emerson, Ralph Waldo. Essays: First Series. 1841. 12
    Feb. 1997 <ftp://ftp.books.com/ebooks/NonFiction/
    Philosophy/Emerson/history.txt>.

Hawthorne, Nathaniel. Twice-Told Tales. Ed. George
    Parsons Lathrop. Boston: Houghton, 1883. 1 Mar.
    1997 <http://www.tiac.net/users/eldred/nh/
    ttt.html>.

Pascal, Blaise. Pensées. Trans. W. F. Trotter. [1910.]
    29 Apr. 1997 <gopher://gopher.vt.edu:10010/02/
    130/1>.

To cite a book that is a part of a scholarly project, give the five
items listed above, as relevant, but follow the information about the
printed book with the publication information for the project (see
6.9.2). Be sure to end with the URL of the book, not that of the project,
if they differ.

Chrétien de Troyes. Le Chevalier de la Charrette. Ed.
    Alfred Foulet and Karl D. Uitti. Paris: Bordas,
    1989. The Charrette Project. Ed. Uitti. 1994.
    Dept. of Romance Langs., Princeton U. 7 Feb. 1997
    <http://www.princeton.edu/~lancelot/
    lancelo2.html>.

Cinderella. New York: Wrigley, [c. 1800-25]. The
    Cinderella Project. Ed. Michael N. Salda. Vers.
    1.0. Feb. 1995. De Grummond Children's Lit.
    Research Collection, U of Southern Mississippi.
    18 Mar. 1997 <http://www-dept.usm.edu/~engdept/
    cinderella/cind2.html>.

Keats, John. Poetical Works. 1884. Project Bartleby.
    Ed. Steven van Leeuwen. Dec. 1995. Columbia U. 5
    Jan. 1997 <http://www.columbia.edu/acis/bartleby/
    keats/>.

Nesbit, E[dith]. Ballads and Lyrics of Socialism.
    London, 1908. Victorian Women Writers Project. Ed.
    Perry Willett. Apr. 1997. Indiana U. 26 Apr. 1997
    <http://www.indiana.edu/~letrs/vwwp/nesbit/
    ballsoc.html>.

Robinson, Mary. <u>Sappho and Phaon</u>. London, 1796. <u>The
    Electronic Text Center</u>. Ed. David Seaman. May
    1995. Alderman Lib., U of Virginia. 14 Feb. 1997
    <http://etext.lib.virginia.edu/britpo/sappho/
    sappho.html>.

If you are citing a part of an online book, place the title or name of
the part between the author's name and the title of the book. If the
part is a work like a poem or an essay, place its title in quotation
marks. If the part is a standard division of the book, such as an introduction or a preface, do not place the title in quotation marks or
underline it; see the entry for Barsky. Be sure to give the URL of the
specific part instead of that of the book if they differ.

Barsky, Robert F. Introduction. <u>Noam Chomsky: A Life of
    Dissent</u>. By Barsky. Cambridge: MIT P, 1997. 8 May
    1997 <http://mitpress.mit.edu/chomsky/intro.html>.
Emerson, Ralph Waldo. "Self-Reliance." <u>Essays: First
    Series</u>. 1841. 12 Feb. 1997 <ftp://ftp.books.com/
    ebooks/NonFiction/Philosophy/Emerson/history.txt>.
Hawthorne, Nathaniel. "Dr. Heidegger's Experiment."
    <u>Twice-Told Tales</u>. Ed. George Parsons Lathrop.
    Boston: Houghton, 1883. 1 Mar. 1997 <http://
    www.tiac.net/users/eldred/nh/dhe.html>.
Keats, John. "Ode on a Grecian Urn." <u>Poetical Works</u>.
    1884. <u>Project Bartleby</u>. Ed. Steven van Leeuwen.
    Dec. 1995. Columbia U. 5 Jan. 1997 <http://
    www.columbia.edu/acis/bartleby/keats/
    keats54.html>.
Nesbit, E[dith]. "Marching Song." <u>Ballads and Lyrics of
    Socialism</u>. London, 1908. <u>Victorian Women Writers
    Project</u>. Ed. Perry Willett. Apr. 1997. Indiana U.
    26 Apr. 1997 <http://www.indiana.edu/~letrs/vwwp/
    nesbit/ballsoc.html#p9>.

6.9.4   An Article in an Online Periodical

Periodical publications online include scholarly journals, newspapers,
and magazines; works and other materials within such publications
include articles, reviews, editorials, and letters to the editor. In general,

follow the recommendations in 6.7 for citing parts of print periodicals, modifying them as appropriate to the electronic source. The typical entry for a work in an online periodical consists of the following items:

1. Author's name (if given)

2. Title of the work or material (if any; a review or letter to the editor may be untitled), in quotation marks

3. Name of the periodical (underlined)

4. Volume number, issue number, or other identifying number

5. Date of publication

6. The number range or total number of pages, paragraphs, or other sections, if they are numbered

7. Date of access and electronic address

If you cannot find some of this information, cite what is available.

a. An Article in a Scholarly Journal (cf. 6.7.1–4)

> Calabrese, Michael. "Between Despair and Ecstasy: Marco Polo's Life of the Buddha." Exemplaria 9.1 (1997). 4 Apr. 1997 <http://www.clas.ufl.edu/english/ exemplaria/calax.htm>.
>
> Flannagan, Roy. "Reflections on Milton and Ariosto." Early Modern Literary Studies 2.3 (1996): 16 pars. 22 Feb. 1997 <http://unixg.ubc.ca:7001/0/ e-sources/emls/02-3/flanmilt.html>.
>
> McDonald, Henry. "The Narrative Act: Wittgenstein and Narratology." Surfaces 4.4 (1994): 21 pp. Jan. 1997 <gopher://surfaces.umontreal.ca:70/00/ Articles/Ascii/Vol4/A-McDonald.txt>.
>
> Pereira, Edimilson de Almeida. "Survey of African-Brazilian Literature." Callaloo 18.4 (1995): 875-80. 11 Apr. 1997 <http://muse.jhu.edu/journals/ callaloo/v018/18.4de_almeida_pereira9.html>.
>
> Trouille, Mary. "La femme mal mariée: Mme Epinay's Challenge to Julie and Emile." Eighteenth-Century Life 20.1 (1996): 42-66. 27 May 1997 <http:// muse.jhu.edu/journals/eighteenth-century_life/ v020/20.1trouille.html>.

b. An Article in a Newspaper or on a Newswire (cf. 6.7.5)

"Actor Urges Film Preservation." <u>AP Online</u> 10 Mar.
　　1997. 10 Mar. 1997 <http://www.nytimes.com/
　　aponline/e/AP-James-Earl-Jones.html>.

Coates, Steve. "A Dead Language Comes to Life on the
　　Internet." <u>New York Times on the Web</u> 28 Oct.
　　1996. 20 Apr. 1997 <http://www.nytimes.com/web/
　　docsroot/library/cyber/week/1028Latin.html>.

c. An Article in a Magazine (cf. 6.7.6)

Landsburg, Steven E. "Who Shall Inherit the Earth?"
　　<u>Slate</u> 1 May 1997. 2 May 1997 <http://slate.com/
　　Economics/97-05-01/Economics.asp>.

McCracken, Elizabeth. "Desiderata." <u>Bold Type</u> Mar.
　　1997. 7 Mar. 1997 <http://www.bookwire.com/
　　boldtype/mccracken/read.article$197>.

d. A Review (cf. 6.7.7)

Angelo, Gretchen V. Rev. of <u>The Book of the Body
　　Politic</u>, by Christine de Pizan. <u>Bryn Mawr Medieval
　　Review</u> 96.1.7 (1996). 26 Jan. 1997 <gopher://
　　gopher.lib.virginia.edu:70/00/alpha/bmmr/v96/
　　96-1-7>.

Debrix, François. "Impassable Passages: Derrida,
　　Aporia, and the Question of Politics." Rev. of
　　<u>Derrida and the Political</u>, by Richard Beardsworth.
　　<u>Postmodern Culture</u> 7.3 (1997): 13 pars. 27 Aug.
　　1997 <http://www.iath.virginia.edu/pmc/
　　current.issue/review-1.597.html>.

Jenkins, James J. "Comprehending Comprehension."
　　Rev. of <u>Language Comprehension as Structure</u>,
　　by M. A. Gernsbacher. <u>Psycoloquy</u> 95.6.26
　　(1995): 5 pars. 3 Feb. 1997 <gopher://
　　gopher.lib.virginia.edu:70/00/alpha/psyc/1995/
　　psyc.95.6.26.language-comprehension.6.jenkins>.

Tommasini, Anthony. "In G. and S., Better to Have More
　　Words, Less Voice." Rev. of <u>The Mikado</u>, by William

> S. Gilbert and Arthur Sullivan. New York City
> Opera. New York State Theater, New York. New York
> Times on the Web 10 Mar. 1997. 10 Mar. 1997
> <http://www.nytimes.com/yr/mo/day/news/arts/
> mikado-opera-review.html>.

e. An Abstract (cf. 6.7.8)

> Kelly, Kathleen Coyne. "Malory's Body Chivalric."
> Arthuriana 6.4 (1996): 52-71. Abstract. 27 Aug.
> 1997 <http://dcwww.mediasvcs.smu.edu/Arthuriana/
> Abstract/Ab_list3.htm>.

f. An Editorial (cf. 6.7.10)

> "Agents of Influence." Editorial. Christian Science
> Monitor 11 Mar. 1997. 11 Mar. 1997 <http://
> www.csmonitor.com/todays_paper/graphical/today/
> edit/edit.1.html>.

g. A Letter to the Editor (cf. 6.7.11)

> Festinger, Trudy. Letter. New York Times on the Web 11
> Mar. 1997. 11 Mar. 1997 <http://www.nytimes.com/
> yr/mo/day/letters/lfesti.html>.

6.9.5   A Publication on CD-ROM, Diskette, or Magnetic Tape

Citations for publications on CD-ROM, diskette, and magnetic tape are similar to those for print sources, with the following important differences.

Publication Medium. Many works are published in more than one format (e.g., print, online, CD-ROM), and the works may not be the same in each. When you cite a publication on CD-ROM, diskette, or magnetic tape, it is important to state the publication medium in order to differentiate the source from its possible print or online counterpart.

Vendor's Name. The persons or groups responsible for supplying the information in publications on CD-ROM, diskette, and magnetic tape are sometimes also the publishers of the works. But many information providers choose instead to lease the data to vendors (e.g., Information Access, SilverPlatter, UMI-Proquest) for distribution. It is important to state the vendor's name in your works-cited list, if it is given in your source, because the information provider may have leased electronic versions of the data to more than one vendor, and the versions may not be identical (see 6.9.5b).

Publication Dates. Many databases published on CD-ROM, diskette, or magnetic tape are updated regularly (e.g., annually, quarterly). Updates add information and may also correct or otherwise alter information that previously appeared in the database. Therefore, a works-cited-list entry for material derived from such a database commonly contains the date of the document used, as indicated in the source, as well as the publication date (or date of the most recent updating) of the database (see 6.9.5b).

The sections below contain recommendations for citing nonperiodical publications on CD-ROM, diskette, or magnetic tape (6.9.5a), materials from periodically published databases on CD-ROM (6.9.5b), and multidisc publications (6.9.5c).

a. A Nonperiodical Publication on CD-ROM, Diskette, or Magnetic Tape. Many publications on CD-ROM, diskette, or magnetic tape are issued as books are—that is, without a plan to update or otherwise revise the work regularly. Cite a nonperiodical publication on CD-ROM, diskette, or magnetic tape as you would a book, but add a description of the medium of publication. Since the information provider and the publisher are usually the same for such publications, no vendor's name appears, and only one publication date is given. The typical works-cited-list entry for the source consists of the following items:

1. Author's name (if given). If only an editor, a compiler, or a translator is identified, cite that person's name, followed by the appropriate abbreviation (*ed., comp., trans.*).
2. Title of the publication (underlined)
3. Name of the editor, compliler, or translator (if relevant)
4. Publication medium (*CD-ROM, Diskette,* or *Magnetic tape*)
5. Edition, release, or version (if relevant)
6. Place of publication
7. Name of the publisher
8. Date of publication

If you cannot find some of this information, cite what is available.

```
Braunmuller, A. R., ed. Macbeth. By William
     Shakespeare. CD-ROM. New York: Voyager, 1994.
English Poetry Full-Text Database. Magnetic tape.
     Rel. 2. Cambridge, Eng.: Chadwyck-Healey, 1993.
Le Robert électronique. CD-ROM. Paris: Robert, 1992.
Thiesmeyer, Elaine C., and John E. Thiesmeyer. Editor:
     A System for Checking Usage, Mechanics,
     Vocabulary, and Structure. Diskette. Vers. 5.2.
     New York: MLA, 1996.
```

If publication information for a printed source or printed analogue is indicated, begin the citation with that information.

```
Aristotle. The Complete Works of Aristotle: The Revised
     Oxford Translation. Ed. Jonathan Barnes. 2 vols.
     Princeton: Princeton UP, 1984. CD-ROM. Clayton:
     Intelex, 1994.
The Oxford English Dictionary. 2nd ed. CD-ROM. New
     York: Oxford UP, 1992.
```

If you are citing only a part of the work, state which part. If the part is a book-length work, underline the title; if the part is a shorter work like an article, an essay, a poem, or a short story, enclose the title in quotation marks. If the source supplies page numbers, paragraph numbers, screen numbers, or some other kind of section numbers, state their total if the numbering starts over with each part (see the entry for Rodes), but state the range of the numbers in the part if a single numbering encompasses all the parts.

```
"Albatross." The Oxford English Dictionary. 2nd ed.
     CD-ROM. Oxford: Oxford UP, 1992.
"Children's Television Workshop." Encyclopedia of
     Associations. Magnetic tape. Detroit: Gale, 1994.
Coleridge, Samuel Taylor. "Dejection: An Ode." The
     Complete Poetical Works of Samuel Taylor
     Coleridge. Ed. Ernest Hartley Coleridge. Vol. 1.
     Oxford: Clarendon, 1912. 362-68. English Poetry
     Full-Text Database. CD-ROM. Rel. 2. Cambridge,
     Eng.: Chadwyck-Healey, 1993.
```

> "Ellison, Ralph." Disclit: American Authors. Diskette.
>   Boston: Hall, 1991.
> "Parque." Le Robert électronique. CD-ROM. Paris:
>   Robert, 1992.
> Rodes, David S. "The Language of Ambiguity and
>   Equivocation." Macbeth. By William Shakespeare.
>   Ed. A. R. Braunmuller. CD-ROM. New York: Voyager,
>   1994. 5 pp.

b. Material from a Periodically Published Database on CD-ROM. Many periodicals (journals, magazines, newspapers) and periodically published reference works, such as annual bibliographies and collections of abstracts, are published both in print and on CD-ROM as databases or as parts of databases. To cite such a work, begin with the publication data for the printed source or printed analogue, as identified in the CD-ROM publication. If the print version is a book or a pamphlet (see the entry for *Guidelines for Family Television Viewing*), follow the guidelines in 6.6; if the print version is an article in a periodical, follow 6.7. The typical works-cited-list entry consists of the following items:

1. Author's name (if given)
2. Publication information for the printed source or printed analogue (including title and date of print publication)
3. Title of the database (underlined)
4. Publication medium (*CD-ROM*)
5. Name of the vendor (if relevant)
6. Electronic publication date

If you cannot find some of this information, cite what is available.

> Brady, Philip. "Teaching Tu Fu on the Night Shift."
>   College English 57 (1995): 562-69. Abstract. ERIC.
>   CD-ROM. SilverPlatter. Sept. 1996.
> Coates, Steve. "Et Tu, Cybernetica Machina User?" New
>   York Times 28 Oct. 1996, late ed.: D4. New York
>   Times Ondisc. CD-ROM. UMI-Proquest. Dec. 1996.
> Guidelines for Family Television Viewing. Urbana: ERIC
>   Clearinghouse on Elementary and Early Childhood
>   Educ., 1990. ERIC. CD-ROM. SilverPlatter. June
>   1993.

Reese, Elaine, Catherine A. Haden, and Robyn Fivush.
"Mothers, Fathers, Daughters, Sons: Gender
Differences in Autobiographical Reminiscing."
Research on Language and Social Interaction 29
(1996): 27-56. Abstract. Sociofile. CD-ROM.
SilverPlatter. Dec. 1996.

Rodríguez, Miguel Angel. "Teatro de los Puppets:
Diversión y educación." Opinión 6 Sept. 1993: 1D.
Ethnic Newswatch. CD-ROM. Dataware Technologies.
1995.

Russo, Michelle Cash. "Recovering from Bibliographic
Instruction Blahs." RQ: Reference Quarterly 32
(1992): 178-83. Infotrac: Magazine Index Plus. CD-
ROM. Information Access. Dec. 1993.

Stephenson, Denise R. "Blurred Distinctions: Emerging
Forms of Academic Writing." DAI 57 (1996): 1700A.
U of New Mexico, 1996. Dissertation Abstracts
Ondisc. CD-ROM. UMI-Proquest. Dec. 1996.

United States. Cong. House. Committee on the Judiciary.
Report on the Fair Use of Copyrighted Works. 11
Aug. 1992. 102nd Cong. 1st session. Congressional
Masterfile 2. CD-ROM. Congressional Information
Service. Dec. 1996.

c. A Multidisc Publication. If you are citing a CD-ROM publication of
more than one disc, follow the publication medium (*CD-ROM*) either
with the total number of discs or with a specific disc number if you use
material from only one.

Perseus 2.0: Interactive Sources and Studies on Ancient
Greece. CD-ROM. 4 discs. New Haven: Yale UP, 1996.

United States. Dept. of State. Patterns of Global
Terrorism. 1994. National Trade Data Bank. CD-ROM.
Disc 2. US Dept. of Commerce. Dec. 1996.

6.9.6   A Work in More Than One Publication Medium

If the work you are citing is published in various media (e.g., a CD-
ROM and a diskette), specify all the media that constitute the publication or cite only the media you used.

223

> Lancashire, Ian, et al. Using TACT with Electronic
>   Texts: A Guide to Text-Analysis Computing Tools.
>   Book, CD-ROM. Vers. 2.1. New York: MLA, 1996.
> Perseus 1.0: Interactive Sources and Studies on Ancient
>   Greece. CD-ROM, videodisc. New Haven: Yale UP,
>   1992.

or

> Mann, Thomas. Tonio Kröger. Ed. Barry Joe. Using TACT
>   with Electronic Texts: A Guide to Text-Analysis
>   Computing Tools. By Ian Lancashire et al. CD-ROM.
>   Vers. 2.1. New York: MLA, 1996.

6.9.7   A Work in an Indeterminate Medium

If you cannot determine the medium of a source—for example, if you access material through a local network and cannot tell whether the work is stored on the central computer's hard drive (where the contents would be subject to revision) or on a CD-ROM—use the designation *Electronic* for the medium. Give whatever relevant publication information you can, as well as the name of the network or of its sponsoring organization and the date of access.

> Bartlett, John. Familiar Quotations. 9th ed. Boston:
>   Little, 1901. New York: Columbia U, Academic
>   Information Systems, 1995. Electronic.
>   ColumbiaNet, Columbia U. 19 Feb. 1997.
> "Brontë, Emily." Discovering Authors. Vers. 1.0. 1992.
>   Electronic. Nutley Public Lib., NJ. 15 May 1997.

6.9.8   Other Electronic Sources

In general, to document other electronic sources, follow the recommendations in 6.8 on citing miscellaneous print and nonprint sources, modifying the guidelines as appropriate (cf. 6.9.2–7). Some kinds of works need identifying labels (*Interview, Map, Online posting*), neither underlined nor enclosed in quotation marks. In documenting a source such as an online posting or a synchronous communication, try to cite an archival version, if one exists, so that the reader can more easily consult the work.

a. A Television or Radio Program (cf. 6.8.1)

> Fishkin, Fred. "The Search for Dot Com." <u>Boot Camp</u>. CBS
>   Radio. WCBS, New York. 7 Aug. 1997. Transcript. 25
>   Aug. 1997 <http://newsradio88.com/boot/archive/
>   august_1997/august_7.html>.
>
> Gardiner, John Eliot. "The Importance of Beethoven."
>   Interview. <u>Charlie Rose</u>. PBS. 25 July 1996.
>   Transcript. <u>Broadcast News</u>. CD-ROM. Primary Source
>   Media. July 1996. 23 screens.

See also the entry for Trudeau in 6.9.8b.

b. A Sound Recording or Sound Clip (cf. 6.8.2)

> Lecuona, Ernesto. "Malagueña." <u>Lecuona Plays Lecuona</u>.
>   BMG, 1997. 2 Feb. 1997 <http://classicalmus.com/
>   bmgclassics/recording-clip/
>   09026-68671-2_011k08bit.aiff>.
>
> Roosevelt, Franklin D. "Americanism." 1920. <u>American
>   Leaders Speak: Recordings from World War I and the
>   1920 Election</u>. 1996. <u>American Memory</u>. Lib. of
>   Congress, Washington. 19 Mar. 1997 <http://
>   lcweb2.loc.gov/mbrs/nforum/9000024.ram>.
>
> Trudeau, Michelle. "Language of Mothers." <u>All Things
>   Considered</u>. Natl. Public Radio. 31 July 1997. 27
>   Aug. 1997 <http://www.npr.org/ramfiles/
>   970731.atc.15.ram>.

c. A Film or Film Clip (cf. 6.8.3)

> Frakes, Jonathan, dir. <u>Star Trek: First Contact</u>.
>   Paramount, 1996. 5 Dec. 1997 <http://
>   firstcontact.msn.com/db/media/STFCTEA2.mov>.
>
> Kurosawa, Akira, dir. <u>Throne of Blood</u>. 1957. <u>Macbeth</u>.
>   By William Shakespeare. Ed. A. R. Braunmuller. CD-
>   ROM. New York: Voyager, 1994.

d. A Work of Art (cf. 6.8.6)

> Delacroix, Eugène. <u>Death of Ophelia</u>. 1853. Louvre,
>   Paris. <u>Shakespeare Illustrated</u>. Ed. Harry Rusche.

Aug. 1996. Emory U. 7 Apr. 1997 <http://
www.cc.emory.edu/ENGLISH/classes/
Shakespeare_Illustrated/Delacroix.Ophelia.html>.

Holbein, Hans. The Ambassadors. Microsoft Art Gallery:
The Collection of the National Gallery, London.
CD-ROM. Redmond: Microsoft, 1994.

Picasso, Pablo. Les demoiselles d'Avignon. 1907.
Museum of Modern Art, New York. 28 Aug. 1997
<http://www.moma.org/paintsculpt/pages/
picasso.demoiselles.html>.

e. An Interview (cf. 6.8.7)

Kamit, Susan. Interview. Bold Type Mar. 1997. 7 Mar.
1997 <http://www.bookwire.com/boldtype/mccracken/
read.article$199>.

See also the entry for Gardiner in 6.9.8a.

f. A Map (cf. 6.8.8)

"Phoenix, Arizona." Map. U.S. Gazetteer. US Census
Bureau. 13 Mar. 1997 <http://www.census.gov/
cgi-bin/gazetteer>.

g. A Cartoon (cf. 6.8.9)

Toles, Tom. "A Fund Raising Addict?" Cartoon. US News
Online. 18 Aug. 1997. 29 Aug. 1997 <http://
www.usnews.com/usnews/issue/970818/18tole.htm>.

h. An Advertisement (cf. 6.8.10)

Lee Mood Ring. Advertisement. 29 Aug. 1997 <http://
www.leejeans.com/cgi-bin/moodring.cgi>.

i. A Manuscript or Working Paper (cf. 6.8.12)

Cacicedo, Al. "Private Parts: Preliminary Notes for an
Essay on Gender Identity in Shakespeare." Working
paper, n.d. 27 Aug. 1997 <http://www.arts.ubc.ca/
english/iemls/shak/PRIVATE_PARTS.txt>.

```
Gregory, Saint. Frontispiece. Moralia in Job. Ms. 2.
    Bibliothèque Municipale, Dijon. 1995. The
    Electronic Beowulf Project. 1 May 1997 <http://
    www.uky.edu/~kiernan/BL/mss.html>.
```

j. An E-Mail Communication (cf. 6.8.13)

To cite electronic mail, give the name of the writer; the title of the message (if any), taken from the subject line and enclosed in quotation marks; a description of the message that includes the recipient (e.g., "E-mail to the author"); and the date of the message.

```
Boyle, Anthony T. "Re: Utopia." E-mail to Daniel J.
    Cahill. 21 June 1997.
Harner, James L. E-mail to the author. 20 Aug. 1996.
```

k. An Online Posting

To cite a posting to an e-mail discussion list, begin with the author's name and the title of the document (in quotation marks), as given in the subject line, followed by the description *Online posting*, the date when the material was posted, the name of the forum (if known; e.g., Humanist Discussion Group), the date of access, and, in angle brackets, the online address of the list's Internet site or, if no Internet site is known, the e-mail address of the list's moderator or supervisor.

```
Holland, Norman. "Overcoming Depression." Online
    posting. 19 Mar. 1997. Psyart. 21 Mar. 1997.
    <http://www.clas.ufl.edu/ipsa/psyart.htm>.
Merrian, Joanne. "Spinoff: Monsterpiece Theatre."
    Online posting. 30 Apr. 1994. Shaksper: The Global
    Electronic Shakespeare Conference. 30 Oct. 1996
    <http://www.arts.ubc.ca/english/iemls/shak/
    shak-L.html>.
Piez, Wendell. "Sustained Reading vs. Synchronic
    Access." Online posting. 23 Jan. 1997. Humanist
    Discussion Group. 24 Jan. 1997 <http://
    www.princeton.edu/~mccarty/humanist/>.
```

Whenever feasible, cite an archival version of the posting, so that your readers can more easily consult your source.

```
Merrian, Joanne. "Spinoff: Monsterpiece Theatre."
    Online posting. 30 Apr. 1994. Shaksper: The Global
```

```
      Electronic Shakespeare Conference. 27 Aug. 1997
      <http://www.arts.ubc.ca/english/iemls/shak/
      MONSTERP_SPINOFF.txt>.
Piez, Wendell. "Sustained Reading vs. Synchronic
      Access." Online posting. 23 Jan. 1997. Humanist
      Discussion Group. 24 Jan. 1997 <gopher://
      lists.princeton.edu:70/OR369820-373704-/humanist/
      logs/log9701>.
```

To cite a posting to a World Wide Web forum, begin with the author's name and the title of the posting (if there is one), in quotation marks, followed by the description *Online posting*, the date when the material was posted, the name of the forum, the date of access, and, in angle brackets, the electronic address.

```
Jackson, Leroy. Online posting. 11 Nov. 1997. Beyond
      the Dictionary: The Best Books for Writers. 24
      Nov. 1997 <http://forums.nytimes.com/webin/
      WebX?14@^5883@.ee7eda0>.
```

To cite a posting to a Usenet news group, begin with the author's name and the title of the document (in quotation marks), as given in the subject line, followed by the description *Online posting*, the date when the material was posted, the date of access, and, in angle brackets, the name of the news group, with the prefix *news:*.

```
Morton, Paul. "Re: Teaching Portuguese." Online
      posting. 25 Feb. 1997. 28 July 1997
      <news:comp.edu.languages.natural>.
```

To cite a document forwarded within a posting, begin with the name of the writer, the title, and the date of the document. Then give the name of the person who forwarded it, preceded by *Fwd. by*. Conclude the entry with the description *Online posting*, the date of the posting in which the material was forwarded, and the appropriate remaining information for a posting to a discussion list, an online forum, or a news group.

```
Chessid, Estelle. "Women Authors: A New List Now
      Available." 29 June 1997. Fwd. by Kevin Berland.
      Online posting. 2 July 1997. Eighteenth Century
      Interdisciplinary Discussion. 5 July 1997 <http://
      cac.psu.edu/~bcj/c18-1.htm>.
```

l. A Synchronous Communication

To cite a synchronous communication posted in a forum such as a MUD (multiuser domain) or MOO (multiuser domain, object-oriented), give the name of the speaker (if you are citing just one), a description of the event, the date of the event, the forum for the communication (e.g., LinguaMOO), the date of access, and the electronic address, with the prefix *telnet://*.

```
Grigar, Dene. Online defense of dissertation
     "Penelopeia: The Making of Penelope in Homer's
     Story and Beyond." 25 July 1995. LinguaMOO. 25
     July 1995 <telnet://lingua.utdallas.edu:8888>.
```

Whenever feasible, cite an archival version of the communication, so that your readers can more readily consult your source.

```
Grigar, Dene. Online defense of dissertation
     "Penelopeia: The Making of Penelope in Homer's
     Story and Beyond." 25 July 1995. LinguaMOO. 1 May
     1997 <http://wwwpub.utdallas.edu/~cynthiah/
     lingua_archive/phd-defense.txt>.
```

m. Downloaded Computer Software

```
MacCASE. Vers. 1.0. 30 Apr. 1997 <ftp://ftp.adfa.oz.au/
     pub/mac/MacCASE/>.
TACT: Text-Analysis Computing Tools. Vers. 2.1 gamma.
     30 Apr. 1997 <gopher://gopher.epas.utoronto.ca:70/
     11/cch/hum_comp/software/TACT>.
```

229

7

DOCUMENTATION: CITING SOURCES IN THE TEXT

7.1 Parenthetical Documentation and the List of Works Cited

7.2 Information Required in Parenthetical Documentation

7.3 Readability

7.4 Sample References
    7.4.1 Citing an Entire Work
    7.4.2 Citing Part of a Work
    7.4.3 Citing Volume and Page Numbers of a Multivolume Work
    7.4.4 Citing a Work Listed by Title
    7.4.5 Citing a Work by a Corporate Author
    7.4.6 Citing Two or More Works by the Same Author or Authors
    7.4.7 Citing Indirect Sources
    7.4.8 Citing Literary Works
    7.4.9 Citing More Than One Work in a Single Parenthetical Reference
    7.4.10 Citing a Book with Signatures and No Page Numbers

7.5 Using Notes with Parenthetical Documentation
    7.5.1 Content Notes
    7.5.2 Bibliographic Notes

7.1   PARENTHETICAL DOCUMENTATION AND THE LIST OF WORKS CITED

While the list of works cited plays an important role in the acknowledgment of sources (see ch. 6), it does not in itself provide sufficiently detailed and precise documentation. You must indicate to your readers not only what works you drew from but also exactly what you derived from each source and exactly where in the work you found the material. The most practical way to supply this information is to insert a brief parenthetical acknowledgment in your paper wherever you incorporate another's words, facts, or ideas. Usually the author's last name and a page reference are enough to identify the source and the specific location from which you borrowed material.

> Medieval Europe was a place both of "raids, pillages,
> slavery, and extortion" and of "traveling merchants,
> monetary exchange, towns if not cities, and active
> markets in grain" (Townsend 10).

The parenthetical reference "(Townsend 10)" indicates that the quotations come from page 10 of a work by Townsend. Given the author's last name, your readers can find complete publication information for the source in the alphabetically arranged list of works cited that follows the text of your work.

> Townsend, Robert M. The Medieval Village Economy.
> Princeton: Princeton UP, 1993.

The sample references in 7.4 offer recommendations for documenting many other kinds of sources.

7.2 INFORMATION REQUIRED IN PARENTHETICAL DOCUMENTATION

In determining the information needed to document sources accurately, keep the following guidelines in mind.

References in the text must clearly point to specific sources in the list of works cited. The information in your parenthetical references in the text must match the corresponding information in the entries in your list of works cited. For a typical works-cited-list entry, which begins with the name of the author (or editor, translator, or narrator), the parenthetical reference begins with the same name. When the list contains only one work by the author cited, you need give only the author's last name to identify the work: "(Patterson 183–85)." If your list contains more than one author with the same last name, you must add the first initial—"(A. Patterson 183–85)" and "(L. Patterson 230)"—or, if the initial is shared too, the full first name. If two or three names begin the entry, give the last name of each person listed:

"(Rabkin, Greenberg, and Olander vii)." If the work has more than three authors, follow the form in the bibliographic entry: either give the first author's last name followed by *et al.*, without any intervening punctuation—"(Lauter et al. 2425–33)"—or give all the last names. If there is a corporate author, use its name, shortened or in full (see 7.4.5). If the work is listed by title, use the title, shortened or in full (see 7.4.4). If the list contains more than one work by the author, add the cited title, shortened or in full, after the author's last name (see 7.4.6).

Identify the location of the borrowed information as specifically as possible. Give the relevant page number or numbers in the parenthetical reference (see esp. 7.4.2) or, if you cite from more than one volume of a multivolume work, the volume and page numbers (see 7.4.3). In a reference to a literary work, it is helpful to give information other than, or in addition to, the page number—for example, the chapter, book, or stanza number or the numbers of the act, scene, and line (see 7.4.8). You may omit page numbers when citing complete works (see 7.4.1), as well as articles in works arranged alphabetically (like encyclopedias) and, of course, unpaginated sources (see esp. 7.4.4). A page reference is similarly unnecessary if you use a passage from a one-page work.

7.3   READABILITY

Keep parenthetical references as brief—and as few—as clarity and accuracy permit. Give only the information needed to identify a source, and do not add a parenthetical reference unnecessarily. Identify sources by author and, if necessary, title; do not use abbreviations such as *ed.*, *trans.*, and *comp.* after the name. If you are citing an entire work, for example, rather than a specific part of it, the author's name in the text may be the only documentation required. The statement "Booth has devoted an entire book to the subject" needs no parenthetical documentation if the list of works cited includes only one work by Booth. If, for the reader's convenience, you wished to name the book in your text, you could recast the sentence: "Booth has devoted an entire book, *The Rhetoric of Fiction*, to the subject."

Remember that there is a direct relation between what you integrate into your text and what you place in parentheses. If, for example, you include an author's name in a sentence, you need not repeat the name in the parenthetical page citation that follows, provided that the reference is clearly to the work of the author you mention. The paired sentences below illustrate alternative ways of identifying authors. Note that sometimes one version is more concise than the other.

AUTHOR'S NAME IN TEXT

Tannen has argued this point (178-85).

AUTHOR'S NAME IN REFERENCE

This point has already been argued (Tannen 178-85).

AUTHORS' NAMES IN TEXT

Others, like Jakobson and Waugh (210-15), hold the opposite point of view.

AUTHORS' NAMES IN REFERENCE

Others hold the opposite point of view (e.g., Jakobson and Waugh 210-15).

AUTHOR'S NAME IN TEXT

Only Daiches has seen this relation (2: 776-77).

AUTHOR'S NAME IN REFERENCE

Only one scholar has seen this relation (Daiches 2: 776-77).

AUTHOR'S NAME IN TEXT

It may be true, as Robertson maintains, that "in the appreciation of medieval art the attitude of the observer is of primary importance [. . .]" (136).

AUTHOR'S NAME IN REFERENCE

It may be true that "in the appreciation of medieval art the attitude of the observer is of primary importance [. . .]" (Robertson 136).

To avoid interrupting the flow of your writing, place the parenthetical reference where a pause would naturally occur (preferably at the end of a sentence), as near as possible to the material documented. The parenthetical reference precedes the punctuation mark that concludes the sentence, clause, or phrase containing the borrowed material.

Benjamin Franklin states in his Autobiography that he prepared a list of thirteen virtues (135-37).

233

A reference directly after a quotation follows the closing quotation mark.

> In the late Renaissance, Machiavelli contended that human beings were by nature "ungrateful" and "mutable" (1240), and Montaigne thought them "miserable and puny" (1343).

If the quotation, whether of poetry or prose, is set off from the text (see 3.9.2–4), type a space after the concluding punctuation mark of the quotation and insert the parenthetical reference.

> John K. Mahon adds a further insight to our understanding of the War of 1812:
>
> > Financing the war was very difficult at the time. Baring Brothers, a banking firm of the enemy country, handled routine accounts for the United States overseas, but the firm would take on no loans. The loans were in the end absorbed by wealthy Americans at great hazard--also, as it turned out, at great profit to them. (385)

> Elizabeth Bishop's "In the Waiting Room" is rich in evocative detail:
>
> > It was winter. It got dark
> > early. The waiting room
> > was full of grown-up people,
> > arctics and overcoats,
> > lamps and magazines. (6-10)

For guidelines on citing literary works, see 7.4.8.

If you need to document several sources for a statement, you may cite them in a note to avoid unduly disrupting the text (see 7.5). If you quote more than once from the same page within a single paragraph—and no quotation from another source intervenes—you may give a single parenthetical reference after the last quotation.

7.4   SAMPLE REFERENCES

Each of the following sections concludes with a list of the works cited in the examples. Note that the lists for the first five sections (7.4.1–5) do not include more than one work by the same author. On citing two or more works by an author, see 7.4.6.

7.4.1   Citing an Entire Work

If you wish to cite an entire work rather than part of the work, it is usually preferable to include the author's name in the text instead of in a parenthetical reference.

BOOKS (cf. 6.6)

McRae's The Literature of Science includes many examples of this trend.

Paul Lauter and his coeditors have provided a useful anthology of American literature.

Gilbert and Gubar broke new ground on the subject.

ARTICLES IN PERIODICALS (cf. 6.7)

But Andrea Henderson has offered another view.

Diction, according to Anthony Tommasini, is more important than vocal prowess in a singer of Gilbert and Sullivan.

MISCELLANEOUS NONPRINT SOURCES (cf. 6.8)

Kurosawa's Rashomon was one of the first Japanese films to attract a Western audience.

I vividly recall Diana Rigg's interpretation of Medea.

Margaret Atwood's remarks drew an enthusiastic response.

ELECTRONIC SOURCES (cf. 6.9)

William J. Mitchell's City of Bits discusses architecture and urban life in the context of the digital telecommunications revolution.

Stempel has tried to develop a "historical sociology"
of sport in nineteenth-century America.

Michael Joyce was among the first to write fiction in
hypertext.

Joanne Merrian reported on a parody of Shakespeare
performed by the Muppets.

Portuguese Language Page has links to helpful
resources.

Works Cited

Atwood, Margaret. "Silencing the Scream." Boundaries of
the Imagination Forum. MLA Convention. Royal York
Hotel, Toronto. 29 Dec. 1993.

Gilbert, Sandra M., and Susan Gubar. The Madwoman in
the Attic: The Woman Writer and the Nineteenth-
Century Literary Imagination. New Haven: Yale UP,
1979.

Henderson, Andrea. "Passion and Fashion in Joanna
Baillie's 'Introductory Discourse.'" PMLA 112
(1997): 198-213.

Joyce, Michael. Afternoon: A Story. Diskette.
Watertown: Eastgate, 1987.

Kurosawa, Akira, dir. Rashomon. Perf. Toshiro Mifune.
Daiei, 1950.

Lauter, Paul, et al., eds. The Heath Anthology of
American Literature. 2nd ed. 2 vols. Lexington:
Heath, 1994.

McRae, Murdo William, ed. The Literature of Science:
Perspectives on Popular Science Writing. Athens:
U of Georgia P, 1993.

Merrian, Joanne. "Spinoff: Monsterpiece Theatre."
Online posting. 30 Apr. 1994. Shaksper: The Global
Electronic Shakespeare Conference. 27 Aug. 1997
<http://www.arts.ubc.ca/english/iemls/shak/
MONSTERP_SPINOFF.txt>.

Mitchell, William J. City of Bits: Space, Place, and

the Informationbahn. Cambridge: MIT P, 1995. MIT P
Electronic Books. 8 May 1997 <http://
mitpress.mit.edu/City_of_Bits>.

Portuguese Language Page. U of Chicago. 1 May 1997
<http://humanities.uchicago.edu/romance/port/>.

Rigg, Diana, perf. Medea. By Euripides. Trans. Alistair
Elliot. Dir. Jonathan Kent. Longacre Theatre, New
York. 7 Apr. 1994.

Stempel, Carl William. "Towards a Historical Sociology
of Sport in the United States, 1825-1875." DAI 53
(1993): 3374A. U of Oregon, 1992. Dissertation
Abstracts Ondisc. CD-ROM. UMI-Proquest. Sept.
1993.

Tommasini, Anthony. "In G. and S., Better to Have More
Words, Less Voice." Rev. of The Mikado, by William
S. Gilbert and Arthur Sullivan. New York City
Opera. New York State Theater, New York. New York
Times 10 Mar. 1997, late ed.: C22.

7.4.2 Citing Part of a Work

If you quote, paraphrase, or otherwise use a specific passage in a book
or article, give the relevant page or section (e.g., paragraph) number or
numbers. When the author's name is in your text, give only the number reference in parentheses, but if the context does not clearly identify
the author, add the author's last name before the reference. Leave a
space between them, but do not insert punctuation or, for a page reference, the word *page* or *pages* or the abbreviation *p.* or *pp.* If you used
only one volume of a multivolume work and included the volume
number in the bibliographic entry, you need give only page numbers
in the reference (see the Lauter et al. example), but if you used more
than one volume of the work, you must cite both volume and page
numbers (see 7.4.3). If your source uses paragraph numbers rather
than page numbers—as, for example, some electronic journals do—
give the relevant number or numbers preceded by the abbreviation
par. or *pars.*; if the author's name begins such a citation, place a comma
after the name (see the Moulthrop example). If another kind of section
is numbered in the source (e.g., screens), either write out the word for
the section or use a standard abbreviation (see ch. 8); if the author's
name begins such a citation, place a comma after the name (see the
Gardiner example).

BOOKS (cf. 6.6)

Brian Taves suggests some interesting conclusions regarding the philosophy and politics of the adventure film (153-54, 171).

The anthology by Lauter and his coeditors contains Stowe's "Sojourner Truth, the Libyan Sibyl" (2425-33).

Among intentional spoonerisms, the "punlike metathesis of distinctive features may serve to weld together words etymologically unrelated but close in their sound and meaning" (Jakobson and Waugh 304).

Although writings describing utopia have always seemed to take place far from the everyday world, in fact "all utopian fiction whirls contemporary actors through a costume dance no place else but here" (Rabkin, Greenberg, and Olander vii).

Another engaging passage is the opening of Isabel Allende's story "Toad's Mouth" (83).

In Hansberry's play A Raisin in the Sun, the rejection of Lindner's tempting offer permits Walter's family to pursue the new life they had long dreamed about (274-75).

ARTICLES IN PERIODICALS (cf. 6.7)

Between 1968 and 1988, television coverage of presidential elections changed dramatically (Hallin 5).

Repetitive strain injury, or RSI, is reported to be "the fastest-growing occupational hazard of the computer age" (Taylor A1).

ELECTRONIC SOURCES (cf. 6.9)

Hypertext, as one theorist puts it, is "all about connection, linkage, and affiliation" (Moulthrop, par. 19).

"The study of comparative literature," Bill Readings wrote, "takes off from the idea of humanity" (6).

Beethoven has been called the "first politically motivated composer," for he was "caught up in the whole ferment of ideas that came out of the French Revolution" (Gardiner, screens 2-3)

Works Cited

Allende, Isabel. "Toad's Mouth." Trans. Margaret Sayers Peden. A Hammock beneath the Mangoes: Stories from Latin America. Ed. Thomas Colchie. New York: Plume, 1992. 83-88.

Gardiner, John Eliot. "The Importance of Beethoven." Interview. Charlie Rose. PBS. 25 July 1996. Transcript. Broadcast News. CD-ROM. Primary Source Media. July 1996. 23 screens.

Hallin, Daniel C. "Sound Bite News: Television Coverage of Elections, 1968-1988." Journal of Communication 42.2 (1992): 5-24.

Hansberry, Lorraine. A Raisin in the Sun. Black Theater: A Twentieth-Century Collection of the Work of Its Best Playwrights. Ed. Lindsay Patterson. New York: Dodd, 1971. 221-76.

Jakobson, Roman, and Linda R. Waugh. The Sound Shape of Language. Bloomington: Indiana UP, 1979.

Lauter, Paul, et al., eds. The Heath Anthology of American Literature. 2nd ed. Vol. 1. Lexington: Heath, 1994.

Moulthrop, Stuart. "You Say You Want a Revolution? Hypertext and the Laws of Media." Postmodern Culture 1.3 (1991): 53 pars. 3 Apr. 1997 <http://muse.jhu.edu/journals/postmodern_culture/v001/1.3moulthrop.html>.

Rabkin, Eric S., Martin H. Greenberg, and Joseph D. Olander. Preface. No Place Else: Explorations in Utopian and Dystopian Fiction. Ed. Rabkin, Greenberg, and Olander. Carbondale: Southern Illinois UP, 1983. vii-ix.

> Readings, Bill. "Translatio and Comparative Literature:
> The Terror of European Humanism." Surfaces 1.11
> (1991): 19 pp. 11 Apr. 1997 <gopher://
> surfaces.umontreal.ca:70/00/Articles/Ascii/
> Vol1/A-Readings-VF.txt>.
>
> Taves, Brian. The Romance of Adventure: The Genre of
> Historical Adventure Movies. Jackson: UP of
> Mississippi, 1993.
>
> Taylor, Paul. "Keyboard Grief: Coping with Computer-
> Caused Injuries." Globe and Mail [Toronto] 27 Dec.
> 1993: A1+.

7.4.3   Citing Volume and Page Numbers of a Multivolume Work

When citing a volume number as well as a page reference for a multi-volume work, separate the two by a colon and a space: "(Wellek 2: 1–10)." Use neither the words *volume* and *page* nor their abbreviations. The functions of the numbers in such a citation are understood. If, however, you wish to refer parenthetically to an entire volume of a multivolume work, there is no need to cite pages. Place a comma after the author's name and include the abbreviation *vol.*: "(Wellek, vol. 2)." If you integrate such a reference into a sentence, spell out *volume*: "In volume 2, Wellek deals with [. . .]."

> The anthology by Lauter and his coeditors contains
> both Stowe's "Sojourner Truth, the Libyan Sibyl"
> (1: 2425-33) and Gilman's "The Yellow Wall-Paper"
> (2: 800-12).

> Between the years 1945 and 1972, the political-party
> system in the United States underwent profound changes
> (Schlesinger, vol. 4).

> Wellek admits in the middle of his multivolume history
> of modern literary criticism, "An evolutionary history
> of criticism must fail. I have come to this resigned
> conclusion" (5: xxii).

> Works Cited
>
> Lauter, Paul, et al., eds. The Heath Anthology of
> American Literature. 2nd ed. 2 vols. Lexington:
> Heath, 1994.

Schlesinger, Arthur M., Jr., gen. ed. <u>History of U.S.</u>
<u>Political Parties</u>. 4 vols. New York: Chelsea,
1973.

Wellek, René. <u>A History of Modern Criticism, 1750–1950</u>.
8 vols. New Haven: Yale UP, 1955–92.

7.4.4   Citing a Work Listed by Title

In a parenthetical reference to a work alphabetized by title in the list of works cited, the full title (if brief) or a shortened version precedes the page or section number or numbers, unless the title appears in your text. When abbreviating the title, begin with the word by which it is alphabetized. Do not, for example, shorten *Glossary of Terms Used in Heraldry* to *Heraldry*, since this abbreviation would lead your reader to look for the bibliographic entry under *h* rather than *g*. If you wish to cite a specific definition in a dictionary entry, give the relevant designation (e.g., number, letter) after the abbreviation *def.* (see the "Noon" example).

BOOKS (cf. 6.6)

A presidential commission reported in 1970 that recent
campus protests had focused on "racial injustice, war,
and the university itself" (<u>Report</u> 3).

The nine grades of mandarins were "distinguished by
the color of the button on the hats of office"
("Mandarin").

ARTICLES IN PERIODICALS (cf. 6.7)

International espionage was as prevalent as ever in the
1990s ("Decade").

A <u>New York Times</u> editorial called Ralph Ellison "a
writer of universal reach" ("Death").

MISCELLANEOUS NONPRINT SOURCES (cf. 6.8)

Even <u>Sixty Minutes</u> launched an attack on modern art, in
a segment entitled "Yes . . . but Is It Art?"

The classical Greek tragedy <u>Medea</u>, one of the most
successful Broadway plays of the 1990s, made a lasting
impression on me.

ELECTRONIC SOURCES (cf. 6.9)

The database <u>Duecento</u> is an invaluable source for texts of medieval Italian poetry.

<u>Perseus 1.0</u> revolutionized the way scholars conduct research on ancient civilizations.

In fresco painting, "the pigments are completely fused with a damp plaster ground to become an integral part of the wall surface" ("Fresco").

Milton's description of the moon at "her highest noon" signifies the "place of the moon at midnight" ("Noon," def. 4b).

Works Cited

"Death of a Writer." Editorial. <u>New York Times</u> 20 Apr. 1994, late ed.: A18.

"Decade of the Spy." <u>Newsweek</u> 7 Mar. 1994: 26-27.

<u>Duecento: Repertorio elettronico della poesia italiana dalle origini a Dante</u>. Ed. Francesco Bonomi. 1996. Si.Lab, Firenze. 19 Apr. 1997 <http://www.silab.it/frox/200/pwhomita.htm>.

"Fresco." <u>Britannica Online</u>. Vers. 97.1.1. Mar. 1997. Encyclopaedia Britannica. 29 Mar. 1997 <http://www.eb.com:180>.

"Mandarin." <u>The Encyclopedia Americana</u>. 1993 ed.

<u>Medea</u>. By Euripides. Trans. Alistair Elliot. Dir. Jonathan Kent. Perf. Diana Rigg. Longacre Theatre, New York. 7 Apr. 1994.

"Noon." <u>The Oxford English Dictionary</u>. 2nd ed. CD-ROM. Oxford: Oxford UP, 1992.

<u>Perseus 1.0: Interactive Sources and Studies on Ancient Greece</u>. CD-ROM, videodisc. New Haven: Yale UP, 1992.

<u>Report of the President's Commission on Campus Unrest</u>. New York: Arno, 1970.

"Yes . . . but Is It Art?" Narr. Morley Safer. <u>Sixty Minutes</u>. CBS. WCBS, New York. 19 Sept. 1993.

7.4.5 Citing a Work by a Corporate Author

To cite a work by a corporate author, you may use the author's name followed by a page reference: "(United Nations, Economic Commission for Africa 79–86)." It is better, however, to include a long name in the text, so that the reading is not interrupted with an extended parenthetical reference.

> According to a study sponsored by the National Research Council, the population of China around 1990 was increasing by more than fifteen million annually (15).

> By 1992 it was apparent that the American health care system, though impressive in many ways, needed "to be fixed and perhaps radically modified" (Public Agenda Foundation 4).

> A study prepared by the United States Department of State defined terrorism as "premeditated, politically motivated violence against noncombatant targets by subnational groups or clandestine agents, usually intended to influence an audience" (lines 14-16).

> In 1963 the United Nations Economic Commission for Africa predicted that Africa would evolve into an advanced industrial economy within fifty years (1-2, 4-6).

Works Cited

National Research Council. China and Global Change: Opportunities for Collaboration. Washington: Natl. Acad., 1992.

Public Agenda Foundation. The Health Care Crisis: Containing Costs, Expanding Coverage. New York: McGraw, 1992.

United Nations. Economic Commission for Africa. Industrial Growth in Africa. New York: United Nations, 1963.

United States. Dept. of State. Patterns of Global Terrorism. 1994. National Trade Data Bank. CD-ROM. Disc 2. US Dept. of Commerce. Dec. 1996.

7.4.6   Citing Two or More Works by the Same Author or Authors

In a parenthetical reference to one of two or more works by the same author, put a comma after the author's last name and add the title of the work (if brief) or a shortened version and the relevant page reference: "(Frye, *Double Vision* 85)," "(Durant and Durant, *Age* 214–48)." If you state the author's name in the text, give only the title and page reference in parentheses: "(*Double Vision* 85)," "(*Age* 214–48)." If you include both the author's name and the title in the text, indicate only the pertinent page number or numbers in parentheses: "(85)," "(214–48)."

PRINT SOURCES

Dreiser's universe, according to E. L. Doctorow, "is composed of merchants, workers, club-men, managers, actors, salesmen, doormen, cops, derelicts--a Balzacian population unified by the rules of commerce and the ideals of property and social position" (Introduction ix).

The brief but dramatic conclusion of chapter 13 of Doctorow's Welcome to Hard Times constitutes the climax of the novel (206-09).

In The Age of Voltaire, the Durants portray eighteenth-century England as a minor force in the world of music and art (214-48).

To Will and Ariel Durant, creative men and women make "history forgivable by enriching our heritage and our lives" (Dual Autobiography 406).

Shakespeare's King Lear has been called a "comedy of the grotesque" (Frye, Anatomy 237).

For Northrop Frye, one's death is not a unique experience, for "every moment we have lived through we have also died out of into another order" (Double Vision 85).

ELECTRONIC SOURCES

Moulthrop sees the act of reading hypertext as "struggle": "a chapter of chances, a chain of detours,

a series of revealing figures in commitment out of
which come the pleasures of the text" ("Traveling").

Hypertext, as one theorist puts it, is "all about
connection, linkage, and affiliation" (Moulthrop, "You
Say," par. 19).

Works Cited

Doctorow, E. L. Introduction. Sister Carrie. By
    Theodore Dreiser. New York: Bantam, 1982. v-xi.
---. Welcome to Hard Times. 1960. New York: Vintage-
    Random, 1988.
Durant, Will, and Ariel Durant. The Age of Voltaire.
    New York: Simon, 1965. Vol. 9 of The Story of
    Civilization. 11 vols. 1933-75.
---. A Dual Autobiography. New York: Simon, 1977.
Frye, Northrop. Anatomy of Criticism: Four Essays.
    Princeton: Princeton UP, 1957.
---. The Double Vision: Language and Meaning in
    Religion. Toronto: U of Toronto P, 1991.
Moulthrop, Stuart. "Traveling in the Breakdown Lane: A
    Principle of Resistance for Hypertext." [19 Apr.
    1995.] 12 Aug. 1997 <http://www.ubalt.edu/www/
    ygcla/sam/essays/breakdown.html>.
---. "You Say You Want a Revolution? Hypertext and the
    Laws of Media." Postmodern Culture 1.3 (1991): 53
    pars. 3 Apr. 1997 <http://muse.jhu.edu/journals/
    postmodern_culture/v001/1.3moulthrop.html>.

7.4.7 Citing Indirect Sources

Whenever you can, take material from the original source, not a secondhand one. Sometimes, however, only an indirect source is available—for example, someone's published account of another's spoken remarks. If what you quote or paraphrase is itself a quotation, put the abbreviation *qtd. in* ("quoted in") before the indirect source you cite in your parenthetical reference. (You may document the original source in a note; see 7.5.1.)

Samuel Johnson admitted that Edmund Burke was an
"extraordinary man" (qtd. in Boswell 2: 450).

> The commentary of the sixteenth-century literary
> scholars Bernardo Segni and Lionardo Salviati shows
> them to be less than faithful followers of Aristotle
> (qtd. in Weinberg 1: 405, 616-17).

Works Cited

Boswell, James. <u>The Life of Johnson</u>. Ed. George
    Birkbeck Hill and L. F. Powell. 6 vols. Oxford:
    Clarendon, 1934-50.

Weinberg, Bernard. <u>A History of Literary Criticism in</u>
    <u>the Italian Renaissance</u>. 2 vols. Chicago: U of
    Chicago P, 1961.

7.4.8   Citing Literary Works

In a reference to a classic prose work, such as a novel or play, that is available in several editions, it is helpful to provide more information than just a page number from the edition used; a chapter number, for example, would help readers to locate a quotation in any copy of a novel. In such a reference, give the page number first, add a semicolon, and then give other identifying information, using appropriate abbreviations: "(130; ch. 9)," "(271; bk. 4, ch. 2)."

> Raskolnikov first appears in <u>Crime and Punishment</u> as a
> man contemplating a terrible act but frightened of
> meeting his talkative landlady on the stairs
> (Dostoevsky 1; pt. 1, ch. 1).

> In one version of the William Tell story, the son urges
> the reluctant father to shoot the arrow (Sastre 315;
> sc. 6).

> In <u>A Vindication of the Rights of Woman</u>, Mary
> Wollstonecraft recollects many "women who, not led by
> degrees to proper studies, and not permitted to choose
> for themselves, have indeed been overgrown children"
> (185; ch. 13, sec. 2).

When you cite an unpaginated source, the chapter number or similar designation may be the only identifying information you can give.

> Douglass notes that he had "no accurate knowledge" of
> his date of birth, "never having had any authentic
> record containing it" (ch. 1).

In citing classic verse plays and poems, omit page numbers altogether and cite by division (act, scene, canto, book, part) and line, with periods separating the various numbers—for example, *"Iliad* 9.19" refers to book 9, line 19, of Homer's *Iliad.* If you are citing only line numbers, do not use the abbreviation *l.* or *ll.,* which can be confused with numerals. Instead, initially use the word *line* or *lines* and then, having established that the numbers designate lines, give the numbers alone.

In general, use arabic numerals rather than roman numerals for division and page numbers. Although you must use roman numerals when citing pages of a preface or other section that are so numbered, designate volumes, parts, books, and chapters with arabic numerals even if your source does not. Some editors prefer roman numerals, however, for citations of acts and scenes in plays (*King Lear* IV.i), but if your editor does not require this practice, use arabic numerals (*King Lear* 4.1). On numbers, see 3.10.

When included in parenthetical references, the titles of the books of the Bible and of famous literary works are often abbreviated (1 Chron. 21.8, *Oth.* 21.3, *Oth.* 4.2.7–13, *FQ* 3.3.53.3). The most widely used and accepted abbreviations for such titles are listed in 8.6. Follow prevailing practices for other abbreviations (*Troilus* for Chaucer's *Troilus and Criseyde,* "Nightingale" for Keats's "Ode to a Nightingale," etc.).

> Chaucer's purpose is "The double sorwe of Troilus to
> tellen, / That was the kyng Priamus sone of Troye"
> (1.1-2).

> Like the bard who made the <u>Ballad of Sir Patrick
> Spence</u>, Coleridge sees the "new-moon winter bright"
> with the "old Moon in her lap, foretelling / The coming
> on of rain and squally blast" (1.9, 13-14).

> In <u>Ballads and Lyrics of Socialism</u>, Nesbit declares,
> "Our arms and hearts are strong for all who suffer
> wrong" ("Marching Song" 11).

> The Dean and Chapter Library manuscript version of
> <u>Octovian</u>, as edited by Frances McSparran, has a more

formal ending than other versions do: "And thus endis
Octouean, / That in his tym was a doghety man
[. . .]" (1629-30).

Shakespeare's Hamlet seems resolute when he asserts,
"The play's the thing / Wherein I'll catch the
conscience of the King" (2.2.633-34).

Works Cited

Chaucer, Geoffrey. Troilus and Criseyde. The Works of
Geoffrey Chaucer. Ed. F. N. Robinson. 2nd ed.
Boston: Houghton, 1957. 385-479.

Coleridge, Samuel Taylor. "Dejection: An Ode." The
Complete Works of Samuel Taylor Coleridge. Ed.
Ernest Hartley Coleridge. Vol. 1. Oxford:
Clarendon, 1912. 362-68. English Poetry Full-Text
Database. Rel. 2. CD-ROM. Cambridge, Eng.:
Chadwyck-Healey, 1993.

Dostoevsky, Feodor. Crime and Punishment. Trans. Jessie
Coulson. Ed. George Gibian. New York: Norton,
1964.

Douglass, Frederick. Narrative of the Life of Frederick
Douglass. Boston, 1845. 30 Jan. 1997 <gopher://
gopher.vt.edu:10010/02/73/1>.

Nesbit, E[dith]. Ballads and Lyrics of Socialism.
London, 1908. Victorian Women Writers Project.
Ed. Perry Willett. Apr. 1997. Indiana U. 26 Apr.
1997 <http://www.indiana.edu/~letrs/vwwp/nesbit/
ballsoc.html#p9>.

Octovian. Ed. Frances McSparran. Early English Text
Soc. 289. London: Oxford UP, 1986. The Electronic
Text Center. Ed. David Seaman. May 1995. Alderman
Lib., U of Virginia. 24 Feb. 1997 <ftp://
etext.virginia.edu/pub/texts/AnoOctC>.

Sastre, Alfonso. Sad Are the Eyes of William Tell.
Trans. Leonard Pronko. The New Wave Spanish Drama.
Ed. George Wellwarth. New York: New York UP, 1970.
165-321.

Shakespeare, William. <u>Hamlet</u>. Ed. Barbara A. Mowat and
Paul Werstine. New York: Washington Square-Pocket,
1992.

Wollstonecraft, Mary. <u>A Vindication of the Rights of</u>
<u>Woman</u>. Ed. Carol H. Poston. New York: Norton, 1975.

7.4.9   Citing More Than One Work in a Single Parenthetical Reference

If you wish to include two or more works in a single parenthetical reference, cite each work as you normally would in a reference, and use semicolons to separate the citations.

(Kaku 42; McRae 101-33)

(National Research Council 25-35; Fitzgerald 330-43)

(Rabkin, Greenberg, and Olander vii; Boyle 96-125)

(Craner 308-11; Moulthrop, pars. 39-53)

(Gilbert and Gubar, <u>Madwoman</u> 1-25; Murphy 39-52)

(Gilbert and Gubar, <u>Norton</u>; Manning)

(<u>Guidelines</u>; Hallin 18-24)

(Lauter et al., vol. 1; Crane)

Keep in mind, however, that a long parenthetical reference such as the following example may prove intrusive and disconcerting to your reader:

(Taylor A1; Moulthrop, pars. 39-53; Armstrong, Yang,
and Cuneo 80-82; Craner 308-11; Kaku 42; Frank; Alston)

To avoid an excessive disruption, cite multiple sources in a note rather than in parentheses in the text (see 7.5.2).

Works Cited

Alston, Robin. "Bodley CD-ROM." Online posting. 15 June
1994. ExLibris. 10 Oct. 1996 <http://
www-cpa.stanford.edu/byform/mailing-lists/
exlibris/1994/06/msg00170.html>.

Armstrong, Larry, Dori Jones Yang, and Alice Cuneo.
"The Learning Revolution: Technology Is Reshaping
Education--at Home and at School." <u>Business Week</u>
28 Feb. 1994: 80-88.

Boyle, Anthony T. "The Epistemological Evolution of
    Renaissance Utopian Literature, 1516-1657." Diss.
    New York U, 1983.

Crane, Stephen. The Red Badge of Courage: An Episode of
    the American Civil War. 1895. Ed. Fredson Bowers.
    Charlottesville: UP of Virginia, 1975.

Craner, Paul M. "New Tool for an Ancient Art: The
    Computer and Music." Computers and the Humanities
    25 (1991): 303-13.

Fitzgerald, John. "The Misconceived Revolution: State
    and Society in China's Nationalist Revolution,
    1923-26." Journal of Asian Studies 49 (1990):
    323-43.

Frank, Holly. Negative Space: A Computerized Video
    Novel. Vers. 1.0. Diskette, videocassette. Prairie
    Village: Diskotech, 1990.

Gilbert, Sandra M., and Susan Gubar. The Madwoman in
    the Attic: The Woman Writer and the Nineteenth-
    Century Literary Imagination. New Haven: Yale UP,
    1979.

---, eds. The Norton Anthology of Literature by Women:
    The Tradition in English. New York: Norton, 1985.

Guidelines for Family Television Viewing. Urbana: ERIC
    Clearinghouse on Elementary and Early Childhood
    Educ., 1990. ERIC. CD-ROM. SilverPlatter. Oct.
    1993.

Hallin, Daniel C. "Sound Bite News: Television Coverage
    of Elections, 1968-1988." Journal of Communication
    42.2 (1992): 5-24.

Kaku, Michio. Hyperspace: A Scientific Odyssey
    through Parallel Universes, Time Warps, and
    the Tenth Dimension. New York: Oxford UP,
    1994.

Lauter, Paul, et al., eds. The Heath Anthology of
    American Literature. 2nd ed. 2 vols. Lexington:
    Heath, 1994.

Manning, Anita. "Curriculum Battles from Left and
    Right." USA Today 2 Mar. 1994: 5D.

McRae, Murdo William, ed. The Literature of Science: Perspectives on Popular Science Writing. Athens: U of Georgia P, 1993.

Moulthrop, Stuart. "You Say You Want a Revolution? Hypertext and the Laws of Media." Postmodern Culture 1.3 (1991): 53 pars. 3 Apr. 1997 <http://muse.jhu.edu/journals/postmodern_culture/v001/1.3moulthrop.html>.

Murphy, Cullen. "Women and the Bible." Atlantic Monthly Aug. 1993: 39-64.

National Research Council. China and Global Change: Opportunities for Collaboration. Washington: Natl. Acad., 1992.

Rabkin, Eric S., Martin H. Greenberg, and Joseph D. Olander. Preface. No Place Else: Explorations in Utopian and Dystopian Fiction. Ed. Rabkin, Greenberg, and Olander. Carbondale: Southern Illinois UP, 1983. vii-ix.

Taylor, Paul. "Keyboard Grief: Coping with Computer-Caused Injuries." Globe and Mail [Toronto] 27 Dec. 1993: A1+.

7.4.10 Citing a Book with Signatures and No Page Numbers

Some books published before 1800 lack page numbers but include letters, numbers, or other symbols, called signatures, at regular intervals at the feet of the pages. These notations were intended to help the bookbinder assemble groups of pages into the proper order. The pages between signatures typically bear the preceding signature symbol with an added numeral (arabic or roman).

In citing books without page numbers but with signatures, indicate the signature symbol, the leaf number, and the abbreviation *r* ("recto") or *v* ("verso") in the parenthetical reference. If no leaf number is printed, supply one: the leaf on which a signature first appears should be considered 1, the next leaf 2, and so forth, until the following signature. The front of a leaf—the side appearing on the reader's right—is the recto; the back of a leaf—the side appearing on the reader's left—is the verso. Thus, A1r is followed by A1v, A2r, A2v, and so on. (On citing books published before 1900, see 6.6.24.)

John Udall, paraphrasing Satan's temptation of Christ, writes, "[T]hrow thy selfe downe" so that "the men of

> Jerusalem" will "receive thee with a common applause"
> (E7v).

Work Cited

> Udall, John. The Combate betweene Christ and the
>   Devill: Four Sermones on the Temptations of
>   Christ. London, 1589.

7.5   USING NOTES WITH PARENTHETICAL DOCUMENTATION

Two kinds of notes may be used with parenthetical documentation:

- Content notes offering the reader comment, explanation, or information that the text cannot accommodate
- Bibliographic notes containing either several sources or evaluative comments on sources

In providing this sort of supplementary information, place a superscript arabic numeral at the appropriate place in the text and write the note after a matching numeral either at the end of the text (as an endnote) or at the bottom of the page (as a footnote). See the examples in 7.5.1–2. For more information on using notes for documentation, see the appendix (sec. A).

7.5.1   Content Notes

In your notes, avoid lengthy discussions that divert the reader's attention from the primary text. In general, comments that you cannot fit into the text should be omitted unless they provide essential justification or clarification of what you have written. You may use a note, for example, to give full publication facts for an original source for which you cite an indirect source and perhaps to explain why you worked from secondary material.

> The commentary of the sixteenth-century literary
> scholars Bernardo Segni and Lionardo Salviati shows
> them to be less-than-faithful followers of Aristotle.[1]

Note

[1] Examples are conveniently available in Weinberg. See Segni, <u>Rettorica et poetica d'Aristotile</u> (Firenze, 1549) 281, qtd. in Weinberg 1: 405, and Salviati, <u>Poetica d'Aristotile parafrasata e comentata</u>, 1586, ms. 2.2.11, Biblioteca Nazionale Centrale, Firenze, 140v, qtd. in Weinberg 1: 616-17.

Work Cited

Weinberg, Bernard. <u>A History of Literary Criticism in the Italian Renaissance</u>. 2 vols. Chicago: U of Chicago P, 1961.

7.5.2   Bibliographic Notes

Use notes for evaluative comments on sources and for references containing numerous citations.

Many observers conclude that health care in the United States is inadequate.[1]

Technological advancements have brought advantages as well as unexpected problems.[2]

Notes

[1] For strong points of view on different aspects of the issue, see Public Agenda Foundation 1-10 and Sakala 151-88.

[2] For a sampling of materials that reflect the range of experiences related to recent technological changes, see Taylor A1; Moulthrop, pars. 39-53; Armstrong, Yang, and Cuneo 80-82; Craner 308-11; Kaku 42; Frank; and Alston.

Works Cited

Alston, Robin. "Bodley CD-ROM." Online posting. 15 June 1994. ExLibris. 10 Oct. 1996 <http://www-cpa.stanford.edu/byform/mailing-lists/exlibris/1994/06/msg00170.html>.

Armstrong, Larry, Dori Jones Yang, and Alice Cuneo.
"The Learning Revolution: Technology Is Reshaping
Education--at Home and at School." <u>Business Week</u>
28 Feb. 1994: 80-88.

Craner, Paul M. "New Tool for an Ancient Art: The
Computer and Music." <u>Computers and the Humanities</u>
25 (1991): 303-13.

Frank, Holly. <u>Negative Space: A Computerized Video
Novel</u>. Vers. 1.0. Diskette, videocassette. Prairie
Village: Diskotech, 1990.

Kaku, Michio. <u>Hyperspace: A Scientific Odyssey through
Parallel Universes, Time Warps, and the Tenth
Dimension</u>. New York: Oxford UP, 1994.

Moulthrop, Stuart. "You Say You Want a Revolution?
Hypertext and the Laws of Media." <u>Postmodern
Culture</u> 1.3 (1991): 53 pars. 3 Apr. 1997 <http://
muse.jhu.edu/journals/postmodern_culture/v001/
1.3moulthrop.html>.

Public Agenda Foundation. <u>The Health Care Crisis:
Containing Costs, Expanding Coverage</u>. New York:
McGraw, 1992.

Sakala, Carol. "Maternity Care Policy in the United
States: Toward a More Rational and Effective
System." Diss. Boston U, 1993.

Taylor, Paul. "Keyboard Grief: Coping with Computer-
Caused Injuries." <u>Globe and Mail</u> [Toronto] 27 Dec.
1993: A1+.

8

ABBREVIATIONS

8.1   Introduction

8.2   Time Designations

8.3   Geographic Names

8.4   Common Scholarly Abbreviations and Reference Words

8.5   Publishers' Names

8.6   Titles of Literary and Religious Works
    8.6.1   Bible
    8.6.2   Works by Shakespeare
    8.6.3   Works by Chaucer
    8.6.4   Other Literary Works

8.7   Names of Languages

8.8   Proofreading Symbols
    8.8.1   Symbols Used in the Text
    8.8.2   Symbols Used in the Margin
    8.8.3   Sample Marked Proof

8.1   INTRODUCTION

Abbreviations are used regularly in the list of works cited and in tables but rarely in the text of a research paper (except within parentheses). In choosing abbreviations, keep your audience in mind. While economy of space is important, clarity is more so. Spell out a term if the abbreviation may puzzle your readers.

When abbreviating, always use accepted forms. In appropriate contexts, you may abbreviate the names of days, months, and other measurements of time (see 8.2); the names of states and countries (see 8.3); terms and reference words common in scholarship (see 8.4);

publishers' names (see 8.5); the titles of well-known literary and religious works (see 8.6); and the names of languages (8.7).

The trend in abbreviation is to use neither periods after letters nor spaces between letters, especially for abbreviations made up of all capital letters.

BC	PhD	S
NJ	CD–ROM	US

The chief exception to this trend continues to be the initials used for personal names: a period and a space ordinarily follow each initial.

```
J. R. R. Tolkien
```

Most abbreviations that end in lowercase letters are followed by periods.

assn.	fig.	Mex.
Eng.	introd.	prod.

In most abbreviations made up of lowercase letters that each represent a word, a period follows each letter, but no space intervenes between letters.

a.m.	i.e.
e.g.	n.p.

But there are numerous exceptions.

mph	os
ns	rpm

8.2   TIME DESIGNATIONS

Spell out the names of months in the text but abbreviate them in the list of works cited, except for May, June, and July. Whereas words denoting units of time are also spelled out in the text (*second, minute, week, month, year, century*), some time designations are used only in abbreviated form (*a.m., p.m., AD, BC, BCE, CE*).

AD   after the birth of Christ (from Lat. *anno Domini* 'in the year of the Lord'; used before numerals ["AD 14"] and after references to centuries ["twelfth century AD"])

a.m.	before noon (from Lat. *ante meridiem*)
Apr.	April
Aug.	August
BC	before Christ (used after numerals and references to centuries: "19 BC," "fifth century BC")
BCE	before the common era (used after numerals and references to centuries)
CE	common era (used after numerals and references to centuries)
cent.	century
Dec.	December
Feb.	February
Fri.	Friday
hr.	hour
Jan.	January
Mar.	March
min.	minute
mo.	month
Mon.	Monday
Nov.	November
Oct.	October
p.m.	after noon (from Lat. *post meridiem*)
Sat.	Saturday
sec.	second
Sept.	September
Sun.	Sunday
Thurs.	Thursday
Tues.	Tuesday
Wed.	Wednesday
wk.	week
yr.	year

8.3 GEOGRAPHIC NAMES

Spell out the names of states, territories, and possessions of the United States in the text, except usually in addresses and sometimes in parentheses. Likewise, spell out in the text the names of countries, with a few exceptions (e.g., USSR). In documentation, however, abbreviate the names of states, provinces, and countries.

AB	Alberta
Afr.	Africa
AK	Alaska
AL	Alabama
Alb.	Albania
Ant.	Antarctica
AR	Arkansas
Arg.	Argentina
Arm.	Armenia
AS	American Samoa
Aus.	Austria
Austral.	Australia
AZ	Arizona
BC	British Columbia
Belg.	Belgium
Braz.	Brazil
Bulg.	Bulgaria
CA	California
Can.	Canada
CO	Colorado
CT	Connecticut
CZ	Canal Zone
DC	District of Columbia
DE	Delaware
Den.	Denmark
Ecua.	Ecuador
Eng.	England
Eur.	Europe

FL	Florida
Fr.	France
GA	Georgia
Ger.	Germany
Gr.	Greece
Gt. Brit.	Great Britain
GU	Guam
HI	Hawaii
Hung.	Hungary
IA	Iowa
ID	Idaho
IL	Illinois
IN	Indiana
Ire.	Ireland
Isr.	Israel
It.	Italy
Jap.	Japan
KS	Kansas
KY	Kentucky
LA	Louisiana
LB	Labrador
Leb.	Lebanon
MA	Massachusetts
MB	Manitoba
MD	Maryland
ME	Maine
Mex.	Mexico
MI	Michigan
MN	Minnesota
MO	Missouri
MS	Mississippi
MT	Montana
NB	New Brunswick
NC	North Carolina

ND	North Dakota
NE	Nebraska
Neth.	Netherlands
NF	Newfoundland
NH	New Hampshire
NJ	New Jersey
NM	New Mexico
No. Amer.	North America
Norw.	Norway
NS	Nova Scotia
NT	Northwest Territories
NV	Nevada
NY	New York
NZ	New Zealand
OH	Ohio
OK	Oklahoma
ON	Ontario
OR	Oregon
PA	Pennsylvania
Pan.	Panama
PE	Prince Edward Island
Pol.	Poland
Port.	Portugal
PQ	Quebec (Province de Québec)
PR	Puerto Rico
PRC	People's Republic of China
RI	Rhode Island
Russ.	Russia
SC	South Carolina
Scot.	Scotland
SD	South Dakota
SK	Saskatchewan
So. Amer.	South America
Sp.	Spain

Swed.	Sweden
Switz.	Switzerland
TN	Tennessee
Turk.	Turkey
TX	Texas
UK	United Kingdom
US, USA	United States, United States of America
USSR	Union of Soviet Socialist Republics
UT	Utah
VA	Virginia
VI	Virgin Islands
VT	Vermont
WA	Washington
WI	Wisconsin
WV	West Virginia
WY	Wyoming
YT	Yukon Territory

8.4 COMMON SCHOLARLY ABBREVIATIONS AND REFERENCE WORDS

The following list includes abbreviations and reference words commonly used in humanities scholarship. Terms within parentheses are alternative but not recommended forms. Terms within brackets are no longer recommended. Most of the abbreviations listed would replace the spelled forms only in parentheses, tables, and documentation.

AAUP	Association of American University Presses
AB	bachelor of arts (from Lat. *artium baccalaureus*)
abbr.	abbreviation, abbreviated
abl.	ablative
abr.	abridgment, abridged
acad.	academy
acc.	accusative
act.	active

adapt.	adapter, adaptation, adapted by
adj.	adjective
adv.	adverb
als	autograph letter signed
AM	master of arts (from Lat. *artium magister*)
Amer.	America, American
Anm.	Ger. *Anmerkung* 'note'
anon.	anonymous
ant.	antonym
app.	appendix
arch.	archaic
art.	article
ASCII	American Standard Code for Information Interchange
assn.	association
assoc.	associate, associated
attrib.	attributive; attributed to
aux.	auxiliary
b.	born
BA	bachelor of arts
Bd., Bde.	Ger. *Band, Bände* 'volume, volumes'
BEd	bachelor of education
BFA	bachelor of fine arts
bib.	biblical
bibliog.	bibliographer, bibliography, bibliographic
biog.	biographer, biography, biographical
BiP	*Books in Print*
bk.	book
BL	British Library, London
BM	British Museum, London (now British Library)
BN	Bibliothèque Nationale, Paris
BS	bachelor of science
bull.	bulletin
©	copyright ("© 1998")

c. (ca.)	circa, *or* around (used with approximate dates: "c. 1796")
cap.	capital, capitalize
CD	compact disc
CD-ROM	compact disc read-only memory
cf.	compare (not "see"; from Lat. *confer*)
ch. (chap.)	chapter
chor.	choreographer, choreographed by
cit.	citation, cited
cl.	clause
cog.	cognate
col.	column
coll.	college
colloq.	colloquial
comp.	compiler, compiled by
compar.	comparative
cond.	conductor, conducted by
conf.	conference
Cong.	Congress
Cong. Rec.	*Congressional Record*
conj.	conjunction
cons.	consonant
Const.	Constitution
cont.	contents; continued
(contd.)	continued
contr.	contraction
d.	died
DA	doctor of arts
DA, DAI	*Dissertation Abstracts, Dissertation Abstracts International*
DAB	*Dictionary of American Biography*
dat.	dative
def.	definition; definite
dept.	department

263

der.	derivative
dev.	development, developed by
DFA	doctor of fine arts
d.h.	Ger. *das heisst* 'that is'
dial.	dialect, dialectal
dict.	dictionary
dim.	diminutive
dir.	director, directed by
diss.	dissertation
dist.	district
distr.	distributor, distributed by
div.	division
DNB	*Dictionary of National Biography*
doc.	document
ed.	editor, edition, edited by
EdD	doctor of education
educ.	education, educational
e.g.	for example (from Lat. *exempli gratia*; rarely capitalized; set off by commas, unless preceded by a different punctuation mark)
e-mail	electronic mail
encyc.	encyclopedia
enl.	enlarged (as in "rev. and enl. ed.")
esp.	especially
et al.	and others (from Lat. *et alii, et aliae*)
etc.	and so forth (from Lat. *et cetera*; like most abbreviations, not appropriate in text)
[et seq., et seqq.]	and the following (from Lat. *et sequens, et sequentes* or *sequentia*)
ex.	example
[f., ff.]	and the following page(s) or line(s) (avoided in favor of specific page or line numbers)
fac.	faculty
facsim.	facsimile
fasc.	fascicle

fem.	feminine
fig.	figure
fl.	flourished, *or* reached greatest development or influence (from Lat. *floruit*; used before dates of historical figures when birth and death dates are not known: "fl. 1200")
[fn.]	footnote
[fol.]	folio
fr.	from
front.	frontispiece
FTP	File Transfer Protocol
fut.	future
fwd.	foreword, foreword by; forwarded (as in "fwd. by")
geb.	Ger. *geboren* 'born'
gen.	general (as in "gen. ed.")
ger.	gerund
gest.	Ger. *gestorben* 'died'
govt.	government
GPO	Government Printing Office, Washington, DC
H. Doc.	House of Representatives Document
hist.	historian, history, historical
HMSO	Her (His) Majesty's Stationery Office, London
HR	House of Representatives
H. Rept.	House of Representatives Report
H. Res.	House of Representatives Resolution
HTML	Hypertext Markup Language
HTTP	Hypertext Transfer Protocol
[ib., ibid.]	in the same place (from Lat. *ibidem*)
i.e.	that is (from Lat. *id est*; rarely capitalized; set off by commas, unless preceded by a different punctuation mark)
illus.	illustrator, illustration, illustrated by
ILMP	*International Literary Market Place*
imp.	imperative

imperf.	imperfect
inc.	including; incorporated
indef.	indefinite
indic.	indicative
infin.	infinitive
[infra]	below
inst.	institute, institution
interjec.	interjective
interrog.	interrogative
intl.	international
intrans.	intransitive
introd.	introduction, introduced by
ips	inches per second (used in reference to tape recordings)
irreg.	irregular
JD	doctor of law (from Lat. *juris doctor*)
jour.	journal
Jr.	Junior
KB	kilobyte
[l., ll.]	line, lines (avoided in favor of *line* and *lines* or, if clear, numbers only)
lang.	language
LC	Library of Congress
leg.	legal
legis.	legislator, legislation, legislature, legislative
lib.	library
lit.	literally; literature, literary
LittB	bachelor of letters (from Lat. *litterarum baccalaureus*)
LittD	doctor of letters (from Lat. *litterarum doctor*)
LittM	master of letters (from Lat. *litterarum magister*)
LLB	bachelor of laws (from Lat. *legum baccalaureus*)
LLD	doctor of laws (from Lat. *legum doctor*)
LLM	master of laws (from Lat. *legum magister*)

LMP	*Literary Market Place*
[loc. cit.]	in the place (passage) cited (from Lat. *loco citato*)
LP	long-playing phonograph record
ltd.	limited
m.	Fr. *mort, morte*; It. *morto, morta*; Sp. *muerto, muerta* 'died'
MA	master of arts
mag.	magazine
masc.	masculine
MB	megabyte
MD	doctor of medicine (from Lat. *medicinae doctor*)
MEd	master of education
MFA	master of fine arts
misc.	miscellaneous
mod.	modern
MOO	multiuser domain, object-oriented (cf. *MUD*)
MS	master of science
ms., mss.	manuscript, manuscripts (as in "Bodleian ms. Tanner 43")
MUD	multiuser domain
n, nn	note, notes (used immediately after the number of the page containing the text of the note or notes: "56n," "56n3," "56nn3–5")
n.	noun. Also Fr. *né, née*; It. *nato, nata*; Lat. *natus, nata*; Sp. *nacido, nacida* 'born'
narr.	narrator, narrated by
natl.	national
NB	take notice (from Lat. *nota bene*; always capitalized)
n.d.	no date of publication
NED	*A New English Dictionary* (cf. *OED*)
no.	number (cf. *numb.*)
nom.	nominative
nonstand.	nonstandard
n.p.	no place of publication; no publisher

n. pag.	no pagination
ns	new series
NS	New Style (calendar designation)
numb.	numbered
ob.	he/she died (from Lat. *obiit*)
obj.	object, objective
obs.	obsolete
OCR	optical character reader; optical character recognition
OED	*The Oxford English Dictionary* (formerly *A New English Dictionary* [*NED*])
o.J.	Ger. *ohne Jahr* 'without year'
o.O.	Ger. *ohne Ort* 'without place'
op.	opus (work)
[op. cit.]	in the work cited (from Lat. *opere citato*)
orch.	orchestra (also It. *orchestra*, Fr. *orchestre*, etc.), orchestrated by
orig.	original, originally
orn.	ornament, ornamented
os	old series; original series
OS	Old Style (calendar designation)
P	Press (also Fr. *Presse*, *Presses*; used in documentation; cf. *UP* and *PU*)
p., pp.	page, pages (omitted before page numbers unless necessary for clarity)
pág.	Sp. *página* 'page'
par.	paragraph
part.	participle
pass.	passive
[passim]	through the work, *or* here and there
perf.	performer, performed by
pers.	person
p. es.	It. *per esempio* 'for example'
p. ex.	Fr. *par exemple* 'for example'

PhD	doctor of philosophy (from Lat. *philosophiae doctor*)
philol.	philological
philos.	philosophical
pl.	plate; plural
por ej.	Sp. *por ejemplo* 'for example'
poss.	possessive
p.p.	past participle
pref.	preface, preface by
prep.	preposition
pres.	present
proc.	proceedings
prod.	producer, produced by
pron.	pronoun
pronunc.	pronunciation
pr. p.	present participle
PS	postscript
pseud.	pseudonym
pt.	part
PU	Fr. *Presse de l'Université, Presses Universitaires* (used in documentation)
pub. (publ.)	publisher, publication, published by
Pub. L.	Public Law
qtd.	quoted
q.v.	which see (from Lat. *quod vide*)
r	righthand page (from Lat. *recto*)
r.	reigned
rec.	record, recorded
refl.	reflexive
reg.	registered; regular
rel.	relative; release
rept.	report, reported by
res.	resolution
resp.	respectively

rev.	review, reviewed by; revision, revised, revised by (spell out *review* where *rev.* might be ambiguous)
rpm	revolutions per minute (used in reference to phonograph recordings)
rpt.	reprint, reprinted by
S	Senate
s.	Ger. *siehe* 'see'
S.	Ger. *Seite* 'page'
sc.	scene (omitted when act and scene numbers are used together: "*King Lear* 4.1")
s.d.	Fr. *sans date*, It. *senza data* 'without date'
S. Doc.	Senate Document
sec. (sect.)	section
ser.	series
sess.	session
s.f.	Sp. *sin fecha* 'without date'
SGML	Standard Generalized Markup Language
sic	thus in the source (in square brackets as an editorial interpolation, otherwise in parentheses; not followed by an exclamation point)
sig.	signature
sing.	singular
s.l.	Fr. *sans lieu*, It. *senza luogo*, Sp. *sin lugar* 'without place'
s.l.n.d.	Fr. *sans lieu ni date* 'without place or date'
soc.	society
spec.	special
Sr.	Senior
S. Rept.	Senate Report
S. Res.	Senate Resolution
st.	stanza
St., Sts. (S, SS)	Saint, Saints
Stat.	Statutes at Large
Ste, Stes	Fr. fem. *Sainte, Saintes* 'saint, saints'

subj.	subject, subjective; subjunctive
substand.	substandard
superl.	superlative
supp.	supplement
[supra]	'above'
s.v.	under the word, under the heading (from Lat. *sub verbo, sub voce*)
syn.	synonym
t.	Fr. *tome*, Sp. *tomo* 'volume'
TEI	Text Encoding Initiative
tls	typed letter signed
trans. (tr.)	transitive; translator, translation, translated by
ts., tss.	typescript, typescripts (cf. *ms.*)
U	University (also Sp. *Universidad*, It. *Università*, Ger. *Universität*, Fr. *Université*, etc.; used in documentation; cf. *PU* and *UP*)
UP	University Press (used in documentation: "Columbia UP")
URL	uniform resource locator
usu.	usually
usw.	Ger. *und so weiter* 'and so on'
v	lefthand page (from Lat. *verso*)
[v.]	see (from Lat. *vide*)
v., vv. (vs., vss.)	verse, verses (cf. *vs. (v.)*)
var.	variant
vb.	verb
[v.d.]	various dates
vers.	version
vgl.	Ger. *vergleiche* 'compare'
v.i.	verb intransitive
[viz.]	namely (from Lat. *videlicet*)
voc.	vocative
vol.	volume
vs. (v.)	versus (*v.* preferred in titles of legal cases)
v.t.	verb transitive

writ.   writer, written by

z.B.   Ger. *zum Beispiel* 'for example'

8.5	PUBLISHERS' NAMES

In the list of works cited, shortened forms of publishers' names immediately follow the cities of publication, enabling the reader to locate books or to acquire more information about them. Since publications like *Books in Print, Literary Market Place,* and *International Literary Market Place* list publishers' addresses, you need give only enough information so that your reader can look up the publishers in one of these sources. It is usually sufficient, for example, to give "Harcourt" as the publisher's name even if the title page shows "Harcourt Brace" or one of the earlier names of that firm (Harcourt, Brace; Harcourt, Brace, and World; Harcourt Brace Jovanovich). If you are preparing a bibliographic study, however, or if publication history is important to your work, give the publisher's name in full.

In shortening publishers' names, keep in mind the following points:

- Omit articles (*A, An, The*), business abbreviations (*Co., Corp., Inc., Ltd.*), and descriptive words (*Books, House, Press, Publishers, Librairie, Verlag*). When citing a university press, however, always add the abbreviation *P* (Ohio State UP) because the university itself may publish independently of its press (Ohio State U).

- If the publisher's name includes the name of one person (Harry N. Abrams, W. W. Norton, John Wiley), cite the surname alone (Abrams, Norton, Wiley). If the publisher's name includes the names of more than one person, cite only the first of the surnames (Bobbs, Dodd, Faber, Farrar, Funk, Grosset, Harcourt, Harper, Houghton, McGraw, Prentice, Simon).

- Use standard abbreviations whenever possible (*Acad., Assn., Soc., UP*; see 8.4).

- If the publisher's name is commonly abbreviated with capital initial letters and if the abbreviation is likely to be familiar to your audience, use the abbreviation as the publisher's name (GPO, MLA, UMI). If your readers are not likely to know the abbreviation, shorten the name according to the general guidelines given above (Mod. Lang. Assn.).

Following are examples of how various types of publishers' names are shortened:

Acad. for Educ. Dev.	Academy for Educational Development, Inc.
ACLS	American Council of Learned Societies
ALA	American Library Association
Basic	Basic Books
CAL	Center for Applied Linguistics
Cambridge UP	Cambridge University Press
Eastgate	Eastgate Systems
Einaudi	Giulio Einaudi Editore
ERIC	Educational Resources Information Center
Farrar	Farrar, Straus and Giroux, Inc.
Feminist	The Feminist Press at the City University of New York
Gale	Gale Research, Inc.
Gerig	Gerig Verlag
GPO	Government Printing Office
Harper	Harper and Row, Publishers, Inc.; HarperCollins Publishers, Inc.
Harvard Law Rev. Assn.	Harvard Law Review Association
HMSO	Her (His) Majesty's Stationery Office
Houghton	Houghton Mifflin Co.
Knopf	Alfred A. Knopf, Inc.
Larousse	Librairie Larousse
Little	Little, Brown and Company, Inc.
Macmillan	Macmillan Publishing Co., Inc.
McGraw	McGraw-Hill, Inc.
MIT P	The MIT Press
MLA	The Modern Language Association of America
NCTE	The National Council of Teachers of English
NEA	The National Education Association
Norton	W. W. Norton and Co., Inc.

PUF	Presses Universitaires de France
Random	Random House, Inc.
Scribner's	Charles Scribner's Sons
Simon	Simon and Schuster, Inc.
SIRS	Social Issues Resources Series
State U of New York P	State University of New York Press
St. Martin's	St. Martin's Press, Inc.
UMI	University Microfilms International
U of Chicago P	University of Chicago Press
UP of Mississippi	University Press of Mississippi

8.6   TITLES OF LITERARY AND RELIGIOUS WORKS

In documentation, you may abbreviate the titles of works and parts of works. It is usually best to introduce an abbreviation in parentheses immediately after the first use of the full title in the text: "In *All's Well That Ends Well* (*AWW*), Shakespeare [. . .]." Abbreviating titles is appropriate, for example, if you repeatedly cite a variety of works by the same author. In such a discussion, abbreviations make for more concise parenthetical documentation —"(*AWW* 3.2.100–29)," "(*MM* 4.3.93–101)"— than the usual shortened titles would: "(*All's Well* 3.2.100–29)," "(*Measure* 4.3.93–101)." For works not on the following lists, you may use the abbreviations you find in your sources, or you may devise simple, unambiguous abbreviations of your own.

8.6.1   Bible

The following abbreviations and spelled forms are commonly used for parts of the Bible (Bib.).

OLD TESTAMENT (OT)

Gen.	Genesis
Exod.	Exodus
Lev.	Leviticus
Num.	Numbers
Deut.	Deuteronomy
Josh.	Joshua

Judg.	Judges
Ruth	Ruth
1 Sam.	1 Samuel
2 Sam.	2 Samuel
1 Kings	1 Kings
2 Kings	2 Kings
1 Chron.	1 Chronicles
2 Chron.	2 Chronicles
Ezra	Ezra
Neh.	Nehemiah
Esth.	Esther
Job	Job
Ps.	Psalms
Prov.	Proverbs
Eccles.	Ecclesiastes
Song Sol. (also Cant.)	Song of Solomon (also Canticles)
Isa.	Isaiah
Jer.	Jeremiah
Lam.	Lamentations
Ezek.	Ezekiel
Dan.	Daniel
Hos.	Hosea
Joel	Joel
Amos	Amos
Obad.	Obadiah
Jon.	Jonah
Mic.	Micah
Nah.	Nahum
Hab.	Habakkuk
Zeph.	Zephaniah
Hag.	Haggai
Zech.	Zechariah
Mal.	Malachi

SELECTED APOCRYPHAL AND DEUTEROCANONICAL WORKS

1 Esd.	1 Esdras
2 Esd.	2 Esdras
Tob.	Tobit
Jth.	Judith
Esth. (Apocr.)	Esther (Apocrypha)
Wisd. Sol. (also Wisd.)	Wisdom of Solomon (also Wisdom)
Ecclus. (also Sir.)	Ecclesiasticus (also Sirach)
Bar.	Baruch
Song 3 Childr.	Song of the Three Children
Sus.	Susanna
Bel and Dr.	Bel and the Dragon
Pr. Man.	Prayer of Manasseh
1 Macc.	1 Maccabees
2 Macc.	2 Maccabees

NEW TESTAMENT (NT)

Matt.	Matthew
Mark	Mark
Luke	Luke
John	John
Acts	Acts
Rom.	Romans
1 Cor.	1 Corinthians
2 Cor.	2 Corinthians
Gal.	Galatians
Eph.	Ephesians
Phil.	Philippians
Col.	Colossians
1 Thess.	1 Thessalonians
2 Thess.	2 Thessalonians
1 Tim.	1 Timothy
2 Tim.	2 Timothy
Tit.	Titus

Philem.	Philemon
Heb.	Hebrews
Jas.	James
1 Pet.	1 Peter
2 Pet.	2 Peter
1 John	1 John
2 John	2 John
3 John	3 John
Jude	Jude
Rev. (also Apoc.)	Revelation (also Apocalypse)

SELECTED APOCRYPHAL WORKS

G. Thom.	Gospel of Thomas
G. Heb.	Gospel of the Hebrews
G. Pet.	Gospel of Peter

8.6.2 Works by Shakespeare

Ado	*Much Ado about Nothing*
Ant.	*Antony and Cleopatra*
AWW	*All's Well That Ends Well*
AYL	*As You Like It*
Cor.	*Coriolanus*
Cym.	*Cymbeline*
Err.	*The Comedy of Errors*
F1	First Folio ed. (1623)
F2	Second Folio ed. (1632)
Ham.	*Hamlet*
1H4	*Henry IV, Part 1*
2H4	*Henry IV, Part 2*
H5	*Henry V*
1H6	*Henry VI, Part 1*
2H6	*Henry VI, Part 2*
3H6	*Henry VI, Part 3*
H8	*Henry VIII*

JC	*Julius Caesar*
Jn.	*King John*
LC	*A Lover's Complaint*
LLL	*Love's Labour's Lost*
Lr.	*King Lear*
Luc.	*The Rape of Lucrece*
Mac.	*Macbeth*
MM	*Measure for Measure*
MND	*A Midsummer Night's Dream*
MV	*The Merchant of Venice*
Oth.	*Othello*
Per.	*Pericles*
PhT	*The Phoenix and the Turtle*
PP	*The Passionate Pilgrim*
Q	Quarto ed.
R2	*Richard II*
R3	*Richard III*
Rom.	*Romeo and Juliet*
Shr.	*The Taming of the Shrew*
Son.	*Sonnets*
TGV	*The Two Gentlemen of Verona*
Tim.	*Timon of Athens*
Tit.	*Titus Andronicus*
Tmp.	*The Tempest*
TN	*Twelfth Night*
TNK	*The Two Noble Kinsmen*
Tro.	*Troilus and Cressida*
Ven.	*Venus and Adonis*
Wiv.	*The Merry Wives of Windsor*
WT	*The Winter's Tale*

8.6.3   Works by Chaucer

BD	*The Book of the Duchess*
CkT	The Cook's Tale

ClT	The Clerk's Tale
CT	*The Canterbury Tales*
CYT	The Canon's Yeoman's Tale
FranT	The Franklin's Tale
FrT	The Friar's Tale
GP	The General Prologue
HF	*The House of Fame*
KnT	The Knight's Tale
LGW	*The Legend of Good Women*
ManT	The Manciple's Tale
Mel	The Tale of Melibee
MerT	The Merchant's Tale
MilT	The Miller's Tale
MkT	The Monk's Tale
MLT	The Man of Law's Tale
NPT	The Nun's Priest's Tale
PardT	The Pardoner's Tale
ParsT	The Parson's Tale
PF	*The Parliament of Fowls*
PhyT	The Physician's Tale
PrT	The Prioress's Tale
Ret	Chaucer's Retraction
RvT	The Reeve's Tale
ShT	The Shipman's Tale
SNT	The Second Nun's Tale
SqT	The Squire's Tale
SumT	The Summoner's Tale
TC	*Troilus and Criseyde*
Th	The Tale of Sir Thopas
WBT	The Wife of Bath's Tale

8.6.4   Other Literary Works

Aen.	Vergil, *Aeneid*
Ag.	Aeschylus, *Agamemnon*

Ant.	Sophocles, *Antigone*
Bac.	Euripides, *Bacchae*
Beo.	*Beowulf*
Can.	Voltaire, *Candide*
Dec.	Boccaccio, *Decameron*
DJ	Byron, *Don Juan*
DQ	Cervantes, *Don Quixote*
Eum.	Aeschylus, *Eumenides*
FQ	Spenser, *The Faerie Queene*
Gil.	*Epic of Gilgamesh*
GT	Swift, *Gulliver's Travels*
Hept.	Marguerite de Navarre, *Heptaméron*
Hip.	Euripides, *Hippolytus*
Il.	Homer, *Iliad*
Inf.	Dante, *Inferno*
LB	Wordsworth, *Lyrical Ballads*
Lys.	Aristophanes, *Lysistrata*
MD	Melville, *Moby-Dick*
Med.	Euripides, *Medea*
Mis.	Molière, *Le misanthrope*
Nib.	*Nibelungenlied*
Od.	Homer, *Odyssey*
OR	Sophocles, *Oedipus Rex* (also called *Oedipus Tyrannus* [*OT*])
Or.	Aeschylus, *Oresteia*
OT	Sophocles, *Oedipus Tyrannus* (also called *Oedipus Rex* [*OR*])
Par.	Dante, *Paradiso*
PL	Milton, *Paradise Lost*
Prel.	Wordsworth, *The Prelude*
Purg.	Dante, *Purgatorio*
Rep.	Plato, *Republic*
SA	Milton, *Samson Agonistes*

SGGK   *Sir Gawain and the Green Knight*

Sym.   Plato, *Symposium*

Tar.   Molière, *Tartuffe*

8.7   NAMES OF LANGUAGES

Abbreviations for the names of languages are used not only in documentation but also in the text of linguistic studies where the context makes the abbreviations clear. Periods are not used in abbreviations containing all capital letters (*ME*), but a period follows an abbreviation ending in a lowercase letter (*Chin.*). An abbreviation that combines two abbreviations and ends in a lowercase letter contains only one period, by convention, at the end; no space is left between the two elements (*OFr.*, *AmerInd.*).

AFr.	Anglo-French
Afrik.	Afrikaans
Alb.	Albanian
AmerInd.	American Indian
AmerSp.	American Spanish
AN	Anglo-Norman
Ar.	Arabic
Arab.	Arabian
Aram.	Aramaic
Arm.	Armenian
Assyr.	Assyrian
Bab.	Babylonian
Beng.	Bengali
Bret.	Breton
Bulg.	Bulgarian
Bur.	Burmese
CanFr.	Canadian French
Cant.	Cantonese
Catal.	Catalan
Celt.	Celtic

Chin.	Chinese
Dan.	Danish
Du.	Dutch
E, Eng.	English
Egypt.	Egyptian
Esk.	Eskimo
Finn.	Finnish
Flem.	Flemish
Fr.	French
Fris.	Frisian
G, Ger.	German
Gael.	Gaelic
Gk.	Greek
Goth.	Gothic
Heb.	Hebrew
HG	High German
Hung.	Hungarian
Icel.	Icelandic
IE	Indo-European
Ind.	Indian
Ir.	Irish
It.	Italian
Jap.	Japanese
Kor.	Korean
L	Late (e.g., *LGk.*, *LHeb.*, *LL*); Low (e.g., *LG*)
L, Lat.	Latin
LaFr.	Louisiana French
M	Medieval (e.g., *ML*); Middle (e.g., *ME*, *MFlem.*, *MHG*, *MLG*)
Maced.	Macedonian
Mal.	Malayan
MexSp.	Mexican Spanish
Mong.	Mongolian
N	New (e.g., *NGk.*, *NHeb.*, *NL*); Norse

Norw.	Norwegian
O	Old (e.g., *OE, OFr., OHG, ON, OProv., OS*)
PaGer.	Pennsylvania German
Pek.	Pekingese
Per.	Persian
PhilSp.	Philippine Spanish
Pol.	Polish
Port.	Portuguese
Prov.	Provençal
Pruss.	Prussian
Rom.	Romanian
Russ.	Russian
S	Saxon
Scand.	Scandinavian
Scot.	Scottish
Serb.	Serbian
Skt.	Sanskrit
Slav.	Slavic
Sp.	Spanish
Swed.	Swedish
Syr.	Syriac
Tag.	Tagalog
Turk.	Turkish
VL	Vulgar Latin
W	Welsh

8.8   PROOFREADING SYMBOLS

Proofreading symbols with marginal corrections are used to correct proof. A list of proofreading symbols and a sample of their application follow. The symbols are divided into two sections: those used in the text and those used in the margin. Every symbol used in the text requires a corresponding symbol or notation in the margin.

8.8.1   Symbols Used in the Text

error‡	Delete a character. The delete symbol is written in the margin.
errăr	Replace a character. The correct character is written in the margin.
er͜ror	Close up a space. The symbol is repeated in the margin.
errͨʝor	Delete a character and close up. The delete-and-close-up symbol is written in the margin.
Love truth, but ꞁɐꞁ pardon error.	Delete or replace more than one character. The delete symbol or the replacement copy is written in the margin.
Love truth꞉th, but pardon error.	Delete more than one character and close up. The delete-and-close-up symbol is written in the margin.
⟨Love truth, but pardon error.⟩	Delete, replace, or correct a block of text. The delete symbol, the replacement copy, or another instruction is written in the margin.
⟨Love truth, but pardon error.⟩	Move a block of text. To indicate the new location, a line is drawn on the proof, or instructions are written in the margin.
Love truth, Ⓑut pardon error.	Lowercase or capitalize text. The abbreviation *lc* or *cap*, circled, is written in the margin.
er͜or	Insert text. The material to be inserted is written in the margin.
Love truth, but|pardon error.	Add a space. The space symbol is written in the margin.

error3✓

Set a letter or number as a superscript. The symbol is repeated in the margin.

Love furth, pardon but error.

Transpose text. The abbreviation *tr*, circled, is written in the margin.

(2nd)error

Spell out a number or an abbreviation. The spelled form or the abbreviation *sp*, circled, is written in the margin.

8.8.2   Symbols Used in the Margin

/   separates corrections in the same line (*ℌ*/#); indicates that a correction is to be made more than once (*ℌ*//)

≡   indicates that an addition is a capital letter (placed under letter)

=   indicates that an addition is a small capital letter (placed under letter)

———   indicates that an addition is italic (placed under characters)

∅   numeral 0, not capital letter O

⌒   close up

ℌ   delete

ℌ   delete and close up

(tr)   transpose

add a space

(more#)   add more space

(less #)   remove space

⊙   add a period

˄   add a comma

⋮   add a colon

;   add a semicolon

˅   add an apostrophe or a single closing quotation mark

˅   add a single opening quotation mark

ᵛ ᵛ	add double quotation marks
⊬ ⊦	add parentheses
〔 〕	add square brackets
⊬	add a slash
⸗	add a hyphen
⊥⌐M	add a one-em dash
⊥⌐N	add a one-en dash
cap	capitalize
sc	make into small capitals
lc	lowercase
ital	italicize
rom	make roman
bf	make boldface
sp	spell out
¶	begin a new paragraph
no ¶	remove a paragraph break, running sentences together
⌐——	move to the left
——⌐	move to the right
⌐—⌐	move up
⌐—⌐	move down
‖	align vertically
stet	let stand as printed
wf	wrong font
Ⓧ	broken letter or dirty proof

8.8.3   Sample Marked Proof

(tr) "Now, waht I want is Facts. Teach
(less #)/# theseOboysand girls nothing but Facts.
(lc)/ℳ FActs alone are are wanted in life. Plarnnt ℳ
ℳ/ℳ nothing else, anmd root oøt everything u
else, You can only form the minds ⊙
(tr)/⌒ reasoning of an imals upon facts| nothing cap/: rom
rom else will ever be of any seyice to them. This r
is the principle on which Ibring up my #/ℳ
ℳ own up my own children, and this is the
principle on which I bring upOthese less #
children. Stick to the Facts, sir!, ℳ/"

APPENDIX:
OTHER SYSTEMS OF
DOCUMENTATION

A   Endnotes and Footnotes
    A.1   Documentation Notes versus the List of Works Cited and
          Parenthetical References
    A.2   Note Numbers
    A.3   Note Form versus Bibliographic Form
    A.4   Endnotes versus Footnotes
    A.5   Sample First Note References: Books and Other
          Nonperiodical Publications
    A.6   Sample First Note References: Articles and Other
          Publications in Periodicals
    A.7   Sample First Note References: Miscellaneous Print and
          Nonprint Sources
    A.8   Sample First Note References: Electronic Publications
    A.9   Subsequent References
B   Author-Date System
C   Number System
D   Specialized Style Manuals

This appendix describes three documentation systems other than the
MLA system. The appendix ends with a selected list of specialized
style manuals.

A   **ENDNOTES AND FOOTNOTES**

Some scholars in the fields of art, dance, history, music, religion, theater, and theology use endnotes or footnotes to document sources.

A.1   Documentation Notes versus the List of Works Cited and Parenthetical References

If you use notes for documentation, you may not need a list of works cited or a bibliography. (Check your editor's preference.) The first note referring to a source includes the publication information found in a bibliographic entry—the author's name, the title, and the publication facts—as well as the page reference identifying the portion of the source you refer to at that point in the text. (Subsequent references to a work require less information; see app., A.9.) A bibliographic entry for a work published as part of a book or periodical usually ends with the inclusive page numbers for the entire work cited, but a documentation note, in contrast, ends with the page number or numbers only of the portion you refer to. Note form differs slightly from bibliographic form in other ways (see app., A.3), and note numbers replace parenthetical references at the points in the text where citations are necessary (see app., A.2). Documentation notes appear either at the end of the text, as endnotes, or at the bottoms of relevant pages, as footnotes (see app., A.4).

A.2   Note Numbers

Number notes consecutively, starting from 1, throughout an essay or, usually, a chapter in a book, except for any notes accompanying special material, such as a figure or a table (see 4.2.7). Do not number them by page or designate them by asterisks or other symbols. Format note numbers as superior, or superscript, arabic numerals (i.e., raised slightly above the line, like this[1]), without periods, parentheses, or slashes. The numbers follow punctuation marks, except dashes. In general, to avoid interrupting the continuity of the text, place a note number, like a parenthetical reference, at the end of the sentence, clause, or phrase containing the material quoted or referred to.

A.3   Note Form versus Bibliographic Form

With some exceptions, documentation notes and bibliographic entries provide the same information but differ in form.

Bibliographic Form. A bibliographic entry has three main divisions, each followed by a period: the author's name reversed for alphabetizing, the title, and the publishing data.

```
Tannen, Deborah. You Just Don't Understand: Women and
    Men in Conversation. New York: Morrow, 1990.
```

Note Form. A documentation note has four main divisions: the author's name in normal order, followed by a comma; the title; the publishing data in parentheses; and a page reference. There is a period only at the end.

> [1] Deborah Tannen, You Just Don't Understand: Women and Men in Conversation (New York: Morrow, 1990) 52.

A.4   Endnotes versus Footnotes

In preparing a manuscript for publication, make all notes endnotes, unless your editor instructs otherwise. As their name implies, endnotes appear after the text, starting on a new page numbered in sequence with the preceding page. Center the title *Notes* one inch from the top, double-space, indent one inch (or five spaces) from the left margin, and add the note number, without punctuation, slightly above the line. Leave a space and give the reference. If the note extends to two or more lines, begin subsequent lines at the left margin. Type the notes consecutively, double-spaced, and number all pages.

Footnotes appear at the bottoms of pages, beginning four lines (or two double spaces) below the text. Single-space footnotes, but double-space between them. When a note continues on the following page, add a solid line across the new page two lines (or one double space) below the last line of the text and continue the note two lines (or one double space) below the solid line. Footnotes for the new page immediately follow the note continued from the previous page, after a double space.

A.5   Sample First Note References: Books and Other Nonperiodical Publications

Bibliographic entries corresponding to the following sample notes appear in the sections indicated in parentheses after the headings. Consult the appropriate section if you need additional information on citing a particular type of reference.

a. A Book by a Single Author (6.6.1)

> [1] David Cressy, Birth, Marriage, and Death: Ritual, Religion, and the Life Cycle in Tudor and Stuart England (New York: Oxford UP, 1997) 32.

b. An Anthology or a Compilation (6.6.2)

[2] Susan Fulop Kepner, ed. and trans., The Lioness in Bloom: Modern Thai Fiction about Women (Berkeley: U of California P, 1996) vii-viii.

c. A Book by Two or More Authors (6.6.4)

[3] Eric S. Rabkin, Martin H. Greenberg, and Joseph D. Olander, eds., No Place Else: Explorations in Utopian and Dystopian Fiction (Carbondale: Southern Illinois UP, 1983) 52-57.

d. A Book by a Corporate Author (6.6.6)

[4] Carnegie Foundation for the Advancement of Teaching, Campus Life: In Search of Community (Princeton: Carnegie Foundation for the Advancement of Teaching, 1990) 69.

e. A Work in an Anthology (6.6.7)

[5] Isabel Allende, "Toad's Mouth," trans. Margaret Sayers Peden, A Hammock beneath the Mangoes: Stories from Latin America, ed. Thomas Colchie (New York: Plume, 1992) 83.

f. An Article in a Reference Book (6.6.8)

[6] "Mandarin," The Encyclopedia Americana, 1994 ed.

g. An Introduction, a Preface, a Foreword, or an Afterword (6.6.9)

[7] Emory Elliott, afterword, The Jungle, by Upton Sinclair (New York: Signet, 1990) 348-50.

h. An Anonymous Book (6.6.11)

[8] A Guide to Our Federal Lands (Washington: Natl. Geographic Soc., 1984) 241-47.

i. An Edition (6.6.12)

[9] Charlotte Smith, The Poems of Charlotte Smith, ed. Stuart Curran (New York: Oxford UP, 1993) 121.

10 Fredson Bowers, ed., The Red Badge of Courage: An Episode of the American Civil War, by Stephen Crane (Charlottesville: UP of Virginia, 1975).

j. A Translation (6.6.13)

11 Laura Esquivel, Like Water for Chocolate: A Novel in Monthly Installments, with Recipes, Romances, and Home Remedies, trans. Carol Christensen and Thomas Christensen (New York: Doubleday, 1992) 1-5.

k. A Book Published in a Second or Subsequent Edition (6.6.14)

12 Geoffrey Chaucer, The Works of Geoffrey Chaucer, ed. F. W. Robinson, 2nd ed. (Boston: Houghton, 1957) 545.

l. A Multivolume Work (6.6.15)

13 Paul Lauter et al., eds., The Heath Anthology of American Literature, 2nd ed., 2 vols. (Lexington: Heath, 1994).

14 Arthur Conan Doyle, The Oxford Sherlock Holmes, ed. Owen Dudley Edwards, vol. 8 (New York: Oxford UP, 1993).

15 René Wellek, A History of Modern Criticism, 1750-1950, vol. 5 (New Haven: Yale UP, 1986) 322-26.

m. A Book in a Series (6.6.16)

16 Marshall R. Pihl, The Korean Singer of Tales, Harvard-Yenching Inst. Monograph Ser. 37 (Cambridge: Harvard UP, 1994) 62.

n. A Republished Book (6.6.17)

17 Margaret Atwood, Surfacing (1972; New York: Fawcett, 1987) 209-12.

o. A Publisher's Imprint (6.6.18)

18 Michael Ondaatje, The English Patient (New York: Vintage-Random, 1992).

p. A Book with Multiple Publishers (6.6.19)

[19] J. Wight Duff, A Literary History of Rome: From the Origins to the Close of the Golden Age, ed. A. M. Duff, 3rd ed. (1953; London: Benn; New York: Barnes, 1967) 88.

q. A Pamphlet (6.6.20)

[20] London (New York: Trip Builder, 1996).

r. A Government Publication (6.6.21)

[21] United Nations, Centre on Transnational Corporations, Foreign Direct Investment, the Service Sector, and International Banking (New York: United Nations, 1987) 4-6.

s. The Published Proceedings of a Conference (6.6.22)

[22] Kira Hall, Michael Meacham, and Richard Shapiro, eds., Proceedings of the Fifteenth Annual Meeting of the Berkeley Linguistics Society, February 18-20, 1989: General Session and Parasession on Theoretical Issues in Language Reconstruction (Berkeley: Berkeley Linguistics Soc., 1989).

t. A Book in a Language Other Than English (6.6.23)

[23] Emanuel Poche, Prazské Palace (Praha [Prague]: Odeon, 1977) 1-5.

u. A Book Published before 1900 (6.6.24)

[24] John Dewey, The School and Society (Chicago, 1899) 104.

v. A Book without Stated Publication Information or Pagination (6.6.25)

[25] Zvi Malachi, ed., Proceedings of the International Conference on Literary and Linguistic Computing ([Tel Aviv]: [Fac. of Humanities, Tel Aviv U], n.d.).

w. An Unpublished Dissertation (6.6.26)

26 Denise R. Stephenson, "Blurred Distinctions: Emerging Forms of Academic Writing," diss., U of New Mexico, 1996, 34.

x. A Published Dissertation (6.6.27)

27 Rudolf F. Dietze, Ralph Ellison: The Genesis of an Artist, diss., U Erlangen-Nürnberg, 1982, Erlanger Beiträge zur Sprach- und Kunstwissenschaft 70 (Nürnberg: Carl, 1982) 168.

A.6 Sample First Note References: Articles and Other Publications in Periodicals

For additional information on citing the following types of sources, consult the related sections on bibliographic entries, indicated in parentheses after the headings.

a. An Article in a Scholarly Journal with Continuous Pagination (6.7.1)

1 Andrea Henderson, "Passion and Fashion in Joanna Baillie's 'Introductory Discourse,'" PMLA 112 (1997): 213.

b. An Article in a Scholarly Journal That Pages Each Issue Separately (6.7.2)

2 Frederick Barthelme, "Architecture," Kansas Quarterly 13.3-4 (1981): 77-78.

c. An Article in a Scholarly Journal That Uses Only Issue Numbers (6.7.3)

3 Karen Stein, "Margaret Atwood's Modest Proposal: The Handmaid's Tale," Canadian Literature 148 (1996): 59.

d. An Article in a Scholarly Journal with More Than One Series (6.7.4)

4 Kathleen Spivack, "Between Two Cultures," Kenyon Review ns 17.3-4 (1995): 119-21.

⁵ Richard Striner, "Political Newtonism: The Cosmic Model of Politics in Europe and America," William and Mary Quarterly 3rd ser. 52 (1995): 590.

e. An Article in a Newspaper (6.7.5)

⁶ Dinitia Smith, "After Four Centuries, Still Gaining Devotees," New York Times 22 Apr. 1997, late ed.: C12.

⁷ Paul Taylor, "Keyboard Grief: Coping with Computer-Caused Injuries," Globe and Mail [Toronto] 27 Dec. 1993: A1.

f. An Article in a Magazine (6.7.6)

⁸ Rick Perlstein, "Abridged Too Far?" Lingua Franca Apr.-May 1997: 23.

g. A Review (6.7.7)

⁹ John Updike, "Fine Points," rev. of The New Fowler's Modern English Usage, ed. R. W. Burchfield, New Yorker 23-30 Dec. 1996: 142-43.

¹⁰ Janet Levarie Smarr, rev. of Authorizing Petrarch, by William J. Kennedy, Journal of English and Germanic Philology 95 (1996): 546.

¹¹ "The Cooling of an Admiration," rev. of Pound/Joyce: The Letters of Ezra Pound to James Joyce, with Pound's Essays on Joyce, ed. Forrest Read, Times Literary Supplement 6 Mar. 1969: 239-40.

¹² Rev. of Anthology of Danish Literature, ed. F. J. Billeskov Jansen and P. M. Mitchell, Times Literary Supplement 7 July 1972: 785.

h. An Abstract in an Abstracts Journal (6.7.8)

¹³ Denise R. Stephenson, "Blurred Distinctions: Emerging Forms of Academic Writing," diss., U of New Mexico, 1996, DAI 57 (1996): 1700A.

i. An Anonymous Article (6.7.9)

[14] "The Decade of the Spy," Newsweek 7 Mar. 1994: 26-27.

j. An Editorial (6.7.10)

[15] "Death of a Writer," editorial, New York Times 20 Apr. 1994, late ed.: A18.

k. A Letter to the Editor (6.7.11)

[16] Cynthia Ozick, letter, Partisan Review 57 (1990): 493-94.

l. A Serialized Article (6.7.12)

[17] Harrison T. Meserole and James M. Rambeau, "Articles on American Literature Appearing in Current Periodicals," American Literature 52 (1981): 704-05; 53 (1981): 164-66.

[18] Michael Winerip, "A Disabilities Program That 'Got out of Hand,'" New York Times 8 Apr. 1994, late ed.: A1; pt. 3 of a series, A Class Apart: Special Education in New York City, begun 6 Apr. 1994.

m. A Special Issue (6.7.13)

[19] Kwame Anthony Appiah and Henry Louis Gates, Jr., eds., Identities, spec. issue of Critical Inquiry 18.4 (1992): 625-884 (Chicago: U of Chicago P, 1995).

[20] Topographies, spec. issue of MLN 109.3 (1994): 345-581.

[21] Christiane Makward, "Reading Maryse Condé's Theater," Maryse Condé, ed. Delphine Perret and Marie-Denise Shelton, spec. issue of Callaloo 18.3 (1995): 681-82.

n. An Article in a Microform Collection of Articles (6.7.14)

[22] Dan Chapman, "Panel Could Help Protect Children," Winston-Salem Journal 14 Jan. 1990: 14, Newsbank: Welfare and Social Problems 12 (1990): fiche 1, grids A8-11.

o. An Article Reprinted in a Loose-Leaf Collection of Articles (6.7.15)

23 Brad Edmondson, "AIDS and Aging," <u>American</u>
<u>Demographics</u> Mar. 1990: 28+, <u>The AIDS Crisis</u>, ed.
Eleanor Goldstein, vol. 2 (Boca Raton: SIRS, 1991)
art. 24.

A.7   Sample First Note References: Miscellaneous Print and Nonprint Sources

For additional information on the following types of documentation,
consult the related sections on bibliographic entries, indicated in
parentheses after the headings.

a. A Television or Radio Program (6.8.1)

1 "<u>Frankenstein</u>: The Making of the Monster," <u>Great</u>
<u>Books</u>, narr. Donald Sutherland, writ. Eugenie Vink,
dir. Jonathan Ward, Learning Channel, 8 Sept. 1993.

b. A Sound Recording (6.8.2)

2 Claudio Abbado, cond., Symphony no. 6 in F, op.
68, and Symphony no. 8 in F, op. 93, by Ludwig van
Beethoven, Vienna Philharmonic, Deutsche Grammophon,
1987.

3 Billie Holiday, "God Bless the Child," rec.
9 May 1941, <u>The Essence of Billie Holiday</u>, Columbia,
1991.

4 Ben Kingsley, narr., <u>Buddhism</u>, audiocassette,
Carmichael, 1994.

5 D. K. Wilgus, Southern Folk Tales, rec. 23-25
Mar. 1965, audiotape, U of California, Los Angeles,
Archives of Folklore, B.76.82.

6 David Lewiston, liner notes, <u>The Balinese</u>
<u>Gamelan: Music from the Morning of the World</u>, LP,
Nonesuch, n.d.

c. A Film or Video Recording (6.8.3)

7 <u>It's a Wonderful Life</u>, dir. Frank Capra, perf.
James Stewart, Donna Reed, Lionel Barrymore, and Thomas
Mitchell, RKO, 1946.

[8] Jean Renoir, dir., <u>Grand Illusion</u> [<u>La grande</u> <u>illusion</u>], perf. Jean Gabin and Erich von Stroheim, 1938, videodisc, Voyager, 1987.

[9] <u>Looking at Our Earth: A Visual Dictionary</u>, sound filmstrip, Natl. Geographic Educ. Services, 1992.

d. A Performance (6.8.4)

[10] Diana Rigg, actor, <u>Medea</u>, by Euripides, trans. Alistair Elliot, dir. Jonathan Kent, Longacre Theatre, New York, 7 Apr. 1994.

[11] Scott Joplin, <u>Treemonisha</u>, dir. Frank Corsaro, cond. Gunther Schuller, perf. Carmen Balthrop, Betty Allen, and Curtis Rayam, Houston Grand Opera, Miller Theatre, Houston, 18 May 1975.

e. A Musical Composition (6.8.5)

[12] Ludwig van Beethoven, Symphony no. 8 in F, op. 93.

f. A Work of Art (6.8.6)

[13] Rembrandt van Rijn, <u>Aristotle Contemplating the</u> <u>Bust of Homer</u>, Metropolitan Museum of Art, New York.

[14] Mary Cassatt, <u>Mother and Child</u>, Wichita Art Museum, Wichita, <u>American Painting: 1560-1913</u>, by John Pearce (New York: McGraw, 1964) slide 22.

g. An Interview (6.8.7)

[15] Federico Fellini, "The Long Interview," <u>Juliet</u> <u>of the Spirits</u>, ed. Tullio Kezich, trans. Howard Greenfield (New York: Ballantine, 1966) 56.

[16] John Updike, interview with Scott Simon, <u>Weekend Edition</u>, Natl. Public Radio, WBUR, Boston, 2 Apr. 1994.

[17] I. M. Pei, personal interview, 22 July 1993.

h. A Map or Chart (6.8.8)

[18] <u>Washington</u>, map (Chicago: Rand, 1995).

[19] Japanese Fundamentals, chart (Hauppauge: Barron, 1992).

i. A Cartoon (6.8.9)

[20] Roz Chast, cartoon, New Yorker 7 Apr. 1997: 72.

[21] Garry Trudeau, "Doonesbury," cartoon, Star-Ledger [Newark] 2 Apr. 1997: 19.

j. An Advertisement (6.8.10)

[22] The Fitness Fragrance by Ralph Lauren, advertisement, GQ Apr. 1997: 111-12.

k. A Lecture, a Speech, an Address, or a Reading (6.8.11)

[23] Margaret Atwood, "Silencing the Scream," Boundaries of the Imagination Forum, MLA Convention, Royal York Hotel, Toronto, 29 Dec. 1993.

[24] Studs Terkel, address, Conf. on Coll. Composition and Communication Convention, Palmer House, Chicago, 22 Mar. 1990.

l. A Manuscript or Typescript (6.8.12)

[25] Mark Twain, notebook 32, ts., Mark Twain Papers, U of California, Berkeley, 50.

m. A Letter or Memo (6.8.13)

[26] Virginia Woolf, "To T. S. Eliot," 28 July 1920, letter 1138 of The Letters of Virginia Woolf, ed. Nigel Nicolson and Joanne Trautmann, vol. 2 (New York: Harcourt, 1976) 437-38.

[27] Thomas Hart Benton, letter to Charles Fremont, 22 June 1847, John Charles Fremont Papers, Southwest Museum Lib., Los Angeles.

[28] Toni Morrison, letter to the author, 19 Mar. 1997.

[29] Daniel J. Cahill, memo to English dept. fac., Brooklyn Technical High School, Brooklyn, NY, 29 May 1996.

n. A Legal Source (6.8.14)

30 Stevens v. National Broadcasting Co., 148 USPQ
755, CA Super. Ct., 1966.

A.8   Sample First Note References: Electronic Publications

For additional information on citing the following types of sources,
consult the related sections on bibliographic entries, indicated in
parentheses after the headings.

a. An Online Scholarly Project, Reference Database, or Professional or Personal Site (6.9.2)

1 Britannica Online, vers. 97.1.1, Mar. 1997,
Encyclopaedia Britannica, 29 Mar. 1997 <http://
www.eb.com/>.

2 The Cinderella Project, ed. Michael N. Salda,
vers. 1.0, Feb. 1995, De Grummond Children's Lit.
Research Collection, U of Southern Mississippi, 18 Mar.
1997 <http://www-dept.usm.edu/~engdept/cinderella/
cinderella.html>.

3 Giacomo da Lentini, "Amor è uno desio che ven da
core," Duecento: Repertorio elettronico della poesia
italiana dalle origini a Dante, ed. Francesco Bonomi,
1996, Si.Lab, Firenze, 19 Apr. 1997 <http://
www.silab.it/frox/200/tree128.htm>.

. 4 "Selected Seventeenth-Century Events," Romantic
Chronology, ed. Laura Mandell and Alan Liu, Oct. 1996,
U of California, Santa Barbara, 22 Nov. 1996 <http://
humanitas.ucsb.edu/projects/pack/rom-chrono/
chronola.htm>.

5 Portuguese Language Page, U of Chicago, 1 May
1997 <http://humanities.uchicago.edu/romance/port/>.

b. An Online Book (6.9.3)

6 Jane Austen, Pride and Prejudice, ed. Henry
Churchyard, 1996, 10 Sept. 1997 <http://
www.pemberley.com/janeinfo/pridprej.html>.

7 Nathaniel Hawthorne, Twice-Told Tales, ed.
George Parsons Lathrop (Boston: Houghton, 1883),

1 Mar. 1997 <http://www.tiac.net/users/eldred/nh/ttt.html>.

[8] Chrétien de Troyes, <u>Le Chevalier de la Charrette</u>, ed. Alfred Foulet and Karl D. Uitti (Paris: Bordas, 1989), <u>The</u> Charrette <u>Project</u>, ed. Uitti, 1994, Dept. of Romance Langs., Princeton U, 7 Feb. 1997 <http://www.princeton.edu/~lancelot/lancelo2.html>.

[9] John Keats, "Ode on a Grecian Urn," <u>Poetical Works</u>, 1884, <u>Project Bartleby</u>, ed. Steven van Leeuwen, Dec. 1995, Columbia U, 5 Jan. 1997 <http://www.columbia.edu/acis/bartleby/keats/keats54.html>.

c. An Article in an Online Periodical (6.9.4)

[10] Roy Flannagan, "Reflections on Milton and Ariosto," <u>Early Modern Literary Studies</u> 2.3 (1996): 16 pars., 22 Feb. 1997 <http://unixg.ubc.ca:7001/0/e-sources/emls/02-3/flanmilt.html>.

[11] Steve Coates, "A Dead Language Comes to Life on the Internet," <u>New York Times on the Web</u> 28 Oct. 1996, 20 Apr. 1997 <http://www.nytimes.com/web/docsroot/library/cyber/week/1028Latin.html>.

[12] Elizabeth McCracken, "Desiderata," <u>Bold Type</u> Mar. 1997, 7 Mar. 1997 <http://www.bookwire.com/boldtype/mccracken/read.article$197>.

[13] Gretchen V. Angelo, rev. of <u>The Book of the Body Politic</u>, by Christine de Pizan, <u>Bryn Mawr Medieval Review</u> 96.1.7 (1996), 26 Jan. 1997 <gopher://gopher.lib.virginia.edu:70/00/alpha/bmmr/v96/96-1-7>.

[14] Kathleen Coyne Kelly, "Malory's Body Chivalric," <u>Arthuriana</u> 6.4 (1996): 52-71, abstract, 27 Aug. 1997 <http://dcwww.mediasvcs.smu.edu/Arthuriana/Abstract/Ab_list3.htm>.

[15] "Agents of Influence," editorial, <u>Christian Science Monitor</u> 11 Mar. 1997, 11 Mar. 1997 <http://www.csmonitor.com/todays_paper/graphical/today/edit/edit.1.html>.

[16] Trudy Festinger, letter, <u>New York Times on the Web</u> 11 Mar. 1997, 11 Mar. 1997 <http://www.nytimes.com/yr/mo/day/letters/lfesti.html>.

d. A Publication on CD-ROM, Diskette, or Magnetic Tape (6.9.5)

[17] A. R. Braunmuller, ed., <u>Macbeth</u>, by William Shakespeare, CD-ROM (New York: Voyager, 1994).

[18] <u>English Poetry Full-Text Database</u>, magnetic tape, rel. 2 (Cambridge, Eng.: Chadwyck-Healey, 1993).

[19] Elaine C. Thiesmeyer and John E. Thiesmeyer, <u>Editor: A System for Checking Usage, Mechanics, Vocabulary, and Structure</u>, diskette, vers. 5.2 (New York: MLA, 1996).

[20] "Albatross," <u>The Oxford English Dictionary</u>, 2nd ed., CD-ROM (Oxford: Oxford UP, 1992).

[21] Steve Coates, "Et Tu, Cybernetica Machina User?," <u>New York Times</u> 28 Oct. 1996, late ed.: D4, <u>New York Times Ondisc</u>, CD-ROM, UMI-Proquest, Dec. 1996.

[22] <u>Guidelines for Family Television Viewing</u> (Urbana: ERIC Clearinghouse on Elementary and Early Childhood Educ., 1990), <u>ERIC</u>, CD-ROM, SilverPlatter, June 1993.

[23] Denise R. Stephenson, "Blurred Distinctions: Emerging Forms of Academic Writing," <u>DAI</u> 57 (1996): 1700A, U of New Mexico, 1996, <u>Dissertation Abstracts Ondisc</u>, CD-ROM, UMI-Proquest, Dec. 1996.

[24] <u>Perseus 2.0: Interactive Sources and Studies on Ancient Greece</u>, CD-ROM, 4 discs (New Haven: Yale UP, 1996).

e. A Work in More Than One Publication Medium (6.9.6)

[25] <u>Perseus 1.0: Interactive Sources and Studies on Ancient Greece</u>, CD-ROM, videodisc (New Haven: Yale UP, 1992).

f. A Work in an Indeterminate Medium (6.9.7)

[26] John Bartlett, <u>Familiar Quotations</u>, 9th ed. (Boston: Little, 1901), New York: Columbia U, Academic

Information Systems, 1995, electronic, ColumbiaNet, Columbia U, 19 Feb. 1997.

g. Other Electronic Sources (6.9.8)

27 John Eliot Gardiner, "The Importance of Beethoven," interview, Charlie Rose, PBS, 25 July 1996, transcript, Broadcast News, CD-ROM, Primary Source Media, July 1996, 23 screens.

28 Franklin D. Roosevelt, "Americanism," 1920, American Leaders Speak: Recordings from World War I and the 1920 Election, 1996, American Memory, Lib. of Congress, Washington, 19 Mar. 1997 <http://lcweb2.loc.gov/mbrs/nforum/9000024.ram>.

29 Jonathan Frakes, dir., Star Trek: First Contact, Paramount, 1996, 1 May 1997 <http://firstcontact.msn.com/db/media/stfctea3.mov>.

30 Hans Holbein, The Ambassadors, Microsoft Art Gallery: The Collection of the National Gallery, London, CD-ROM (Redmond: Microsoft, 1994).

31 Susan Kamit, interview, Bold Type Mar 1997, 7 Mar. 1997 <http://www.bookwire.com/boldtype/mccracken/read.article$199>.

32 "Phoenix, Arizona," map, U.S. Gazetteer, US Census Bureau, 13 Mar. 1997 <http://www.census.gov/cgi-bin/gazetteer>.

33 Al Cacicedo, "Private Parts: Preliminary Notes for an Essay on Gender Identity in Shakespeare," working paper, n.d., 27 Aug. 1997 <http://www.arts.ubc.ca/english/iemls/shak/PRIVATE_PARTS.txt>.

34 James L. Harner, e-mail to the author, 20 Aug. 1996.

35 Wendell Piez, "Sustained Reading vs. Synchronic Access," online posting, 23 Jan. 1997, Humanist Discussion Group, 24 Jan. 1997 <gopher://lists.princeton.edu:70/OR369820-373704/humanist/logs/log9701>.

36 Dene Grigar, online defense of dissertation "Penelopeia: The Making of Penelope in Homer's Story

and Beyond," 25 July 1995, LinguaMOO, 1 May 1997
<http://wwwpub.utdallas.edu/~cynthiah/lingua_archive/
phd-defense.txt>.

    [37] TACT: Text-Analysis Computing Tools, vers.
2.1 gamma, 30 Apr. 1997 <gopher://
gopher.epas.utoronto.ca:70/11/cch/hum_comp/software/
TACT>.

A.9   Subsequent References

After fully documenting a work, use a shortened form in subsequent notes. As in parenthetical references (see 7.2), include enough information to identify the work. The author's last name alone, followed by the relevant page numbers, is usually adequate.

    [4] Frye 345-47.

If you cite two or more works by the same author—for example, Northrop Frye's *Anatomy of Criticism* and his *The Double Vision*—include a shortened form of the title following the author's last name in each reference after the first.

    [8] Frye, Anatomy 278.
    [9] Frye, Double Vision 1-3.

Repeat the information even when two references in sequence refer to the same work. The abbreviations *ibid.* and *op. cit.* are not recommended.

B   AUTHOR-DATE SYSTEM

The author-date system, used in the social sciences and in many of the physical sciences, requires that a parenthetical reference include the author's last name, a comma, the work's year of publication, another comma, and the page reference, preceded by the abbreviation *p.* or *pp.*: "(Wilson, 1992, p. 73)." Information cited in the text is omitted from the parenthetical reference. The authoritative guide to this documentation system is the *Publication Manual of the American Psychological Association* (see the list of specialized style manuals in app., D), and the system is often called APA style.

    APA and MLA bibliographic forms differ in a number of ways: in APA style, only the initials of the first and middle names are given; the year of publication, in parentheses, follows the author's name; for a book, only proper nouns and the first word of the title and of the subtitle are capitalized; the names of some publishers, such as university presses and associations, are spelled out; and the first line of the entry is indented, while the second and subsequent lines are flush with the left margin.

> Tannen, D. (1990). <u>You just don't understand:</u>
> <u>Women and men in conversation</u>. New York: Morrow.

If the book is edited, the abbreviation *Ed.* or *Eds.*, in parentheses, precedes the year of publication.

> Tannen, D. (Ed.). (1985). <u>Gender and</u>
> <u>conversational interaction</u>. New York: Oxford
> University Press.

If there are two or more authors, each name is reversed, and an ampersand (*&*), not the word *and*, precedes the final name.

> Durant, W., & Durant, A. (1977). <u>A dual</u>
> <u>autobiography</u>. New York: Simon and Schuster.

Titles of essays, book chapters, and articles in periodicals are capitalized like titles of books but are neither put in quotation marks nor underlined. Journal titles, however, are capitalized in a manner consistent with MLA capitalization style (see 3.7.1) and are underlined. The volume number, also underlined, follows the journal title and a comma; the issue number, if needed, appears in parentheses after the volume number; a comma and the inclusive page numbers for the article complete the entry.

> Craner, P. M. (1991). New tool for an ancient art:
> The computer and music. <u>Computers and the Humanities</u>,
> <u>25</u>, 303-13.

If the list of works cited includes more than one work by an author, the entries are arranged chronologically, and the author's name is repeated in each entry. If two or more works by the same author were published in a year, each is assigned a lowercase letter: "(1998a)," "(1998b)." For a multivolume work, the range of volume numbers is given in parentheses, preceded by the abbreviation *Vols.*: "(Vols. 1–4)."

The following parenthetical references and corresponding list of works cited demonstrate the author-date system.

Between 1968 and 1988, television coverage of presidential elections changed dramatically (Hallin, 1992, p. 5).

Eighteenth-century England was a "humble satellite" in the world of music and art (Durant & Durant, 1965, pp. 214-48).

Frye defined the alazon as a "self-deceiving or self-deceived character in fiction" (1957a, p. 365).

Wellek admits in the middle of his multivolume history of modern literary criticism, "An evolutionary history of criticism must fail. I have come to this resigned conclusion" (1955-92, Vol. 5, p. xxii).

There are several excellent essays in the book Sound and Poetry (Frye, 1957b).

To Will and Ariel Durant, creative men and women make "history forgivable by enriching our heritage and our lives" (1977, p. 406).

Works Cited

Durant, W., & Durant, A. (1965). The age of Voltaire. New York: Simon and Schuster.

Durant, W., & Durant, A. (1977). A dual autobiography. New York: Simon and Schuster.

Frye, N. (1957a). Anatomy of criticism: Four essays. Princeton: Princeton University Press.

Frye, N. (Ed.). (1957b). Sound and poetry. New York: Columbia University Press.

Hallin, D. C. (1992). Sound bite news: Television coverage of elections, 1968-1988. Journal of Communication, 42 (2), 5-24.

Wellek, R. (1955-92). A history of modern criticism, 1750-1950. (Vols. 1-8). New Haven: Yale University Press.

C   NUMBER SYSTEM

Disciplines such as chemistry, mathematics, medicine, and physics use the number system, which varies from field to field (see the list of specialized style manuals by discipline in app., D). In the number system, arabic numerals designate entries in the list of works cited and appear in parenthetical documentation followed by commas and the relevant volume and page references, which are preceded by the appropriate abbreviations: "(13, Vol. 5, p. 259)." With this system, the year of publication remains at the end of the bibliographic entry, and the works are usually listed not in alphabetical order but in the order in which they are first cited in the text. Titles generally follow APA style (app., B).

But Peter Scotto has offered another view (1).

Frye defined the <u>alazon</u> as a "self-deceiving or self-deceived character in fiction" (2, p. 365).

Wellek admits in the middle of his multivolume history of modern literary criticism, "An evolutionary history of criticism must fail. I have come to this resigned conclusion" (3, Vol. 5, p. xxii).

Eighteenth-century England was a "humble satellite" in the world of music and art (4, pp. 214-48).

To Will and Ariel Durant, creative men and women make "history forgivable by enriching our heritage and our lives" (5, p. 406).

Works Cited

1. Scotto, P. Censorship, reading, and interpretation: A case study from the Soviet Union. <u>PMLA</u> 109 (1994): 61-70.
2. Frye, N. <u>Anatomy of criticism: Four essays</u>. Princeton: Princeton University Press, 1957.
3. Wellek, R. <u>A history of modern criticism, 1750-1950</u>. 8 vols. New Haven: Yale University Press, 1955-92.
4. Durant, W., and Durant, A. <u>The age of Voltaire</u>. New York: Simon and Schuster, 1965.

5. Durant, W., and Durant, A. <u>A dual autobiography</u>. New York: Simon and Schuster, 1977.

D   SPECIALIZED STYLE MANUALS

Every scholarly field has its preferred style. MLA style, as presented in this manual, is widely accepted in humanities disciplines. The following manuals describe the styles of other disciplines.

BIOLOGY
Council of Biology Editors. *CBE Style Manual: A Guide for Authors, Editors, and Publishers in the Biological Sciences*. 6th ed. Bethesda: Council of Biology Editors, 1994.

CHEMISTRY
American Chemical Society. *The ACS Style Guide: A Manual for Authors and Editors*. Washington: Amer. Chemical Soc., 1986.

GEOLOGY
United States. Geological Survey. *Suggestions to Authors of the Reports of the United States Geological Survey*. 7th ed. Washington: GPO, 1991.

LINGUISTICS
Linguistic Society of America. *LSA Bulletin*, Dec. issue, annually.

MATHEMATICS
American Mathematical Society. *A Manual for Authors of Mathematical Papers*. 8th ed. Providence: Amer. Mathematical Soc., 1990.

MEDICINE
American Medical Association. *AMA Manual of Style*. 8th ed. Chicago: Amer. Medical Assn., 1990.

PHYSICS
American Institute of Physics. *Style Manual for Guidance in the Preparation of Papers*. 4th ed. New York: Amer. Inst. of Physics, 1990.

PSYCHOLOGY
American Psychological Association. *Publication Manual of the American Psychological Association*. 4th ed. Washington: Amer. Psychological Assn., 1994.

There are also style manuals that address primarily editors and concern procedures for preparing a manuscript for publication:

The Chicago Manual of Style. 14th ed. Chicago: U of Chicago P, 1993.

United States. Government Printing Office. *Style Manual.* Rev. ed. Washington: GPO, 1984.

Words into Type. By Marjorie E. Skillin, Robert M. Gay, et al. 3rd ed. Englewood Cliffs: Prentice, 1974. New ed. in preparation.

For other style manuals and authors' guides, see John Bruce Howell, *Style Manuals of the English-Speaking World* (Phoenix: Oryx, 1983).

Sources of Examples in 3.4–5

Page 67—"Synonyms have": adapted from Frederic G. Cassidy, "Learning from Dictionaries," *Language Variation in North American English: Research and Teaching*, ed. A. Wayne Glowka and Donald M. Lance (New York: MLA, 1993) 67.

Page 67—"Inexpensive examples": Paula R. Feldman, "How Their Audiences Knew Them: Forgotten Media and the Circulation of Poetry by Women," *Approaches to Teaching British Women Poets of the Romantic Period*, ed. Stephen C. Behrendt and Harriet Kramer Linkin, Approaches to Teaching World Lit. 60 (New York: MLA, 1997) 37.

Page 67—"Priests, conjurers": Thomas L. Clark, "Using Toponymic Onomastics in a Pedagogical Setting to Demonstrate Phonological Variation (An Essay on Names)," *Language Variation in North American English: Research and Teaching*, ed. A. Wayne Glowka and Donald M. Lance (New York: MLA, 1993) 72.

Page 67—"To some writers": adapted from William Costanzo, "Reading, Writing, and Thinking in an Age of Electronic Literacy," *Literacy and Computers: The Complications of Teaching and Learning with Technology*, ed. Cynthia L. Selfe and Susan Hilligoss (New York: MLA, 1994) 16.

Page 67—"Originally the plantations": adapted from Salikoko S. Mufwene, "Investigating Gullah: Difficulties in Ensuring 'Authenticity,'" *Language Variation in North American English: Research and Teaching*, ed. A. Wayne Glowka and Donald M. Lance (New York: MLA, 1993) 178.

Pages 67–68—"Perhaps the most ambitious": Jahan Ramazani, "The Wound of History: Walcott's *Omeros* and the Postcolonial Poetics of Affliction," *PMLA* 112 (1997): 406.

Page 68—"For men": adapted from Karin A. Wurst, introduction, *Adelheit von Rastenberg: An English Translation*, by Eleonore Thon, trans. George F. Peters, Texts and Trans. 4 (New York: MLA, 1996) xxv.

Page 68—"The dialogue": Karin A. Wurst, introduction, *Adelheit von Rastenberg: An English Translation*, by Eleonore Thon, trans. George F. Peters, Texts and Trans. 4 (New York: MLA, 1996) vii.

Page 68—"A title": Lev Petrovich Yakubinsky, "On Dialogic Speech," trans. Michael Eskin, *PMLA* 112 (1997): 252.

Page 68—"It is not": Angelika Bammer, letter, *PMLA* 111 (1996): 1151.

Page 68—"Baron François-Pascal-Simon Gérard": Joan DeJean, introduction, *Ourika: An English Translation*, by Claire de Duras, trans. John Fowles, introd. DeJean and Margaret Waller, Texts and Trans. 3 (New York: MLA, 1994) viii–ix.

Page 69—"All these subjects": adapted from James Thorpe, introduction, *Relations of Literary Study: Essays on Interdisciplinary Contributions*, ed. Thorpe (New York: MLA, 1967) viii.

Page 69—"A brief comparison": Karin A. Wurst, introduction, *Adelheit von Rastenberg: An English Translation*, by Eleonore Thon, trans. George F. Peters, Texts and Trans. 4 (New York: MLA, 1996) xvii.

Page 69—"After the separation": Joan DeJean, introduction, *Letters from a Peruvian Woman*, by Françoise de Graffigny, trans. David Kornacker, introd. DeJean and Nancy K. Miller, Texts and Trans. 2 (New York: MLA, 1993) x.

Page 69—"In this charged atmosphere": adapted from Philip Fisher, "American Literary and Cultural Studies since the Civil War," *Redrawing the Boundaries: The Transformation of English and American Literary Studies*, ed. Stephen Greenblatt and Giles Gunn (New York: MLA, 1992) 233.

Page 70—"When Zilia": Nancy K. Miller, introduction, *Letters from a Peruvian Woman*, by Françoise de Graffigny, trans. David Kornacker, introd. Joan DeJean and Miller, Texts and Trans. 2 (New York: MLA, 1993) xx.

Page 70 —"Fin de siècle Spain": adapted from Joyce Tolliver, introduction, *"Torn Lace" and Other Stories*, by Emilia Pardo Bazán, trans. María Cristina Urruela, Texts and Trans. 5 (New York: MLA, 1996) xiv.

Page 70 —"Sometimes this is where": Angelika Bammer, letter, *PMLA* 111 (1996): 1151.

Page 70 —"Alexander Pope": adapted from John B. Vickery, "Literature and Myth," *Interrelations of Literature*, ed. Jean-Pierre Barricelli and Joseph Gibaldi (New York: MLA, 1982) 69.

Page 70 —"What makes Sartre's theory": adapted from Matei Calinescu, "Literature and Politics," *Interrelations of Literature*, ed. Jean-Pierre Barricelli and Joseph Gibaldi (New York: MLA, 1982) 135.

Page 70 —"In 1947": adapted from Harold B. Allen, "American English Enters Academe," *Language Variation in North American English: Research and Teaching*, ed. A. Wayne Glowka and Donald M. Lance (New York: MLA, 1993) 6.

Pages 70–71 —"Bakhtin's notion": adapted from Carrie Noland, "Poetry at Stake: Blaise Cendrars, Cultural Studies, and the Future of Poetry in the Literature Classroom," *PMLA* 112 (1997): 41.

Page 71 —"Miller has taken": adapted from Matthew C. Roudané, "Materials," *Approaches to Teaching Miller's* Death of a Salesman, ed. Roudané, Approaches to Teaching World Lit. 52 (New York: MLA, 1995) 16.

Page 71 —"In the afterlife": adapted from Paula Bennett, "Phillis Wheatley's Vocation and the Paradox of the 'Afric Muse,' " *PMLA* 113 (1998): 71.

Page 71 —"From his darkness": adapted from Ann Paton, *"King Lear* in a Literature Survey Course," *Approaches to Teaching Shakespeare's* King Lear, ed. Robert H. Ray, Approaches to Teaching World Lit. 12 (New York: MLA, 1986) 76.

Page 71 —"The current political": adapted from Eric Gadzinski, "The Year of Living Dangerously; or, Not Just an Adventure, but a Job," *ADE Bulletin* 117 (1997): 35.

Page 72 —"Shelley remarks": adapted from Susan J. Wolfson, "Feminist Inquiry and *Frankenstein*," *Approaches to Teaching Shelley's* Frankenstein, ed. Stephen C. Behrendt, Approaches to Teaching World Lit. 33 (New York: MLA, 1990) 59.

Page 72 —"Thérèse, the washerwoman": adapted from Rosemarie Garland Thomson, "Speaking about the Unspeakable: The Representation of Disability as Stigma in Toni Morrison's Novels," *Courage and Tools: The Florence Howe Award for Feminist Scholarship, 1974–1989*, ed. Joanne Glasgow and Angela Ingram (New York: MLA, 1990) 250.

Page 72 —"All five": adapted from Richard Pilgrim, "The *Tale of Genji* in a Religio-Aesthetic Perspective," *Approaches to Teaching Murasaki Shikibu's* The Tale of Genji, ed. Edward Kamens, Approaches to Teaching World Lit. 47 (New York: MLA, 1993) 48.

Page 72 —"As Emerson's friend": adapted from Joel Conarroe, introduction, *Introduction to Scholarship in Modern Languages and Literatures*, ed. Joseph Gibaldi (New York: MLA, 1981) xi.

Page 73 —"Most such standards": Paul Hernadi, "Literary Theory," *Introduction to Scholarship in Modern Languages and Literatures*, ed. Joseph Gibaldi (New York: MLA, 1981) 110.

Page 73 —"Atwood's other visual art": Thomas B. Friedman and Shannon Hengen, "Materials," *Approaches to Teaching Atwood's* The Handmaid's Tale *and Other Works*, ed. Sharon R. Wilson, Friedman, and Hengen, Approaches to Teaching World Lit. 56 (New York: MLA, 1996) 15.

Page 73 —"The new art relation": adapted from Jon D. Green, "Determining Valid Interart Analogies," *Teaching Literature and Other Arts*, ed. Jean-Pierre Barricelli, Joseph Gibaldi, and Estella Lauter (New York: MLA, 1990) 10.

Page 73 —"The human race": Linda Kauffman, "Special Delivery: Twenty-First-Century Epistolarity in *The Handmaid's Tale*," *Courage and Tools: The Florence Howe Award for Feminist Scholarship, 1974–1989*, ed. Joanne Glasgow and Angela Ingram (New York: MLA, 1990) 234.

Page 74 —"Most newcomers": adapted from Thomas L. Clark, "Using Toponymic Onomastics in a Pedagogical Setting to Demonstrate Phonological Variation (An Essay on Names)," *Language Variation in North American English: Research and Teaching*, ed. A. Wayne Glowka and Donald M. Lance (New York: MLA, 1993) 73.

Page 74 —"Whether we locate": adapted from Annette Kolodny, "Dancing through the Minefield: Some Observations on the Theory, Practice, and Politics of a Feminist Literary Criticism," *Courage and Tools: The Florence Howe Award for Feminist Scholarship, 1974–1989*, ed. Joanne Glasgow and Angela Ingram (New York: MLA, 1990) 95.

Page 77 —"Teachers often": adapted from Teresa Vilardi, "Bard College: Freshman Workshop in Language and Thinking," *New Methods in College Writing Programs: Theories in Practice*, ed. Paul Connolly and Vilardi (New York: MLA, 1986) 8.

Page 78 —"Baillie relies": Andrea Henderson, "Passion and Fashion in Joanna Baillie's 'Introductory Discourse,'" *PMLA* 112 (1997): 208.

Page 78 —"One commentator": adapted from Neil ten Kortenaar, "Beyond Authenticity and Creolization: Reading Achebe Writing Culture," *PMLA* 110 (1995): 41.

Page 78 —"From its inception": adapted from Stephen Barker, "The Crisis of Authenticity: *Death of a Salesman* and the Tragic Muse," *Approaches to Teaching Miller's* Death of a Salesman, ed. Matthew C. Roudané, Approaches to Teaching World Lit. 52 (New York: MLA, 1995) 82.

Page 78 —"During the Meiji period": adapted from John Whittier Treat, "Beheaded Emperors and the Absent Figure in Contemporary Japanese Literature," *PMLA* 109 (1994): 106.

Page 78 —"In a 1917 letter": Richard Heinemann, "Kafka's Oath of Service: 'Der Bau' and the Dialectic of Bureaucratic Mind," *PMLA* 111 (1996): 257.

Page 79 —"The editor": adapted from Francis I. Andersen, "The Hebrew Bible (Old Testament)," *Scholarly Editing: A Guide to Research*, ed. D. C. Greetham (New York: MLA, 1995) 47.

Page 79 —"The essay": adapted from Joseph A. Boone, "Vacation Cruises; or, The Homoerotics of Orientalism," *PMLA* 110 (1995): 103.

Page 79 —"The class": adapted from Wendy Steiner, "Literature and Painting," *Teaching Literature and Other Arts*, ed. Jean-Pierre Barricelli, Joseph Gibaldi, and Estella Lauter (New York: MLA, 1990) 42.

Page 81 —"The exercise": adapted from Mary Fuller and Donald A. Daiker, "Miami University: Freshman Composition Program," *New Methods in College Writing Programs: Theories in Practice*, ed. Paul Connolly and Teresa Vilardi (New York: MLA, 1986) 80.

INDEX

a *See* articles
AAUP   *See* Association of American University Presses
abbreviations 8
  in addresses (geographic) 8.3
  of French titles of persons 3.6.5
  of geographic names 8.3
  guidelines for use of 8.1
  in lists of works cited 6.6.1
  for literary works 8.6.2–4
    Chaucer 8.6.3
    classics 8.6.4
    in parenthetical references 7.4.8
    Shakespeare 8.6.2
  lowercase 8.1
  of names of languages 8.7
  of names of persons (initials) 3.6.5, 6.6.1, 7.2, 8.1
  with numbers 3.10.2
  in parenthetical documentation 7.2, 7.4.8, 8.6
  plurals of 3.4.7g, 8.1
  for proofreading 8.8
  of publishers' names 8.5
  punctuation with 8.1
    French titles of persons 3.6.5
    plurals 3.4.7g
  for religious works 8.6.1
  scholarly 8.4
  spacing with 8.1
  for time 3.10.5, 8.2
  of titles of works 3.8.6, 8.6
  uppercase 8.1
  use of 8.1
abridged editions
  in lists of works cited 6.6.14
  in note references A.5k (app.)
abstracts
  of dissertations 5.5.2–3, 5.6.2
  journals of 6.7.8
  in lists of works cited
    from abstracts journals 6.7.8

abstracts, in lists of works cited *(cont.)*
    on CD-ROM, diskette, magnetic tape 6.9.5
    online 6.9.4e
  in note references
    from abstracts journals A.6h (app.)
    on CD-ROM, diskette, magnetic tape A.8c (app.)
    online A.8c (app.)
  in parenthetical references 7.4.1
abstracts journals 6.7.8
accents, on foreign words
  in alphabetization of German 3.3.5
  reproducing 3.3.4–5
access, dates of, for electronic sources 6.9.1
acknowledgments
  in books 4.1.2
  in dissertations 5.5.3
acronyms   *See* abbreviations
acts, legal
  in lists of works cited 6.8.14
  in note references A.7n (app.)
  titles of 3.8.5
acts, of plays
  mentioned in text 3.7.1, 3.8.5
  numbers for 3.10.7, 7.4.8
actual malice 2.3.4
AD, in dates 8.2
  placement of 3.10.5
adaptations, in lists of works cited 6.8.1–3
addresses (geographic)
  abbreviations of 8.3
  numbers with 3.10.2
  punctuation with 3.10.3
addresses (network) 6.9.1
addresses (speeches)   *See* speeches
addresses (street) 3.10.2–3
adjectives
  capitalization of, in titles 3.7.1
  compound 3.4.6a–f
  coordinate 3.4.2c
  in French 3.7.2

adjectives *(cont.)*
  in German 3.7.3
  in Italian 3.7.4
  numbers in 3.4.6d
  in Portuguese 3.7.5
  punctuation with
    commas 3.4.2c
    hyphens 3.4.6a–f
  in Russian 3.7.6
  in Spanish 3.7.7
adverbs
  in German 3.7.3
  in Italian 3.7.4
  as phrases, punctuation of 3.4.2e
advertisements
  for books 1.6.6
  in lists of works cited 6.8.10
    electronic sources 6.9.8h
  in note references A.7j (app.)
    electronic sources A.8g (app.)
Aeneid, abbreviation for 8.6.4
Aeschylus, abbreviations for works of 8.6.4
afterwords
  in lists of works cited 6.6.9
  mentioned in text 3.7.1, 3.8.5
  in note references A.5g (app.)
Agamemnon, abbreviation for 8.6.4
agents, literary 1.5.4, 2.2.1
Agreement on Trade-Related Aspects of Intel-
    lectual Property Rights 2.1.16
agreements, publication *See* contracts, publi-
    cation
aircraft, names of 3.8.2
All rights reserved 2.1.9
alphabetization 6.5
  a, an, the in 6.5, 6.6.11, 6.7.9
  of indexes 1.6.3
  letter by letter 1.6.3, 6.5
  in lists of works cited 6.5, 6.6.1, 6.6.11
    anonymous works 6.5, 6.6.11, 6.7.7,
      6.7.9
    coauthors 6.5
    multiple works by same author 6.6.3
  of names of persons 6.5
    Dutch 3.6.4
    French 3.6.5
    German 3.6.4
    Hungarian 3.6.7
    Italian 3.6.8
    punctuation 6.6.1
    Spanish 3.6.10
  word by word 1.6.3
a.m. 8.1–2

American Chemical Society style manual
  D (app.)
American Heritage Dictionary, The 3.3.1
American Institute of Physics style manual
  D (app.)
American Library Association romanization
  tables 3.11
American Mathematical Society style manual
  D (app.)
American Medical Association style manual
  D (app.)
American Psychological Association (APA)
  documentation style B (app.)
Amharic 3.11
an See articles
and, comma before 3.4.2a–b
angle brackets, with URLs 6.9.1
annotated bibliographies, preparing 1.5.2
annotated lists of works cited 6.3, 6.5
annotations, in lists of works cited 6.3, 6.6.1
anonymous submission of manuscripts, format
  for 1.4.4, 4.2.5
anonymous works
  in lists of works cited 6.6.1
    alphabetization 6.5, 6.6.11, 6.7.7
    articles 6.7.9
    books 6.6.11
    online publications 6.9.2
  in note references
    articles A.6i (app.)
    books A.5h (app.)
    online publications A.8a (app.)
  in parenthetical references 7.4.4, 7.4.9
anthologies (entire works)
  copyright and 2.1.2, 2.1.5, 2.1.9
  editing 1.5.2
  in lists of works cited 6.6.2
    electronic sources 6.9.2–3, 6.9.5
  in note references A.5b (app.)
    electronic sources A.8a, b, d (app.)
  of original essays, compiling 1.5.2
  in parenthetical references 7.4.1–3, 7.4.9
  of previously published essays, compiling
    1.5.2
  types of 1.5.2
anthologies, works in
  compensation for contributing 2.2.2
  copyright and 2.1.2, 2.1.5, 2.1.9
  in lists of works cited 6.6.7
    electronic sources 6.9.2–3, 6.9.5
  in note references A.5e (app.)
    electronic sources A.8a, b, d (app.)
  publication contracts for 2.2.2

anti-, hyphen with 3.4.6h
Antigone, abbreviation for 8.6.4
APA (American Psychological Association) documentation style B (app.)
Apocrypha, abbreviations for 8.6.1
apostrophes 3.4.7
  for contractions 3.4.7
  for possessives 3.4.7a–f
  with proper nouns 3.4.7e–f
appendixes (of works)
  in books 4.1.2
  mentioned in text 3.7.1, 3.8.5
Arabic
  capitalization in 3.7.9
  transliteration of 3.11
arabic numerals 3.10.1
Aristophanes, *Lysistrata*, abbreviation for 8.6.4
Armenian 3.11
art, documentation style in field of A (app.)
  See also artworks
articles (*a, an, the*)
  in abbreviations of publishers' names 8.5
  in alphabetization 6.5, 6.6.11, 6.7.9
  introductory, in titles of periodicals 3.7.1, 6.7.1, 6.7.5
  lowercasing of, in titles 3.7.1
articles, periodical
  anonymous *See* anonymous works
  in lists of works cited 6.7
    abstracts 6.7.8
    from anthologies 6.6.7
    on CD-ROM, diskette, magnetic tape 6.9.5
    editorials 6.7.10
    from journals 6.7.1–4
    letters to editor 6.7.11
    from loose-leaf collections 6.7.15
    from magazines 6.7.6
    from microform collections 6.7.14
    from newspapers 6.7.5
    online 6.9.4
    page numbering 6.7.1–2
    from reference books 6.6.8
    reprints 6.7.15
    reviews 6.7.7
    serialized articles 6.7.12
  in note references A.6 (app.)
    from anthologies A.5e (app.)
    electronic sources A.8c–d (app.)
    from reference books A.5f (app.)
  in parenthetical references
    entire articles 7.4.1, 7.4.9

articles, periodical, in parenthetical references (*cont.*)
    listed by title 7.4.4
    part of 7.4.2, 7.4.6, 7.4.9
  titles of 3.7.1, 3.8.3–4
  types of scholarly 1.4.2
  See also encyclopedia articles; journal articles; magazine articles; newspaper articles
artworks
  in lists of works cited 6.8.6
    electronic sources 6.9.8d
  in note references A.7f (app.)
    electronic sources A.8g (app.)
  reproduced in manuscripts 4.2.7
  titles of 3.8.2
ASCII 4.4
Asian names 3.6.12
Assamese 3.11
Association of American University Presses
  directory 1.5.3
  guidelines for manuscripts 4.3
associations, as authors 6.6.6
audience for scholarly writing, assessing 3.1
audiocassettes
  in lists of works cited 6.8.2
  in note references A.7b (app.)
  titles of 3.8.2
audiotapes
  in lists of works cited 6.8.2
  in note references A.7b (app.)
author-date (APA) system, of documentation B (app.)
authors, names of 3.6
  initials 6.6.1, 8.1
  in lists of works cited 6.6.1, 6.6.3, 6.7.1, 6.9.3–5
    corporate 6.6.6, 6.6.21
    multiple 6.6.4
  on manuscripts 4.2.5
  in note references A.5a (app.)
    corporate A.5d, r (app.)
    multiple A.5c (app.)
  in parenthetical references 7.2–3
    corporate 7.4.5
    multiple 7.4.1–2, 7.4.6, 7.4.9
  pseudonyms 3.6.3
  spelling out, in documentation 6.6.1
  See also anonymous works

Bacchae, abbreviation for 8.6.4
ballets *See* dance performances
BC, in dates 8.2
  placement of 3.10.5

BCE, in dates 8.2
  placement of 3.10.5
Beckley Newspapers Corp. v. Hanks 2.3.4
Belorussian 3.11
Bengali 3.11
Beowulf, abbreviation for 8.6.4
Berne Convention 2.1.7–9, 2.1.16
Bible
  abbreviations for 7.4.8, 8.6.1
  citing 3.8.5
  in parenthetical references 7.4.8
  titles of books and versions of 3.8.5
bibliographic notes, in text 7.5.2
bibliographies
  annotated, preparing 1.5.2
  on CD-ROM, documentation of 6.9.5b
  in manuscripts *See* works cited, lists of
Bibliography, as heading 6.3
bills, in lists of works cited 6.6.21
binding
  of books 1.6.5
  of manuscripts 4.2.9
  of theses and dissertations 5.5.6
biology, style manual for D (app.)
BiP (*Books in Print*) 1.5.3
Blue Book, The 6.8.14
Boccaccio, *Decameron*, abbreviation for 8.6.4
book reviews *See* reviews
books
  anonymous *See* anonymous works
  copyright and 2.1.1–16
  design of 1.6.4
  divisions of, mentioned in text 3.7.1, 3.8.5
  indexes for, preparing 1.6.3
  in lists of works cited 6.6
    anthologies 6.6.2, 6.6.7
    on CD-ROM, diskette, magnetic tape 6.9.5
    by corporate author 6.6.6
    in foreign language 6.6.23
    with long titles 6.6.1
    missing information 6.6.25
    by more than three authors 6.6.4
    multiple works by single author 6.6.3
    multivolume 6.6.15
    online 6.9.3
    published before 1900 6.6.24
    reference 6.6.8
    republished 6.6.17
    in series 6.6.16
    by single author 6.6.1
    by two or more authors 6.6.4
    two or more by same authors 6.6.5

books *(cont.)*
  manuscripts for
    acceptance of 1.5.7
    copyediting of 1.6.1
    evaluation of 1.5.6
    submitting 1.5.5
  marketing of 1.6.6
  in note references A.5
    electronic sources A.8b, d (app.)
  in parenthetical references
    entire books 7.4.1
    listed by title 7.4.4
    no page numbers 7.2, 7.4.2, 7.4.8, 7.4.10
    parts of 7.4.2
    published before 1800 7.4.10
    signatures and no page numbers 7.4.10
  parts of, mentioned in text 3.7.1, 3.8.5
  printing and binding of 1.6.5
  production of 1.6.1–5
  proofreading of 1.6.2
  prospectus for 1.5.4
  publication contracts for 2.2.1
  titles of 3.7.1, 3.8.1–2, 3.8.4
    shortened 3.8.6, 6.6.1
  typesetting of 1.6.5
  types of scholarly 1.5.2
Books in Print 1.5.3
brackets *See* angle brackets, with URLs;
      square brackets
Brazilian Portuguese 3.7.5
Buenos Aires Convention 2.1.9
buildings, names of 3.8.5
Bulgarian 3.11
bulletin boards, electronic
  copyright and 2.1.17
  in lists of works cited 6.9.8k
  in note references A.8g (app.)
Burmese 3.11
Burrow-Giles Lithographic Co. v. Sarony 2.1.2
but, comma before 3.4.2a
by 6.6.9, 6.6.12–13
Byron, *Don Juan*, abbreviation for 8.6.4

c. (*circa*), with dates of publication 6.6.25
calls for papers 1.4.3
Candide, abbreviation for 8.6.4
capitalization
  of *edition* 3.7.1
  of entire words in titles 3.7.1
  in French 3.7.2
  in German 3.7.3
  in Italian 3.7.4
  in Latin 3.7.8

capitalization *(cont.)*
  of names of parts of works 3.7.1
  in Portuguese 3.7.5
  in Russian 3.7.6
  of *series* 3.7.1
  in Spanish 3.7.7
  of titles of works 3.7.1
    in author-date (APA) style B (app.)
captions, in manuscripts 4.2.7
carets 4.2.8
cartoons
  in lists of works cited 6.8.9
    electronic sources 6.9.8g
  in note references A.7i (app.)
    electronic sources A.8g (app.)
cases, law *See* laws and legal sources
CD-ROM, diskette, or magnetic tape, publications on
  in lists of works cited 6.9.5, 6.9.8
  in note references A.8d, g (app.)
  in parenthetical references
    corporate author 7.4.5
    entire works 7.4.1, 7.4.4–5, 7.4.9
    listed by title 7.4.4, 7.4.9
    no page numbers 7.2, 7.4.2, 7.4.8–9
    parts of 7.4.2, 7.4.8
CDs (compact discs), titles of 3.8.2 *See also* musical compositions; sound recordings
CE, in dates 8.2
  placement of 3.10.5
centuries
  hyphens with 3.10.5
  in Italian 3.7.4
Cervantes, *Don Quixote*, abbreviation for 8.6.4
chapters, of books
  mentioned in text 3.7.1, 3.8.5
  titles of 3.8.3
characters, fictional, names of 3.6.3
charts
  as illustrations in manuscripts 4.2.7
  in lists of works cited 6.8.8
  in note references A.7h (app.)
Chaucer, abbreviations for works of 8.6.3
chemistry
  documentation style in C (app.)
  style manual for D (app.)
Chicago Manual of Style, The, on indexing 1.6.3
Chinese
  capitalization in 3.7.9
  names of persons in 3.6.1, 3.6.12
  romanization of 3.11
choreographers, in lists of works cited 6.8.4

Church Slavonic 3.11
circa 6.6.25
citations *See* parenthetical documentation
clauses, punctuation of 3.4.2a–b, 3.4.2e–f, 3.4.3a
co-, hyphen with 3.4.6h
coding, of electronic manuscripts 4.4–5
collaboration, in publishing 1.1
collections *See* anthologies (entire works); anthologies, works in
colons 3.4.4
  before lists, elaborations, rules, principles 3.4.4a
    dashes instead of 3.4.5c
  after place of publication 6.6.1
  with quotation marks 3.9.7
  before quotations 3.4.4b, 3.9.2, 3.9.7
  before subtitles 3.7.1, 6.6.1
colophons 6.6.23
commas 3.4.2
  between adjectives 3.4.2c
  with alternative or contrasting phrases 3.4.2g
  clauses and 3.4.2a–b, e–f
  before coordinating conjunctions (*and, but, for, nor, or, yet, so*) 3.4.2a
  in dates 3.4.2l–m, 3.10.5
  after introductory phrases 3.4.2f
  with nonrestrictive (nonessential) modifiers 3.4.2e
  in numbers 3.10.3
  with parenthetical comments 3.4.2d
  with quotations 3.9.7
  to separate words, phrases, clauses 3.4.2b
commissions, as authors 6.6.6
committees, as authors 6.6.6
common knowledge, omitting documentation for 6.1
compact discs, titles of 3.8.2 *See also* musical compositions; sound recordings
compilations *See* anthologies (entire works); anthologies, works in
compilers
  in lists of works cited 6.6.1–3, 6.6.7, 6.6.21
    electronic sources 6.9.3, 6.9.5
  in note references A.5b–c, e (app.)
composers
  in lists of works cited 6.8.1–5
  in note references A.7b–e (app.)
composition (typesetting), of books 1.6.5
compound subjects, objects, and verbs, commas with 3.4.2j
compound words, hyphens with 3.4.6
  adjectives 3.4.6a–f, 3.4.10

computer networks *See* online publications
computer software
  for indexing 1.6.3
  in lists of works cited
    on CD-ROM or diskette 6.9.5
    downloaded 6.9.8m
  in note references A.8d, g (app.)
  word processors, word wrapping in 3.3.2
concerts
  in lists of works cited 6.8.4
  in note references A.7d (app.)
  See also musical compositions; perfor-
    mances; reviews
conductors
  in lists of works cited 6.8.1–4
  in note references A.7b, d (app.)
Conference on Fair Use 2.1.13
conferences
  electronic
    in lists of works cited 6.9.8k
    in note references A.8g (app.)
  proceedings of
    in lists of works cited 6.6.22
    in note references A.5s (app.)
  titles of 3.8.5
CONFU (Conference on Fair Use) 2.1.13
congressional publications
  in lists of works cited 6.6.21
  in note references A.5r (app.)
conjunctions
  capitalization of, in titles 3.7.1
  commas before coordinating (*and, but, for,*
    nor, or, yet, so) 3.4.2a
consent as defense, in privacy action 2.4.4
Constitution *See* historical documents
consultant readers
  for book publishers 1.5.6
  for journals 1.4.5
contents, tables of, in books 4.1.2
contractions 3.4.7
contracts, publication
  for books 1.5.7, 1.6.3, 2.2.1
  for contributions to edited works 2.2.2
  guides on 2.5
  for journal articles 1.4.6, 2.2.2
contributors, notes on, in books 4.1.2
copyediting, of manuscripts 1.6.1, 4.3
  of indexes 1.6.3
  preparations for 1.3, 3.3.1
copyright 2.1
  actions for infringement of 2.1.8
  compilations and 2.1.2, 2.1.5, 2.1.9
  computer networks and 2.1.9, 2.1.11, 2.1.17
  contracts with publisher and 2.2

copyright *(cont.)*
  co-ownership of 2.1.4
  damages for infringing 2.1.8, 2.1.15
  dates, citing as publication years 6.6.1
  of dissertations 5.6.3
  fair use and 2.1.13
  guides on 2.5
  inheritance of 2.1.10, 2.1.12
  international 2.1.16
  law, development of 2.1.1, 2.1.16
  material objects and 2.1.6
  notices of 2.1.9
    in dissertations 5.6.3
  online publications and 2.1.9, 2.1.11,
    2.1.17
  pages for notice of 4.1.2
  and permission requests 2.1.14
  protection, scope of 2.1.2
  registration of 2.1.8
  renewal of 2.1.9–10
  rights encompassed by 2.1.11
  symbol 2.1.9, 2.1.16
  terms of 2.1.7
  transferring 2.1.4–5, 2.1.10, 2.1.12
  works made for hire and 2.1.3, 2.1.12
Copyright, as word in copyright notice 2.1.9
corporate authors 6.6.6
  in lists of works cited 6.6.6, 6.6.21
  in note references A.5d, r (app.)
  in parenthetical references 7.4.5, 7.4.9
corrections
  in manuscripts 4.2.8
  in proofs 8.8
Council of Biology Editors style manual
  D (app.)
Council of Editors of Learned Journals 1.4.6
countries, abbreviations for 8.3
  in lists of works cited 6.6.1
courses, titles of 3.8.5
court cases *See* laws and legal sources
cross-references, in lists of works cited 6.6.10
Curtis Publishing Co. v. Butts 2.3.4
Cyrillic script, languages in 3.11

DA (Dissertation Abstracts)
  in lists of works cited 6.7.8
  in note references A.6h (app.)
DAI (Dissertation Abstracts International) 5.6.2
  in lists of works cited 6.7.8
  in note references A.6h (app.)
dance, documentation style in field of A (app.)
dance performances
  in lists of works cited 6.8.4–5
  in note references A.7d (app.)

dance performances *(cont.)*
  reviews of
    in lists of works cited 6.7.7
    in note references A.6g (app.)
  titles of 3.8.2
Dante, abbreviations for works of 8.6.4
dashes 3.4.5
databases *See* CD-ROM, diskette, or magnetic
    tape, publications on; electronic publi-
    cations; online publications
dates, of access, for online sources 6.9.1
dates, of publication
  anthologies, works in 6.6.7
  approximated 6.6.25
  for books 6.6.1, 6.9.3
  c. (circa) with 6.6.25
  for electronic publications
    on CD-ROM, diskette, magnetic tape
      6.9.5
    online 6.9.1–4
  for multivolume works 6.6.15
  not given
    in lists of works cited 6.6.25
    in note references A.5v
  for periodicals 6.7.1, 6.9.4
  for reprints 6.6.7, 6.6.17
  to date 6.6.15
  for works in progress 6.6.15
dates, writing of
  abbreviations 8.2
  with *AD, BC, BCE, CE* 3.10.5
  as adjectives before nouns 3.10.5
  capitalization
    in French 3.7.2
    in Italian 3.7.4
    in Portuguese 3.7.5
    in Russian 3.7.6
    in Spanish 3.7.7
  centuries 3.10.5
  decades 3.10.5
  format for 3.10.5
  numerals 3.10.2, 3.10.5
  punctuation 3.4.2l–m, 3.10.3, 3.10.5
  ranges of years 3.10.6
  seasons 3.4.2m
days
  abbreviations for 8.2
  capitalization of
    in French 3.7.2
    in German 3.7.3
    in Italian 3.7.4
    in Portuguese 3.7.5
    in Russian 3.7.6
    in Spanish 3.7.7

Decameron, abbreviation for 8.6.4
decimal fractions, numerals in 3.10.2
Declaration of Independence *See* historical
    documents
dedications, in books 4.1.2
defamation 2.3
  guides on 2.5
definitions, dictionary *See* dictionary
    entries
degrees, academic
  abbreviations for 8.4
  in lists of works cited 6.6.1
design, of publications 1.6.4
  publisher as arbiter of 2.2.1
deuterocanonical works, abbreviations for
    8.6.1
diacritical marks, reproducing 3.3.4–5
diaereses, reproducing 3.3.5
diagonals (/) *See* slashes
dialogue, quotations of 3.9.4
dictionaries, use of 3.3.1–3
dictionary entries
  in lists of works cited 6.6.8
    electronic sources 6.9.2, 6.9.5
  in note references A.5f (app.)
    electronic sources A.8a, d (app.)
  in parenthetical references 7.2
dioramas, in lists of works cited 6.8.8
directors, of films
  in lists of works cited 6.8.3
  in note references A.7c (app.)
*Directory of Electronic Journals, Newsletters, and
    Academic Discussion Lists* 1.4.3
discriminatory language 3.2
  guides on avoiding 3.12
discussion lists, e-mail
  in lists of works cited 6.9.8k
  in note references A.8g (app.)
diskette, publications on *See* CD-ROM,
    diskette, or magnetic tape, publica-
    tions on
Dissertation Abstracts
  in lists of works cited 6.7.8
  in note references A.6h (app.)
Dissertation Abstracts International 5.6.2
  in lists of works cited 6.7.8
  in note references A.6h (app.)
dissertations
  abstracts of, writing 5.6.2
  binding of 5.5.6
  copyright of 5.6.3
  electronic publication of 5.7
  format of 5.2, 5.5
  guidelines for 5.2

dissertations *(cont.)*
  in lists of works cited
    abstracts 6.7.8
    published 6.6.27
    unpublished 6.6.26
  in note references A.5w–x (app.)
  in parenthetical references 7.4.9
  permissions needed for 5.6.4
  preparing 5
  prospectus for 5.4
  publishing 1.5.2, 5.6–7
  topics for 5.3
  University Microfilms International, as publisher of 5.6, 6.6.27
Divehi 3.11
divisions
  of books, mentioned in text 3.7.1, 3.8.5
  of manuscripts 4.1
    for articles 4.1.1
    for books 4.1.2
  of theses and dissertations 5.5.2
  of words 3.3.2
documentation, methods of
  American Psychological Association style B (app.)
  author-date system B (app.)
  endnotes and footnotes A (app.)
  manuals about D (app.)
  MLA style 6.2, 7.1
  number system C (app.)
  See also endnotes and footnotes; note references; parenthetical documentation; works cited, lists of
documentation, parenthetical   *See* parenthetical documentation
documents, government
  in lists of works cited 6.6.21
  in note references A.5r (app.)
Don Juan, abbreviation for 8.6.4
Don Quixote, abbreviation for 8.6.4
double-spacing
  of manuscripts 4.2.4
  in theses and dissertations 5.5.5
Dr. 3.6.2
dramas   *See* plays
drawings, as illustrations in manuscripts 4.2.7
Dutch, names of persons in 3.6.4

ed. 6.6.2, 6.6.7, 6.6.12, 6.6.14, 6.9.2–3, 6.9.5
edition, capitalizing 3.7.1
editions
  abridged or revised
    in lists of works cited 6.6.14
    in note references A.5k (app.)

editions *(cont.)*
  facsimile, in lists of works cited 6.6.12
  first or subsequent
    in lists of works cited 6.6.14
    in note references A.5k (app.)
    in parenthetical references 7.4.1–4, 7.4.8–9
  governed by publication contracts 2.2.1
  of newspapers 6.7.5
  no edition given 6.6.14
  scholarly
    conventions of 3.1
    definition of 6.6.12
    in lists of works cited 6.6.12
    in note references A.5i (app.)
    in parenthetical references 7.4.8–9
    preparing 1.5.2
    types of 1.5.2
editorial boards
  for book publishers 1.5.6
  for journals 1.4.1, 1.4.5
editorials
  in lists of works cited 6.7.10
    electronic sources 6.9.4f
  in note references A.6j (app.)
    electronic sources A.8c (app.)
  in parenthetical references 7.4.4
editors 1.1–2
  in author-date (APA) system B (app.)
  at book publishers 1.5.1, 1.5.4–7
  of collections 1.5.2
  ed. 6.6.2, 6.6.7, 6.6.12, 6.6.14, 6.9.2–3, 6.9.5
  on journal staffs 1.4.5–6
  in lists of works cited
    of anthologies 6.6.2, 6.6.7
    in cross-references 6.6.10
    of electronic publications 6.9.2–3, 6.9.5
    general editors 6.6.15
    of scholarly editions 6.6.12
  in note references A.5b, e, i, l (app.)
    electronic publications A.8a, b, d (app.)
  in parenthetical references 7.4.1–3, 7.4.8–9
  queries from, answering 1.6.1
  of scholarly editions 1.5.2
electronic mail   *See* e-mail
electronic manuscripts 4.3–5
  underlining in 3.5
electronic publications
  assessing 6.9.1
  in lists of works cited 6.9
    on CD-ROM, diskette, magnetic tape 6.9.5, 6.9.8
    in an indeterminate medium 6.9.7
    in more than one medium 6.9.6
    online 6.9.2–4, 6.9.8

electronic publications *(cont.)*
  media of, distinguishing 6.9.5
  in note references A.8 (app.)
  numbering sections of 4.4, 6.9.1, 6.9.5
  in parenthetical references
    entire works 7.4.1, 7.4.6, 7.4.9
    listed by title 7.4.4, 7.4.9
    no page numbers 7.2, 7.4.2, 7.4.6, 7.4.8–9
    parts of 7.4.2, 7.4.6, 7.4.8–9
  scholarly manuscripts as 4.4–5
  theses and dissertations as 5.7
  See also CD-ROM, diskette, or magnetic tape,
    publications on; online publications
ellipses
  in long titles 6.6.1
  in quotations 3.9.5
e-mail
  in lists of works cited 6.9.8j
    discussion lists 6.9.8k
  in note references A.8g (app.)
emphasis, italics for 3.5.3
encyclopedia articles
  in lists of works cited 6.6.8
    electronic sources 6.9.2, 6.9.5
  in note references A.5f (app.)
    electronic sources A.8a, d (app.)
  in parenthetical references 7.4.4
  titles of 3.8.3
endnotes and footnotes A.1–4 (app.)
  line spacing A.4 (app.)
  vs. lists of works cited A.1 (app.), A.3 (app.)
  numbers for 7.5, A.2 (app.)
  placement of 7.5, A.4 (app.)
  punctuation of A.2–3 (app.)
  See note references *for specific formats*
English, capitalization in 3.7.1
Epic of Gilgamesh, abbreviation for 8.6.4
epigraphs, in books 4.1.2
essays
  compiling collections of 1.5.2
  in lists of works cited 6.6.7
    electronic sources 6.9.5
  in note references A.5e (app.)
    electronic sources A.8b–d (app.)
  titles of 3.8.3–4
et al.
  in lists of works cited 6.6.4
  in parenthetical references 7.2
Eumenides, abbreviation for 8.6.4
Euripides, abbreviations for works of 8.6.4
evaluation, of manuscripts
  by book publishers 1.5.6
  by journals 1.4.5
examples, musical, in manuscripts 4.2.7

exclamation points 3.4.11
  with quotation marks 3.9.7
  in quotations 3.9.7
exhibits
  in lists of works cited 6.8.8
  for marketing books 1.6.6

facsimile editions, in lists of works cited
    6.6.12
Faerie Queene, The, abbreviation for 8.6.4
fair use, of copyrighted works 2.1.13
false-light tort 2.4.3
*Feist Publications, Inc., v. Rural Telephone Service,
    Inc.* 2.1.2
fictional characters, names of 3.6.3
figures (illustrations), in manuscripts 4.2.7
films
  in lists of works cited 6.8.3
    online or on CD-ROM 6.9.8c
  in note references A.7c (app.)
    online or on CD-ROM A.8g (app.)
  in parenthetical references 7.4.1
  reviews of, in lists of works cited 6.7.7
    electronic sources 6.9.4d
  reviews of, in note references A.6g (app.)
    electronic sources A.8c (app.)
  titles of 3.8.2
flash cards, in lists of works cited 6.8.8
footnotes   *See* endnotes and footnotes; *see* note
    references *for specific formats*
for, comma before 3.4.2a
foreign countries   *See* countries, abbreviations
    for
foreign languages   *See specific languages*
foreign languages, works in
  in lists of works cited 6.6.23
  in note references A.5t (app.)
foreign words
  accents and special characters with
    in alphabetization of German 3.3.5, 3.6.4
    reproducing 3.3.4–6
  in Danish 3.3.6
  in Dutch 3.6.4
  in French 3.3.4, 3.3.6, 3.6.5, 3.7.2
  in German 3.3.5–6, 3.6.4, 3.7.3
  in Greek 3.6.6
  in Hungarian 3.6.7
  in Italian 3.6.8, 3.7.4
  italics and 3.5.2
  in Latin 3.6.11, 3.7.8
  in Norwegian 3.3.6
  in Portuguese 3.7.5
  in Russian 3.6.9, 3.7.6
  in Spanish 3.6.10, 3.7.7

foreign words *(cont.)*
  spelling of 3.3.4–6
  translations of 3.4.8b
forewords
  in books 4.1.2
  in lists of works cited 6.6.9
  mentioned in text 3.7.1, 3.8.5
  in note references A.5g (app.)
  page numbers of 3.10.7
format, of manuscripts
  in electronic form 4.3–5
  in printed form 4.1.1–3, 4.2
forwarded electronic documents 6.9.8k
fractions, numerals in 3.10.2
French
  capitalization in 3.7.2
  names of persons in 3.6.5

galley proofs *See* proofreading
games, in lists of works cited 6.8.8
gender, in language 3.2
  guides on 3.12
general editors, in lists of works cited 6.6.15
genres, of scholarly writing 3.1
geographic names *See* names, of places
geology, style manual for D (app.)
Georgian 3.11
German
  capitalization in 3.7.3
  diaereses in 3.3.5
  ligatures in 3.3.6
  names of persons in 3.6.4
globes, in lists of works cited 6.8.8
glossaries, in books 4.1.2
Government Printing Office 6.6.21
government publications
  in lists of works cited 6.6.21
  in note references A.5r (app.)
GPO (Government Printing Office) 6.6.21
grammar
  software for checking 4.2.8
  See also punctuation
graphs, as illustrations in manuscripts 4.2.7
Greek
  names of persons in 3.6.6
  transliteration of 3.11
guides, on writing 3.12
Gujarati 3.11
Gulliver's Travels, abbreviation for 8.6.4

handbooks, on writing 3.12
headings, in manuscripts 4.1.1–3, 4.2.5
Hebrew 3.11

Heptaméron, abbreviation for 8.6.4
Her Majesty's Stationery Office 6.6.21
Hindi 3.11
Hippolytus, abbreviation for 8.6.4
His Majesty's Stationery Office 6.6.21
historical documents
  in lists of works cited 6.8.14
  in note references A.7n (app.)
history, documentation style for A (app.)
HMSO (Her [or His] Majesty's Stationery
    Office) 6.6.21
home pages *See* World Wide Web, publica-
    tions on
Homer, abbreviations for works of 8.6.4
house style 1.6.1
HTML 4.4–5
humanities, documentation style for 6.2,
    D (app.)
Hungarian, names of persons in 3.6.1, 3.6.7
Hypertext Markup Language (HTML) 4.4–5
hyphenation (word division) 3.3.2
hyphens 3.4.6
  with centuries 3.10.5
  between coequal nouns 3.4.6g
  in compound terms 3.4.6, 3.4.10
  in dates as adjectives 3.10.5
  for dates of works in progress 6.6.15
  in French names of persons 3.6.5
  three, for names in lists of works cited
    6.6.3–5

ibid., avoiding A.9 (app.)
Iliad, abbreviation for 8.6.4
illustrations
  lists of, in books 4.1.2
  in manuscripts 1.4.4, 1.5.4, 4.2.7
ILMP (*International Literary Market Place*) 1.5.3–4
imprints, publishers'
  definition of 6.6.18
  in lists of works cited 6.6.18
  in note references A.5o (app.)
inclusive numbers 3.10.6–7
indentations
  for dialogue quotations 3.9.4
  for first words of paragraphs 4.2.3
  parenthetical references and 7.3
  for poetry quotations 3.9.3
  for prose quotations 3.9.2
indexes
  in books 4.1.2
  mentioned in text 3.7.1, 3.8.5
  preparing 1.6.3
    governed by publication contracts 2.2.1

indirect sources, in parenthetical references
7.4.7
Inferno, abbreviation for 8.6.4
infinitives, capitalization of, in titles 3.7.1
initials, for names of persons 8.1
in lists of works cited 6.6.1
periods with 8.1
insertions, in manuscripts 4.2.8
installments, articles published in 6.7.12
International Literary Market Place 1.5.3–4
Internet   *See* online publications; World Wide
Web, publications on
interviews
in lists of works cited 6.8.7
electronic sources 6.9.8e
in note references A.7g (app.)
electronic sources A.8g (app.)
in parenthetical references 7.4.2
introductions
in books 4.1.2
in lists of works cited 6.6.9, 6.6.12
mentioned in text 3.7.1, 3.8.5
in note references A.5g (app.)
page numbers of 3.10.7
in parenthetical references 7.4.6
invasion of privacy 2.4
warranties on, in publication contracts 2.2.1
issues, of periodicals
in lists of works cited 6.7.1–3
page numbering 6.7.1–2
special issues 6.7.13
in note references A.6b–c (app.)
special issues A.6m
Italian
capitalization in 3.7.4
names of persons in 3.6.8
italics 3.5   *See also* underlining

Japanese
capitalization in 3.7.9
names of persons in 3.6.1, 3.6.12
romanization of 3.11
jargon 3.2
journal articles
compensation for contributing 2.2.2
copyright and 2.1.5
in lists of works cited 6.7.1
anonymous 6.7.9
on CD-ROM, diskette, magnetic tape
6.9.5
editorials 6.7.10
issues 6.7.1–3
letters to editor 6.7.11

journal articles, in lists of works cited *(cont.)*
from loose-leaf collections 6.7.15
from microform collections 6.7.14
with multiple series 6.7.3
online 6.9.4a
page numbering 6.7.1–2
reviews 6.7.7
serialized 6.7.12
manuscripts for
acceptance of 1.4.6
evaluation of 1.4.5
copyediting of 1.6.1
submitting 1.4.4
in note references A.6a–d, g, i–l, n–o (app.)
electronic sources A.8c–d (app.)
in parenthetical references 7.4.1–2, 7.4.6, 7.4.9
proofreading of 1.6.2
publication contracts for 2.2.2
titles of 3.7.1, 3.8.3–4
typesetting of 1.6.5
types of 1.4.2
See also articles, periodical
journals
copyright and 2.1.5
definition of 1.4.1–2, 6.7.1
design of 1.6.4
editorial boards of 1.4.1, 1.4.5
editors of 1.4.5–6
printing and binding of 1.6.5
readers, consultant, for 1.4.5
selecting for submissions 1.4.3
special issues of
calls for submissions to 1.4.3
in lists of works cited 6.7.13
in note references A.6m
submitting manuscripts to 1.4
titles of 3.8.2
Jr., punctuation with 6.6.1
justification of lines, in manuscripts 4.2.1

Kannada 3.11
Kashmiri 3.11
Khmer 3.11
kits, in lists of works cited 6.8.8
Korean
names of persons in 3.6.1, 3.6.12
romanization of 3.11
Kurdish 3.11

labels, in manuscripts 4.2.7
language, of scholarly writing 3.1–2
copyediting and 1.6.1
guides on usage and style 3.12, D (app.)

language, of scholarly writing *(cont.)*
  nonsexist 3.2
  software for checking 4.2.8
languages, names of
  abbreviations for 8.7
  capitalization of
    in French 3.7.2
    in German 3.7.3
    in Italian 3.7.4
    in Russian 3.7.6
    in Spanish 3.7.7
languages, other than English   *See* foreign languages, works in; foreign words; *and specific languages*
Lao 3.11
Latin
  capitalization in 3.7.8
  names of persons in 3.6.11
laws and legal sources
  in lists of works cited 6.8.14
    Blue Book, The 6.8.14
    law cases 6.8.14
  in note references A.7n (app.)
  titles of 3.8.5
lectures   *See* speeches
legal issues, in scholarly publishing 2
Lepcha 3.11
letters (correspondence)
  in lists of works cited 6.8.13
    to editor 6.7.11, 6.9.4g
  in note references A.7m (app.)
    to editor A.6k (app.), A.8c (app.)
letters, of the alphabet
  plurals of 3.4.7
  referred to as letters 3.5.1
libel 2.3
  guides on 2.5
  warranties on, in publication contracts 2.2.1
Library of Congress
  requirement for deposit of published works 2.1.8
  romanization tables 3.11
librettos
  in lists of works cited 6.8.2
  in note references A.7b (app.)
ligatures, reproducing 3.3.6
Limbu 3.11
line numbers
  abbreviations with, avoiding 7.4.8
  commas omitted from 3.10.3
  in parenthetical references 7.4.8
linguistics, style manual for D (app.)
Linguistic Society of America style manual D (app.)

lists
  punctuation introducing
    colons 3.4.4a
    dashes 3.4.5c
  of works cited   *See* works cited, lists of
Literary Agents of North America 1.5.4
Literary Market Place 1.5.3–4
literary works, documentation of
  abbreviations for 8.6.4
  Chaucer 8.6.3
  classics 8.6.4
  religious works 8.6.1
  Shakespeare 8.6.2
  in parenthetical references 7.4.8
Literature Cited, as heading 6.3
LMP (Literary Market Place) 1.5.3–4
loose-leaf collections of articles
  in lists of works cited 6.7.15
  in note references A.6o (app.)
LSA Bulletin D (app.)
Lyrical Ballads, abbreviation for 8.6.4
Lysistrata, abbreviation for 8.6.4

Macedonian 3.11
magazine articles
  in lists of works cited 6.7.6
    anonymous 6.7.9
    on CD-ROM, diskette, magnetic tape 6.9.5
    editorials 6.7.10
    letters to editor 6.7.11
    from loose-leaf collections 6.7.15
    from microform collections 6.7.14
    online 6.9.4c
    reviews 6.7.7
    serialized 6.7.12
  in note references A.6f–g, i–l, n–o (app.)
    electronic sources A.8c–d (app.)
  in parenthetical references 7.4.4, 7.4.9
  titles of 3.8.3
  See also articles, periodical
magazines, titles of 3.8.2
magnetic tape, publications on   *See* CD-ROM, diskette, or magnetic tape, publications on
MAI Systems Corp. v. Peak Computer, Inc. 2.1.17
Malayalam 3.11
malice 2.3.4
manuals, style, specialized D (app.)
manuscripts
  acceptance of
    books 1.5.7
    journal articles 1.4.6
  authors' names on 4.2.5

manuscripts *(cont.)*
  binding 4.2.9
  citing, in lists of works cited 6.8.12
    online sources 6.9.8i
  citing, in note references A.7l (app.)
    online sources A.8g (app.)
  conventions of 3.1
  copyediting of 1.6.1, 1.6.3, 4.3
  correcting 4.2.8
  divisions of
    for articles 4.1.1
    for books 4.1.2
  in electronic form 3.5, 4.3–5
  electronic publication of 4.4–5
  evaluation of
    books 1.5.6
    journal articles 1.4.5
  format of
    in electronic form 4.3–5
    in printed form 4.1.1–3, 4.2
  headings in 4.1.1–3, 4.2.5
  margins of 4.2.3
  printing 4.2.1–2
  print publication of 4.3
  revising 1.4.6, 1.5.7, 4.2.8
    last chance for 1.6.1
  running heads of 4.2.6
  submitting 1.3
    to book publishers 1.5.5
    to journals 1.4.4
  tables and illustrations in 4.2.7
  titles on 4.2.5
  typesetting of 4.3
maps
  as illustrations in manuscripts 4.2.7
  in lists of works cited 6.8.8
    online sources 6.9.8f
  in note references A.7h (app.)
    online A.8g (app.)
Marathi 3.11
margins
  of manuscripts 4.2.3
    captions and 4.2.7
    indentations from 3.9.2–4, 4.2.3
  of theses and dissertations 5.5.4
Marguerite de Navarre, *Heptaméron*, abbreviation for 8.6.4
marketing, of books 1.6.6
material objects, and copyright 2.1.6
mathematics
  documentation style in C (app.)
  style manual for D (app.)
measurement, units of 3.10.2
Medea, abbreviation for 8.6.4

medicine
  documentation style in C (app.)
  style manual for D (app.)
Melville, *Moby-Dick*, abbreviation for 8.6.4
memos
  in lists of works cited 6.8.13
  in note references A.7m (app.)
Merriam-Webster's Collegiate Dictionary 3.3.1
microfiche, publications on
  in lists of works cited 6.7.14
  in note references A.6n (app.)
microfilming, of dissertations 5.6
microfilms *See* microform, publications on
microform, publications on
  in lists of works cited 6.7.14
  in note references A.6n (app.)
Middle English, special characters in 3.3.6
Milton, abbreviations for works of 8.6.4
misanthrope, Le, abbreviation for 8.6.4
Miss 3.6.2
mistakes, correcting
  in manuscripts 4.2.8
  in proofs 8.8
MLA Directory of Periodicals 1.4.3
MLA Directory of Scholarly Presses in Language and Literature 1.5.3
MLA style 6.2, 7.1
Moby-Dick, abbreviation for 8.6.4
models, in lists of works cited 6.8.8
modifiers, restrictive vs. nonrestrictive 3.4.2e
  See also adjectives
Molière, abbreviations for works of 8.6.4
money, numerals for 3.10.2, 3.10.4
Mongolian 3.11
months
  abbreviations for 8.2
  capitalization of
    in French 3.7.2
    in Italian 3.7.4
    in Portuguese 3.7.5
    in Russian 3.7.6
    in Spanish 3.7.7
monuments, names of 3.8.5
MOOs, postings in
  in lists of works cited 6.9.8l
  in note references A.8g (app.)
Moplah 3.11
moral rights, of authors 2.1.16
movies *See* films
Mr. 3.6.2
Mrs. 3.6.2
Ms. 3.6.2
MUDs, postings in
  in lists of works cited 6.9.8l

MUDs, postings in *(cont.)*
    in note references A.8g (app.)
multi-, hyphen with 3.4.6h
multiple authors *See under* authors, names of
multiple publication media, works in
    in lists of works cited 6.9.6
    in note references A.8e
    in parenthetical references 7.4.4, 7.4.9
multiple publishers 6.6.19
multiple submissions, of manuscripts
    of books 1.5.5
    of journal articles 1.4.4
multivolume works
    in lists of works cited 6.6.15
        dates of publication 6.6.15
    in note references A.5l (app.)
    in parenthetical references 7.4.3, 7.4.7, 7.4.9
museum dioramas, in lists of works cited
        6.8.8
music, documentation style in field of A (app.)
musical compositions
    divisions of, mentioned in text 3.7.1, 3.8.5
    examples from, in manuscripts 4.2.7
    in lists of works cited 6.8.5
        librettos 6.8.2
        performances 6.8.4
        published scores 6.8.5
        songs 6.8.2
        sound recordings 6.8.2
    in note references A.7e (app.)
        performances A.7d (app.)
        sound recordings A.7b (app.)
    titles of
        long 3.8.2, 3.8.5
        short 3.8.3
musical examples, in manuscripts 4.2.7

names
    abbreviations of 6.6.1
        initials 6.6.1, 8.1
        places 8.3
        titles of persons 3.6.2, 3.6.5
    of aircraft 3.8.2
    alphabetization of *See* alphabetization
    of authors
        in lists of works cited 6.6.1
        on manuscripts 4.2.5
        in parenthetical references 7.3
        pseudonyms 3.6.3
        simplified 3.6.3
        transliterated 3.6.13
    of fictional characters 3.6.3
    of languages, abbreviations for 8.7
    on manuscripts, authors' 4.2.5

names *(cont.)*
    of persons 3.6
        Chinese 3.6.1, 3.6.12
        Dutch 3.6.4
        famous 3.6.1
        first uses vs. subsequent 3.6.1–2
        French 3.6.5
        German 3.6.4
        Greek 3.6.6
        Hungarian 3.6.1, 3.6.7
        initials 6.6.1, 8.1
        Italian 3.6.8
        Japanese 3.6.1, 3.6.12
        Korean 3.6.1, 3.6.12
        Latin 3.6.11
        possessive forms 3.4.7d–f
        Russian 3.6.9
        Spanish 3.6.10
        suffixes with 6.6.1
        with titles of nobility 3.6.2, 6.6.1
        with titles of persons 3.6.2
        Vietnamese 3.6.1, 3.6.12
        women's 3.6.2
    of places
        abbreviations 8.3
        French 3.7.2
        Italian 3.7.4
        Portuguese 3.7.5
        Russian 3.7.6
        Spanish 3.7.7
        transliterations and romanizations 3.7.9
    possessive forms of 3.4.7d–f
    of ships 3.8.2
    of societies 3.8.5
    of spacecraft 3.8.2
narrators
    in lists of works cited 6.8.1–2
    in note references A.7a–b (app.)
nationalities, capitalization of
    in Italian 3.7.4
    in Spanish 3.7.7
n.d. (*no date of publication given*) 6.6.25, 6.8.2
networks, computer *See* online publications
Newsbank, in lists of works cited 6.7.14
news group postings
    in lists of works cited 6.9.8k
    in note references A.8g (app.)
newspaper articles
    in lists of works cited 6.7.5
        anonymous 6.7.9
        on CD-ROM, diskette, magnetic tape
            6.9.5
        editions 6.7.5
        editorials 6.7.10

newspaper articles, in lists of works cited
(cont.)
letters to editor 6.7.11
from loose-leaf collections 6.7.15
from microform collections 6.7.14
online 6.9.4b, d, f–g
page numbering 6.7.5
reviews 6.7.7
serialized 6.7.12
in note references A.6e, g, i–l, n–o (app.)
electronic sources A.8c–d (app.)
in parenthetical references 7.4.1–2, 7.4.4, 7.4.9
titles of 3.8.3
See also articles, periodical
newspapers, titles of 3.7.1, 3.8.2
newswire articles, online 6.9.4b
New Testament 8.6.1
New York Times Co. v. Sullivan 2.3.4
Nibelungenlied, abbreviation for 8.6.4
no date of publication 6.6.25, 6.8.2
non-, hyphen with 3.4.6h
nonsexist language 3.2
guides on 3.12
no pagination 6.6.25
no place of publication 6.6.25
no publisher 6.6.25
nor, comma before 3.4.2a
note references A (app.)
abbreviations in 8.1
abstracts in
from abstracts journals A.6h (app.)
on CD-ROM, diskette, magnetic tape
A.8c (app.)
online A.8c (app.)
addresses (speeches) in A.7k (app.)
electronic sources A.8g (app.)
advertisements in A.7j (app.)
electronic sources A.8g (app.)
afterwords in A.5g (app.)
anonymous works in
articles A.6i (app.)
books A.5h (app.)
online publications A.8a (app.)
anthologies in A.5b (app.)
electronic sources A.8a, b, d (app.)
works in A.5e (app.)
articles, periodical, in A.6 (app.)
electronic sources A.8c–d (app.)
artworks in A.7f (app.)
electronic sources A.8g (app.)
audio recordings in A.7b (app.)
ballets in A.7d–e (app.)
books in A.5
electronic sources A.8b, d (app.)

note references *(cont.)*
bulletin boards, electronic, in A.8g (app.)
cartoons in A.7i (app.)
electronic sources A.8g (app.)
CD-ROM, publications on, in A.8d, g
charts in A.7h (app.)
commissions as authors in A.5d (app.)
committees as authors in A.5d (app.)
compilations in A.5b (app.)
electronic sources A.8a, b, d (app.)
works in A.5e (app.)
computer networks, material from, in
A.8a–c, g (app.)
computer software in A.8d, g (app.)
concerts in A.7d (app.)
conferences in
electronic A.8g (app.)
proceedings of A.5s (app.)
congressional proceedings and publications
in A.5r (app.)
corporate authors in A.5d, r (app.)
databases, electronic, in A.8a, d (app.)
dictionary entries in A.5f (app.)
electronic sources A.8a, d (app.)
diskette, publications on, in A.8d, g
dissertations in A.5w–x (app.)
editions in
of books A.5i, k (app.)
of newspapers A.6e (app.)
editorials in A.6j (app.)
electronic sources A.8c (app.)
e-mail in A.8g (app.)
encyclopedia articles in A.5f (app.)
electronic sources A.8a, d (app.)
essays in A.5e (app.)
electronic sources A.8b–d (app.)
films in A.7c (app.)
electronic sources A.8g (app.)
foreign language works in A.5t (app.)
forewords in A.5g (app.)
format for A.2–3 (app.)
government publications in A.5r (app.)
imprints, publishers', in A.5o (app.)
information missing in works in A.5v (app.)
interviews in A.7g (app.)
electronic sources A.8g (app.)
introductions in A.5g (app.)
journal articles in A.6a–d (app.)
electronic sources A.8c–d (app.)
lectures in A.7k (app.)
electronic sources A.8g (app.)
legal sources in A.7n (app.)
letters (correspondence) in A.7m (app.)
to editor A.6k (app.), A.8c (app.)

note references *(cont.)*
librettos in A.7b (app.)
line spacing in A.4 (app.)
vs. lists of works cited A.1 (app.), A.3 (app.)
loose-leaf collections of articles in A.6o (app.)
magazine articles in A.6f (app.)
electronic sources A.8c–d (app.)
magnetic tape, publications on, in A.8d, g
manuscripts in A.7l (app.)
online A.8g (app.)
maps in A.7h (app.)
online A.8g (app.)
memos in A.7m (app.)
microform, publications on, in A.6n (app.)
multiple publication media, works in, in A.8e (app.)
multiple publishers, works with, in A.5p (app.)
multivolume works in A.5l (app.)
musical compositions in A.7e (app.)
performances A.7d (app.)
sound recordings A.7b (app.)
newspaper articles in A.6e (app.)
electronic sources A.8c–d (app.)
notes, editors' explanatory, in A.5i (app.)
online publications in A.8a–c, g (app.)
operas in A.7e (app.)
performances A.7d (app.)
sound recordings A.7b (app.)
page numbers cited in A.1 (app.), A.3 (app.)
books with no page numbers A.5v (app.)
pamphlets in A.5q (app.)
paperbacks in A.5n (app.)
vs. parenthetical documentation A.1 (app.)
performances in A.7d (app.)
periodical articles in A.6 (app.)
plays in A.7d (app.)
electronic sources A.8a–b, d (app.)
poetry in A.5e (app.)
electronic sources A.8a–b, d (app.)
prefaces in A.5g (app.)
pre-1900 publications in A.5u (app.)
proceedings of conferences in A.5s (app.)
publishers' imprints in A.5o (app.)
punctuation of A.3 (app.)
radio productions in A.7a (app.)
electronic sources A.8g (app.)
interviews A.7g (app.)
readings (oral presentations) in A.7k (app.)
electronic sources A.8g (app.)
recordings in
sound A.7b (app.), A.8g (app.)
video A.7c (app.)

note references *(cont.)*
reference works in A.5f (app.)
electronic sources A.8a, d (app.)
reprints of articles in
anthologies A.5e (app.)
loose-leaf collections A.6o (app.)
republished books in A.5n (app.)
reviews in A.6g (app.)
electronic sources A.8c (app.)
serialized articles in A.6l (app.)
series in
books A.5m (app.)
journals A.6d (app.)
television and radio A.7a (app.)
short stories in A.5e (app.)
electronic sources A.8b, d (app.)
software in A.8d, g (app.)
songs in A.7b (app.)
sound recordings in A.7b (app.)
online A.8g (app.)
special issues of journals A.6m
speeches in A.7k (app.)
electronic sources A.8g (app.)
subsequent references in A.9 (app.)
television productions in A.7a (app.)
electronic sources A.8g (app.)
interviews A.7g (app.)
translated works in A.5j (app.)
electronic sources A.8a–d (app.)
two or more works by same author in A.9 (app.)
typescripts in A.7l (app.)
video recordings in A.7c (app.)
volume numbers in
journals A.6a–b (app.)
multivolume books A.5l (app.)
See also endnotes and footnotes; notes, with parenthetical references
notes
in books 4.1.2
editors' explanatory
in lists of works cited 6.6.12
in note references A.5i (app.)
with parenthetical references 7.5
bibliographic 7.5.2
content 7.5.1
See also endnotes and footnotes; note references
for tables and illustrations 4.2.7
nouns
capitalization of, in titles 3.7.1
coequal, hyphen with 3.4.6g
in German 3.7.3
in Italian 3.7.4

nouns *(cont.)*
  in Portuguese 3.7.5
  possessive 3.4.7a–f
  in Russian 3.7.6
  in Spanish 3.7.7
novels
  in lists of works cited
    afterwords to 6.6.9
    anthologized 6.6.7
    in book series 6.6.16
    introductions to 6.6.9
    in languages other than English
      6.6.23
    with multiple publishers 6.6.19
    online 6.9.3
    publishers' imprints and 6.6.18
    republished 6.6.17
    scholarly editions of 6.6.12
    translated 6.6.13
  in parenthetical references 7.4.8
n.p. (no place of publication given, no publisher
    given) 6.6.25
n. pag. (no pagination given) 6.6.25
ns (new series) 6.7.4
numbers 3.10
  with abbreviations or symbols 3.10.2
  for acts and scenes in plays 3.10.7
  in addresses (geographic) 3.10.2–3
  as adjectives 3.4.6d
  arabic numerals for 3.10.1
  at beginning of sentence 3.10.2
  in dates 3.10.2, 3.10.5–6
  in fractions 3.10.2
  inclusive (number ranges) 3.10.6–7
  large 3.10.2
  in line references 3.10.3, 7.4.8
  for money 3.10.4
  in names of persons 3.10.7
  in page references 3.10.2, 7.4.2
  for percentages 3.10.4
  plurals of 3.4.7g, 3.10.2
  punctuation with 3.4.7g
    commas 3.10.3
    hyphens 3.4.6d
  range of 3.10.6
  roman numerals for 3.10.7
  superscript 7.5
  in times of the day 3.10.5
  for units of measurement 3.10.2
  words vs. numerals for 3.10.2, 3.10.5
number system, of documention C (app.)

OCR (optical character reader) 1.6.5
Odyssey, abbreviation for 8.6.4

Oedipus Rex (Oedipus Tyrannus), abbreviation
  for 8.6.4
Old English, special characters in 3.3.6
Old Testament 8.6.1
omitted material, in quotations 3.9.5
online postings *See* postings, online
online publications
  assessing 6.9.1
  coding for World Wide Web 4.4–5
  copyright and 2.1.9, 2.1.11, 2.1.17
  HTML 4.4–5
  institutions associated with 6.9.2–3
  in lists of works cited 6.9.1–4, 6.9.8
    advertisements 6.9.8h
    artworks 6.9.8d
    books 6.9.3
    cartoons 6.9.8g
    discussion forums 6.9.8k
    e-mail 6.9.8j
    films 6.9.8c
    interviews 6.9.8e
    manuscripts 6.9.8i
    maps 6.9.8f
    news groups 6.9.8k
    periodicals 6.9.4
    poems 6.9.2–3
    postings 6.9.8k
    radio productions 6.9.8a
    reference databases 6.9.2
    scholarly projects 6.9.2
    short stories 6.9.2–3
    software, downloaded 6.9.8m
    sound recordings 6.9.8b
    synchronous communications (e.g., in
      MOOs and MUDs) 6.9.8l
    television productions 6.9.8a
    Usenet postings 6.9.8k
    working papers 6.9.8i
    on World Wide Web 6.9.2–4
  in note references A.8a–c, g (app.)
  numbering sections of 4.4, 6.9.1
  in parenthetical references
    entire works 7.4.1, 7.4.6, 7.4.9
    listed by title 7.4.4
    no page numbers 7.2, 7.4.2, 7.4.8–9
    parts of 7.4.2, 7.4.6, 7.4.8–9
  publication dates of 6.9.1–4
  scholarly manuscripts as 4.4–5
  theses and dissertations as 5.7
  URLs of, citing 6.9.1
op. cit., avoiding A.9 (app.)
operas
  in lists of works cited
    librettos 6.8.2

operas, in lists of works cited *(cont.)*
    performances 6.8.4
    published scores 6.8.5
    sound recordings 6.8.2
  in note references A.7e (app.)
    performances A.7d (app.)
    sound recordings A.7b (app.)
  titles of 3.8.2
  See also reviews
opinion, statements of, and defamation 2.3.2
optical character reader 1.6.5
options, on author's next work 2.2.1
or, comma before 3.4.2a
Oresteia, abbreviation for 8.6.4
Oriya 3.11
os (original series) 6.7.4
Ottoman Turkish 3.11
out-of-print publications, rights in 2.2.1
over-, hyphen with 3.4.6h

page numbers, of dissertations 5.5.3
page numbers, in documentation
  commas in 3.10.3
  in lists of works cited 6.6.1, 6.6.7, A.1 (app.)
    abbreviations with, avoiding 6.6.7
    anthologies, works in 6.6.7
    books with no page numbers 6.6.25
    cross-references 6.6.10
    dictionaries 6.6.8
    encyclopedia articles 6.6.8
    interrupted page numbering 6.7.1, 6.7.5,
      6.7.6
    journals 6.7.1–2
    magazines 6.7.6
    multivolume works 6.6.15
    newspapers 6.7.5
    periodicals 6.7.1–2, 6.7.5–6, 6.7.12
    placement of 6.6.1
    serialized articles 6.7.12
  in note references A.1 (app.), A.3 (app.)
    books with no page numbers A.5v (app.)
  numerals for
    commas in 3.10.3
    instead of words 3.10.2
    roman 3.10.7
  in parenthetical references 7.1–2, A.1 (app.)
    literary works 7.4.8
    no page numbers 7.2, 7.4.2, 7.4.8
    parts of articles or books 7.4.2
page numbers, of manuscripts 4.2.6
  abbreviations with, avoiding 4.2.6
  in endnotes section A.4 (app.)
  in lists of works cited 6.4
page numbers, of theses and dissertations 5.5.3

page proofs *See* proofreading
pages, World Wide Web *See* World Wide Web,
    publications on
paintings *See* artworks
Pali 3.11
pamphlets
  in lists of works cited 6.6.20
  in note references A.5q (app.)
  titles of 3.8.2
paper, for manuscripts 4.2.2
paperbacks, as republished works
  in lists of works cited 6.6.17
  in note references A.5n (app.)
Paradise Lost, abbreviation for 8.6.4
Paradiso, abbreviation for 8.6.4
paragraphs
  indentation of first words of 4.2.3
  numbered, in electronic publications 4.4
  par. for, in parenthetical references 7.4.2,
    7.4.6, 7.4.9
paraphrasing 3.9.1
  and copyright infringement 2.1.13
parentheses 3.4.5
  within parentheses 3.4.9
  square brackets with 3.4.9
parenthetical documentation 7
  authors' names in 7.2–3
    corporate authors 7.4.5
    more than three authors 7.2
    multiple authors with same name 7.2
    one author with multiple works 7.4.6
    two or three authors 7.2
    when to include 7.3
  of entire works 7.4.1
  guidelines for 7.1–4
  of indirect sources 7.4.7
  information required in 7.2
  of literary works 7.4.8
  of multiple works in single reference 7.4.9
  of multivolume works 7.4.3
  notes with 7.5
  page numbers in 7.1–2, A.1 (app.)
  of parts of works 7.4.2
  placement of 7.3
  of poetry 3.9.3, 7.4.8
  punctuation in 3.9.5, 3.9.7, 7.3
  with quotations 3.9.7, 7.3
    drama 3.9.4
    ellipsis 3.9.5
    poetry 3.9.3
    prose 3.9.2
  readability of 7.3
  title, sources listed by 7.4.4
parts of works, mentioned in text 3.7.1, 3.8.5

pen names
  of authors in text 3.6.3
  in lists of works cited 6.6.1
percentages, numerals vs. words for 3.10.2,
      3.10.4
performances
  in lists of works cited 6.8.4
    reviews 6.7.7
  in note references A.7d (app.)
    reviews A.6g (app.)
  in parenthetical references 7.4.1, 7.4.4
periodicals
  definition of 6.7.1
  in lists of works cited 6.7
    a, an, the in titles 6.7.1
    microform collections 6.7.14
    online 6.9.4
    page numbering 6.7.1–2, 6.7.5
    publication dates 6.7.1
    reprints 6.7.14
    series, journals in 6.7.4
    special issues of journals 6.7.13
  in note references A.6b–c, m (app.),
      A.8c–d (app.)
  in parenthetical references 7.4.1–2, 7.4.4,
      7.4.6, 7.4.9
  titles of 3.7.1, 3.8.2
  See also articles, periodical
periods 3.4.11
  with abbreviations 8.1
  in ellipsis 3.9.5
  ending a sentence 3.4.11
  parenthetical references and 3.9.2, 3.9.7
  after quotations 3.8.4, 3.9.7
permission, to reproduce material 2.1.13–14
  in dissertations 5.6.4
  required by publication contracts 2.2.1–2
  sample letters to request figs. 2–3 (pp. 31–32)
  when to obtain 1.3, 1.5.7
Persian 3.11
persons *See* names, of persons; titles, of
      persons
photographs
  as illustrations in manuscripts 4.2.7
  in lists of works cited
    of artworks 6.8.6
    slide programs 6.8.3
phrases, punctuation of
  alternative or contrasting 3.4.2g
  introductory 3.4.2f
  restrictive vs. nonrestrictive 3.4.2e
  in series 3.4.2b
physics
  documentation style in C (app.)

physics *(cont.)*
  style manual for D (app.)
pinyin system 3.6.12
place-names *See* names, of places
places, of publication 6.6.1
  abbreviations for 6.6.1
  more than one city 6.6.1
  not given 6.6.25
plagiarism 6.1
Plato, abbreviations for works of 8.6.4
Playboy Enterprises, Inc., v. Frena 2.1.17
plays
  acts and scenes of
    mentioned in text 3.7.1, 3.8.5
    numbers for 3.10.7, 7.4.8
  in lists of works cited
    in anthologies 6.6.7
    editions of 6.6.12
    electronic sources 6.9.2–3, 6.9.5
    performances of 6.8.4
  in note references A.7d (app.)
    electronic sources A.8a–b, d (app.)
  in parenthetical references 7.4.1–2, 7.4.4,
      7.4.8
  quotations from 3.9.4
  titles of 3.8.2
  See also reviews
plurals
  of abbreviations 3.4.7g, 8.1
  of letters of alphabet 3.4.7
  of numbers 3.4.7g, 3.10.2
  possessives of
    common nouns 3.4.7b–c
    proper nouns, 3.4.7f
  spelling of 3.3.3, 3.4.7, 3.10.2
p.m. 8.1–2
PMLA
  Directory of Useful Addresses in 1.4.6
  editorial policy of 3.2
  Journal Notes in 1.4.3
poetry
  in lists of works cited
    in anthologies 6.6.7, 6.6.10
    books of 6.6.5
    editions of 6.6.12, 6.6.14
    electronic sources 6.9.2–3, 6.9.5
    forewords and introductions to books of
        6.6.9
    translations of 6.6.10, 6.6.13
  in note references A.5e (app.)
    electronic sources A.8a–b, d (app.)
  in parenthetical references 3.9.3, 7.3, 7.4.8
  quotations of 3.9.3
    ellipsis 3.9.5

poetry, quotations of *(cont.)*
    indenting 3.9.3
    omitted material 3.9.5
    slashes (/) 3.9.3
  titles of
    first line as title 3.7.1
    long vs. short poems 3.8.2–3
    poems published as books 3.8.2
    underlining vs. quotation marks 3.8.2–3
political documents, titles of 3.8.5
Portuguese, capitalization in 3.7.5
possessions, territorial, of the United States,
    abbreviations for 8.3
possessives, forming
  with apostrophes 3.4.7
  of names of persons 3.4.7d–f
  of nouns in series 3.4.7d
  of plural common nouns 3.4.7b–c
  of plural proper nouns 3.4.7f
  of singular common nouns 3.4.7a
  of singular proper nouns 3.4.7e
post-, hyphen with 3.4.6h
postings, online
  in lists of works cited 6.9.8k
  in note references A.8g (app.)
  in parenthetical references 7.4.1, 7.4.9
Prakrit 3.11
pre-, hyphen with 3.4.6h
prefaces
  in books 4.1.2
  in lists of works cited 6.6.9
  mentioned in text 3.7.1, 3.8.5
  in note references A.5g (app.)
  page numbers of 3.10.7
prefixes, hyphens with 3.4.6h
Prelude, The, abbreviation for 8.6.4
prepositions
  in German 3.7.3
  lowercasing of, in titles 3.7.1
presses *See* publishers
printing
  and binding of publications 1.6.5
  of manuscripts 4.2.1–2
privacy, right of 2.4
  guides on 2.5
proceedings of conferences
  in lists of works cited 6.6.22
  in note references A.5s (app.)
production, of books 1.6.1–5
Professor 3.6.2
pronouns
  capitalization of, in titles 3.7.1
  clarification of, in quotations 3.9.6
  in French 3.7.2

pronouns *(cont.)*
  in German 3.7.3
  in Italian 3.7.4
  in Latin 3.7.8
  in Portuguese 3.7.5
  in Russian 3.7.6
  in Spanish 3.7.7
proofreading 1.6.2
  described in publication contracts 2.2.1–2
  symbols for 8.8
proofs *See* proofreading
prose quotations *See* quotations
prose style *See* language, of scholarly writing
prospectuses, for books 1.5.4
proverbs, omitting documentation for 6.1
provinces, abbreviations for 8.3
pseudonyms
  of authors in text 3.6.3
  in lists of works cited 6.6.1
psychology
  documentation style in B (app.)
  style manual for B (app.), D (app.)
publication, dates of *See* dates, of publication
publication, places of *See* places, of publication
publicity, unreasonable 2.4.2
Public Law numbers 6.8.14
publishers
  finding
    for books 1.5.3
    for journal articles 1.4.3
  in lists of works cited 6.6.1
    abbreviations for 8.5
    as authors 6.6.6
    multiple 6.6.19
    names of 6.6.1
    not given 6.6.25
    omitting, for pre-1900 works 6.6.24
    pre-1900 publication 6.6.24
    shortening names of 6.6.1, 8.5
  in note references A.5d, p, u–v (app.)
  role of 1.1
  types of 1.5.1
  See also imprints, publishers'
punctuation 3.4
  with abbreviations 8.1
  in note references A.3 (app.)
  in parenthetical references 3.9.5, 3.9.7, 7.3
  See also angle brackets, with URLs; apostro-
    phes; colons; commas; dashes; excla-
    mation points; hyphens; parentheses;
    periods; question marks; quotation
    marks, double; quotation marks,
    single; semicolons; slashes; square
    brackets

Punjabi 3.11
Purgatorio, abbreviation for 8.6.4
Pushto 3.11

qtd. in 7.4.7
question marks 3.4.11
   with quotation marks 3.4.11, 3.9.7
quotation marks, double 3.4.8, 3.9
   omitting after *so-called* 3.4.8
   with parenthetical references 3.9.7, 7.3
   for poetry quotations 3.9.3
   for prose quotations 3.9.2
   punctuation with 3.9.7
      commas 3.9.7
      periods 3.8.4, 3.9.7
      question marks 3.4.11, 3.9.7
   within quotations 3.9.7
   for quotations run into text 3.9.7
   with single quotation marks 3.9.7
   for special meanings 3.4.8a
   for titles 3.8.3–4
   for translations 3.4.8b, 3.9.8
   vs. underlining, for non-English phrases
      3.5.2
   unnecessary 3.4.8a
quotation marks, single
   with double quotation marks 3.9.7
   with indented quotations 3.9.7
   punctuation with 3.9.7
   for quotations within quotations 3.9.7
   for quotations within titles 3.8.4
   for titles within titles 3.8.4
   for translations 3.4.8, 3.9.8
quotations 3.9
   accuracy of 3.9.1
   acknowledging sources of 6.1
   added comments with 3.9.6
   copyright and 2.1.13–14
   of dialogue 3.9.4
   drama 3.9.4
   ellipsis in 3.9.5
   fair use of 2.1.13
   format for
      indentation 3.9.2–3
      spacing 3.9.2–3
   from indirect sources 7.4.7
   introducing 3.9.2–3, 3.9.7
   omitting documentation of 6.1
   omitting material from 3.9.5
   original spelling in 3.3.1, 3.9.1
   parenthetical references and 7.3
      poetry 3.9.3, 7.3
      prose 3.9.2, 7.3
      punctuation 3.9.2, 3.9.7

quotations *(cont.)*
   permission for 2.1.13–14
      in dissertations 5.6.4
      required by publication contracts 2.2.1–2
      sample letters to request figs. 2–3 (pp.
         31–32)
      when to obtain 1.3, 1.5.7
   from plays 3.9.4
   poetry 3.9.3, 7.3
   prose 3.9.2, 7.3
   punctuation with 3.9.7
      colons 3.4.4b, 3.9.2, 3.9.7
      commas 3.9.7
      exclamation points 3.9.7
      periods 3.8.4, 3.9.2, 3.9.7
      question marks 3.4.11, 3.9.7
      square brackets 3.9.6
   within quotations 3.9.7
   romanization of 3.11
   sic with 3.9.6
   slashes to separate lines in 3.9.3
   within titles 3.8.4
   translations of 3.9.8
   transliteration of 3.11
   use of 3.9.1
   See also quotation marks, double; quotation
      marks, single

radio productions
   in lists of works cited 6.8.1
      electronic sources 6.9.8a
      interviews 6.8.7
   in note references A.7a (app.)
      electronic sources A.8g (app.)
      interviews A.7g (app.)
   titles of
      episodes 3.8.3
      programs 3.8.2
      series 3.8.5
*Random House Dictionary of the American
   Language* 3.3.1
re-, hyphen with 3.4.6h
readability, of manuscripts
   content notes and 7.5.1
   parenthetical references and 7.3
readers, consultant
   for book publishers 1.5.6
   for journals 1.4.5
readings (oral presentations)   *See* speeches
recordings   *See* reviews; sound recordings;
      video recordings
refereed publication 1.2
   of books 1.5.6
   of journal articles 1.4.5

references, parenthetical   *See* parenthetical
 documentation
reference works
 in lists of works cited 6.6.8
  electronic sources 6.9.2, 6.9.5
 in note references A.5f (app.)
  electronic sources A.8a, d (app.)
 in parenthetical references 7.2
 preparing 1.5.2
registration, of copyright 2.1.8
religion, documentation style in field of
 A (app.)
religious affiliations, in lists of works cited
 6.6.1
religious works
 abbreviations for 8.6
 titles of 3.8.5
 See also Bible
renewal, of copyright 2.1.10
reports
 congressional
  in lists of works cited 6.6.21
  in note references A.5r (app.)
 readers'   *See* readers, consultant
reprinted works
 in lists of works cited
  articles in loose-leaf collections 6.7.15
  republished books 6.6.17
  works in anthologies 6.6.7
 in note references A.5e, n (app.),
  A.6o (app.)
Republic, abbreviation for 8.6.4
republished books
 in lists of works cited 6.6.17
 in note references A.5n (app.)
research articles, conventions of 3.1
resolutions, congressional
 in lists of works cited 6.6.21
 in note references A.5r (app.)
Reverend 3.6.2
reviews
 in lists of works cited 6.7.7
  electronic sources 6.9.4d
 in marketing of books 1.6.6
 in newspapers, conventions of 3.1
 in note references A.6g (app.)
  electronic sources A.8c (app.)
 in parenthetical references 7.4.1
 writing 1.4.2
revised editions
 of books 6.6.14
 governed by publication contracts 2.2.1
revisions, of manuscripts 4.2.8
Roberson v. Rochester Folding Box Co. 2.4.1

romanization
 capitalization and 3.7.9
 of Chinese names 3.6.12
 guides on 3.7.9, 3.11
roman numerals 3.10.7
 for acts and scenes in play 7.4.8
 in outlines 3.10.7
 as page numbers 3.10.7
 for persons in series 3.10.7
royalties 1.5.4, 1.5.7, 2.2.1–2
running heads, in manuscripts 4.2.6
Russian
 capitalization in 3.7.6
 names of persons in 3.6.9
 transliteration of 3.11

sacred writings   *See* Bible; religious works
Samson Agonistes, abbreviation for 8.6.4
Sanskrit 3.11
Santali 3.11
sayings, familiar, omitting documentation for
 6.1
scenes, in play
 mentioned in text 3.7.1, 3.8.5
 numerals for 3.10.7, 7.4.8
science
 documentation style in B–D (app.)
 style manuals for D (app.)
scores, musical, in lists of works cited 6.8.5
sculpture   *See* artworks
seasons, punctuation with 3.4.2m
sections of works, mentioned in text 3.7.1,
 3.8.5
semi-, hyphen with 3.4.6h
semicolons 3.4.3
 between independent clauses 3.4.3a
 with quotation marks 3.9.7
 in series with commas 3.4.2b, 3.4.3b
seminars, titles of 3.8.5
Serbian 3.11
serialized articles
 in lists of works cited 6.7.12
 in note references A.6l (app.)
series
 in lists of works cited
  books 6.6.1, 6.6.16
  journals 6.7.4
  television and radio 6.8.1
 in note references
  books A.5m (app.)
  journals A.6d (app.)
  television and radio A.7a (app.)
 titles of 3.8.5
series, capitalizing 3.7.1

sexist language 3.2
  guides on avoiding 3.12
SGML 4.4–5
Shakespeare, abbreviations for works of 8.6.2
ships, names of 3.8.2
short stories
  in lists of works cited 6.6.7
    electronic sources 6.9.2–3, 6.9.5
  in note references A.5e (app.)
    electronic sources A.8b, d (app.)
  in parenthetical references 7.4.2–3
  titles of 3.8.3
sic, in quotations 3.9.6
signatures of book, citing 7.4.10
simultaneous submission, of manuscripts
  of books 1.5.5
  of journal articles 1.4.4
Sindhi 3.11
single-spacing, in theses and dissertations 5.5.5
Sinhalese 3.11
Sir Gawain and the Green Knight, abbreviation
    for 8.6.4
SIRS (Social Issues Resources Series) 6.7.15
sites, World Wide Web   *See* World Wide Web,
    publications on
slander 2.3.1
slashes (/)
  for paired alternatives 3.4.10
  in poetry quotations 3.9.3
  in URLs 6.9.1
slide programs
  in lists of works cited 6.8.3
  in note references A.7c (app.)
so, comma before 3.4.2a
Social Issues Resources Series 6.7.15
social sciences
  documentation style in B (app.)
  style manual for B (app.)
societies, names of 3.8.5
software   *See* computer software
songs
  in lists of works cited 6.8.2
  in note references A.7b (app.)
  titles of 3.8.3
Sophocles, abbreviations for works of 8.6.4
sound recordings
  in lists of works cited
    booklets with 6.8.2
    on CD, cassette, tape, LP 6.8.2
    online 6.9.8b
  in note references
    booklets with A.7b (app.)
    on CD, cassette, tape, LP A.7b (app.)
    online A.8g (app.)

sound recordings *(cont.)*
  titles of 3.8.2
sources
  acknowledgment of 6.1, 7.1
  annotated lists of 6.3
  comments on, in notes 7.5
  failure to acknowledge 6.1
spacecraft, names of 3.8.2
spacing
  in abbreviations 8.1
  of lines in manuscripts 4.2.4–5
    endnotes and footnotes A.4 (app.)
    lists of works cited 6.4
    notes to tables 4.2.7
    quotations 3.9.2–4
  in theses and dissertations 5.5.5
Spanish
  capitalization in 3.7.7
  names of persons in 3.6.10
special characters, reproducing 3.3.6
special issues, of journals
  calls for submissions to 1.4.3
  in lists of works cited 6.7.13
  in note references A.6m
speeches
  in lists of works cited 6.8.11
    electronic sources 6.9.8b
  in note references A.7k (app.)
    electronic sources A.8g (app.)
  in parenthetical references 7.4.1
  titles of 3.8.3
spelling 3.3
  accents and 3.3.4
  consistency of 3.3.1
  of foreign words 3.3.4–6
  of plurals 3.3.3, 3.4.7, 3.10.2
  software for checking 4.2.8
Spenser, *The Faerie Queene*, abbreviation for
    8.6.4
square brackets
  for added material in quotations 3.9.6
  for ellipsis 3.9.5
  for information missing in cited works
    6.6.1, 6.6.25
  for parenthesis in parenthesis 3.4.9
Standard Generalized Markup Language
    (SGML) 4.4–5
states, in the United States, abbreviations for
    8.3
statistics, numerals vs. words for 3.10.2, 3.10.4
statutes
  in lists of works cited 6.8.14
  in note references A.7n (app.)
Statutes at Large numbers 6.8.14

stet, in proofreading 8.8.2
street addresses 3.10.2–3
street names, capitalization in
  in French 3.7.2
  in Italian 3.7.4
  in Portuguese 3.7.5
  in Russian 3.7.6
  in Spanish 3.7.7
style, writing *See* language, of scholarly
  writing
style manuals, specialized D (app.)
sub-, hyphen with 3.4.6h
submission, of manuscripts 1.3
  to book publishers 1.5
  to journals 1.4
  to multiple publishers 1.4.4, 1.5.5
subsidiary rights, in publications 2.2.1
subtitles 3.7.1, 6.6.1
  in French 3.7.2
  in German 3.7.3
  in Italian 3.7.4
  in Latin 3.7.8
  in lists of works cited 6.6.1
  in Portuguese 3.7.5
  in Russian 3.7.6
  in Spanish 3.7.7
suffixes, with names of persons
  in lists of works cited 6.6.1
  roman numerals as 3.10.7
Swift, *Gulliver's Travels*, abbreviation for
  8.6.4
symbols, proofreading 8.8
Symposium, abbreviation for 8.6.4
symphonies
  in lists of works cited
    performances 6.8.4
    published scores 6.8.5
    sound recordings 6.8.2
  in note references
    performances A.7d (app.)
    published scores A.7e (app.)
    sound recordings A.7b (app.)
  titles of 3.8.2, 3.8.5
  See also reviews
synchronous communications, online (e.g., in
  MOOs and MUDs)
  in lists of works cited 6.9.8l
  in note references A.8g (app.)

tables
  in books 4.1.2
  in manuscripts 4.2.7
tagging, of electronic manuscripts 4.4–5
Tamil 3.11

Tartuffe, abbreviation for 8.6.4
TEI (Text Encoding Initiative) 4.4–5
telephone interviews 6.8.7
television productions
  in lists of works cited 6.8.1
    electronic sources 6.9.8a
    interviews 6.8.7
  in note references A.7a (app.)
    electronic sources A.8g (app.)
    interviews A.7g (app.)
  in parenthetical references 7.4.2, 7.4.4
  titles of 3.8.2
    episodes 3.8.3
    programs 3.8.2
    series 3.8.5
Telugu 3.11
terminations, of contracts 2.1.12
territories, of the United States, abbreviations
  for 8.3
textbooks, writing of 1.5.2
Text Encoding Initiative 4.4–5
Thai 3.11
that clauses 3.4.2e
the *See* articles
theater, documentation style in field of
    A (app.) *See also* plays; reviews
theology, documentation style in field of
    A (app.)
theses
  electronic publication of 5.7
  format of 5.2, 5.5
  prospectus for 5.4
  selecting topics for 5.3
  See also dissertations
Tibetan 3.11
Tigrinya 3.11
time of day, abbreviations for 3.10.5, 8.2 *See*
  also dates, writing of
title pages
  of books 4.1.2
  of dissertations 5.5.2
titles, for tables and illustrations in manuscripts 4.2.7
titles, of persons
  abbreviations of French 3.6.5
  capitalization of
    French 3.7.2
    Italian 3.7.4
    Portuguese 3.7.5
    Russian 3.7.6
    Spanish 3.7.7
  for nobility 3.6.2
    French 3.6.5, 3.7.2
    in lists of works cited 6.6.1

titles, of works 3.8
 articles 3.8.3
 audiocassettes 3.8.2
 ballets 3.8.2
 books 3.8.1–2
 CD-ROM, publications on 6.9.5
 chapters of books 3.8.3
 compact discs 3.8.2
 conferences 3.8.5
 courses 3.8.5
 diskette, publications on 6.9.5
 essays 3.8.3
 films 3.8.2
 in foreign languages
  French 3.7.2
  German 3.7.3
  Italian 3.7.4
  Latin 3.7.8
  Portuguese 3.7.5
  Russian 3.7.6
  Spanish 3.7.7
 format for
  abbreviations 3.8.6, 8.6
  capitalization 3.7.1
  changed titles 6.6.7, 6.6.17, 6.7.12
  introductory *a, an, the* 3.7.1, 6.7.1, 6.7.5
  in parenthetical references 7.4.4
  quotation marks 3.8.3–4
  shortening 3.8.6, 6.6.1, 7.4.4
  titles within titles 3.8.4
  underlining (italicization) 3.5, 3.8.2
  works within works 3.8.3
 journals 3.7.1, 3.8.1–2
 laws 3.8.5
 lectures 3.8.3
 long, shortening for lists of works cited 6.6.1
 magazines 3.7.1, 3.8.1–2
 on magnetic tape 6.9.5
 musical compositions 3.8.2–3, 3.8.5
 newspapers 3.7.1, 3.8.2
 online publications 6.9.2–4
 operas 3.8.2
 paintings 3.8.2
 pamphlets 3.8.2
 periodicals 3.7.1, 3.8.1–2
  French 3.7.2
  Portuguese 3.7.5
  Russian 3.7.6
  Spanish 3.7.7
 plays 3.8.2
 poems
  first line as title 3.7.1
  long vs. short 3.8.2–3
 political documents 3.8.5

titles, of works *(cont.)*
 radio productions
  episodes 3.8.3
  programs 3.8.2
  series 3.8.5
 record albums 3.8.2
 religious works 3.8.5
 scholarly journals 3.7.1, 6.7.1
 sculpture 3.8.2
 seminars 3.8.5
 series 3.8.5
 short stories 3.8.3
 songs 3.8.3
 speeches 3.8.3
 television productions
  episodes 3.8.3
  programs 3.8.2
  series 3.8.5
 within titles 3.8.4
 unpublished works 3.8.3
titles, on manuscripts 4.2.5
to date, for multivolume works in progress
 6.6.15
transcripts, of broadcasts
 in lists of works cited 6.8.1
  electronic sources 6.9.8a
 in note references A.7a (app.)
  electronic sources A.8g (app.)
 in parenthetical references 7.4.2
transfers, of contracts 2.1.12
translated works
 in lists of works cited 6.6.13
  electronic sources 6.9.2–3
 in note references A.5j (app.)
  electronic sources A.8a–d (app.)
 in parenthetical references 7.4.8
 preparing for publication 1.4.2, 1.5.2
 See also translators
translations, of words
 in lists of works cited 6.6.23
 in note references A.5t (app.)
 in text 3.4.8b, 3.9.8
translators
 in lists of works cited 6.6.1–3, 6.6.7, 6.6.10,
  6.6.13
  electronic sources 6.9.2–3, 6.9.5
 in note references A.5b, e, j (app.)
  electronic sources A.8a–d (app.)
 in parenthetical references 7.4.8
transliterated names, citing 3.6.13
transliteration
 capitalization and 3.7.9
 guides on 3.7.9, 3.11
 of Russian names 3.6.9

TRIPS (Agreement on Trade-Related Aspects of Intellectual Property Rights) 2.1.16
truth, as defense in libel action 2.3.3
typefaces, choosing
    for manuscripts 4.2.1
    for theses and dissertations 5.5.1
typescripts
    in lists of works cited 6.8.12
    in note references A.7l (app.)
typesetting, of manuscripts 1.6.5, 4.3

Uighur 3.11
Ukrainian 3.11
Ulrich's International Periodicals Directory 1.4.3
UMI (University Microfilms International) 5.6, 6.6.27
umlauts, reproducing 3.3.5
un-, hyphen with 3.4.6h
under-, hyphen with 3.4.6h
underline character, in electronic manuscripts 3.5
underlining 3.5
    continuous, for titles of works 3.8.1–2
    in electronic manuscripts 3.5
    for emphasis 3.5.3
    of foreign words 3.5.2
    to indicate italics 3.5
    in lists of works cited 6.6.1
    of titles of works 3.8.1–2, 6.6.1
    of words and letters referred to as words and letters 3.5.1
uniform resource locators (URLs), citing 6.9.1
United States Code 6.8.14
United States Geological Survey style manual D (app.)
Universal Copyright Convention 2.1.9, 2.1.16
University Microfilms International 5.6, 6.6.27
university presses, abbreviations for 8.5
unpublished works
    fair use and 2.1.13
    titles of 3.8.3
Urdu 3.11
URLs, citing 6.9.1
usage, English   *See* language, of scholarly writing
USC (United States Code) 6.8.14
Usenet postings
    in lists of works cited 6.9.8k
    in note references A.8g (app.)

van, van der, van den 3.6.4
variant spellings 3.3.1
vendors of electronic publications, citing 6.9.5

verbs, capitalization of, in titles 3.7.1
Vergil, *Aeneid*, abbreviation for 8.6.4
verse   *See* poetry
verse plays 7.4.8
video recordings
    in lists of works cited 6.8.3
    in note references A.7c (app.)
    in parenthetical references 7.4.4, 7.4.9
    titles of 3.8.2
    See also reviews
Vietnamese names of persons 3.6.1, 3.6.12
Voltaire, *Candide*, abbreviation for 8.6.4
volume numbers, of journals
    in lists of works cited 6.7.1–2
        more than one series 6.7.4
        not used 6.7.3
        page numbering 6.7.1–2
    in note references A.6a–d (app.)
volume numbers, of multivolume books
    in lists of works cited 6.6.1, 6.6.15
    in note references A.5l (app.)
    in parenthetical references 7.4.3
    vol. 7.4.3
von 3.6.4

Wade-Giles system 3.6.12
Webster's Third New International Dictionary 3.3.1
which clauses 3.4.2e
who, whom, whose clauses 3.4.2e
women, names of 3.6.2
word division 3.3.2
word processors
    for indexing 1.6.3
    word wrapping in 3.3.2
words, referred to as words 3.5.1
Wordsworth, abbreviations for works of 8.6.4
working papers   *See* manuscripts, citing
works cited, lists of
    abbreviations in 8.1
    abstracts in
        from abstracts journals 6.7.8
        on CD-ROM, diskette, magnetic tape 6.9.5
        online 6.9.4e
    addresses (speeches) in 6.8.11
        electronic sources 6.9.8b
    advertisements in 6.8.10
        electronic sources 6.9.8h
    afterwords in 6.6.9
    alphabetization in   *See* alphabetization
    annotations in 6.3, 6.6.1
    anonymous works in 6.6.1
        articles 6.7.9

works cited, lists of, anonymous works in
 (cont.)
 books 6.6.11
 online publications 6.9.2
anthologies in 6.6.2
 electronic sources 6.9.2–3, 6.9.5
 works in 6.6.7
arrangement of entries in 6.5
articles in *See* articles, periodical
artworks in 6.8.6
 electronic sources 6.9.8d
audio recordings in 6.8.2
authors' names in *See* authors, names of
ballets in 6.8.4–5
books in *See* books
bulletin boards, electronic, in 6.9.8k
cartoons in 6.8.9
 electronic sources 6.9.8g
CD-ROMs in 6.9.5, 6.9.8
charts in 6.8.8
commissions as authors in 6.6.6
committees as authors in 6.6.6
compilations in 6.6.2
 electronic sources 6.9.2–3, 6.9.5
 works in 6.6.7
computer networks, material from, in
 6.9.1–4, 6.9.8
computer software in
 on CD-ROM or diskette 6.9.5
 downloaded 6.9.8m
concerts in 6.8.4
conferences in
 electronic 6.9.8k
 proceedings of 6.6.22
congressional proceedings and publications
 in 6.6.21
content of 6.3
corporate authors in 6.6.6, 6.6.21
cross-references in 6.6.10
databases, electronic, in 6.9.2, 6.9.5
dictionary entries in 6.6.8
 electronic sources 6.9.2, 6.9.5
dioramas in 6.8.8
diskette, publications on, in 6.9.5, 6.9.8
dissertations in
 abstracts of 6.7.8
 published 6.6.27
 unpublished 6.6.26
as divisions in books 4.1.2
editions in
 of books 6.6.12, 6.6.14
 of newspapers 6.7.5
editorials in 6.7.10
 electronic sources 6.9.4f

works cited, lists of *(cont.)*
 editors in
 anthologies 6.6.2, 6.6.7
 cross-references 6.6.10
 electronic publications 6.9.2–3, 6.9.5
 general editors 6.6.15
 scholarly editions 6.6.12
 e-mail in 6.9.8j
 discussion lists 6.9.8k
encyclopedia articles in 6.6.8
 electronic sources 6.9.2, 6.9.5
essays in 6.6.7
 electronic sources 6.9.5
et al. in 6.6.4
films in 6.8.3
 online or on CD-ROM 6.9.8c
flash cards in 6.8.8
foreign language works in 6.6.23
forewords in 6.6.9
format for entries in 6.6–9
games in 6.8.8
globes in 6.8.8
government publications in 6.6.21
heading of 6.3–4
imprints, publishers', in 6.6.18
information missing in works in 6.6.1, 6.6.25
 electronic sources 6.9.1
interviews in 6.8.7
 electronic sources 6.9.8e
introductions in 6.6.9, 6.6.12
journal articles in 6.7.1–4
 electronic sources 6.9.4a, 6.9.5
kits in 6.8.8
lectures in 6.8.11
 electronic sources 6.9.8b
legal sources in 6.8.14
letters (correspondence) in 6.8.13
 to editor 6.7.11, 6.9.4g
librettos in 6.8.2
line spacing of 6.4
loose-leaf collections of articles in 6.7.15
magazine articles in 6.7.6
 electronic sources 6.9.4c, 6.9.5
magnetic tape, publications on, in 6.9.5,
 6.9.8
manuscripts in 6.8.12
 online sources 6.9.8i
maps in 6.8.8
 online sources 6.9.8f
memos in 6.8.13
mentioned in text 3.7.1, 3.8.5
microfiche, publications on, in 6.7.14
microform, publications on, in 6.7.14
models in 6.8.8

works cited, lists of *(cont.)*
  multiple publication media, works in, in
    6.9.6
  multiple publishers, works with, in 6.6.19
  multivolume works in 6.6.15
  musical compositions in 6.8.5
    librettos 6.8.2
    performances 6.8.4
    published scores 6.8.5
    songs 6.8.2
    sound recordings 6.8.2
  names for 6.3
  newspaper articles in 6.7.1, 6.7.5
    electronic sources 6.9.4b, d, f–g, 6.9.5
  notes, editors' explanatory, in 6.6.12
  operas in 6.8.4–5
  online publications in 6.9.1–4, 6.9.8
  page numbers cited in *See* page numbers,
    in documentation
  page numbers of 6.4
  pamphlets in 6.6.20
  paperbacks in 6.6.17
  with parenthetical references 6.2
  performances in 6.8.4
  periodical articles in 6.7
  placement of, in manuscripts 6.4
  plays in
    in anthologies 6.6.7
    electronic sources 6.9.2–3, 6.9.5
    performances of 6.8.4
  poetry in 6.6.7
    electronic sources 6.9.2–3, 6.9.5
  prefaces in 6.6.9
  pre-1900 publications in 6.6.24
  proceedings of conferences in 6.6.22
  pseudonyms in 6.6.1
  publication information in, for articles
    journals 6.7.1
    magazines 6.7.6
    newspapers 6.7.5
  publication information in, for books 6.6.1
    dates 6.6.1, 6.6.7, 6.6.15
    editions 6.6.1, 6.6.12, 6.6.14
    missing or uncertain 6.6.25
    multiple publishers 6.6.19
    names of publishers 6.6.1
    places of publication 6.6.1, 6.6.25
    punctuation 6.6.1
  publication information in, for electronic
    sources
    on CD-ROM, diskette, or magnetic tape
      6.9.5, 6.9.8
    online publications 6.9.1–4, 6.9.8
  publishers' imprints in 6.6.18

works cited, lists of *(cont.)*
  punctuation in 6.6.1, 6.7.1
  radio productions in 6.8.1
    electronic sources 6.9.8a
    interviews 6.8.7
  readings (oral presentations) in 6.8.11
    electronic sources 6.9.8b
  recordings in
    sound 6.8.2, 6.9.8b
    video 6.8.3
  reference works in 6.6.8
    electronic sources 6.9.2, 6.9.5
  reprints of articles in
    anthologies 6.6.7
    loose-leaf collections 6.7.15
  republished books in 6.6.17
  reviews in 6.7.7
    electronic sources 6.9.4d
  serialized articles in 6.7.12
  series in
    books 6.6.1, 6.6.16
    journals 6.7.4
    television and radio 6.8.1
  short stories in 6.6.7
    electronic sources 6.9.2–3, 6.9.5
  slide programs in 6.8.3
  software in
    on CD-ROM or diskette 6.9.5
    downloaded 6.9.8m
  songs in 6.8.2
  sound recordings in
    booklets with 6.8.2
    on CD, cassette, tape, LP 6.8.2
    online 6.9.8b
  spacing in 6.4
    in manuscripts 4.2.4
    in theses and dissertations 5.5.5
  special issues of journals in 6.7.13
  speeches in 6.8.11
    electronic sources 6.9.8b
  television productions in 6.8.1
    electronic sources 6.9.8a
    interviews 6.8.7
  text references to 3.8.5
  titles of works in 3.8
    books 6.6.1
    CD-ROM, diskette, or magnetic tape,
      publications on 6.9.5
    changed 6.6.7
    journal articles 6.7.1
    long 6.6.1
    online publications 6.9.2–4
  transcripts of broadcasts in 6.8.1
    electronic sources 6.9.8a

works cited, lists of *(cont.)*
   translated works in 6.6.13
     electronic sources 6.9.2–3
   translations of words in 6.6.23
   typescripts in 6.8.12
   video recordings in 6.8.3
   volume numbers in
     journals 6.7.1–2
     multivolume books 6.6.1, 6.6.15
works consulted, lists of 6.3, 6.5
workshops, titles of 3.8.5
works made for hire 2.1.3
World Wide Web, publications on
   in lists of works cited 6.9.2–4
   in note references A.8a–c (app.)

World Wide Web, publications on *(cont.)*
   in parenthetical references
     entire works 7.4.1, 7.4.6, 7.4.9
     listed by title 7.4.4
     no page numbers 7.2, 7.4.2, 7.4.8–9
     parts of 7.4.2, 7.4.6, 7.4.8–9
writing style   *See* language, of scholarly
   writing

years
   abbreviations for 8.2
   AD, BC, BCE, CE with 3.10.5
   punctuation with 3.4.2l–m, 3.10.3, 3.10.5
   ranges of 3.10.6
Yiddish 3.11